The Supreme Court and the
Idea of Constitutionalism

Democracy, Citizenship, and Constitutionalism

Rogers M. Smith, Series Editor

In 1787, revolutionaries in Philadelphia invented a new political identity: citizenship in a large-scale constitutional democracy. That combination, once new and rare, is today being imitated around the globe. Yet despite its great prestige, constitutional democratic citizenship is fraught with tensions that are becoming ever more acute. The series seeks to publish the best empirical and normative explorations of citizenship, democracy, and constitutionalism from scholars in many disciplines, including political science, law, history, sociology, philosophy, anthropology, communications, literature, and education.

The Supreme Court and the Idea of Constitutionalism

Edited by
Steven Kautz, Arthur Melzer,
Jerry Weinberger, and M. Richard Zinman

PENN
University of Pennsylvania Press
Philadelphia

Published by
University of Pennsylvania Press
Philadelphia, Pennsylvania 19104-4112

Printed in the United States of America on acid-free paper
10 9 8 7 6 5 4 3 2 1

Library of Congress Cataloging-in-Publication Data
The Supreme Court and the idea of constitutionalism / edited by
Steven Kautz . . . [et al.].
    p. cm. — (Democracy, citizenship, and constitutionalism)
  Includes bibliographical references and index.
  ISBN 978-0-8122-4166-2 (alk. paper)
    1. United States. Supreme Court. 2. Judicial power—United States. 3.
Constitutional law—United States. 4. Constitutional law—Philosophy. 5. Judicial
review—United States. I. Kautz, Steven J.
  KF5130.S87 2009
  347.73'12—dc22

                                                          2009005978

Contents

Part III. Comparative Perspectives

Part IV. Constitutionalism and Democracy

Part V. Constitutionalism and Politics

Introduction
The Idea of Constitutionalism

Steven Kautz, Arthur Melzer, Jerry Weinberger, and
M. Richard Zinman

After the death of Chief Justice Rehnquist, the retirement of Justice O'Connor, and the debates over the confirmations of their replacements, Chief Justice Roberts and Justice Alito, the question of the place of the United States Supreme Court in our constitutional order is once again near the top of the nation's political agenda. Indeed, during the past half-century—from *Brown v. Board of Education* to *Roe v. Wade* to *Bush v. Gore*—the Supreme Court has assumed an increasingly prominent and controversial place in American political life. At least among party activists, few questions today divide the Democratic Party from the Republican Party more profoundly than the question of the proper tasks of the Supreme Court, as protector of our liberties and guardian of our constitutional design. If the nation is today in the midst of a "culture war," the party contest over the Constitution is certainly one of the principal battlefields in that war.

What is at stake in this struggle over the meaning of the Constitution of the United States and over the role of the United States Supreme Court as interpreter of that Constitution?

The contributors to this volume approach our political and intellectual ferment from some distance. They approach the problems of constitutionalism from a variety of disciplinary or methodological perspectives—historical, philosophical, comparative, and social scientific, as well as legal and jurisprudential. In bringing together these essays, we aim to move the debate beyond the questions that divide the parties of the day, or at least to raise those presently urgent questions in the light of more fundamental questions about the nature of constitutionalism in general and of American constitutionalism in particular. This volume includes chapters on the philosophical and historical origins of the idea of constitutionalism; chapters on the development of theories of constitutionalism in American history in particular; comparative analyses of practices of constitutionalism around the world; and chapters on the parallel emergence of (and the persistent tensions between) constitutional politics and democratic politics in the modern world.

Constitutions, both ancient and modern, establish the rule of law and thereby tame the rule of party or faction in political communities. Constitutions aim to thwart the unjust rule of a part over the whole and thus to establish a moderate politics where the rulers serve the common good.[1] Modern constitutions employ a particular strategy to achieve these ends. Modern constitutions are liberal democratic constitutions; but the *liberal* and the *democratic* aspects of modern constitutionalism are often in some tension. On one hand, modern constitutions are liberal constitutions, whose aim is to depoliticize politics. A liberal constitution seeks to limit government in various ways, but above all by withdrawing from political controversy the great moral and religious questions that could become a source of civil strife (and that had given rise to religious civil wars in the seventeenth century). A liberal constitution aims to reduce politics to a struggle over (mere) interest. Big questions about justice and salvation would be set aside for the sake of civil peace. On the other hand, modern constitutions constitute democracies and thus seek to empower "the people" against their partisan rivals. What the authors of the *Federalist Papers* said about the people of America might in time be said, with appropriate allowances for difference of circumstance, about peoples around the world: only a "strictly republican" form of government "would be reconcilable with the genius of the people of America; with the fundamental principles of the Revolution; or with that honorable determination which animates every votary of freedom, to rest all our political experiments on the capacity of mankind for self-government." Liberal ends would now, necessarily, be achieved by democratic means. But in liberal democratic constitutions, the vindication of democracy, of the rule of the people, is purchased at a price: the people's rule must be limited by various sorts of liberal restrictions on majority rule and the ends of politics. It is thus not at all surprising that we citizens of modern liberal democracies have an ambivalent stance toward modern constitutionalism. We prize our (liberal) freedoms while chafing against the enervation of our (democratic) politics. In this introduction, we consider these aspects of liberal democratic constitutionalism in turn.

Constitutionalism and Politics

Constitutions tame politics. Modern constitutions do so in at least two ways. First, constitutions limit government to the pursuit of agreed-upon ends (and sometimes limit authorized means to achieve those ends). Modern constitutionalism is associated with the rise of liberal ideas of limited government. Our own Constitution limits government both directly (through prohibitions against governmental intrusions on liberties specified in the Constitution and Bill of Rights) and indirectly (through structural fences against usurpation, such as the separation of powers). Second, constitutionalism tames politics by establishing as fundamental and incontestable those bedrock principles of political life that unite all citizens. In the case of the polity established by the Constitution of the United States, those fundamental principles include religious freedom, republican government, equal protection of the laws, due process rights of the accused, the priority of certain individual rights (freedom of speech, property) to majority rule, and so on. By putting certain potentially divisive questions beyond the party fray, constitutionalism tames politics by encouraging partisans, even or especially in times of emergency or civil strife, to moderate partisan claims by requiring fidelity to a nonpartisan framework within which all party claims must be advanced.

These twin purposes of constitutionalism are related: in the best case, a constitution might be said to establish (or reflect) an all-party agreement to take certain questions "off the table" and thereby to limit normal (or nonconstitutional) politics to questions that do not challenge that fundamental consensus about the limits and purposes of government and about the first principles of the polity. When Jefferson said in his first inaugural address, "We are all Republicans, we are all Federalists," he captured this spirit of constitutionalism: on some fundamental matters, there is or should no longer be a party contest; the Constitution unites, it does not divide.[2] To the extent, then, that a constitution itself becomes a matter of deep partisan controversy, there is some risk that the purposes of liberal constitutionalism will be undermined: as bigger and bigger questions are put back "on the table," the stakes contested in ordinary political life rise.[3] There have, of course, been polities where the ruling parties, or the parties contending for rule, did not recognize constitutional constraints of these kinds, where (as Keith Whittington puts it in his chapter in this volume) "everything could be on the table." Liberal political philosophers and statesmen of the seventeenth century embraced constitutionalism partly in order to escape from the hardships of a politics where everything could be on the table.

But perhaps this account of the purposes of constitutionalism is naïve. Is not our own Constitution, or any constitution, inescapably contested in politics? Constitutions are of course not self-executing or self-interpreting. Constitutional government therefore requires the establishment of authoritative interpreters of the constitution, and it is not surprising that both the identity of that authority (or those authorities) and the principles of interpretation that should guide it (or them) have been contested in politics, in *party* politics.[4] Of course politics matters. As Whittington writes in his chapter: the *meaning* of a constitution "must be won, and it must be won within politics." There simply is no place to stand outside of politics, no neutral arbiter of the meaning of the constitution to which one can appeal in constitutional contestation. It is hard to imagine a political actor who stands outside politics and who nevertheless possesses the legitimacy and the power to interpret the meaning of the constitution for a people authoritatively. Indeed, in some cases, the project of constitutionalism is itself an avowedly partisan project, whose aim is to establish a liberal polity in the face of a political culture that is at least somewhat resistant to liberalism. Consider, for example, Gary Jacobsohn's account in his chapter in this volume of "subversive" constitutionalism in India; or the project of constitutionalism in Iraq today.[5] Agreement on this basic idea—that the meaning of any constitution "must be won, and it must be won within politics"—unites almost all of the chapters in this volume. Reflection on the character of the *politics* of constitutionalism is the overarching theme of this volume.

Politics matters: there is no constitution beyond politics. But if the meaning of the constitution is inescapably contested within politics, as many of the contributors to this volume argue—among other things, if the aspiration to discover a neutral arbiter of the meaning of the constitution is doomed to failure—then why not dispense with the idea of constitutionalism altogether? How far can constitutionalism tame politics if the meaning of the constitution is itself, often or always, a party question?

We can specify this problem of constitutionalism more fully. Where politics impinges on debate about the meaning of the constitution too much, the line between constitutional questions and questions of ordinary politics will soon become murky. The considerable achievements of constitutionalism—limiting government and putting certain questions beyond party as matters of unalienable principle—are undermined. In contrast, when politics impinges too little on debate about the meaning of the constitution, other sorts of pathologies can emerge. In democracy in particular, the triumph of constitutionalism can be politically enervating, giving rise to popular frustration in face of the appearance of judicial oligarchy, or to a widespread sense among citizens of democratic inefficacy (consider the recent plight of European constitutionalism), or even to impatience with the forms of constitutionalism altogether (which come to be seen as the rule of the "dead hand of the past" thwarting present democratic aspiration). We therefore turn next to consideration of the relation of democracy and constitutionalism, with a view to further specifying the meaning of a constitutionalism that is neither beyond politics nor simply identical to ordinary party politics.

Constitutionalism and Democracy

Almost all modern constitutions purport to establish, and many do in fact establish, constitutional democracies. But as constitutions tame politics, so constitutional democracy tames democracy. Or it might be said that constitutional democracy thwarts and diminishes democracy. The pathologies of modern democracy are well known, and many of them can be traced, at least in part, to our constitutionalism. We have already alluded to some of these pathologies. Many lament the enervation of politics and citizenship in modern democracy. Constitutional democracy imposes a wide range of restrictions on majority rule, and so it is not altogether surprising that the experience of modern democracy is often one of inefficacy or incapacity, of "democratic deficit." The repeated popular revolts against the constitutional treaty in Europe might, from this point of view, be seen as protests against an extreme form of a pathology built into the modern constitutional project of liberal democracy. And if, as many argue, popular vigilance against threats to liberty is necessary to sustain liberal democracy, then even liberals must be troubled by the enervation of democratic citizenship that constitutionalism sometimes seems to produce.[6]

Others are troubled by the apparent triumph of elites in modern democracy. If constitutional debate is often merely a masked form of partisan political struggle, then the contest over the meaning of the constitution will often be won by the powerful; the argument from "the constitution" will prove to be a weapon in the hands of the powerful.[7] Perhaps it would be better to unmask the players and reveal the inescapably partisan character of all contestation over the meaning of the constitution. (On the other hand, the necessity of masks can sometimes itself serve as a moderating force.) Indeed, as various contributors to this volume suggest, the suspicion of judicial elites is increasingly widespread, on both the Right and the Left, although there is of course disagreement among the critics about the character of the elites who seek protection from democratic choices through entrenchment of "constitutional" privileges, with some more troubled by cultural elites and others more troubled by economic elites.[8]

To repeat: reflection on the character of the *politics* of constitutionalism is *the* theme of this volume. But our contributors are particularly worried about the politics of constitutionalism in *democracy*. Given the threats posed by constitutionalism to democratic politics (enervation of citizenship; elite dominance), what is the case for constitutional restraint in democratic politics?[9] Our contributors address both the question how constitutionalism works (by limiting and taming politics) and the question whether constitutionalism is, for a democratic people, a good thing.

As to the first sort of question: how is it possible to defend the idea of constitutionalism while acknowledging that all constitutional contestation is at some level political contestation? If struggle over the meaning of the constitution is inescapably political, is it nevertheless still a political struggle *over the constitution*? Is a more sophisticated defense of the naïve view of constitutionalism—that it limits government in part by establishing a nonpartisan consensus on questions of first principle, interpreted and enforced in a reasonably nonpartisan way—possible? We do not here propose to canvass the various views on that question defended by the contributors to this volume, but we do want to observe this unifying theme, that many of our contributors appeal in one way or another to the idea of a *constitutional politics*, between ordinary party politics on one hand and the unreal neutrality of a constitutionalism outside of politics on the other hand. Partisan conflict over the meaning of constitutionalism is inevitable; and it is sometimes dangerous, sometimes salutary. Indeed, the American experience of constitutionalism has been in part an agreement to constitutionalize partisan disagreement by fostering a political culture in which certain sorts of political questions are treated as constitutional or legal questions. That strategy for taming our politics arose almost at the beginning, when the former anti-Federalists agreed to shift from attacking the Constitution to debating its meaning (as, for example, in the contest over the Bill of Rights). And it was quickly solidified when the participants in the earliest "party" debates (e.g., Hamilton, Jefferson, and Madison) framed their battles as contests over the meaning of the Constitution.[10] But it is also evident that the constitutionalization of partisan disagreement can sometimes be dangerous, as in the case of the struggle over the meaning of the Constitution that culminated in secession and the Civil War. The contributors to this volume help us to navigate these difficult waters: to discern the character of a constitutional politics, especially in a democracy, and to explain how such a politics can sometimes serve and sometimes undermine liberal and democratic aspirations.

We conclude with a further reflection on the question of whether constitutionalism is, all things considered, good for a democratic people. In its origins, the idea of constitutionalism was a liberal idea, not a democratic idea. Arguably, the first constitutional government, achieved through the Glorious Revolution, was a constitutional monarchy, not a democracy. But in spite of these liberal origins, or perhaps because of them, the rise of constitutionalism in the modern world has been accompanied by the rise of democracy. Indeed, several of our contributors discuss the emergence in recent years of a distinctive form of modern democracy, "juristocracy."[11]

A democratic constitution might be thought of as an act of popular self-restraint. In a democracy, says Montesquieu, the people are both monarch and subject, ruler and ruled.[12] It follows, he argues, that *self-government* must supply the defect of *government* in a democracy. Democracy must for this reason, says Montesquieu, be animated by the republican virtue of citizens, the spirit of self-abnegation, the capacity of citizens to subordinate their private interest to the public good. But perhaps that asks too much of human beings. In any case, modern liberal democracy is founded on a more modest conception of virtue—self-interest rightly understood. Democratic constitutionalism (the institutional form of self-interest rightly understood) might be said to offer an alternative to the austerity (and unnaturalness) of republican virtue. A prudent people recognizes that it is capable of folly and vice; anticipating the temptation to act rashly, it restrains itself in advance by means of constitutional limits, including a willingness to subject itself to judicial elites or to endure an enervated citizenship. From one point of view, juristocracy—or, more generally, democratic constitutionalism—appears to be a kind of oligarchy. But from another point of view, democratic constitutionalism is an honorable exercise of the power of the people by which that people at the same time restrains itself.

Self-restraint is a willing refusal to exercise a power that one is capable, but for the self-restraint, of exercising. Any account of the constitutional politics of a democracy must do justice to both sides of this story, both the power of the people to govern itself and the self-restraint of a people capable of subjecting itself to constitutional limits. That is the paradox of a constitutional politics. On one hand, as Lincoln said (in a remark quoted by James Stoner in his chapter in this volume), "the candid citizen must confess that if the policy of the government, upon vital questions affecting the whole people, is to be irrevocably fixed by decisions of the Supreme Court, the instant they are made, in ordinary litigation between parties, . . . the people will have ceased to be their own rulers." On the other hand, it is a virtue of a moderate or constitutional people, aware of its own capacity for folly and vice, to submit to constitutional limits and to refrain, except in exceptional cases, from exercising that power in constitutional matters. When such a people throws off these self-imposed restraints, "politics" intrudes on the constitution and constitutional contestation will be politicized. There are good reasons for the people, as a general rule, to refrain from "politics" in constitutional matters. But there are also occasions when constitutional politics is inescapable and salutary.[13]

It is a virtue of the chapters in this volume, we submit, that they avoid what James Stoner calls the "oscillat[ion] between assertions of judicial supremacy and threats of civil disobedience" that characterizes much of the contemporary debate on the meaning of the Constitution of the United States and the role of the Supreme Court in our constitutional politics. We believe that this volume will contribute to ongoing debates about the character of the difficult terrain between politics and constitutional law, advancing our understanding of their necessary relation but without reducing one to the other.

PART I

Philosophical Perspectives

Chapter One
Ideas of Constitutionalism Ancient and Modern

Nathan Tarcov

The Supreme Court's constitutional jurisprudence is presumably both justified and guided by the idea of constitutionalism. There is, however, no single idea of constitutionalism but a bewildering variety of competing ideas of constitutionalism. Not only are there competing ideas of constitutionalism today, but the history of political philosophy reveals an even broader range and deeper opposition of ideas, most manifestly a division between ancient and modern ideas of constitutionalism. The intention of this chapter is to explore what we might learn from both that might help us to think more clearly and comprehensively about the dilemmas of constitutionalism. In particular, it will examine the ideas of constitutionalism of the two greatest ancient political philosophers, Plato and Aristotle, the problematic constitutionalism of the first great modern political philosopher, Machiavelli, the Lockean constitutionalism that laid the foundations for American ideas of constitutionalism, and conclude with the idea of constitutionalism present in *The Federalist,* the classic exposition of American constitutionalism.

Ancient Ideas of Constitutionalism

According to the modern idea of constitutionalism that shaped the American founding and that is supposed to guide the constitutional jurisprudence of the Supreme Court, a constitution is a fundamental law superior to ordinary laws because it expresses the will of the whole people granting and limiting powers to the government to secure the rights of all, and those who govern in accordance with it, therefore, act as representatives of the whole people. This idea stands in sharp contrast with the idea of a constitution (*politeia*) in classical political philosophy, which is the form of a political community defined by the part that rules over and forms the other parts, determining the goals of the whole regime and of the individuals in it. One is tempted to conclude that the ancient idea of a constitution was not by modern standards a constitution at all.[1]

There is, however, sufficient resemblance between the ancient idea of the *mixed* constitution or regime and the modern idea of constitutionalism for us to consider the former as the ancient idea of constitutionalism, just as there is sufficient difference between them for us to hope to learn something from their comparison.[2] For an articulation of that ancient idea of constitutionalism we cannot turn to the most famous work of ancient political philosophy entitled *Politeia* or *Constitution,* traditionally translated as the *Republic* of Plato, since the rule of philosopher-kings in that work can hardly be said to exemplify an idea of constitutionalism or of the mixed regime. We must first turn instead to Plato's *Laws.*

Book III of Plato's *Laws* offers a historical, or rather mythical (681a, 683d), account of the origins of constitutions (676a).[3] The first constitution described in any detail in this account is that of the Dorian League among Argos, Messene, and Lacedaimon (Sparta). The kings and peoples (*dēmoi*) of the three cities swore oaths "in accordance with the common laws they set up for ruling and being ruled" to prevent the king and people of any one of the cities from doing injustice to one another (683d–684b). The kings swore not to make their rule more violent and the peoples swore in turn not to overthrow their kings. The advantage of this federal constitution was that its guarantee of a restrained monarchical form of government was to be enforced against any one party in violation, whether king or people, by both parties in the other two cities in combination. The Athenian Stranger, the chief speaker in the *Laws,* contrasts the legislation of these cities with the usual procedure of lawgivers, who establish only such laws as the peoples and majorities willingly accept: for Plato, popular consent is a potential obstacle to a good constitution or good laws, not their source or guarantee.

Despite the high praise Plato's Athenian Stranger seems to bestow on the Dorian League, he notes that the constitutions and laws of Argos and Messene, two of the three federated cities, were rapidly corrupted (685a). He contrasts their reliance on oaths with the Spartan mixture of a dual kingship, a council of twenty-eight elders, and the elected ephors (691e–692a). Their insufficiently experienced lawgivers, he argues, mistakenly thought that by means of oaths they could keep within measured bounds a young soul that had obtained a rule which might become tyrannical; as a result their kings fell prey to the desire to have more (pleonexia) than the laws allowed, hubris, and injustice (691a–692b). Their reliance on oaths rather than on countervailing institutions failed to take account of the universal human desire to have all things happen in accord with the commands of one's own soul (687), the universal human inclination toward tyranny.[4] The insufficiency of oaths may have cosmological as well as psychological premises in that the gods cannot be counted on to act directly to enforce them. The Athenian Stranger politely does not mention to his Spartan interlocutor that the collapse of the Dorian League included not only the corruption of the constitutions and laws of Argos and Messene, but also the Spartan conquest and enslavement of their Messenian confederates (but compare 698e and 777c).

Plato's Athenian Stranger describes the mixed constitution as a mixture not only of institutions, such as the Spartan dual monarchy, senate, and ephorate, but also of goals: "a city should be free and prudent and a friend to itself" (693b). He also puts it as a mixture of the "two mothers of constitutions," monarchy and democracy, which must both be present for a constitution to have freedom, friendship, and prudence (693d; also 756e–758a). He illustrates this mixture by the examples of the Persian monarchy and his own Athenian democracy, and in doing so shifts to calling this mixture one of slavery or despotism with freedom. These provocative terms underline the element of constraint involved in obedience to law by both rulers and ruled, an essential element of constitutionalism, which constrains the freedom of both rulers and ruled. Under Cyrus the Persians possessed the proper amount of slavery and freedom since "the rulers shared their freedom with the ruled and drew toward equality," which made the ruled more friendly toward the rulers (particularly the soldiers toward their generals), and the king allowed freedom of speech to the prudent (694ab). The Athenian Stranger says nothing of any countervailing institutions among the Persians like the Spartan dual monarchy, senate, and ephorate, but he reports instead that the Persian monarchy degenerated under Cyrus's heirs owing to their bad education and hence bad character and bad behavior (694c–695b). Darius restored friendship (nothing is said of freedom and prudence) by establishing a sort of general equality through laws and making gifts to the populace, until it degenerated again under Xerxes (695ce). By depriving the people of freedom, the Persian rulers destroyed friendship within the community, made policy no longer for the sake of the ruled and the people but for their own rule, and established complete slavery and despotism (697c–698a). According to this Platonic constitutionalism, freedom must be shared with the people to ensure civic friendship and free speech for the prudent must be protected so the rulers will receive prudent counsel, but good institutions are insufficient without good education, good character, and good behavior on the part of the rulers.

The Athenian constitution, according to the Athenian Stranger, in contrast, declined from a willingness on the part of the people not to be sovereign over everything but to live as slaves of the laws and a strong sense of civic friendship (intensified by the Persian threat) to a total freedom from all rule (698b–700a). The loss of the willingness by the people to be enslaved to rulers, parents, elders, laws, and oaths, he argues, originated in the sphere of "music" or culture, in the replacement of the previous "aristocracy in music," in which the majority of the audience deferred to knowledgeable judges, by a "theatocracy" in which the poets catered to the pleasures of the majority (700a–701c). Insofar as Platonic constitutionalism depends on character and education as well as on countervailing institutions to preserve rule of law and prevent tyranny, it thereby depends on cultural character-formation and hence on some kind of censorship formal or informal.

When the Athenian Stranger asks his Spartan and Cretan interlocutors what sorts of constitutions their cities have, they are at a loss to say whether their constitutions are democratic, oligarchic, aristocratic, monarchic, or even tyrannical since their constitutions contain elements of each of those other kinds (712ce). The Athenian explains that this is because theirs are truly constitutions whereas the other unmixed kinds are not truly constitutions, but rather the rule of despots over slaves (712e–713a). He denies that every form of rule deserves to be called a constitution, as maintained by those who define justice as the advantage of the stronger (714b–715b; cf. also *Republic* 338c–339a, 422e–23a). When one party wins in civil strife and refuses to share rule, instead ruling violently over unwilling subjects and making laws in its own interest rather than for the common good—as the demos does in a democracy, the wealthy do in an oligarchy, or the tyrant does in a tyranny—that is not a constitution but rule of a faction (715b, 832bc). Prescriptive constitutional*ism* differs from mere description of all the different kinds of rule as constitutions in that it uses the term constitution as a term of distinction that denies that high status to unconstitutional forms of rule. In a constitution properly so called, those usually called rulers are instead "servants of the laws," for the law must be despot over the rulers and they must be slaves of the law (715cd).

Rule of law is necessary because "human nature is not at all capable of regulating the human things when it possesses autocratic authority over everything, without becoming swollen with insolence [hubris] and injustice" (713c). Rule of law is necessary in the first place because "there is no one among human beings whose nature grows so as to become adequate both to know what is in the interest of human beings as regards a constitution and, knowing this, to be able to and willing always to do what is best"; even one who knows that it is in both the common and the private interest that the common interest prevail over the private would never adhere to this conviction if he were able to rule autocratically, but would give way to pleonexia and prefer his own pleasure to what is juster and better (875ac). If a human being adequate in nature were ever born, the Athenian Stranger continues, he could rule over everything without laws (like the philosopher-kings of the *Republic*), but since no one like that actually exists, one must choose rule of law as second-best (875cd). The Athenian Stranger recognizes that he and his interlocutors are not, like the ancient mythical lawgivers, children of gods legislating for children of gods, but human beings legislating for human beings to rule human beings (713a–14a, 853c). Although he sometimes speaks of sanctifying the laws and making them unchangeable, as if the original laws were a sort of permanent constitution, he allows future law guardians to be legislators and make continual changes, improving on the deficiencies of the original laws while obscuring the difference between such alterations and keeping them perfect (769c–771a, 951c, 952b).

For Plato's Athenian Stranger, the ordering of a constitution has two forms: the establishment of ruling offices and the giving of laws, roughly similar to modern distinctions between constitutions and laws (751ab). The proper establishment of the offices is insufficient unless both those elected to fill them and those electing them are well educated in lawful habits: well-founded laws will be harmful if the officials chosen to look after them are unfit (751bc). Education is paramount (765e–766c).

The conservative aspect of Platonic constitutionalism is further elucidated by the arguments on behalf of rule of law made by the Eleatic Stranger, the chief speaker in Plato's *Statesman*. Although the only right rule and constitution in the strictest sense would be that of those who possess political science, regardless of whether they rule with or without laws and over willing or unwilling subjects, and even regardless of whether they rule or not, such rulers are not to be found (292b–93e, 301de). Even though law in its generality and permanence is unable to grasp and ordain what is best for all and forever owing to the dissimilarities among human beings and the flux that attends human things, it is still necessary because no one is capable of prescribing precisely what is suitable for each individual (294a–95b). Rule must be in conformity with laws laid down on the basis of experience and persuasion of the multitude, rather than in accord with whatever the rulers think best, which would amount to tyranny (296a, 297de, 300bd, 301bd). Accordingly, Plato's Eleatic Stranger distinguishes kingship from tyranny, aristocracy from oligarchy, and good from bad democracy on the basis of whether they rule by force or consent, lawfully or lawlessly (291d–92a, 301ac, 302ce). Platonic constitutionalism gives a privileged status to the existing laws both as the presumed result of experience and persuasion and as the best safeguard against tyranny.

Plato's Eleatic Stranger praises the lawful forms of rule by one, few, or many but without endorsing a mixture of the three like the Athenian Stranger in the *Laws*. Instead he proposes that the statesman and legislator weave together the naturally discordant virtues of courage and moderation both in marriages and in offices (305e–11c). Offices entrusted to single individuals must be given to those who possess both virtues, while offices occupied by more than one person should mix moderate and courageous officials. We see again that the proper establishment of offices is insufficient without concern for the character of those who hold them, though it is also possible that different offices could be designed to foster different virtues (e.g., a generalship for courage, a senate for moderation).

What may be called Platonic constitutionalism, in summary, distinguishes a true constitution as a sharing of rule for the common good by means of law from factional or tyrannical rule. It relies not on oaths but on countervailing institutions, education, and character to restrain the universal human inclination toward tyranny. It is a mixture of institutions or the rule of one, few, and many (and hence is not identical with simple democracy as the rule of the many), but also of different goals and virtues. Platonic constitutionalism emphasizes the prevention of tyranny, but does not simply serve the maximization of freedom: rather it mixes freedom with civic friendship and prudence and even with slavery to the laws. It gives the benefit of the doubt to existing laws over the prospect of improvement or the possibility of prudent exceptions. Platonic constitutionalism aspires to be the rule of law and not of men, but it does so with full consciousness that laws are made and applied by human beings whose education and character therefore matter and that the rule of human law is necessarily imperfect and second-best to the unavailable rule of divine wisdom.[5]

For Aristotle in his *Politics* a political community (*polis*) is a community (*koinonia*) of citizens (*politēs*) in a constitution (*politeia*): the constitution is the form that makes the political community what it is (1276b1–13). A constitution is the arrangement of offices, especially the sovereign office, of a political community; it is the governing body (*politeuma*) of that community; it determines the goal of the political community and is its way of life (1278b8–11, 1279a25–27, 1289a15–18, 1295a40). For Aristotle, the constitution is more fundamental than the laws, not as a higher law that can be appealed to against the laws but as the fundamental political fact that shapes the laws (1281a36–39, 1282b8–13). Aristotle distinguishes right constitutions from their perversions: kingship, aristocracy, and constitutional government (*politeia*) are the rule of one, the few, or the many for the common advantage, whereas tyranny, oligarchy, and democracy are the rule of one, the few (the rich), or the many (the poor) for their own advantage (1279a17–b10).

Aristotle's constitutionalism, like Plato's, is thus not a merely descriptive typology of constitutions, but an evaluative one in which "constitution" is a term of distinction. He denies that the perversions are constitutions at all since they are despotic, resembling rather the rule of a master (*despotēs*) over slaves, whereas a political community is a community of free persons (1279a21). He declares that the extreme form of democracy, in particular, in which the demos rules by particular decrees rather than being ruled by general laws, is not a constitution, for "where laws do not rule there is no constitution" (1292a4–37). This applies also to the extreme form of oligarchy and to tyranny (1292b5–10, 1293a30–34, b27–30, 1309b31–34).

Aristotle's willingness to grant the generic name *politeia* to the right rule of the many singles it out as being constitutional government par excellence (1279a37–39). He defines such constitutional government not only as rule by the many for the common good, but also paradoxically as a mixture of oligarchy and democracy, two of the perverted constitutions (1293b33–34). The mark of a well-mixed constitution is that it can be described as either a democracy or an oligarchy or both or neither (1294b14–17, 34–36), much as the Spartan and Cretan interlocutors in Plato's *Laws* were at a loss when asked what kind of constitutions their cities possessed. Whereas democracies pick officials by lot to ensure that they are representative in the sense of being typical and oligarchies elect them on the basis of a property qualification to ensure that they are rich, mixed or constitutional governments (as well as aristocracies) mix the two methods by using election like oligarchies but without a property qualification like democracies, presumably in the hope that they will be virtuous and prudent (1294b6–13)—the same method generally used by modern representative democracies.[6]

A mixed constitution, according to Aristotle, is preserved because it enjoys the support not merely of a majority, but of all parts of the political community, with none wishing for a different kind of constitution (1294b36–40). The survival of such a constitution requires that no part of the political community be oppressed. This is a practical requirement rather than a doctrine of popular sovereignty or the derivation of all just powers from the consent of the governed. The mixture of two perversions can therefore produce a right constitution, because whereas oligarchy excludes and oppresses the poor and democracy excludes and oppresses the rich, a mixed constitution includes both, shares rule between them, and oppresses neither. The mixture of freedom, the principle of democracy, with wealth, the principle of oligarchy, can even open room for virtue, the principle of aristocracy.

Aristotle defines constitutional government in yet a third way in addition to rule by the many for the common good and a mixture of oligarchy and democracy: as a constitution in which the middle class predominates, which has a similar effect to that of the mixing of democracy and oligarchy (1295a34–1296a8). The middle class virtues, according to Aristotle, are a mean between the despotic hubris and contempt characteristic of the rich and the slavish humility and envy characteristic of the poor, making possible the friendship among free and equal persons needed in a political community rather than a despotic one of masters and slaves.

The hallmark of Aristotle's constitutional government in all its guises is inclusion of all parts of the political community in rule rather than factional rule. His criteria for distinguishing right constitutions from their perversions are clarified further by his explication of the different kinds of democracies and oligarchies (1290a30–1292b21). He ranks higher those kinds of democracy or oligarchy that share rule with the opposite part (the rich in a democracy, the poor in an oligarchy) and ranks lower those kinds that exclude and oppress the opposite part. He also ranks higher those kinds of democracy or oligarchy ruled by laws and lowest those not ruled by law. For Aristotle, the case for rule of law or constitutionalism rests on the superiority of the generality of law to the particularity of rule by decree and the superiority of rule by reason to rule by passion (1281a34–36, 1287a28–32); but it also rests on the less lofty recognition of the dependence of law on habit and the consequent need for stability over long periods of time such that laws should be changed only with the utmost caution (1269a8–26).[7]

For Aristotle, as for Plato, a constitution depends not only on laws and institutions, but above all on education. He explains that the greatest means for preserving a constitution is education with a view toward that constitution, for there is no benefit in the most salutary laws unless the citizens are habituated and educated for that constitution (1310a12–17). Education for the constitution is not, however, an education simply directed by the distinctive principle of that constitution, but rather an education that makes it more mixed and inclusive. Education with a view toward oligarchy or democracy, for example, should be directed not toward doing whatever the oligarchs or democrats please, but rather toward doing what preserves the constitution—for example, by making oligarchy more inclusive of and just toward the demos and making democracy more inclusive of and just toward the rich (1310a19–35; compare 1309a15–30). Aristotle shares with Plato a recognition that a constitution depends on education and character as well as institutions, but he develops more fully the practical importance of letting all parts of a political community share in rule, especially the opposed economic classes.

Modern Ideas of Constitutionalism

Machiavelli is one of the founders of modern political thought, but there is only a hint of constitutionalism in *The Prince*. His greatest examples of new princes or founders of new states introduce "new orders," which he also calls their "constitutions" (*constituzioni*) (VI).[8] These new orders or constitutions are revolutionary or transformative in that they must combat the previous old orders and those who benefited from them. New princes or founders order things in such a mode that the people can be made to believe by force and observe those constitutions for a long time. Machiavellian constitutions are the fundamental orders that provide for the force needed for any orders to be observed: he stresses the necessary element of force at the basis of all constitutions.

   The Prince comes closest to constitutionalism in its discussions of France. Machiavelli contrasts France with Turkey: whereas the Turkish sultan governs with ministers who are his servants or slaves, the king of France governs with "an ancient multitude of lords, acknowledged in that state by their subjects and loved by them: they have their privileges, and the king cannot take them away without danger to himself" (IV). France is one of the "well-ordered and governed" kingdoms of his times, and the first of the "infinite good institutions (*constituzioni*) on which the liberty and security of the king depend" is the parlement (a court) and its authority (XIX). The orders of that kingdom constituted (*constituí*) the parlement as "a third judge" to beat down the great so as to secure the people against their ambition and insolence without the king incurring any blame (we are not altogether unfamiliar with courts taking the blame for making decisions for which another branch of government is unwilling to take the blame). Machiavelli concludes that "this order could not be better, or more prudent, or a greater cause of the security of the king and the kingdom." An independent judiciary provides the people with security, but apparently provides both security and liberty only to the constitutional monarch himself.[9]

In his *Discourses on Livy* Machiavelli further explains that the kingdom of France "lives secure because of nothing other than that the kings are obligated by infinite laws in which the security of all its peoples is included," so that apart from arms and money, which the kings can dispose of in their own mode, they are not able to act "except as the laws order" (I 16.5; see also 58.2). [10] He reveals further that the parlement sometimes condemns the king in its verdicts (III 1.5), though it condemns the king's actions on the basis of laws rather than condemning laws on the basis of a constitution in the mode of modern judicial review. Machiavelli stresses the superiority in stability and prudence of a king or a ruling multitude "shackled by laws" to an unshackled prince or multitude (I 58.2–4). Rulers for Machiavelli are strengthened rather than weakened by constitutional restraints.

Machiavelli presents the Roman constitution as a mixture of the kingly power of the consuls, the Senate of the optimates, and the popular government of the tribunes (I 2.7). In this he follows the classical notion of the mixed constitution, in particular as it came down through Polybius, but "contrary to the opinion of many" he traces this constitutional perfection not to concord or harmony, but to disunion or enmity between the plebs and the Senate (I 3–6). Internal discord or enmity is at the root of liberty and perfect constitutional order.[11] Machiavelli reveals the extent to which constitutional government is the continuation of civil war by other means.

Machiavelli distinguishes between "the orders of the state" of ancient Rome (namely, "the authority of the people, of the Senate, of the tribunes, of the consuls; the mode of soliciting and creating the magistrates; and the mode of making the laws") and "the laws that checked the citizens" (I 18.2). He regards the orders of the state, what might be called the constitution, as more fundamental than the laws, but his point is not constitutionalist in the sense of subordinating the laws to an unchanging constitution. On the contrary, he makes this distinction between orders and laws so as to complain that in ancient Rome only the laws were changed, whereas the orders also needed to be changed to check corruption (I 18.1–4).

Machiavelli emphasizes the importance of including within the constitution dangerous practices necessary for its preservation rather than leaving them unconstitutional. He argues for including within the orders of a republic a mode by which the citizens can vent their indignation against those who "sin in anything against the free state," so they may be vented by "ordinary" rather than "extraordinary" modes, which produce much worse effects (I 7). Similarly, he defends the Roman institution of the dictatorship on the grounds that "magistrates that are made and authorities that are given through extraordinary ways, not those that come through ordinary ways, hurt republics," as if republics remain healthy so long as their constitutions are observed and are hurt only by violation of their constitutions (I 34.1). He argues that every republic should include among its orders an authority like the Roman dictatorship, able to decide things quickly in urgent dangers (I 34.3). He does not leave it at asserting that only extra-constitutional, not constitutional, authorities hurt republics: a constitutionally elected authority can be dangerous if it is both unlimited in power and given for a lengthy term (more than a year, he warns) (I 35). Machiavelli argues for observing constitutional procedures rather than resorting to extra-constitutional means: "For when a like mode is lacking in a republic, it is necessary either that it be ruined by observing the orders or that it break them so as not to be ruined. In a republic, one would not wish anything ever to happen that has to be governed with extraordinary modes. Although the extraordinary mode may do good then, nonetheless the example does ill; for if one sets up a habit of breaking the orders for the sake of good, then later, under that coloring, they are broken for ill." Similarly, he argues that "it should never be ordered in a city that the few can hold up any of those decisions that ordinarily are necessary to maintain the republic" (I 50). A well-ordered constitution should be marked by fetters, not by gridlock.

For Machiavelli, laws depend not only on the force necessary to enforce them, but also on customs that reinforce them: "as good customs have need of laws to maintain themselves, so laws have need of good customs so as to be observed" (I 18.1). Customs are in effect a part of the constitution that shapes how the orders and laws function in practice. This may help to explain why Machiavelli argues that it is so difficult for a people used to living under a prince that becomes free to preserve its freedom or for a prince to govern by violence a city used to living freely (I 16.1, II 4.1, 23.4, *Prince* V).

Machiavelli pronounces what may be considered one of the guiding principles of constitutionalism in declaring that "it is necessary to whoever disposes a republic and orders laws in it to presuppose that all men are bad, and that they always have to use the malignity of their spirit whenever they have a free opportunity for it" (I 3.1). Men "never work any good unless through necessity"; they can be made good, that is to say deprived of the opportunity to show their wickedness, by customs or laws or orders (3.2; also *Prince* XXIII end). Since "necessity produces virtue," founders should give laws to impose necessity on their peoples (I 1.4). Good orders or constitutions impose necessity on rulers as good laws impose necessity on subjects. Machiavelli relies ultimately on necessity, not on nature or even education: he notes "how easily men are corrupted and make themselves assume a contrary nature, however good and well brought up" (I 42). He shares the ancient appreciation of the importance of customs and education (I 4.1, II 2.2, III 27.2, 30.1, 31.3, 43, 46), but stresses their insufficiency without effective orders or institutions.

According to Machiavelli, prudent orders give princely government, aristocratic government, and popular government each their part so they may guard each other and keep each other good, or rather prevent each other from showing their wickedness (I 2). Similarly, the Roman people did not have to fear ambitious men because they too guarded one another (I 30.2). The Senate, consuls, and tribunes, for example, were like a guard on the dictator "to make him not depart from the right way" (I 35, 40.7).

Machiavelli thus sets forth these basic principles of a form of modern constitutionalism: he praises the constitutional monarchy of France for shackling its king with laws and protecting the people through an independent judiciary; he regards discord between opposed classes as the source of liberty; and he declares that constitutions must presuppose all men are bad and compel them to be good by necessity, institutional checks, and vigilance on the part of both the people and ambitious competitors. Ultimately, however, one cannot strictly term Machiavelli a constitutionalist, given his emphasis on the need for new orders "every day" (I 49.3 and III 49) and for recourse to "extraordinary" means "such as violence and arms" to reorder a corrupt city so as to live in freedom (I 17.3, 18.4). He writes that a wise understanding will never reprove anyone for any "extraordinary" action that he uses to "order" a kingdom or constitute a republic (I 9.2). Machiavelli never seems willing to let us forget the extraordinary at the root of the ordinary, the radical innovation and violence at the root of the most stable constitution, and the need for occasional return to those roots.[12]

John Locke formulated many of the fundamental principles of the modern idea of constitutionalism that informed the American founding: the natural liberty and equality of human beings; individual rights to life, liberty, and property; government by consent; limited government; rule of law; and the right of revolution. The fundamental hypothesis of his *Second Treatise of Government* is the state of nature, his claim that the natural condition of all human beings is one of freedom and equality (II 4–5).[13] By nature human beings are free to act, constrained only by their own reason (the dictates of which Locke calls the law of nature) and not by the will of any other human being (I 67, II 4, 6). This hypothesis contrasts sharply with Aristotle's view that human beings are by nature members of a political community and that natural inequalities subordinate some human beings to be ruled or even enslaved by others. In the state of nature, individuals possess and defend rights to life, liberty, and property. Liberty is the basic fence protecting life, so any threat to one's liberty may be resisted as an attack on one's life and no one can reasonably consent to slavery (II 17, 23). Since in the state of nature the enjoyment of the rights to life, liberty, and property is very insecure, reasonable individuals establish civil society (II 20, 21, 123). All rightful political power exists only by consent (II 95, 104, 134, 189, 192). This contrasts with any justification derived from conquest, as well as with the classical view that superiority in wisdom or virtue carries with it a right to rule (II 54, 70).

For Locke the end of government is the protection of the lives, liberties, and properties of all the members of society as far as possible (II 88, 123, 131, 134, 159). This limited end of government is the heart of modern liberalism and contrasts sharply with classical and medieval conceptions of the end of government as the inculcation of virtue or the salvation of souls.[14] The limited end of government in turn entails limits on its powers: it may not possess absolute arbitrary power over the lives and property of the people; or exercise rule by decree or without promulgated laws and authorized judges; or take away property without the consent of the majority or their representatives (II 131, 135–40, 221–22). Once individuals have consented to government, political power belongs to the people acting by majority decision unless or until they establish another form of government (II 95–99, 132). The people are not sovereign: the limitations on the end and power of government bind even the people.

Locke's principles of government by consent with limited end and power laid the ground for modern liberal constitutionalism. The people by majority decision establish the form of government through a voluntary grant of power which Locke calls "the first and fundamental positive Law" or "the Original Constitution" (II 134, 153–56). Because this constitution is the original and supreme or fundamental act of the society, antecedent to all positive laws, and because it depends wholly on the people, no inferior power can alter it. Thus Locke establishes the basis of the position that a constitution is the supreme law of the land: it is prior to ordinary laws, it authorizes the legislature to make them, and it is the act of the people themselves rather than of the legislature. Although Locke insists on "indifferent and upright judges" (II 131), he does not discuss whether they should judge according to the original constitution rather than ordinary laws.[15] Locke is a constitutionalist rather than a populist in that, for him, once the people delegate their authority through the constitution to the constituted authorities, they do not resume that authority as long as that constitution and government last (II 168, 243).

Locke is not, however, a doctrinaire constitutionalist. He recognizes that the uncertainty and variableness of human affairs may prevent the framers of a government from settling all important questions in the original constitution by a steady fixed rule and compel them instead to entrust such matters to the prudence of later governors (II 156). He also recognizes that the original constitution may possess faults and defects that the people are slow to amend, so much more powerful is custom than reason (II 157, 223).

Locke propounds a limited and constitutional conception of the powers of government, but he does not require a simply democratic form of government. He claims that the majority may exercise legislative power themselves as a perfect democracy, put it into the hands of a few men and their heirs or successors as an oligarchy, give it to one man as a monarchy, or make a mixed form, as they think good (II 132), but he rules out absolute monarchy as inconsistent with civil society since by uniting all legislative and executive power in one man it leaves him still in the state of nature with those under his dominion (II 90–94). Furthermore, the same persons should not have in their hands the legislative and executive powers, since it is dangerous to allow the persons charged with making laws to exempt themselves from their execution, and the legislature should include a number of persons (II 143). The legislature should be supreme over the executive since the power that can give laws to another must be superior to the power that merely executes those laws (II 134, 150). Locke's stipulation that government may not take property without the consent of the majority or their representatives effectively requires every form of government to include a democratic branch (II 138–40, 142, 213, 221–22).

Locke's constitutionalism, like Machiavelli's, incorporates extralegal, even extra-constitutional elements. He argues that since it is impossible to foresee and provide by laws for all accidents and necessities, the good of the society requires that many things be left to the discretion of the executive to be ordered for the public good where law is silent and sometimes even against the law (II 156–68). Locke's executive prerogative, like Machiavelli's dictatorship, remains, however, within a legal framework, for the people may judge whether its exercise tends toward their good and if necessary limit it through laws passed by the legislature (II 162–66).[16] Although the executive power is in itself subordinate to the legislative power, what Locke calls the "federative" power (the power over war and peace, leagues and alliances, and all transactions with persons and communities outside the commonwealth) is much less capable of being directed by antecedent laws and so necessarily must be left to the prudence and wisdom of those in whose hands it is (II 145–48). Finally, behind and above the original constitution is the power of the people that originally constituted it. Although the legislative is the supreme power within any form of government, it is a fiduciary power given by the people as a trust to be employed for their good, and they retain the power to remove or alter it when it is used contrary to that trust (II 149, 171, 221–22, 240). Political power then reverts to the society acting through its majority, which must establish a new government before society itself dissolves in the absence of civil government and under the pressure of tyranny (II 220).[17] Ultimately the constitution cannot be self-enforcing, but depends on its enforcement by the people.

The American Declaration of Independence affirmed the fundamental principles of Lockean constitutionalism: human equality; individual rights to life, liberty, and the pursuit of happiness; securing of those rights as the end of government; derivation of the powers of government from consent of the governed; and the right of the people to alter or abolish any government destructive of these ends and institute new government on such principles and in such form as to them shall seem most likely to effect their safety and happiness. That most authoritative exposition of the American Constitution, *The Federalist,* in turn reaffirms those fundamental principles: government originates from the consent of individuals in a state of nature (51, pp. 321–22), the consent of the people is the "original fountain of all legitimate authority," and the people retain "the transcendent and precious right" to "abolish or alter their governments as to them shall seem most likely to effect their safety and happiness" (22, p. 148, 40, p. 249; also 28, p. 176, 43, p. 276, 78, p. 468).[18] Because popular consent is the source of all legitimate authority, the ratification of the Constitution by conventions specially elected by the people rather than by ordinary legislatures, a mode recently pioneered by the states, was crucial to its legitimation (22, p. 148, 49, pp. 310–11). *The Federalist* both opens and closes by remarking that for a whole people so to choose their constitution by voluntary consent, far from being typical, is an unprecedented prodigy (1, p. 27, 85, p. 526). This new mode of popular consent to the institution of government formalized Locke's idea of the constitution as the original and supreme act of the society depending wholly on the people. It provides a peaceful, certain, and solemn alternative to violent and irregular acts, but remains ultimately an expression of the same fundamental right of the people to alter or abolish their form of government. Madison almost admits that adoption of the Constitution was authorized not by the Articles of Confederation but only by popular consent as an exercise of revolutionary right (40, p. 249). He invokes the "important distinction so well understood in America between a Constitution established by the people and unalterable by the government, and a law established by the government and alterable by the government," which he notes "seems to have been little understood and less observed in any other country" (53, p. 328). This distinction, the basis of which Locke established, is the essence of modern constitutional government.

The Federalist echoes the Athenian Stranger's reminder that framers are human beings who give laws for human beings to rule human beings (*Laws* 853c), in remarking that they were "framing a government which is to be administered by men over men," and that "if men were angels, no government would be necessary. If angels were to govern men, neither external nor internal controls on government would be necessary" (51, p. 319). *The Federalist* accordingly relies on the external control of a dependence on the people through elections and the internal control of a government so structured as to make ambition counteract ambition rather than on "moral or religious motives" (10, p. 75). Underlying these controls is the interplay of a multiplicity of interests and a multiplicity of sects protecting civil and religious liberty (10, p. 78, 51, p. 321), much as for Machiavelli the discord between the nobles and the plebes was the source of Roman liberty. And much as the Athenian Stranger refused to trust in oaths, so *The Federalist* does not trust to "parchment barriers" to restrain "the encroaching spirit of power" (48, 305; also 25, p. 163, 73, p. 441). But it does not simply "presuppose that all men are bad," as for Machiavelli whoever orders laws for a republic must do. On the contrary, Madison affirms that "as there is a degree of depravity in mankind which requires a certain degree of circumspection and distrust, so there are other qualities in human nature which justify a certain portion of esteem and confidence. Republican government presupposes the existence of these qualities in a higher degree than any other form." He argues that if there were not "sufficient virtue among men for self-government," then "nothing less than the chains of despotism" could "restrain them from destroying and devouring one another" (55, p. 343). Indeed he maintains that "the aim of every political constitution is, or ought to be, first to obtain for rulers men who possess most wisdom to discern, and most virtue to pursue, the common good of the society; and in the next place, to take the most effectual precautions for keeping them virtuous" (57, p. 348). Similarly, the functioning of the Constitution depends on "the vigilant and manly spirit which actuates the people of America—a spirit which nourishes freedom, and in return is nourished by it" (57, p. 350). The people that constitutes the constitution must first be constituted by the spirit and creed of enlightened liberty (26, p. 164).

As Machiavelli urged that every republic include among its orders an authority able to decide things quickly in urgent danger, since otherwise it would either be ruined by observing its orders or set the bad example of violating them, so does Hamilton warn that "the circumstances that endanger the safety of nations are infinite, and for this reason no constitutional shackles can wisely be imposed on the power to which the care of it is committed" (23, p. 149). He explains further that "nations pay little regard to rules and maxims calculated in their very nature to run counter to the necessities of society. Wise politicians will be cautious about fettering the government with restrictions that cannot be observed, because they know that every breach of the fundamental laws, though dictated by necessity, impairs that sacred reverence which ought to be maintained in the breast of rulers toward the constitution of a country, and forms a precedent for other breaches" (25, p. 163). A constitution should not run counter to the requirements of national survival or impose restrictions that cannot and should not be observed. It should not be a suicide pact, in the words of Justice Jackson in *Terminiello v. Chicago*.

Hamilton defends the doctrine of judicial review, that laws contrary to the Constitution are void and can be declared so by the courts, on the Lockean grounds that the people is superior to the legislature, and the Constitution is made by the people, whereas the laws are made only by the legislature (78, pp. 465–67). He argues that a limited constitution can be preserved in no other way than by courts whose duty it is to declare void all acts contrary to the manifest tenor of the Constitution. A limited constitution is one that contains specified limitations on legislative authority; the necessity of judicial review for Hamilton is derived from the need to preserve constitutional limits on legislative rather than executive authority. His constitutionalism is not simply democratic: judicial review serves to guard the Constitution and the rights of individuals not only from a legislature acting contrary to the intention of the people, but also from the "ill humors" of the people themselves, though only until they give way to "better information, and more deliberate reflection," or until the people by "some solemn and authoritative act" exercise their right to amend or annul the Constitution (78, pp. 468–70). The republican principle demands that the cool and deliberate sense of the community should prevail, but it does not require "unqualified complaisance to every sudden breeze of passion, or to every transient impulse" of a popular majority (63, pp. 382–83, 71, pp. 430–31). This sense that should prevail must be cool and deliberate, but it must also be that of the community to be consonant with the republican principle. The Supreme Court's right to declare laws void as against the Constitution derives only from the status of the Constitution as the deliberate sense of the people, not from the superior wisdom of judges or professors of law or philosophy or even political science. The United States would not be a republic, according to *The Federalist,* if the judges were not "a remote choice of the people themselves" (39, p. 242). *The Federalist,* after all, rejects the option of protecting minority rights by creating a will independent of society, a will that might as readily espouse the unjust views of the majority as the rights of the minority or turn against them both (51, pp. 320–21).

The identification of the Constitution, let alone the results of judicial review, with the will of the people becomes problematic, however, once the people who ordained and established the Constitution are long dead. Jefferson suggested in a letter to an unpersuaded Madison that all constitutions naturally expire every generation (September 8, 1789). Madison in reply adduced the danger of faction and the need of even the most rational government for the prejudice that results from stability (February 4, 1790). In *The Federalist* Madison had a twofold reply to a related proposal of Jefferson, that conventions be held to correct breaches of the Constitution: "a nation of philosophers is as little to be expected as the philosophical race of kings wished for by Plato," so "the most rational government" will need "to have the prejudices of the community on its side" and "it is the reason, alone, of the public, that ought to control and regulate the government" (49, pp. 311–12, 314). Similarly, Aristotle argued for the rule of law both as reason and as habit. It seems that the authority of the Constitution must rest both on the aspiration of the people to be rational and on its habitual reverence for a Constitution that has stood the test of time.

Ideas of Constitutionalism Ancient and Modern

The ancient ideas of constitutionalism of Plato and Aristotle share enough of the insights of the modern ideas of constitutionalism that we are not precluded from learning something from them. They are not based on a naïve or idealistic faith in the goodness of human nature or the efficacy of oaths and parchment barriers: on the contrary, they recognize the necessity of countervailing institutions to check the universal human inclination toward tyranny, hubris, and pleonexia. We may profit from their emphasis on constitutional government as second-best *mixed* government, mixing not only countervailing institutions and clashing social classes, but diverse goals by combining freedom with civic friendship and prudence and even with restraint and slavish obedience to law, and giving their due to both reason and habitual reverence, improvement and stability. Above all, ancient constitutionalism stresses the importance of education, culture, and character for the functioning of constitutional government. As we consider the prospects for constitutionalism in places divided by deep ethnic and sectarian enmities, we should recall Plato and Aristotle's lesson that popular ratification alone cannot guarantee such a constitution unless it serves the common good rather than the interests of a faction and that constitutional government must be not the rule of a majority, but rule shared by those groups otherwise likely to be oppressed.

Machiavelli may remind us of the elements of force and conflict behind all constitutions. He would note that the people that ordained and established the American Constitution was itself constituted by a bloody revolution that was also a civil war, with much of the losing party going into exile, and was reconstituted anew by another even bloodier civil war. He highlights the need to incorporate the extraordinary within the constitutional order if it is to survive, a lesson that Locke and *The Federalist* taught less spectacularly. We can try to reread *The Federalist* and rethink our own ideas of constitutionalism in the light not only of their Lockean roots in human equality, individual rights, and popular consent, but of their ancient and Machiavellian inheritances or forgotten lessons.

Chapter Two
On Liberal Constitutionalism

Steven Kautz

The Constitution of the United States is a distinctively modern ("liberal") constitution. "We the People of the United States," having somehow constituted ourselves as "one politic society" (Locke, *Second Treatise*, §211; cf. §§95–99), instituted new government by means of a written constitution: a government deriving its just powers from the consent of the governed, whose ultimate purpose would be to secure the blessings of liberty to ourselves and our posterity. That's the familiar liberal story.

Political life is untidy. We should not take too seriously any parallel between the liberal political theory of Locke and early American political history. Nevertheless, there is a Lockean account of that history that some of the principal founders were themselves inclined to propound: the constitution of "one politic society" was achieved prior to 1787, through a declaration of shared political principles, through the joint experience of a war for independence, and on the basis of certain favorable circumstances of common ancestry, language, religion, and custom (see *Federalist* 2 [Jay], on "one united people"). So too, Lincoln: "four score and seven years ago" (and thus "a new nation") recalls 1776, not 1787. The first and fundamental constitution of "one politic society" was not achieved by means of law; but the subsequent institution of a form of government was achieved, and is best achieved, by a written constitution, a kind of law. The question of the relation between these two constitutions, the unwritten constitution of "one politic society" and the written constitution of a form of government, is one of the themes of this chapter.

A liberal constitution like the Constitution of the United States is ordinarily a written constitution: that is because it is a kind of law. Such a written constitution has authority as the act of a people, of "We the People": that is, there is (already) a "people" that is capable of acting authoritatively, in its constitutional capacity. But who is this "people," this constitution-making "We the People"? The very distinction between a constitutional people and a partisan people—between "We the People" and the *demos*—is alien to classical constitutionalism; it is a discovery or invention of modern liberal constitutionalism. A written constitution is, on one hand, an act of democratic self-assertion, by means of which "We the People" establish a *limited* government and then disperse the limited powers of government to officers authorized to exercise those powers in various, separate spheres. It is, on the other hand, and probably more importantly, an act of democratic self-restraint, by means of which "We the People" restrain ourselves, restrain the *demos*—or, perhaps more precisely, by means of which the constitutional people restrains the partisan people.

As Madison puts the point in *Federalist* 63, speaking here of the "political constitutions" of the "ancients": "The true distinction between these [ancient constitutions] and the American governments, lies *in the total exclusion of the people, in their collective capacity, from any share in the latter.*" And in *Federalist* 51, Madison writes on the same question: "In framing a government which is to be administered by men over men, the great difficulty lies in this: you must first enable the government to control the governed; and in the next place oblige it to control itself." The priority is somewhat surprising, emphasizing as it does that democratic self-restraint is at least as important as democratic self-assertion in liberal constitutionalism. Liberal constitution-making is designed to enable the people both to govern and to govern itself.

A liberal constitution establishes a fundamental law, superior in dignity and authority to ordinary law, that grants and then limits the power of government. But limited government requires not only that the powers of government be limited: the powers of the people must also be limited. The paradox of liberal constitutionalism is that the rulers and the ruled are, in this decisive respect, the same human beings; a liberal constitution is for this reason an act of democratic self-restraint, of government as self-government, of a kind of virtue.[1] For a liberal, there is no alternative to government as self-government, as self-mastery, owing to our natural condition of equality: "wherein all the power and jurisdiction is reciprocal, no one having more than another; there being nothing more evident, than that creatures of the same species and rank, promiscuously born to all the same advantages of nature, and the use of the same faculties, should also be equal one amongst another without subordination or subjection" (*Second Treatise*, §4).[2] There is no rule by nature; we must therefore learn to rule ourselves. It is at least unsurprising, and perhaps even necessary, that *law* should be the form of this self-government, that law should be the form of the virtue of a people that has come to understand that it must govern itself.[3] The "first" defect of the state of nature, where the equality of "private judgment" that makes self-government necessary is a terrible inconvenience, is the want of "an established, settled, known law, received and allowed by common consent to be the standard of right and wrong" (*Second Treatise*, §124). Where all claims to rule on the basis of superior "private judgment" (on the basis of some claim to wisdom or prudence) must be excluded, the only legitimate form of rule is founded on a "common consent" regarding standards of right and wrong—that is, on a fundamental law that "We the People" give to ourselves.

The character of the liberal constitution as fundamental law distinguishes modern constitutionalism from ancient constitutionalism. I begin with an account of the liberal case for the "rule of law" and then turn to the classical account of the same idea, the rule of law, with a view to criticizing and further elaborating the liberal alternative to ancient constitutionalism.

Classical Liberalism and the Rule of Law

Classical liberalism is the view that liberty is the fundamental political good because it is the most certain means to *peace* among natural foes who must learn to live together as civil friends.[4] Liberalism, strictly speaking, is the doctrine that *liberty* is *the* fundamental political good. Where there is no liberty, all other political goods—justice, virtue, prosperity, equality—are quite beyond our reach. And *what is liberty*? "Political liberty," says Montesquieu, "is that tranquility of spirit which comes from the opinion each citizen has of his security"; "in order for him to have this liberty the government must be such that one citizen cannot fear another citizen" (*The Spirit of the Laws*, 11.6). That is liberty: *one citizen must not fear another citizen.*

And this is so whether that other citizen is a ruler or a common thief: "The Injury and the Crime is equal," says Locke, "whether committed by the wearer of a Crown, or some petty Villain." "Should a Robber break into my House, and with a Dagger at my Throat, make me seal Deeds to convey my Estate unto him, would this give him any Title?" Surely not. But "the Title of the Offender, and the Number of his Followers make no difference in the Offence, unless it be to aggravate it. The only difference is, Great Robbers punish little ones, to keep them in their Obedience, but the great ones are rewarded with Laurels and Triumphs, because they are too big for the weak hands of Justice in this World, and have the power in their own possession, which should punish Offenders" (*Second Treatise*, §176). And so, the first task of the liberal polity is to secure citizens against robbers: above all, against the tyrant, who sometimes comes in numbers (the "tyranny of the majority") and who would strike at our lives and liberties under color of law. Thus, both the law-and-order conservative and the civil libertarian have essential and respectable places in the liberal polity, each with a task that will be from time to time more urgent than the other's. Defeat the (lawless) petty criminal; restrain the (lawless) tyrannical magistrate.

So, what is the place of the "rule of law" in this liberal understanding? The principal root of the insecurity of human beings, which liberalism seeks to ameliorate, is the *lawlessness* of the most natural human passions—or, more precisely, *the inefficacy of the law of nature* in the state of nature, in the absence of a common power to secure obedience to law. The great task of liberal political theory and liberal statesmanship is to secure obedience to law, or to teach the reasonableness of obedience to law. The rule of law has pride of place in the liberal understanding because the fundamental problem of political life is to remedy the insecurity that follows inescapably from the natural lawlessness of human beings. If the end of political life is liberty understood as security, and if security is threatened above all by the natural lawlessness of human beings, then establishment of the rule of law will be the principal means to achieve the end of liberty. Consider Montesquieu's radical but precise formulation of the point: "Liberty is the right to do everything the laws permit; and if one citizen could do what they forbid, he would no longer have liberty because others would likewise have this same power" (*The Spirit of the Laws*, 11.3). On this account, liberty is mutual obedience to law—no more, no less.

Let's follow this classical liberal argument a little further. Locke argues that the natural passions of human beings will drive us, in various ways, toward disobedience of the law of nature, which would teach us "Peace, Good Will, Mutual Assistance, and Preservation," if we could attend to it. But we cannot. And this is so, perversely, in spite of our natural desire for self-preservation and security, toward which obedience to the law of nature would of itself tend. Consider, for example, the crucial problem of the executive power in the state of nature. Locke argues that, where there is no common power, every human being retains an equal right to punish violators of the law of nature. This follows immediately from the natural equality of human beings: if anyone were to claim an exclusive executive power in the state of nature, he would thereby claim a natural right to rule; but no one is entitled to rule by nature, since we are by nature equals. Yet this arrangement of the executive power, the power to punish those who violate the law of nature, ensures the inefficacy of the law of nature, Locke argues. Human beings who feel aggrieved will ordinarily "use a Criminal when he has got him in his hands, according to the passionate heats, or boundless extravagancy of his own Will," and not "as calm reason and conscience dictates." That is, human beings will often neglect their best self-interest, misled by a blind (angry and intemperate) self-love. Escalation is inevitable: my enemies will respond to the "passionate heats and boundless extravagancy" of my friends, who will respond in kind, and so on and on and on (*Second Treatise*, §8). Thus, "*the State of War once begun, continues*," with no end in prospect (*Second Treatise*, §20). Innocent bystanders who are neither friends nor enemies will prudently shy away from such quarrels: the inefficacy of any imaginable arrangement for neutral arbitration of disputes is one of the fundamental defects of the state of nature. Locke concludes: "*Civil Government* is the proper Remedy for the Inconveniences of the State of Nature, which must certainly be Great, where Men may be Judges in their own Case" (*Second Treatise*, §13). That is, civil government is first and fundamentally the *rule of law*: where men may not be judges in their own case; where there is government of laws, not of men. Law has an unusually distinguished place in the liberal understanding of politics above all because the natural lawlessness of the human passions is the principal threat to a civilized politics; the rule of law is the necessary remedy for this natural disorder.

Further, the law of nature can be known only to its "Studier[s]," says Locke: and who has time to study in our ordinary state of penury and insecurity (*Second Treatise*, §12)? More precisely, reason must be made to come to the aid of the liberal passions, for Locke; but human reason is too easily vanquished by ordinary passions and prejudices. Thus, when Locke surveys the nations of the world, he sees an extraordinary diversity of human institutions, but rather few pleasing spectacles and many follies and brutalities; he has "but little Reverence for the Practices which are in use and in credit amongst Men," he says, for these most often have their roots in the conceits of the passions and the imagination, bolstered over time by custom and authority—and not in the calm reason that teaches a reasonable love of liberty. This Lockean pessimism regarding the power of reason appears in a remarkable passage from the *First Treatise* (§58):

Thus far can the busie mind of Man carry him to a Brutality below the level of Beasts, when he quits his reason, which places him almost equal to angels. Nor can it be otherwise in a Creature, whose thoughts are more than the Sands, and wider than the Ocean, where fancy and passion must needs run him into strange courses, if reason, which is his only Star and compass, be not that he steers by. The imagination is always restless and suggests variety of thoughts, and the will, reason being laid aside, is ready for every extravagant project; and in this State, he that goes farthest out of the way, is thought fittest to lead, and is sure of most followers: And when Fashion hath once Established, what Folly or craft began, Custom makes it Sacred, and 'twill be thought impudence or madness, to contradict or question it. He that will impartially survey the Nations of the World, will find so much of their Governments, Religions, and Manners brought in and continued amongst them by these means, that he will have but little Reverence for the Practices which are in use and credit amongst Men.

There is little place for the reasonable love of liberty in this mad world, ruled as it is by imagination, fancy, passion, folly, craft, custom, religion, and not by reason: indeed, perhaps the love of liberty will itself "be thought impudence or madness." A politics of liberty can be achieved only at the end of this sorry history, when the madness is evident to all: only then can peaceful reason supply the defect of the peaceful passions, by teaching human beings who have grown tired of endless war the necessity of the rule of law, limited government, self-restraint of political parties and religious sects, mutual respect for rights, and so on.

But, and this is among the most crucial of the differences between ancient and modern constitutionalism: it would be unreasonable, on this liberal view, to permit "reason" to rule directly, so to speak—or, put otherwise, to submit to the rule of putatively wise rulers. Locke makes this clear in his account of the natural history of political communities (in Chapter VIII of the *Second Treatise*). At first, says Locke, rulers were "Fathers" and then "Generals," apparently trustworthy elders who seemed wise and strong to our more innocent forebears; the view that government is by nature monarchical and that the wise and strong are entitled to rule is, so to speak, a natural confusion. But soon enough, these trusted rulers began to behave treacherously, motivated by "vain ambition," the wicked love of gain, and "evil Concupiscence," among other vices. After this historical progress, "Men found it necessary to examine more carefully *the Original* and Rights of *Government*; and to find out ways to *restrain the Exorbitances*, and *prevent the Abuses* of that Power which they having intrusted in another's hands only for their own good, they found was made use of to hurt them" (*Second Treatise*, §110–11). History, too, teaches that government of men, however (seemingly) wise and trustworthy, must be replaced by government of laws.

This conclusion of Locke's "impartial survey of the nations of the world"—his natural history of liberty, so to speak—bolsters the theoretical conclusion derived from Locke's account of the natural equality of human beings, that the rule of "private judgment" must be excluded in the constitution of a liberal polity.

Ancient Constitutionalism and the Rule of Law

The liberal case for the rule of law is vulnerable to criticism on at least two grounds: that the rule of law is inferior to the discretion or judgment of wise and beneficent rulers; and that the so-called rule of law is often or always a mask for party rule.[5] I consider each objection in turn.

The Rule of Law Versus Private Judgment

There is a respectable alternative to the rule of law. Aristotle asks in the *Politics* "whether it is more advantageous to be ruled by the best man or by the best laws." He concludes—surprisingly, on the liberal view—that there is no certain answer to this question. On one hand, "law is intellect without appetite." Since the passions often "pervert rulers and [even] the best men," the rule of law must be superior even to the rule of good and prudent statesmen. On the other hand, laws are too rigid and "do not command with a view to circumstances." Sometimes the law judges poorly, because the law is blind to particulars; for this reason, "the best regime is not one based on written . . . laws," but authorizes wise and virtuous rulers to judge with a view to circumstances (Aristotle, *Politics*, 1286a5–10, 1287a25–1287b35). That Aristotle would reach a conclusion that differs from Locke's is of course unsurprising. The case for the rule of law is surely strongest where the end of political life is liberty, or liberty understood as security. But suppose (against the liberal) that the salvation of souls or the inculcation of virtue is the true end of political life. In that case, it is not at all clear that the rule of law would be superior to the rule of certain human beings: say, the pious, or the wise, or the virtuous. Of course there is an ancient case for the rule of law, discussed by Nathan Tarcov in his discussion of the ancient idea of constitutionalism in his chapter in this volume. But that argument does not rest on the liberal doctrine of natural equality (and its corollary, the liberal doctrine of consent). For this reason, the ancient argument for the rule of law is contingent. One might say that the end, for ancient constitutionalism, is political moderation or public-spirited rule in pursuit of a common good; the rule of law is a means to that end.

Locke argues that rule by consent is safer than the rule of the putatively wise, or even than the rule of law understood, in the spirit of classical moderation, as a rule of thumb (an exaggeration, but perhaps not much and certainly in the right direction). Wisdom is rare; and who can tell the difference between wisdom and a clever fraud? Better to trust ourselves: we may not know our own best interests as well as a philosophical statesman (or a Solomonic judge), but we can be sure that we have our own best interests at heart.

Here's the danger: the claim of wisdom is too readily a mask for partisan or sectarian mystification. The natural condition of human beings, in the absence of a common judge who can enforce common judgments about political right, is an incipient war of all against all. But this is surely an unstable situation, one that almost inevitably leads to the establishment of tumultuous and illiberal political communities, where petty warfare is replaced by partisan and sectarian warfare—often between rich and poor, sometimes among religious sects or other parties animated by one or another of the opinions contrived by some "wise" leader of a party or sect. There is a kind of communitarian logic about war: human beings at war seek allies because they have enemies. Alliances, parties, and sects will soon conceive the ideologies or dogmas that are necessary to justify oppressing their enemies, thus arming the warlike passions by civilizing them. (This is the natural origin of "community.") Here, then, is a task for the so-called wise, on the liberal view that seeks to demystify claims to wisdom: to teach the myths and ideologies that constitute illiberal communities. "And when Fashion hath once Established, what Folly or craft began, Custom makes it Sacred, and 'twill be thought impudence or madness, to contradict or question it." So-called wisdom is often or always the craft of demagogues, ideologues, or sectarians.

What is called wisdom is mere "private judgment," says Locke, and private judgment is not to be trusted. Hence, the liberal social contract: "all private judgment of every particular Member being excluded, the Community comes to be Umpire, by settled standing Rules, indifferent, and the same to all Parties, . . . concerning any matter of right." Liberal government is government established by the consent of free and equal persons, with no privileges granted to any species of private judgment. As Walter Berns argues, "each man agrees that his opinions of good and bad, right and wrong, justice and injustice are just that—private opinions—and the principle of equality requires him to acknowledge that other opinions, even if they are contrary to his own, have as much (or as little) dignity as his own. . . . Leave other men alone in exchange for the promise, which the sovereign will enforce, to leave you alone." Thus, "in a world where all opinions of justice and injustice are understood to be merely private opinions, no man can rationally agree to an arrangement where another man is authorized to convert his opinion into fundamental law."[6] There is thus a second reason for the unusual respect for the rule of law of liberal theorists: an abiding suspicion of all "private judgment," even the private judgment of the putatively wise. For this reason, too, government of laws is superior to government of men: rule by consent ensures greater security than the rule of the wise exercising private judgment beyond consent.

Few liberals would deny, I think, that this particular aspect of the case for the "rule of law" is contingent—to some extent an acknowledgment of unfortunate necessity rather than a celebration of something good for its own sake. If there were Solomons, and if we could reliably recognize them, who would not want to be ruled by them, when it mattered? No one thinks, for example, that the principle of the "rule of law" should govern in the family, except so far as the "rule of law" in a family can serve as a heuristic device, to prepare children and young adults for responsible life as adult citizens and human beings; but that is the sort of exception that proves the rule: "rule of law" in the family is a tool of the (putatively) wise parent, not a genuine alternative principle of rule, at least until the child reaches such maturity as to be acknowledged, by the parents, to be capable of governing himself. There is, of course, a ready answer to this question: that freedom to govern oneself, even at risk of error, is the necessary condition of an autonomous moral life. Happy children are nevertheless children; the child's life in the family is not yet a fully human life. True enough, as even Aristotle goes some way toward acknowledging (see *Politics*, 1279a5–20 and 1281a25–35). But so far as this argument gives way in the face of the possibility of grave errors, even in politics, it cannot be the whole story of political legitimacy, even in a liberal polity. And of course mature adults can and do acknowledge the necessity of submitting to the rule of the wise or to expertise, as when we hand ourselves over to doctors in medical emergency.

The liberal principle of consent is therefore qualified in many ways in liberal practice, and above all in the practice of *judicial discretion* and *executive prerogative*, both of which are present surprisingly often in our practice, though we liberals properly have a guilty conscience about their necessity. Let us begin by considering the practice of judicial discretion.

Justice Antonin Scalia, in a well-known essay called "The Rule of Law as a Law of Rules," describes and mostly decries the Solomonic temptation sometimes indulged by judges who seek to achieve justice by "dispensing justice case-by-case."[7] Scalia criticizes the unbridled practice of judicial discretion (in the context, as he says, of "law that is made by the courts," which is surely the toughest context for critics of judicial discretion); and his argument is more faithful to classical liberal fear of "private judgment" than are the arguments of those who would enhance the power of judges simply because, what is obviously true but not dispositive, "every rule of law has a few corners that do not fit." As Montesquieu argues in his classic statement of the liberal case for judicial independence, the judicial magistracy is most terrible where it is seen (and the appearance is enough) as an instrument of party: "the power of judging, so terrible among men, being attached neither to a certain state nor to a certain profession, becomes, so to speak, invisible and null. Judges are continually in view; one fears the magistracy, not the magistrates." The best means of achieving the requisite appearance of party neutrality is to cabin the discretion of those who wield judicial power, says Montesquieu, and this is so in spite of the hard fact that law is a crude instrument: "It could happen that the law, which is simultaneously clairvoyant and blind, might be too rigorous in certain cases. But the judges of the nation are, as we have said, only the mouth that pronounces the words of the law, inanimate beings who can moderate neither its force nor its rigor" (*The Spirit of the Laws*, 11.6). Better to rely on the nonjudicial power of pardon, and otherwise to permit here and there an unfortunate man to suffer, than to liberate judges to serve justice directly: because the legitimacy of courts, and above all the popular sense that the power of judging is not "terrible" (as it is by nature, since here is where the threat of deprivation of life and liberty is most immediate) but rather "invisible and null," depends on denying to judges, and being seen to deny, the power to exercise "private judgment" and thereby (inescapably) to seem to speak for party interest. As Scalia puts the point: "parents know that children will accept quite readily all sorts of arbitrary substantive deprivations—no television in the afternoon, or no television in the evening, or even no television at all. But try to let one brother or sister watch television when the others do not, and you will feel the fury of the fundamental sense of justice unleashed." And where that fury and fear is attached to the most "terrible" business of the state, its ability to deprive citizens of life, liberty, and property, the practice of judicial discretion will very likely be seen as a party tool, not only or even especially in the context of criminal prosecutions.[8]

All of which is not to deny that there is a place for judicial discretion even in a liberal polity founded on the rule of law. It seems to me that the liberal common sense of the matter, at least as informed by a classical (Aristotelian) doubt about the justice of simple fidelity to the rule of law, would embrace something like the following division of duties: greater judicial discretion is appropriate in the context of the development of ordinary law (as opposed to constitutional law, where party interest is nearer to the surface of legal disputes), and even here outside the context of criminal law, where the "terrible" character of the power of the state is at its peak; in contexts where party interest is for whatever reason muted, which may vary from time to time, such as, say, tort law[9] or commercial law; and in contexts of common democratic temptations to folly or vice (e.g., in the context of sentencing of convicted criminals and so perhaps in the currently controversial area of sentencing discretion, see Locke, *Second Treatise*, §§8, 11, or in the context of "prejudice against discrete and insular minorities," see *United States v. Carolene Products Co.*, 304 U.S. 144 (1938), footnote 4). There is room for disagreement about the role of judicial discretion in a liberal regime of rule of law; I mean here only to specify the liberal principles that should frame the argument.[10]

Next, consider the case of executive prerogative.[11] Again, let us begin from the general Aristotelian principle: "One who asks law to rule, therefore, is held to be asking god and intellect alone to rule, while one who asks man adds the beast"; "hence law is intellect without appetite" (*Politics*, 1287a25–35). So Aristotle's rule of thumb, like Locke's, is that the "rule of law" is usually superior to the discretionary rule of human beings. But there are so many exceptions, for Aristotle, that those exceptions might seem to swallow the rule. "Some things can be encompassed by the laws and others cannot"; "laws only speak of the universal and do not command with a view to circumstances"; "to legislate concerning matters of deliberation is impossible"; "to rule in accordance with written rules is foolish in any art"; some human beings (probably neither one nor many, but rather the few) are able to "deliberate in finer fashion concerning particulars": so "the best regime is not one built on written rules and laws" (*Politics*, 1286a5–1286b20; 1287a20–1287b30). It is hard to know where Aristotle finally stands on the question whether it is better to be ruled by excellent laws or excellent human beings. Perhaps something like this: the better the regime (that is, the better the rulers), the less one should rely predominantly on the rule of law, and the reverse. Thus, in the case of the most defective forms of democracy, where the people under sway of demagogues rule by decree rather than law, Aristotle says, not quite in his own name but with some sympathy: "For where the laws do not rule there is no regime" (*Politics*, 1292a30–35). As for the "best regime": "the best regime is not one built on written rules and laws."

However that might be, Locke's analysis of the same set of questions is simpler and the place for what he calls "prerogative" *on grounds of the superior judgment of a ruler* considerably narrower. Locke and his liberal successors are less troubled than Aristotle by what might called the problem of judgment or "deliberation." For Locke, whether because of a deep subjectivism about the human good (and thus skepticism about whether any human beings can truly be said to "deliberate in finer fashion concerning particulars") or because of radical egalitarianism in faculties of human beings (and thus skepticism about any claim that one human being might know better than another what is good for that other), superiority of political judgment is never a legitimate title to rule. There simply is no political science in the old-fashioned sense, of superior political *understanding* possessed by a few acute students of politics, the great statesmen and historians; there is only the new political science that designs the institutional machine that structures the forms in which our *will* can take shape and be expressed: there is no political *judgment*, there is only political *will*.

It follows that both the virtues and the vices of the rule of law are principally *formal*, not *substantive*. As a formal matter, the rule of law (or, more precisely, a written constitution that is well designed according to the teachings of the new "science of politics" [see *Federalist* 9]) confers legitimacy because it is the most secure form of self-government by consent. Its virtue is the formal quality of ordering the people's wills in such a way as to establish a peaceful, stable government that secures our liberties (above all, protected private space for "pursuits of happiness" privately defined: even "securing liberty" is principally a formal achievement of liberal politics, not a substantive one). But there are cases where the formal qualities of the "rule of law" prove to be destructive of the stability and liberty that it is designed to secure, and where "prerogative" (the "power to act according to discretion, for the public good, without the prescription of the law, and sometimes even against it" [*Second Treatise*, §160]) is the needed remedy. Locke first introduces the idea of prerogative in relation to malapportionment in the legislature (§158) and tends thereafter to focus on cases where rigid adherence to the rule of law undermines security (e.g., the pardon power exercised for political purposes and to mitigate the severity of the law is a prerogative power). He consistently disparages, on the other hand, prerogative understood as the rule of "wisdom" (cf. §§163–68, §§105–12).[12]

Probably this argument is false. Or rather, the liberal doctrine, it is tolerably clear, is more edifying than true. But the false doctrine itself serves a liberal purpose and is therefore defensible: the popular temptation to submit too readily to strong executives, perhaps especially wise princes (compare the passages just cited with §§223–30), requires efforts to sustain popular vigilance whenever it might be expected to fade, and therefore requires a political science that exaggerates the distinction between Aristotelian and Lockean understandings of prerogative.[13] Consider on this point the example of Lincoln, whose statesmanship is more Aristotelian than Lockean, as I argue elsewhere.[14]

It seems to me that the liberal case here withstands the classical criticism, perhaps even that the Lockean analysis of the limits of the discretionary rule of the wise achieves Aristotelian purposes more reliably than Aristotelian ambivalence regarding the rule of law. Especially decisive, it seems to me, at least in our democratic times, is the Lockean argument that "the people" are naturally conservative and naturally compliant to rule—that is, that the opportunities for ideologues and demagogues to exercise tyrannical power over a compliant people are greatly enhanced when those tyrants can claim to rule on the basis of some superior wisdom, however acquired.

But a tougher challenge looms.

Indirect Government Versus Party Rule: Who Are "We the People"?

"We the People," we say. But who are "We the People"? The orthodox liberal answer to this question, founded on the radical individualism of classical liberal political theory (as reflected, say, in the state of nature teachings of Locke), is that "We the People" is all of us. But everyone knows that this pretense is a bit of a myth. So: why take it seriously?[15]

Let us begin with the myth. Its radical individualism is famously the Achilles' heel of liberal political philosophy. That individualism—which is, in one way or another, the foundation of liberal ideas about consent, individual (inalienable) rights, limited government, and the rest—seems to be both sociologically and psychologically untrue, or so many critics of liberalism contend (and many liberals now agree). The image of solitary, free and equal individuals in a state of nature does not do justice to the evidence that we are constituted in various important ways by history, by culture, by family, by religion, and so on. The political implication (to narrow the present question) of these sociological and psychological falsehoods is that the orthodox liberal claim that "We the People" is an undifferentiated aggregation of free and equal individuals—that is, that "We the People" is not the name of one or more parties within the polity, but rather simply *is* the whole polity—is something of a pretense. Thoughtful liberals are aware of the problem. So, for example, the authors of *The Federalist Papers* acknowledge, even trumpet, the fact that ordinarily in republican politics, including in liberal republican politics, "the people" are animated by passions, interests, and opinions that might—if not "controlled"—produce majority faction, a kind of tyranny. So, from a more "realistic" point of view, "We the People" is best understood as a party—and even as a party naturally tempted to act on impulses that are "adverse to the rights of other citizens, or to the permanent and aggregate interests of the community." Indeed, the danger of majority faction is so permanent and fundamental in republican political life, including in its modern liberal form, that it is one of the "diseases most incident to republican government" (see *Federalist* 9–10). It is no exaggeration to say that the central task of modern constitutionalism, of the new "science of politics," is to tame or moderate or "control the effects" of the ruling authority of the *party* of "the people," while nevertheless enabling the people *as a constitutional being* to rule—by means of the principal institutions of modern constitutional politics (representation, separation of powers, an independent judiciary, extending the sphere, and so on).

That is, the authors of *The Federalist Papers* might seem to concede the essential truth of the Aristotelian understanding of "the people." "We the People" is the ruling authority in a democratic regime. For better or worse (depending on the quality of "the people"), on the Aristotelian view, the character of our or any democratic regime is governed by the ruling authority of the people, which rules on the basis of a partial (among other partialities, democratic) conception of justice ("justice is held to be equality, and it is, but for equals and not for all," *Politics*, 1280a10–15) and in its own interest (*Politics*, 1279b5–10). As in any "regime," the ruling party gives the polity its character: it commands with a view to establishing as the collective good of the polity certain ways of life, tastes, and moral aspirations that are favored by the dominant party. Every "people" is different, Aristotle acknowledges, and so the relevant set of dominant or privileged ways of life will vary from one democracy to another. Aristotle thus speaks in the *Politics* of a great range of democratic regimes: a democracy of farmers, a democracy of the urban poor, a democracy of the middle class, a democracy of citizen soldiers, and so on, each of which has its particular and distinctive character,

way of life, (partial) conception of justice, and the rest. One of these democracies, by the way—the rule of the middle class of a certain quality—is "best
for most cities and most human beings" (see *Politics*, 1295a25–1296b15; cf.
1281a40–1282b15). But what is not possible, on Aristotle's account, is the rule
of "We the People" *beyond party*: the rule of party, the rule of a part over the
whole for its own advantage and on the basis of its own partial conception
of justice, is the natural condition of political life.[16] To the extent that the
rule of party can be tamed and the partial character of a regime moderated,
that aim is best achieved (on this classical understanding) by establishing
a "mixed regime" of one sort or another, where two or more parties are
(somehow) judiciously balanced in order to permit competing conceptions
of the good life to flourish side by side and thereby to provide some space
for the practice of freedom by citizens in their choice of a way of life and for
the emergence of a variety of forms of human excellence—or at least, what
might be good enough for us liberals, with some space for diversity and
idiosyncrasy.[17]

Now what is at stake in this dispute about the true or deepest meaning
of "We the People"? Let's return, in this light, to the idea of the "rule of law."
Plato's Thrasymachus famously remarks, at the beginning of the *Republic*,
that "justice is the advantage of the established ruling body." And then he
provides a gloss that makes it clear that democracy is in no way exempt
from this fundamental vice of regimes: *all political justice is the justice of
party* (*Politics*, 1281a15–20). In brief, the classical view is pessimistic about
the prospect that "the rule of law" can serve as a path beyond party, toward
a neutral set of rules that provide equal protection of the laws to each individual, regardless of party. Polities are everywhere constituted by parties,
not by individuals: that is the central tenet of ancient constitutionalism.
There are thus democratic laws in democracy, oligarchic laws in oligarchy,
and so on, and all of these laws are "partial" (and therefore in some measure unjust). The claim that "We the People" could somehow escape this
necessity, by imagining ourselves as constituting something more than a
party, as speaking with one voice for the polity as a whole in defense of a
common good beyond party, is a self-delusion. The best we can do, Aristotle
concludes, is something like a "mixed regime": in the judicious mixture of
forms of injustice or partiality, some approximation of justice, of an almost
truly common good, might be achieved.

How might the liberal respond? First, we should, I think, concede that
there is some truth to the Aristotelian critique of the liberal idea of "indirect
government" through the "rule of law." A second Achilles' heel of liberal

political philosophy is the tendency of liberals to want to deny what is plain to honest eyes, that liberal democratic polities systematically privilege some ways of life and conceptions of the good over others. Liberalism is not truly "neutral" in respect of its consequences for how liberal citizens choose to live their private and public lives. Certain ways of life and moral opinions are disfavored and others privileged. Commerce, equality, the health and comfort of the body, bourgeois virtues, rights, and privacy are in; the virtues and ways of life of priests and aristocrats are out. A thousand proofs are available and have over the years been offered by critics of liberalism and acknowledged by its friends. Here, I will let one example stand for the whole argument, because it is especially illuminating as to the difficulty of relying on "the rule of law" as a path to neutrality. Tocqueville's *Democracy in America* is a masterly Aristotelian portrait of modern (liberal) democracy and of the qualities of the democratic soul that our regime—our party—produces. Early in the first volume, in a section entitled "That the Salient Point of the Social State of the Anglo-Americans Is Its Being Essentially Democratic," Tocqueville writes: "it was estate law that made equality take its last step."[18] The consequences of this democratic law (providing for equal partition of the family inheritance among all the children) are pervasive, and in no way neutral.

I am astonished that ancient and modern political writers have not attributed to estate laws a greater influence on the course of human affairs. These laws belong, it is true, to the civil order; but they ought to be placed at the head of all political institutions, for they have an incredible influence on the social state of people, of which political laws are only the expression. . . . The legislator regulates the estates of citizens and he rests for centuries: motion having been given to his work, he can withdraw his hand from it; the machine acts by its own force and is directed as if by itself toward a goal indicated in advance. Constituted in a certain manner, it gathers, it concentrates, and it groups around some head property and soon after power; in a way, it makes aristocracy shoot up from the soil. Guided by other principles and launched on another track, its action is more rapid still; it divides, it partitions, it disperses goods and power. . . . It crushes or shatters all that comes across its path, it rises up and falls back incessantly on the earth until all that can be seen is a shifting and impalpable dust on which democracy sits. (p. 47)

There is, in brief, no path to party neutrality in respect of such regime-constitutive laws. And the consequences of such laws are not merely material: "the law of equal partition does not exert its influence only on the fate of goods; it acts on the very souls of property owners and calls their passions to its aid." Family spirit "materialized in the land" is destroyed; individual selfishness is redirected from the aspiration "to immortalize oneself in one's remote posterity" to the present purpose of securing material well-being; attachment to the sort of family that has a history is destroyed. Any vestige of hereditary distinction, and of the aristocratic ways of life that are made possible by the preservation of an aristocratic class, is destroyed: "today the sons of these opulent citizens are men of commerce, attorneys, doctors"; "there does not exist in America, therefore, any class in which the penchant for intellectual pleasures is transmitted with comfort and inherited leisure, and which holds the work of the intellect in honor."[19] If the nonpartisan conception of "We the People" is to be defended, it must nevertheless be possible to concede the truth of the criticisms thus far considered.

Second, it seems to me that we liberals should accept Aristotle's aid and seek to defend a conception of liberal democracy as "mixed regime." Vestiges of aristocratic and religious ways of life are worth preserving and even promoting, as a counterweight to prevailing democratic aspirations, tastes, and moral opinions. The principal lesson of ancient constitutionalism is that protecting dissenting ways of life and moral opinions is a source of political moderation. One source of the continuing vitality of liberal democracy in America, it seems to me, is that even now our politics is partly constituted by a fruitful tension between a party of liberty and a party of equality, and to a lesser extent between a party of religion and a party of secular liberalism.[20]

And yet, perhaps all of this is to concede too much to classical constitutionalism. Liberal constitutionalism should not work, if the "We the People" idea and its "rule of law" corollaries are mostly imaginations; and yet it does. The rule of the party of the people in liberal democracy is certainly not as direct or raw as the classical portrait of democracy suggests it should be (cf. *Federalist* 9 or the portrait of democracy in Plato's *Republic*), and not only because American democracy is a kind of "mixed regime." That is, the argument for classical constitutionalism against the liberal conception of the "rule of law" does not quite defeat the liberal argument discussed above, however much it requires us to qualify that argument. Above all, certain institutional features of the "new science of politics" are designed to enable the people to conceive of itself in two political moments, so to speak: both as a constitutional people and as a political party. The habit of thinking constitutionally, learning to distinguish between what is appropriate in constitutional contestation and what is appropriate in ordinary political contestation, is an essential condition of liberal moderation.[21] It is, moreover, a sign of health that both of our principal political parties still have "constitutionalist" wings, whose purpose is to defend, say, religious liberty or freedom of speech or structural constitutional principles such as federalism or separation of powers, sometimes without regard to immediate party advantage. And, from this point of view, a more-than-rational reverence for the "Founding Fathers" and the Constitution they brought forth is probably salutary (see *Federalist* 49 for the classic defense of this particular political mystification). For now, I leave the argument here: that the task of defenders of liberal constitutionalism is to discover ways of preserving the distinction, in theory and practice, between a constitutional "We the People" and the sort of *demos* that governs as a party and that constitutes a partisan regime, in the face of the sorts of objections from the point of view of classical constitutionalism that I have considered here.

Conclusions: Regarding Constitutionalism

Let me conclude, then, by sketching a few consequences of this analysis of the problematic character of the liberal ideas of the "rule of law" and "We the People." The core of liberal constitutionalism, I have argued, is the distinction between "We the People" understood as a constitutional people and "the people" understood as the party that constitutes our democratic regime. How might that distinction be sustained in our habits of constitutional reasoning?

- To preserve the distinction between a constitutional people and the people as a party, it is necessary to insist upon the exceptional and foundational character of constitutional judgments and enactments. A certain wariness about constitutional change is therefore desirable (see *Federalist* 49) and the natural conservatism of the people in constitutional matters ought to be cultivated.
- The aspect of liberal constitutionalism that calls on "We the People" to conceive of itself as sometimes acting in a constitutional capacity requires attention, on the part of citizens and judges and legislators, to the conditions of democratic self-mastery or self-restraint. A liberal people is, in the best case, "populist" only in ordinary politics, not in constitutional politics, and since the temptations of populism may bleed from the one sphere to the other, liberal constitutionalism requires a wariness about populist impulses.

- Constitutional gag rules of various sorts ("Congress shall make no law . . ."), by which the people compels itself to renounce certain party ends as beyond the sphere of limited, constitutional government, are a key means for the people acting in its constitutional capacity to restrain its populist impulses, and so constitutional doctrines that permit the people to set aside such rules through processes of ordinary politics threaten to undermine the distinction between the constitutional people and the partisan people.
- Structural constitutionalism—strict fidelity to the rules of the game that prevent the people from acting as a party beyond certain limits (for example, federalism, separation of powers, and the delegation of legislative powers in Article I of the Constitution)—is an important formal complement to the substantive restraints of constitutional gag rules, and so liberal constitutionalists should be wary of the sort of populism that chafes against merely formal rules, whether in the name of democracy or in the name of some substantive claim of justice.
- The principle of consent is bedrock for liberal constitutionalists, because of the dangers of "private judgment" discussed above, but that consent, properly understood, is the consent of a constitutional people acting in its constitutional capacity, not the consent of the people acting through ordinary legislation or the constructive consent of the people acting by political acquiescence to constitutional developments not formally adopted.

One final point: the strategy that I have sketched here for thinking about liberal constitutionalism presents a middle way, it seems to me, between two trends in constitutional reasoning that are prevalent on the Right and the Left today. The Right is perhaps sometimes too indulgent of democracy, advocating judicial restraint in the culture wars, but without sufficiently recognizing the necessary distinction between the people toward which liberal constitutionalism requires deference (the constitutional people) and the partisan people that liberal constitutionalism aims to restrain. When the people acts in its constitutional capacity, certainly liberal principles of constitutionalism require judges to suspend their "private judgment" and defer to the will of that constitutional people. It seems to me a fair criticism of contemporary constitutional jurisprudence, from the Right, that our judges have too often failed to acknowledge the sovereignty of the constitutional people. And yet, this deference to democracy sometimes leads constitutional theorists on the Right to confer constitutional status on popular enactments and judgments where the people cannot be said to have acted in its constitutional capacity—that is, where the people has acted as a party ("adverse to the rights of other citizens, or to the permanent and aggregate interests of the community"). In contrast, constitutional theorists on the Left are sometimes too hasty in advocating the exercise of judicial power to oppose the excesses of democracy in the name of liberal philosophy ("a fusion of constitutional law and moral theory"), without sufficiently acknowledging the importance of the same distinction. Where the people has acted in its constitutional capacity, the will of the people must be the final word for a liberal constitutionalist, whatever its wisdom. And the question of whether the people has acted in its constitutional capacity or as a party will very often be best settled by attention to the formal properties of the popular enactment, not its substantive content. For the liberal constitutionalist, form will often trump substance, even in matters of constitutional right. Constitutional theorists of the Left have very often chafed against these formal principles of liberal constitutionalism, in defense of substantive (liberal) principles of right, but that is to employ illiberal means to achieve liberal ends. Liberal constitutionalism, properly conceived, offers a middle ground between the democratic constitutionalism of some on the Right and the philosophical constitutionalism of some on the Left.[22]

PART II

Historical Perspectives: American Constitutional History

Chapter Three
Judicial Review and the Incomplete Constitution: A Madisonian Perspective on the Supreme Court and the Idea of Constitutionalism

Michael P. Zuckert

It is now often remarked that we live in the age of the stealth nominee. The reason that not having a public record is increasingly among the most important qualifications for appointment to the Supreme Court is not difficult to state: the Court has become so controversial, the role of the Court so contested, the fate of certain issues and the future of important constitutional doctrines so dependent on the particular composition of the Court that all sectors of American political society are readily mobilized to foster or hinder the candidacies of those perceived to be favorable or not to the causes promoted by the activists. To leave the sleeping dogs to their slumber, to avoid excessive bloodletting, presidents, ever since the infamous Bork debacle, have sought candidates with a smaller footprint, with fewer targets to aim at, for in our age every achievement is, in the eyes of some beholders, a blemish and a reason for opposition. Thus in our age we are unlikely to see individuals like John Marshall or Roger Brooke Taney, or Charles Evans Hughes, men with large public records, appointed to the Court.

Thus it is tempting to think of ours as an age of especial conflict around the Court, but that is, to a large degree, an illusion. The Supreme Court, by design the least political branch, and by proclamation of one of the leading founders "the least dangerous branch," has been politically controversial at almost every moment of its history.[1] The sainted Marshall Court was the target of great hostility emanating from the Jeffersonian Republican Party. The Taney Court was even more despised by the new Republican Party of the 1850s. FDR's Democrats intensely opposed the Court of their day; bill-boards across America sought to "impeach Earl Warren"; and we need no reminders of how controversial the more recent Courts of *Roe v. Wade*[2] and *Planned Parenthood v. Casey*[3] have been.

As striking as the continuity of opposition is the great discontinuity and variety in the nature and direction of the opposition. The Jeffersonians were centered in the South and favored strict construction. The Republicans were centered in the North and tended to favor a looser construction. The FDR Democrats were centered in the Northeast and the South, definitely favored loose construction, and disagreed with the Court mostly over economic issues. The opposition to the Warren Court was perhaps most focused in the South and Midwest, and fought over civil rights and civil liberties. The most recent opposition is less regional, although perhaps the "red state" coalition captures the core of it. The battles are now largely over social issues.

The great variety of the sources of opposition to the Court at different times is no doubt responsible for a general failure to appreciate how controversial the Court has *always* been. The center of opposition, politically and geographically, has varied greatly, and the issues that prompted opposition have varied just as much; the favored approach to the Constitution has likewise varied. Yesterday's opponents have become today's supporters and today's neutrals have become tomorrow's partisans. Thus no group or region or philosophic persuasion has felt consistently out of sorts with the Court and thus no one notices how much the court has been politically buffeted since its founding.

The most recent source of controversy is remarkable, however, for producing, if not quite a consensus, then a surprising convergence of thinking on the Court. The keynote of this convergence is contained in the title to Mark Tushnet's book *Taking the Constitution Away from the Courts.*[4] What is remarkable is not that some are calling for court curbing of one sort or another—this has been a fairly constant feature of reaction to the Court—but that those calls are now coming from the Left—as with Tushnet—and from the Right—as with Robert Bork's proposal to limit the Court.[5] An important part of this recent expression of discontent with the role and actions of the Court in our day is a looking back to the founding for guidance on what the institution was intended to be, and how it was supposed to behave. Thus we have seen a large number of reconsiderations of old and, as one would have thought, well-worn questions, such as was the power of judicial review intended to be held by the Court, or was it some sort of usurpation? If judicial review was intended, what sort of review? Was it the sort of review the Court claimed for itself in *Cooper v. Aaron,*[6] that is, the power to interpret the Constitution with an authority binding on all the political actors in the Constitutional system? Or was it some version of departmentalism, as was defended in different forms by some of the great figures in America's political past—Jefferson, Jackson, and Lincoln among them? If judicial review was intended, that is, if the Court has a special task to interpret the Constitution, what mode of interpretation ought it to deploy: "originalism" or some more "living" kind of constitutional hermeneutics? If originalism was the original intent, does original intent have the authority to require the use of original intent? In other words, many look back to the founding, seeking from the founders some sort of guidance, neutral authority, on how we should conduct the judicial function today.

I intend to join those looking back to the founding, but my intent differs from most of the others in two specific ways. My attention will rest on only one of the founders, James Madison. He was, after all, the "father of the Constitution," and most important he understood the overall logic of the new order better than anyone else at the time. He is not a legal authority—he was just one man, and on the losing side of many important battles over the new Constitution. But he was the man who developed the core insights that made the new federalism, and the new kind of separation of powers system. Moreover, he promoted the new theory of the extended republic as a means for securing individual rights and the common good in a "wholly republican" order. Not only did he have an unparalleled understanding of the political nature of the Constitution, but he also had an unexcelled understanding of what judicial review was to be in the new system—and of what was problematic about it.

Rousseau in his *Social Contract* sought to explain not how naturally free human beings came to possess their chains, but rather how those chains might be rendered legitimate. My undertaking here is nearly the reverse and differs from that of many of the others who have looked back to the founders by seeking not so much a way to render legitimate the court's role, but rather attempting to explain how it came to play a role, which, more often than not, is necessarily viewed as illegitimate by large segments of the American public, and which, judging from the range of literature on the subject, has never been rendered quite legitimate in the eyes of students of the Court.

Madison: Judicial Review and the Incomplete Constitution

The place to begin is with Madison in the months just at and after the end of the Constitutional Convention, a gathering in which he had personally played such a large and decisive role. Strange to say, Madison was not so pleased with the convention's handiwork as one might expect, given his importance to the proceedings. In early September 1787, not long before the convention was to complete its work, Madison wrote to his friend and fellow Virginian, Thomas Jefferson, then in Paris conducting his nation's diplomatic business. After sketching the new constitutional plan, he commented: "These are the outlines. The extent of them may surprise you:" Madison recognized that the convention had gone far and done much. Nonetheless, he continued, "I hazard an opinion . . . that the plan should it be adopted will neither effectually answer its national object nor prevent the local mischiefs which everywhere excite disgust agst. [*sic*] the state governments."[7] That is to say, whatever the convention had accomplished, it had not achieved the two things Madison thought most essential: it neither provided for an adequate union of the states nor supplied an adequate remedy for the misgovernment within the states, two formidable failings. As it turns out, these failings had much to do with the birth of judicial review and with its amazingly tangled history.

In order to discover the relation between Madison's pessimistic diagnosis of the new Constitution and judicial review, it helps to begin by recalling that judicial review is normally identified as one of the major innovations of the American founding. It was not the only novelty, however. Indeed, Madison used the phrase "a system without a precedent, ancient or modern," to describe the new constitutional order.[8] Alexander Hamilton, Madison's coauthor in *The Federalist,* was also very impressed with these novelties. Indeed, he announced in *Federalist* 9 that were it not for these innovations, the "friends of liberty" would not be able to support a republican form of government, for the historical record of republics was not, to that date, very favorable to liberty. The novelties in question, Hamilton announced, were the products of "the science of politics," which, like many other sciences in the eighteenth century, had made great improvements recently.[9] A glance at the improvements Hamilton lists there makes it clear that the practitioner of the "science of politics" he has in mind, or the one who called attention to all these improvements, is Montesquieu, the French political philosopher who published his classic text, *On the Spirit of the Laws,* about forty years before the Constitutional Convention. Montesquieu's was the cutting-edge political science of the mid- to late eighteenth century, and his book was the chief authority for all sides in America at the time of the founding.

The Americans, the *Federalist* and other sources made clear, were fol-

lowers of Montesquieu, but it is equally clear that they were not mere followers. They were innovators, too, partly from necessity, partly from conviction.
There were, however, unexpected and even perplexing consequences that
resulted from the American combination of following and then departing
from Montesquieu.

The chief adapter of Montesquieu was James Madison. In preparing a
plan for the upcoming constitutional convention, he had developed a com-
prehensive analysis of what needed to be done in America, together with
concrete proposals for reform.[10] He prevailed upon the Virginia delegation
to make most (though not quite all) of his scheme theirs, which they did
when Governor Randolph presented it to the convention on behalf of his
state's delegation at the opening of proceedings.[11] Madison proposed, but
the convention disposed—one can discern the main outlines of Madison's
thinking in the final Constitution, but many important changes were made
by the convention as a whole, changes inspired in part by the play of conflicting interests, in part by doubts about some of Madison's theories and
proposals, in part by cold feet. The convention's retreat from Madison's proposals was the immediate cause of his near-despairing letter to Jefferson.

Madison had worked out a daring synthesis of certain themes in Montesquieu, which synthesis in turn required, according to Madison, three
absolutely essential institutions: a council of revision, a congressional negative on state law on behalf of federalism, and a congressional negative on
state laws on behalf of individual rights and justice. The convention rejected
all three, and since Madison believed they were essential, he concluded the
Constitution would not survive. Nonetheless, the convention did not leave
matters at merely turning down Madison's three proposals; with little fore-
thought or overall planning the delegates turned the jobs that Madison's
three institutions were to do over to the judiciary. They thus produced one
of the most notable and at that time unique and novel institutions—a judiciary powerful beyond any seen before, because it was armed with the power
of constitutional review.

An apt slogan for the situation as Madison saw it comes from Robert
Burns's famous "To a Mouse": "The best laid schemes o' mice and men / Gang
aft a-gley." Madison had well-laid schemes indeed, but in their "gang[ing]
aft a-gley" we ended up with an institution nobody quite planned and one
beset with insuperable tensions and even contradictions.

The Best Laid Schemes

Madison's "well-laid scheme" was, as I have suggested, an adaptation of Montesquieuean political science. In taking Montesquieu seriously Madison was not in the least singular. *The Spirit of the Laws* was the beginning point for all critical thinking about political construction in late eighteenth-century America. The prominence of Montesquieu at the time has been well documented. In his citation analysis of eighteenth-century political writings in America, Donald Lutz discovered that Montesquieu was the single most widely cited political thinker of the entire founding era.[12]

Three of Montesquieu's central ideas had a particularly great impact on Madison, and, again, not on him alone. First, he had a theory of republicanism, the model for which was ancient Sparta. Second, he spoke of a federal union of republics as a requirement of maintaining the liberty of republics. And third, he spoke of a different kind of constitution, called a "free constitution," that is, a constitution organized internally to provide liberty. The model for a free constitution was modern Britain.

For Montesquieu the republic and the free constitution were by no means identical, as is evident from the immense difference between Sparta and eighteenth-century Britain. He says in fact that the republic is not inherently free, and he shows that the free constitution is at best only partly republican.[13] The free constitution, the British constitution, has a republican element, the popular House of Commons, but it mixes that with a hereditary and aristocratic House of Lords, and a hereditary monarchy. The free constitution must, Montesquieu argued, contain a mixture of elements of this sort—it must be like the old sorts of mixed regimes that political scientists since Aristotle had been recommending. He added the idea that the mix of monarchic, aristocratic, and democratic elements must be superimposed on a new-fangled distinction among legislative, executive, and judicial powers. Montesquieu is the first to develop the theory that what makes a free constitution free is the separateness of the powers. But, he insisted, this separation could succeed only if the powers were divided among the different elements (democratic, aristocratic, etc.). The free constitution must also be a mixed constitution.

Republics, especially the sort Montesquieu called democratic republics (Athens would be an example), located political power in the hands of the great body of the people and had minimal and mostly ineffective separation of powers. They were not and could not be "free societies": in addition to lacking separation of powers they required rigorous training and control of citizens in order to produce republican "virtue." They also required thorough control of economic life in order to maintain equality of wealth, simplicity of manners, and frugality—all requirements of republics.[14] According to Montesquieu, then, the republic and the free constitution were really quite different from each other.

The Americans, Madison included, opted after the Revolution for a form Montesquieu had implied was impossible—a synthesis of the republican and free models. As Madison put it in the *Federalist* they sought a system "wholly republican," that is, a system that derived all political power directly or indirectly from the great body of the people and had no hereditary or grossly oligarchic authority in it, a system that would be at the same time a "free constitution" in Montesquieu's sense.[15] Thus like most Americans in the 1780s, Madison wanted to construct an order that was at once *free, republican,* and *federal.* He was the greatest political scientist of his time because he saw that Montesquieu might be a good point of departure, but that his solutions were inadequate, especially in light of the American commitment to all three together.

For a constitution to be free meant, at a minimum, that it had to have a genuine separation of powers.[16] For a constitution to be republican meant (according to Madison and the other Americans) that it have no branches not derived from the people.[17] The two commitments interacted in a way that exacerbated a difficulty inherent in all separation of powers schemes. Such schemes have two natural problems requiring some sort of resolution: on the one hand, any system of divided power implies the possibility of conflict over who possesses what powers. Some mode of settling such conflicts is necessary. Secondly, there is an inevitable danger that the separation will be undone in one way or another. For example, in the actual operating English constitution of the eighteenth century, the executive possessed the ability to make "side-payments" that allowed it to dominate parliament. The eighteenth-century British opposition thinker John Trenchard, writing as Cato, diagnosed the problem as follows: "What with the crowd of offices in the gift of the crown . . . ; what with the promises and expectations given to those who by court influence, and often by court money, carried their elections; what with luxurious dinners, and rivers of burgundy, champagne, and tokay, thrown down the throats of gluttons; and what with pensions and other personal gratifications; I say, by all these corrupt arts, the representatives of the English people . . . have been brought to betray the people, and to join with their oppressors. So much are men governed by artful applications to their private passions and interest."[18] When this happens, the liberty-serving virtues of separated powers are lost. The American states in the past decade had revealed even more direct instances of violation of the separation of powers when, for example, legislatures intervened in pending court cases, or even passed laws overturning the decisions made by courts. Encroachments on the executive power were also common, although most state executives were so weak it was not always easy to tell an encroachment from business as usual. So, in sum, separation of powers schemes pose problems of both conflict of powers and encroachment, both requiring something like a policeman to deal with.

The attempt to build a free constitution that is "wholly republican" exacerbates the problem and at the same time removes the solution Montesquieu had hit upon. Although the three separated powers possess a theoretical equality, that is not the case in practice: the legislative power has a certain natural supremacy. It makes the laws on the basis of which the other branches operate, and, according to Montesquieuean theory, one branch of the legislature is necessarily popular, drawn from the great body of the people. The people collectively being the most numerous, wealthy, and ultimately most powerful element in the society, their branch, the legislature, has a natural weight in a separated powers system that reinforces the primacy of the legislative over the other functions. This actual primacy of the legislature is much increased in a wholly republican system because here only the people have a call on political power. In the "wholly republican" version, Madison speculated, what he called the "legislative vortex" is especially prone and capable of drawing to itself the other powers.[19]

In part because of the natural advantages of the legislature, Montesquieu had posited the British mixed model (rather than a republic) as the only workable version of the free constitution. A monarchy (likely hereditary) and a hereditary House of Lords, containing old families and great wealth, could have the political weight to retain their independence. In case of conflict among the powers, moreover, Montesquieu saw the upper house of the legislature holding the balance of power between the popular lower house and the monarchical executive; it could thus serve as umpire and ultimately maintain the system of separated powers.[20]

But the wholly republican version of the free constitution took that option off the table—there would be no nonpopular branches to contain and constrain the popular branch, and thus to maintain the separation. An early solution Americans of the revolutionary generation hit upon was to declare firmly, as the Virginia Constitution did, that no branch should exercise the powers of the other branches. Madison rightly had contempt for such a solution—it was a classic example of what he sneered at as a "parchment barrier," a declaration on paper with no means provided to make it effective in practice.[21]

Thomas Jefferson, also seeing this problem, proposed that an appeal be made to a special popular assembly in order to adjudicate conflicts among the branches and to enforce the separation. Madison more gently sneered at this proposal of his good friend—it was setting the foxes to guard the henhouse.[22] Jefferson did not understand that placing political power in the people was not the solution to every problem, but was itself a primary fact that created many problems.

Madison's proposed solution, as contained in the Virginia Plan, was a Council of Revision—a body sitting atop the pyramid of governmental powers, armed with a qualified (i.e., overrideable) veto on the acts of the legislature. The council was to consist of the "executive head" and "some number of judges."[23] Madison thought that the executive and the judges together would possess the weight, the competence, and the incentives to operate as preservers and umpires of the separation of powers scheme. He feared that unless the two other branches were joined together as he proposed, the function would be ill-done, if done at all. Although tempted to it, the convention ultimately rejected Madison's Council of Revision.

Madison's scheme was also a federal scheme. This too was a direct development from Montesquieuean theory. The French thinker had argued that republics, necessarily small and therefore weak relative to nonrepublican neighbors, were required to federate in order to maintain their liberty.[24] The struggle with Britain, of course, drove home to the Americans the value of union. Federal systems, which divide powers on a vertical axis parallel to the horizontal division of separation of powers, raise many of the same issues of conflict and encroachment that separation of powers schemes do. Going beyond Montesquieu, and building in part on the American experience in the decade since 1776, Madison concluded that one set of parties was specially advantaged in these conflicts. The member states had an inevitable tendency to fly out of the orbit of the general government of the union. The states normally had both the capability and the incentive to encroach on each other and on the central authorities.[25] The federal system, Madison concluded, needed "an enforcer," an umpire, too.

Just as with the problem posed by the attempt to construct a free constitution, so with the problem posed by federalism, the decision to have "wholly republican" political systems exacerbated the difficulties. The people were naturally and, Madison feared, perhaps inevitably, attached to their states far more than to the union—think of the relative attachments of Americans today to the United States as opposed to NATO or the United Nations. Popular attachment to the state republics would encourage and support the individual states in their natural tendency to self-aggrandizement at the expense of federation partners and the federation authorities.

The most important solution Madison proposed to the centrifugal tendencies of federal systems was a very radical institution now mostly forgotten. In the Virginia Plan he proposed that Congress be armed with an unqualified power to veto all laws of the states, which, in Congress' opinion, overstepped the bounds of state constitutional power by trenching on the powers of other states or of the union itself.[26] Although Congress was composed of representatives of the people in the states just as much as each state legislature was, Madison counted on the likelihood that the ambitious attachments members of Congress would form to their offices in the federation government would supply them with sufficient incentive to resist state encroachments.[27] Moreover, Madison understood well the dynamics of the collective choice issues involved. Each state acting individually has an incentive to resist the central authorities or to encroach on others, but the group of states as a whole (and thus their representatives gathered in Congress) had an incentive to keep the union together and effective. He was not, however, able to prevail on his fellow delegates to include his proposed negative in their proposed constitution.

Finally, Madison concluded in an argument that has certainly not been forgotten (although I think often misunderstood) that republican systems have a natural tendency to violate rights, which their republican form does not cure, but indeed exacerbates. As he argued in *Federalist* 10, republics have a tendency to faction, that is, to break down into groups and interests hostile to the rights of others or the common needs of the community. Montesquieu recognized the problem and for that reason had recommended small, homogeneous, rigorously regulated polities like Sparta as the republican solution to the problem of faction. Many Americans at the time of the founding were profoundly ambivalent toward Montesquieu's solution. Many of the existing states were already far larger and more diverse than Sparta, and even the strongest partisans of republican virtue held back from endorsing the kind of restrictive state this sort of republic had to be.

Madison thought the issue through more ruthlessly than his contemporaries, many of whom were willing to settle for halfway measures tempered with hope for the best. Madison pushed the analysis further by showing that republican systems, especially smaller ones, are particularly prone to succumb to the evil of majority faction, for the principle of operation of republics, majority rule, acts to empower factious majorities.[28]

Madison famously argued that the large or extended, socially, economically, and religiously heterogeneous republic could avoid this problem and, almost by magic, produce only good or at least much better majorities (nonfactious majorities) than could smaller, more homogeneous republics.[29] Madison applied this thought to his America as follows: the smaller states are more likely to be dominated by factious majorities than the larger union. Congressional majorities are more likely than state majorities to be just, that is, not to violate the rights of others, and to be compatible with the long-term common good.

Some scholars, such as Gordon Wood and Martin Diamond, concluded that this analysis must have made Madison a full-scale nationalist, that is, a supporter of transfer of complete sovereignty to the government of the union from the states, or of as much authority as he could get away with transferring.[30] This view profoundly misses Madison's real scheme. Rather than seeking to transfer authority to Congress, Madison rather sought a policeman within the states, just as he also sought institutions to police the federal system and the separation of powers system. This "umpire" was to intervene and adjudicate, in effect, in disputes between governing majorities in the states and the minorities they might otherwise oppress. Congress was not to govern directly, but rather to act the umpire by correcting the states.[31] Here was Madison's most audacious scheme—he wanted Congress, the institution most likely to have nonfactious majorities, to possess a veto over all laws in the states, not just those that encroached on the federal system. The aim would be to protect rights by correcting unjust, improvident, overly changeable legislation in the states.

This proposal for a universal veto was another incredibly creative adaptation of a Montesquieuean idea. In the latter's model of a free constitution, the nonrepublican elements—monarch and aristocratic upper house—would be empowered to thwart potentially oppressive acts of the more popular lower house. Madison saw Congress playing a role in the de facto constitution of each state especially analogous to the role of the monarch in the free mixed regime. Instead of transferring state powers to the nation as Wood or Diamond have it, Madison would make Congress part of the constitutions of each state. The model for this idea, a model which must have made Madison believe this plan to be workable, was the pre-Revolutionary imperial Constitution. Before the revolution, the king, acting through his Privy Council, had such a veto over the acts of the colonial legislatures.[32]

Perhaps in part because of the imperial precedent, Madison's proposal proved far too bold for his fellow delegates. Although it was debated at the Convention on several occasions, it could not muster enough support to make it into the Constitution.

"Gang[ing] Aft A-Gley"

Madison saw three great needs in the complex type of political order he and his fellow delegates were putting in place. He proposed three institutions to supply those needs; he saw his fellows reject all three. It was clear from Madison's letter to Jefferson that it was the convention's failure to adopt these favored devices that led him to be so pessimistic about the new Constitution. He in effect judged that however remarkable the achievements of the convention, it had failed at the two most important tasks—the establishment of a proper separation of powers system, and the proper division of power between the general government and the states.

He spent most of his space decrying the absence of the two congressional negatives. In explaining himself he recapitulated two of the most important political analyses he is known for—the analysis underlying the new kind of federalism contained in the Constitution, and the analysis of the need for a large rather than a small republic. This latter analysis, so famous as the core of *Federalist* 10, was explicitly attached here and everywhere else Madison ever presented it (except *Federalist* 10) to the proposal for a congressional negative on state laws, a negative meant to secure private rights. It is a strange quirk of history that Madison's political thought in the Constitution-making years is so often misunderstood due to the fact that the extended republic argument came to be known from the one place where it was detached from the actual application Madison made of it.

It would take us too far afield to explore in detail the reasons for the convention's rejection of Madison's three famed institutions. In part, the failure of the negatives must be attributed to Madison's success in impressing on his colleagues the new principle that should govern the operation of the new constitution: that one level of government (the general government) should not operate on the other level of government (the states), but rather on individuals. Madison's beloved negatives would violate his own principle, and the expedient settled on in place of the negatives, the empowerment of the judiciary to carry on these functions, seemed to many to be more in accord with the true Madisonian principle of the new order.[33]

Perhaps more significant for our immediate theme is the debate on

Madison's proposed Council of Revision. The council was debated on four different occasions. It was first defeated on June 4 in the convention's first sweep through the provisions of the Virginia Plan.[34] Instead of Madison's call for a council to be composed of some number of judges in addition to the executive head, the convention adopted an alternate proposal sponsored by Elbridge Gerry to omit the judges and vest the power in the executive alone. Gerry's substitute proposal won decisively; eight states to two, with Madison unable to prevail even within his home-state delegation.[35]

The issue came up again very soon, when James Wilson of Pennsylvania on June 6 urged the restoration of the judges to the Council of Revision.[36] He and Madison made strong speeches in favor of reconsidering the decision to drop the judges made two days earlier. The result was little different the second time; however, this time the Madisonian version of the council went down eight states to three, with his home state this time supporting him.[37]

So strongly did Madison and his allies feel about the council, however, that despite these two decisive defeats they raised the issue yet again on July 21, when Wilson once again moved to add the judiciary to the executive veto power.[38] Both Madison and Wilson again made lengthy and strong defenses of the institution as they would have it; again their fellow delegates were unconvinced. This time, however, three states supported them, four opposed, and three were evenly divided. It seemed, finally, that they were making progress.

It is therefore not altogether surprising that they tried yet one more time: on August 15 Madison moved a revised version of his council, a revision meant to respond to some of the concerns expressed in the earlier debates.[39] If Madison and his allies thought that things were positioned for a more favorable outcome this time around, they must have been greatly disappointed by the final vote: eight states against and only three for them.

The August defeat seems to have settled the fate of the Madisonian council, although as we shall soon see, Madison himself did not give up his conviction that such a council was needed for a proper operation of a free government. For the moment, however, what is most significant about the repeated defeats of the council is the set of reasons that was advanced against the proposal. There were many arguments raised, but the key one for our purposes was raised by Elbridge Gerry in the very first speech on the council. As Madison reported Gerry's intervention in his convention debate notes: "Mr. Gerry doubts whether the Judiciary ought to form a part of it, as they will have a sufficient check against encroachments on their own department by their exposition of the laws, which involved a power of deciding on their constitutionality. In some states the Judges had (actually) set aside laws as being against the constitution. This was done too with general approbation."[40] Gerry's point was repeated many times in the debates and was one of the main arguments that was deployed against Madison's proposal. Judicial involvement would be neither necessary nor proper, for the judges would have a power to pass on constitutional violations in the course of their ordinary duties. A prospective involvement in making laws would compromise their proper business of expounding the laws made by others, a thought quite consistent with the Montesquieuean theory of separation of powers.

As several of the recent scholarly reconsiderations of the origins of judicial review have noted, however, this view of the judicial function was neither unanimously held nor unambiguous on the scope or the nature of the judicial power being affirmed. William Lowry Clinton appears to see the debate as general support for his thesis that judicial power to pass on constitutionality was limited to the defense of the judicial branch itself and to the enforcement of certain very specific and explicit limitations on congressional and state power. He is especially eager to show that the members of the convention drew a very sharp distinction between judicial or legal questions and political or policy questions and thought it quite improper for judges to exercise anything like the latter powers. Thus they supported the narrower and tighter version of judicial review.[41] Similarly, Sylvia Snowiss, who also sees a limited kind of judicial review affirmed in the convention, found the delegates' "notions not always clear": it was not clear "whether speakers endorsing judicial review were supporting a general power over legislatures or are limited to defense of the Court's Constitutional sphere."[42] She also pointed out that there was no unanimity on whether the Court did possess such a power.[43]

Three comments are in order regarding these scholars' observations on these debates. First, it is true that the discussion of judicial review was unsystematic and at least potentially ambiguous. Second, it is true that some did express reservations about the Court's possessing such a power. Those reservations were most explicitly stated during the last of the four debates on the council. John Mercer of Maryland made the most express statement: "He disapproved of the Doctrine that the Judges as expositors of the Constitution should have authority to declare a law void."[44] What is striking about this comment is its very ambiguity. Does he mean to say that judges *are to be* "expositors of the Constitution," but should not, in that capacity, "have authority to declare a law void." Or does he mean they should not be "expositors of the Constitution"? Most significantly, note that the whole is in the form of an ought: the Court *should* not have such an authority. Does that mean that as things stand, they *do* have that power? As we shall see, that is the position that Madison articulates at the end of the convention. It also seems to be the position of John Dickinson of Delaware, who spoke soon after Mercer on August 15: "Mr. Dickinson was strongly impressed with the remarks of Mr. Mercer as to the power of the Judges to set aside the law. He thought no such power *ought* to exist. He was at a loss what expedient to substitute. The Justiciary of Aragon he observed became by degrees the law giver."[45] Dickinson presents himself as agreeing with and reinforcing Mercer's point. He is even clearer than Mercer, however, in accepting the notion that under the Constitution as it is, the judiciary has such a power, however improper or unwise it might be that such a power exist. For it not to have that power, some "expedient" would have to be substituted, but of what sort he could not say.[46] His comment, and in its light Mercer's, thus do not seem to be evidence against the claim that Court does possess the power of judicial review, but rather protests that it should not, a very different matter. Madison thought states should not have equal representation in the Senate, but they do. Madison's position on judicial review, we shall see, was in fact quite close to the Mercer-Dickinson position, with the difference that in the months just after the convention broke up he thought up an "expedient" of the sort Dickinson could not. In any case, the non-unanimity over the existence, rather than the propriety, of judicial review is much overstated, once we look at the actual evidence.

As for the ambiguity over the scope of judicial review, that is real but also overstated in the recent literature. Let us look again at Gerry's initial statement opposing the Council of Revision. He concedes that the judges have a power of constitutional review, but he identifies this as "a sufficient check agst. encroachments on their own department."[47] That is, Gerry seems to endorse the view that constitutional review concerns only the powers and perquisites of the judiciary itself. That, I believe, is a *mis*reading, however. Gerry is speaking, we must recall, on the proposed Council of Revision, which was being promoted in the first instance as an instrument for maintaining the separation of powers, for preventing the legislature from encroaching on either the executive or judiciary. One idea behind the council was that the legislature has such an advantage over the other branches that the others can protect themselves only by acting in concert when threatened by "the most dangerous branch."

Gerry's point is that the judiciary can protect itself through its power of constitutional review, that is, "by their exposition of the laws, which involved a power of deciding on their Constitutionality."[48] One goal sought to be achieved through the council, protection of the independence and integrity of the branches, can be achieved through a different power. But it does not follow logically or from what Gerry says here that the power to expound the Constitution is limited in any way to those provisions directly concerning the judiciary. Indeed, he speaks of a general "exposition of the laws," all of them, "which involved a power of deciding on their Constitutionality."

So, it seems, one reason for the defeat of the Council of Revision is indeed the expectation or affirmation that the Courts do possess the power of judicial review, rendering their involvement in the Council either superfluous or inappropriate, or both.

Madison saw three great needs in the complex type of political order he and his fellow delegates were putting in place; he proposed three institutions to supply these needs; he saw his fellows reject all three. Perhaps surprisingly, the Supreme Court inherited the task of meeting all three needs, sharing the job of umpire of the separation of powers system with the president via the executive veto. These powers resulted to the Court almost but not quite by default; it was generally understood at the convention that the Court would take on these functions. As Edward Corwin, one of the classic students of the Court, put it: "That the members of the Convention of 1787 thought the Constitution secured to Courts in the United States the right to pass on the validity of acts of Congress under it cannot reasonably be doubted."[49]

The delegates even explicitly added features to the Constitution that expedited the judiciary's capacity to fill these three roles. In place of Madison's proposal to use Congress to police the federal system, the convention adopted the supremacy clause, a declaration that the Constitution, laws, and treaties of the United States are supreme over state constitutions and laws. This provision was too much of a parchment barrier for Madison's taste, but the clause explicitly bound state judges to uphold this provision and since state decisions would be appealed to the Supreme Court, the ultimate enforcement of this clause, and thus the ultimate umpiring of the federal system, would fall to the U.S. Supreme Court.[50]

Correcting the republican systems in the states also fell to the Supreme Court when the convention substituted for Madison's proposed congressional veto on state laws the provisions of Article I, section 10, prohibiting the states from engaging in a specified set of actions (e.g., impairing the obligations of contract) that had been of particular concern to Madison and others when they thought of rights violations in the states. The convention also put into the Constitution Article IV, which contained provisions dealing with the relations between the states. Some of these, such as the guarantee of "privileges and immunities" of citizens, like the guarantees of Article I, section 10, also seem to fall primarily to the Court to enforce.

Without anybody quite planning it, the Supreme Court thus became the recipient of an impressive array of powers, and these were located at strategic choke points in the overall constitutional scheme. The extent and significance of these powers became much greater when the framers of the Bill of Rights gave courts rights protecting provisions to enforce, and then even more when the framers of the Fourteenth Amendment, building on the general scheme in the original Constitution, added substantially to the Court's powers by including provisions securing privileges and immunities, due process and equal protection of the laws within the states. But the original Constitution had already sewn up quite large britches for the Supreme Court, independent of this substantial letting out of the seams after the Civil War.

Madison on the Illegitimate Legitimacy of Judicial Review

On several occasions subsequent to the convention, Madison commented on the judicial role in the new constitutional order. The earliest and most revealing, far preceding any of the partisan battles of the 1790s, occurred in the context of his response to a request for his advice about a constitution for the new state of Kentucky. Some of the Kentuckians were thinking of adopting some version of a draft constitution Jefferson had prepared some years earlier. Madison thus gave the Kentuckians his assessment of Jefferson's draft.

Madison's most important and paradoxical comments occur as part of his advocacy for his pet Council of Revision. His repeated losses on this issue at the convention did nothing to cool his ardor for it. As was the case in the debates at the convention, Madison sees the council as (in part) an alternative to judicial review: "A revisionary power is meant as a check to precipitate, to unjust, and to unconstitutional laws." Madison's new proposal for a council would make explicit provision for constitutional interpretation and for resolution of what to do in the case of conflict of interpretation among different authorities. He means to remedy a serious deficiency in the existing constitution: "in the state Constitution and indeed in the Federal one also, no provision is made for the case of disagreement in expositing them, and as the courts are generally the last in making their decision, it results to them, by refusing or not refusing to execute a law, to stamp it with its final character."[51]

Madison is thus quite clear that there is such a power in the courts of the states and of the union. It is a power that does not require an explicit grant, it seems, for it results to the courts from a combination of elements that are part of the constitutional orders themselves. First, courts, like all the other branches, engage in exposition of the Constitution in the course of carrying out their ordinary duties. The Constitution is an instrument expressing the powers of and governing all the branches of government. The Constitution, however, is law, like any other law. Otherwise the courts would not have constitutional interpretation as part of its ordinary task, for its task is expounding and applying law.

The power to expound the Constitution includes the power to disregard or set aside laws that are not in accord with the Constitution—the courts may and do "refuse or not refuse to execute a law." The judicial function thus includes the comparing of laws and giving effect to the one that is valid. Moreover, the Constitution is not merely law but a superior law, for in the interpretation of the Constitution courts set aside or refuse to execute laws incompatible with it, rather than setting aside provisions of the Constitution incompatible with the law. This is merely to express the meaning of a constitution.

So far, most of what has been said of courts applies to the other branches as well. Congress must consider its constitutional powers when it considers laws. The Executive branch must do the same, and so on. The special role of the courts results from the specific character of the separation of powers/functions system. The courts are the last to pronounce on a given case, and they give the final statement of what the law is as it applies to the case. One of the staples of separation of powers theory is that neither the legislative nor the executive branch can apply laws without the cooperation of the judiciary, and that no branch may step in to reverse or act contrary to a judicial determination. Thus Madison and many others found among the great abuses requiring constitutional reform prior to the Constitutional Convention was the practice of state legislatures to interfere with, ignore, or reverse judicial decisions. Proper separation of powers schemes gave the courts the last say. That is, it was emphatically the province and duty of the judiciary "to say what the law is," including the law of the Constitution.

Thus there is no need for a special grant of the power of judicial review, for it flows from the nature of this kind of constitution as law, as supreme or superior law (see Article VI), and the role of the courts as possessors of the judicial power. The courts have a special, but not a unique role. They are only one among several expositors of the Constitution, but their place is special and in most (but not all) cases more authoritative than the others because they are final. Madison articulates essentially the same view of things as does John Marshall in *Marbury*,[52] but decidedly not the position taken by the Warren Court in *Cooper v. Aaron*.[53]

In his comments on Jefferson's draft Constitution, Madison does not end with his affirmation of the power of judicial review. He goes on to express grave reservations about it: "This makes the Judiciary Department paramount in fact to the legislature, which was never intended, and can never be proper."[54] In rejecting judicial review as improper, Madison reminds us of Mercer and Dickinson at the convention. But in rejecting it as "never intended" he puzzles us, for he has himself just presented an account of how the power derives to courts from the logic of the Constitution, if not from explicit intent. Perhaps that is what he means to say: that judicial review was not so much intended as an implication of other constitutional principles and structures that were intended.

More likely, however, what Madison has in mind as "never intended" is judicial supremacy over the legislature. That is to say, judicial review may have been implicit in the logic or even explicit in the minds of the Constitution makers (consider the various comments in the debate over the Council of Revision), but whichever it was, judicial "paramountcy" was not intended. They may have meant or implied judicial review without appreciating that this makes the judiciary "paramount." Madison is saying that judicial review is a legitimate power of the courts, that is, a power correctly inferred from the constitutional text and structure. It is, however, in a deeper sense, illegitimate. That is the paradox of Madison's position on judicial review. Madison recognizes that judicial review is a part of the Constitution and moreover is the substitute for the three institutions he could not get the convention to accept. He sees it as an illegitimate or improper substitute, and at the same time, he also finds it to be an inadequate substitute.

In his letter to Jefferson of October 1787, Madison explains his reservations about judicial review as a replacement for his congressional negative on behalf of federalism. "It may be said," he said, "that the judicial authorities under our new system will keep the states within their proper limits, and supply the place of a negative on their laws." Madison thus confirms an earlier observation that the judiciary was handed the task his negative was to serve. "The answer is," he answers, "that it is more convenient to prevent the passage of a law, than to declare it void after it is passed; that this will be particularly the case, where the law aggrieves individuals, who may be unable to support an appeal agst. a State to the Supreme Judiciary."[55] That is to say, Madison recognizes that the judicial solution turns into a judicial process, requiring that standard case and controversy rules be met. These requirements mean that many actions by states that are violations of the federal provisions of the Constitution may not be able to be brought to the "umpire" who is supposed to keep the boundary lines clear. Thus many abuses of the federal system, itself so prone to abuse, may occur and never be corrigible.

Moreover, Madison continues, "a State which would violate the legislative rights of the Union, would not be very ready to obey a Judicial decree in support of them, and that a recourse to force, which in the event of disobedience would be necessary, is an evil which the new Constitution meant to exclude as far as possible."[56] Madison fears that the judicial solution comes too close to returning the new Constitution to the inadequacies of the old Articles of Confederation system, where the states ignored the mandates of the Articles Congress and any effort to actually enforce them threatened civil war. Madison is assuming that member states are far more likely to ignore the commands of the "weakest branch," the judiciary, than those of Congress, with all the moral authority that the elected representative legislature for the whole union could bring to bear.

Madison also recognized that the courts had been given responsibility for the protection of private rights, which the extended republic, operating through the congressional negative, was meant by him to secure against hostile state legislation. "The restraints against paper emissions and violations of contracts are not sufficient."[57] These two were among the chief evils complained of during the 1780s and both found explicit protection in Article I, section 10, the chief repository of the constitutional substitution for Madison's rights-protecting negative. The protections of Article I, section 10, are, Madison thinks, "short of the mark." The problem is that "injustice may be effected by such an infinitude of legislative expedients, that where the disposition exists it can only be controlled by some provision which reaches all cases whatsoever. The partial provisions made supposes the disposition which will evade it."[58] No strictly constitutional provision in the sense of a legal prohibition can suffice. The faces of injustice are infinite and even if the judicial check works (a likelihood Madison doubts) one can never specify all the possible acts of injustice one wishes to prevent. Only a constitutional solution in the sense of a political device or institution can work. Only the congressional negative, for reasons contained in the famous argument about factions in an extended republic, can reasonably be expected to protect against injustice. The combination of the small republics (the states exercising their legislative powers) and the large republic (Congress exercising its negative) can produce the neutrality and democratic dependence that will be safe and just.[59] The judgment that is needed, Madison thought, is a political judgment about justice and wisdom, and includes such matters as whether a law is properly drafted, or whether a state is passing too many laws. These are not judgments that courts are well suited to make, nor, in Madison's view, are they appropriately legal questions for courts to answer.

Finally, Madison also thought the Constitution's replacements for his Council of Revision to be inadequate. These were the executive veto supplemented by judicial review. His primary reason for preferring the council was the danger of the "legislative vortex": "Experience in all the states had evinced a powerful tendency in the legislature to absorb all power into its vortex. This was the real source of danger to the American Constitution; and suggested the necessity of giving every defensive authority to the other departments that was consistent with republican principles."[60] He feared that neither of the branches alone could resist the legislature; indeed, he feared that "notwithstanding this cooperation of the two departments, the legislature would still be an overmatch for them."[61]

Developing a sufficient power of resistance to defend the separateness of the separated powers was not Madison's only reason for wishing to join the judiciary with the executive in his council. It would inspire the executive with confidence, and thus allow him to act firmly, but more to the point, "it would be useful to the legislature [or to legislation] by the valuable assistance it would give in preserving a consistency, conciseness, perspicuity, and technical quality in the laws, qualities peculiarly necessary; and yet shamefully wanting in our republican codes."[62] These are qualities that the judges can bring to bear on legislation to a far higher degree than can the executive. As Oliver Ellsworth said in this same debate, the judges "will possess a systematic and accurate knowledge of the laws, which the Executive can not be expected always to possess."[63]

The contribution of the judges acting as part of a Council of Revision can go far beyond these somewhat technical matters. Their participation, Madison added, "would be useful to the community at large as an additional check agst. a pursuit of those unwise and unjust measures which constituted so great a portion of our calamities."[64] James Wilson, the convention's other most persistent advocate for a council, stated most clearly the greater advantages of the council over judicial involvement via constitutional review.

"The Judiciary ought to have an opportunity of remonstrating agst. projected encroachments on the people as well as on themselves. It had been said that the Judges, as expositors of the laws would have an opportunity of defending their constitutional rights. There was weight in this observation; but this power of the Judges did not go far enough." And what more was needed that constitutional review would hardly be able to supply? "Laws may be *unjust,* may be *unwise,* may be *dangerous,* may be *destructive;* and yet not be so unconstitutional as to justify the Judges in refusing to give them effect. Let them have a share in the Revisionary power, and they will have an opportunity to take notice of these characters of a law, and of counteracting, by the might of their opinion the improper views of the Legislature."[65]

As we have already seen, Madison not only considered the convention's substitutions for his three institutions to be inadequate, but he also found judicial review in particular to be improper. In his assessment of Jefferson's draft Constitution he identified the impropriety with judicial "paramountcy" over the legislature. This is improper because there is a certain primacy to the legislature over the other two powers—the executive and judiciary take their bearings from the laws the legislature makes. Or, if not legislative primacy, then at least an equality of the branches that is contravened if the judiciary is paramount.

Behind his concern for the formal equality of the three branches lay a more fundamental concern yet. Madison gave best expression to that concern in his well-known *Federalist* 51. In that essay, he returns to one of the concerns so central to his argument in *Federalist* 10 and in his defenses of the congressional negative. "It is of great importance in a republic, not only to guard the society against the oppression of its rulers; but to guard one part of society against the injustice of the other part . . . there are but two methods of providing against this evil: the one by creating a will in the community independent of the majority, that is, of the society itself."[66] The other method is the extended republic, which produces majorities relatively neutral but not independent of the society itself.

"The first method prevails in all governments possessing an hereditary or self-appointed authority." Madison considered this sort of will not only "a precarious security," for it could turn against the whole or any part of the society at will, but also deeply illegitimate. As Madison said in *Federalist* 39, only the republican form of government is compatible "with the fundamental principles of the revolution," that is, with the Declaration of Independence, which states the fundamental principles of political right. A republic is one where the government is "derived from the great body of the society, not from an inconsiderable proportion, or a favored class of it." Thus a republic cannot contain any hereditary powers.

The judiciary under the Constitution qualifies as a republican institution, for it is "indirectly" derived from the people, that is, its members are nominated by the (indirectly) elected president and confirmed by the (indirectly) elected Senate. Given its technical function as expositor of the law, this attenuated republicanism is sufficient. But it is not sufficient to justify that the Supreme Court be paramount over the elected legislature. Madison thought reliance on such a will independent of society to be highly illegitimate in a republic, despite the appeal many friends of judicial activism make to Madison's doubts about pure majoritarianism. Madison wanted to correct the evils of majoritarian politics, but he set himself the requirement that the principle of majoritarianism not be violated in doing so. Madison thus would not join the judicial activists who claim to march in his army and under his banner.

Madison thus concedes that in the Constitution as written and adopted the courts do indeed possess the power of constitutional review, not alone it is true, but in a particularly authoritative manner. He was not friendly to this power, however, regretting both its limitations relative to his preferred institutions, and decrying its impropriety or even illegitimacy. He could never fix all that was wrong with the U.S. Constitution, but he did recommend a practice for the state of Kentucky that would solve some of the problems of judicial review, in particular the legitimacy problem. He urged the Kentuckians not to follow the example of the constitutions in place all over America, but instead to institute a version of the Council of Revision. Bills should be "separately communicated to the Exec. and Judicy. depts. If either of these object, let 2/3, if both 3/4 of each House be necessary to override the objection; and if either or both protest against a bill as violating the Constitution, let it moreover be suspended, notwithstanding the overruling proposition of the assembly, until there shall have been a subsequent election of the H[ouse] of D[elegates] and a repassage of the bill by 2/3 or 3/4 of both Houses, as the case may be."[67] But the truly relevant point comes next: "It [should] not be allowed the Judges or the Ex[ecutive] to pronounce a law thus enacted, unconstitutional and invalid." This complex scheme would replace judicial review as implicit in the Constitution. Notice that it is Madison's view that unless the courts are forbidden to exercise the power, it falls to them from the logic of the Constitution. It would be worth pondering whether Madison provides here a viable plan for dealing with this institution, judicial review, which has proven so controversial over its entire history. Carrying Madison's idea into our time is a task for another day, however.

Conclusion

In conclusion, I would like to emphasize the chief points that setting the institution of judicial review into the context of Madisonian constitutional theory allows us to see.

That requires first comparing Madison's original proposed three political institutions and practices with the Supreme Court as successor legal institution. Madison's three institutions functioned in a solely negative manner—the Council of Revision and the two forms of congressional umpiring power were solely powers to say no to actions taken elsewhere on matters entrusted to others. Second, the three institutions were all political in the sense that they were all elective offices, ultimately responsible to the people. All three were political also in the sense that they were not asked to apply legal principles and provisions, but to exercise a kind of judgment typical of political rather than legal decision, and operating in the fluid and less structured context of politics rather than a suit at law.

The Supreme Court differs, more or less, on all three grounds. Although it operates primarily in a nay-saying role when it exercises these functions, it does not do so exclusively. When, for example, it fashions remedies, the line between negative and positive powers can become exceedingly blurry, as we have seen in the past several decades with courts, for example, running schools and prisons and redrawing electoral districts. The Court, furthermore, is not political in the sense that Congress and the presidency are; indeed, it is intentionally constituted to be the most distant and politically insulated institution of governance in the whole system. Finally, the Supreme Court plays its part only in the course of hearing legal cases and controversies and is bound, at least in theory, to making decisions on the basis of legal rules, not broad political considerations.

Judicial review goes too far, Madison thought, in giving the judiciary a paramountcy it should not have, but it also, Madison believed, did not go far enough: if the courts stick to their own constitutional power, the power that in turn gives them access to the power of constitutional review, they consider only legal, that is, narrowly constitutional issues, raised in genuine legal cases. They do not address the over-haste or injustice or foolishness of a law, as Madison's Council of Revision and negative over the states would.

More important and more interesting, however, is the way Madison's analysis helps lay bare the deeper anomaly the Supreme Court embodies: it is a legal body, with a certain legal claim (the power of the "last say," as Madison put it) to the power of constitutional review. But the Court's position in the system is more deeply defined by the fact that it is the body entrusted with the three keystone political functions within the complex institutional array of the American Constitution. There is a built-in disproportion between the political tasks and the legal tools with which these are supposed to be accomplished. The Court faces the choice of sticking to the narrow legal basis, for example, following the rule of the "clear mistake" or applying a strictly originalist approach to cases; or attempting to fulfill the broader, political, trans-legal system needs thrown into its lap by the Constitution. It has the implicit duty to be more than a legal institution; it has the explicit duty to be nothing but a legal institution. Responding to this dual imperative, to this dilemma built into its very structure and function, the Court is constantly driven beyond the bounds of strict legality in order to do its political work.

Chapter Four

Constitutionalism as Judicial Review: Historical Lessons from the U.S. Case

Leslie Friedman Goldstein

Constitutionalism as World Trend

The sharp recent rise in "the power of judges" the world over has attracted considerable notice. Titles such as *The Global Expansion of Judicial Power*[1] and terms such as "juristocracy"[2] and "courtocracy"[3] proliferate because this power has spread around the globe, in a development that seriously began only after World War II and that took on real momentum in the past thirty-five years.

Before World War I, and again as of 1942, only the United States and Norway had a court with power to throw out laws adopted by the national legislature.[4] Today more than eighty countries do.[5] This rapidity of the transformation of constitutions around the globe is nothing short of remarkable.

In both the United States (1803) and Norway (1866) this power came not explicitly from the written constitution, but from court precedent.[6] The Weimar Republic, Austria, Spain, and—in Alec Stone Sweet's phrase—"some states in Eastern Europe[,] had possessed constitutional courts of varying effectiveness in the interwar years," which were ended by the wartime constitutions.[7] In 1943 Iceland joined this tiny judicial review club, making it a threesome.[8]

During the 1940s and 1950s, the postwar wave of (in Ran Hirschl's term) "reconstruction" constitutions that instituted judicial review included Austria, Italy, Germany, France, and Japan.[9] The decolonization of Africa and Asia in the 1950s and 1960s brought judicial review in several "independence" constitutions of Africa and Asia.[10] A wave of democratization in southern Europe brought judicial review to Spain, Portugal, and Greece in the 1970s, and then, in the late 1980s and early 1990s, to new constitutions in the Republic of South Africa and in several Latin America countries. Yet another wave struck in the 1990s, as the Soviet, Soviet bloc, and Yugoslavian republics adopted liberal democratic constitutions that included judicial review. As part of no specifically classifiable trend, several additional countries in the period between 1979 and 1994 adopted new constitutions or new constitutional guarantees of fundamental rights to be enforced via judicial review: Sweden, 1979; Egypt, 1980; Canada, 1982; Belgium, 1985; New Zealand, 1990; Mexico, 1994; Israel, 1992–95. (By 1995 the Israeli Supreme Court announced that the 1992 Basic Laws could be applied by courts to strike down ordinary legislation, giving the courts of Israel the power of judicial review.)[11]

Complicating the trend toward handing to judges via judicial review a policy-making power that had once belonged exclusively to legislatures (i.e., the power to determine the constitutional reach of the legislative power) was an additional trend enhancing judicial power, one that extended from the 1960s through the 1990s. Transnational courts in Europe in particular (the European Court of Justice and the European Court of Human Rights), and to a lesser degree other supranational tribunals, took on the power under various multilateral treaties to identify conflicts between national laws and transnational treaties, with rulings that indicated that such conflicting laws should be eliminated in the home country.[12] In effect, these transnational courts were behaving as though the treaty were a higher-law constitution. Ordinary member-state courts that had enjoyed no previous exercise of judicial review power cooperated in this transformation, and began declaring void their own country's laws.

These developments make clear that to the degree that the world has been undergoing a wave of democratization for the past six decades, the worldwide craving for "democracy" appears to be a craving for not just any variety of the genre, but specifically for *constitutional* democracy. And, for better or worse, constitutionalism the world over is increasingly seen as constitutionalism guarded or enforced by the practice of judicial review under a written constitution. While most of these new judicial review systems adopt mechanical arrangements more akin to that of Germany than of the United States (in that they have a specialized constitutional court for judicial review rather than using their ordinary highest appellate court for the practice), there can be no reasonable doubt that America's lengthy history of judicial-review-guarded liberty played an inspirational role in this worldwide trend toward judicially guarded constitutionalism.

The First Laboratory of Modern Constitutionalism: The United States

Thus it is worth a close look at how the practice of judicial review has played out within the U.S. context in order to understand how this phenomenon of judicially guarded constitutionalism is likely to play out over the long run worldwide.[13] By this examination I do not mean to give a detailed history of specific U.S. Supreme Court cases over 215 years. What I mean to do here is to understand what judicial-review-guarded constitutionalism has meant in the U.S. context by examining its high points and low points, its hits and misses so to speak, as judged by long-term reputation.

There is an important sense in which informed scholarly opinion, and the public opinion that it guides, themselves over time constitute U.S. constitutionalism. Over the long run, the fact that certain Supreme Court decisions remain widely admired or widely condemned shapes the decisions that are to come. Whether this fact should be called social construction, or scholarly construction, or a kind of Burkean traditionalism, it does constitute our polity—perhaps even as much as the written text of our Constitution or the structure of governmental institutions does. In other words, the long-run reception of the products of judicial review itself is one of the constituters of constitutionalism.

This chapter, then, examines three formative points of U.S. constitutionalism: two that are widely regarded as peaks of excellence in the history of judicial review and one that is widely regarded as one of its nadirs. The two that I am calling peaks of excellence can be thought of as iconic in U.S. jurisprudence in the sense that they are so widely admired that constitutional theorists make it a point to design their theories to be, in one way or another, broad enough to encompass them—to do otherwise in effect brands oneself as outside the mainstream. These two icons of U.S. constitutionalism are (1) the jurisprudence of John Marshall, and (2) the decision in *Brown v. Board of Education*, 347 U.S. 483 (1954).

The iconic status of John Marshall's jurisprudence is attested to by the frequency with which constitutional theorists defend their own theories by claims that they echo that of John Marshall. Thus in the 1980s Suzanna Sherry defended extratextualism by the claim that John Marshall, at least until 1819, followed an extratextual approach to constitutional theory,[14] while Gary Jacobsohn claimed Marshall as a textualist, as part of his defense of his own aspirational version of textualism.[15] In the 1990s, Robert Bork defended his own original-understanding textualism with, among other arguments, the claim that it fit John Marshall's jurisprudence (with the sole exception of the *Fletcher v. Peck,* 10 U.S. 87 [1810] decision).[16] Christopher Wolfe makes the same claim.[17] And in the same decade, Sotirios Barber defended his moral-philosophy-based jurisprudence, by claiming the mantle of John Marshall for it.[18] This beat goes on into the twenty-first century, as the 2007 volume by Jim Fleming and Sotirios Barber notes that their defense of a jurisprudence following Ronald Dworkin is strengthened by, inter alia, the fact that it is the jurisprudence that Marshall used.[19]

As for the iconic status of *Brown v. Board,* it is such a widely admired decision, as to its holding if not its reasoning, that even those theorists who insist that it was wrongly decided find ways to say we should nonetheless retain it and honor it as a precedent. Two originalists, Raoul Berger and Christopher Wolfe, might be viewed as the exceptions that prove this rule. Both initially develop theories of interpretation that condemn *Brown v. Board.* Raoul Berger claims it was wrongly decided because it did not follow the specific original intent of the framers of the Fourteenth Amendment,[20] and Christopher Wolfe says that the rule proclaimed by it and its immediate sequelae of the late 1950s—the rule that government may not discriminate on the basis of race—is belied by the text of the Fourteenth Amendment, which anticipated (and permitted) such discrimination as to the franchise.[21] But then both theorists nonetheless maintain that, in contrast to certain other longstanding precedents, it should be retained.[22] They do this not on the grounds of what might be called initial interpretive theory, but on the basis of a theory about how judges should treat precedents. Still, the latter theory comes to modify their initial interpretive theory, so one might say that their net, or completed, interpretive theory ends up endorsing *Brown v. Board.*

At the other end of the scale, that is, the near-universally condemned precedent, one might offer up an important section of the *Slaughterhouse Cases,* 83 U.S. 36 (1873). In this decision, the specific holding involving state legislative restrictions on the practice of slaughtering animals was innocuous, and received little notice, but the reasoning was notoriously bizarre: The Supreme Court interpreted the privileges or immunities clause as having added no new meaning to the Constitution, but as simply having underlined what the supremacy clause had already established, namely that the states were forbidden to abridge rights that the national Constitution or national laws created.[23] Without ever overruling the decision, the Supreme Court within a short time began to interpret the due process and equal protection clauses as doing the work the privileges or immunities clause was meant to do—namely, protecting the fundamental rights of citizens from abridgment by state government.

The point of this chapter is to attempt to articulate what the jurisprudence of John Marshall and the ruling of the Supreme Court in *Brown v. Board* have in common that makes them exemplars of admirable judicial review, and also to characterize what it is that makes the widely condemned decisions bad judicial review. My guess is that if scholars can achieve these goals, we will have gone a long way toward explaining the meaning of constitutionalism, at least in the sense of judicial-review-guarded constitutionalism—the version of constitutionalism that appears to be sweeping the globe.

What Was Admirable in Marshall's Jurisprudence

The accomplishments for which John Marshall's jurisprudence is renowned consist more in the ways that his Court shaped the fundamental contours of the U.S. polity—that is, constitutional structure—than in specific modes of reasoning displayed on various occasions by the Marshall Court. As to those modes of reasoning, they in fact shifted from one case to another.

For instance, the political crisis created by President Jefferson's public flouting of the law that led to William Marbury's justice of the peace appointment pushed Marshall in *Marbury v. Madison* to announce strained readings of both the text of 1789 Judiciary Act[24] and of Article III, Section 2, clause 2.[25] It is highly unlikely that the Court majority would have stretched these texts in these ways, had the Court not been *politically* pressed to strengthen the rule of law and for that reason to strengthen judicial authority. Judicial review of federal law was openly anticipated by a number of speakers at the Constitutional Convention and in the print war over ratification between the Anti-Federalists and the Federalists, *and* it is at least compatible with, if not demanded by, the words of the Constitution, *and* it fits the overall constitutional structure; therefore, it almost certainly would have come along sooner or later. Still, without the pressures of Jefferson's lawless behavior, the Court would likely have waited for a more plainly unconstitutional law before asserting this power.

What is admirable about *Marbury* is precisely that, against all political odds, Marshall managed to strengthen judicial authority and thereby the rule of law in that decision. With a similar result, Marshall, during his tenure on the Court, managed to convince his fellow justices to cease issuing *seriatim* opinions in every case, and instead to unite most of the time around a single Court opinion. This practice of uniting around a single "opinion of the Court" made it much more clear to the public what was the law of a given case, thereby also enhancing the rule of law. A third contribution of the Marshall Court to enhancing federal judicial authority and thereby to the rule of law at the federal level was the Court's insistence on its authority, an authority affirmed by Congress in the Judiciary Act of 1789, to overrule state high courts on interpretations of federal law.[26] This insistence made feasible the rendering of clear federal rules for governing the new nation.

Again, one can observe John Marshall engaged in a stretching of text in the contracts clause (Article I, section 10, clause 1) cases of *Fletcher v. Peck* (1810) and *Dartmouth College v. Woodward*, 17 U.S. 518 (1819), to make the clause cover, respectively, those sales of state land known as "land grants" and privileges granted by states in corporate charters. It is highly improbable that most readers of the constitutional text in, say, 1800, would have said that the command, "No state shall impair the obligation of contracts" itself meant that states may not ever alter property rights.[27] On the other hand, an outright state-governmental taking of privately owned real estate would have generally been viewed as wrong, despite the constitutional silence on this subject. Marshall compensated for that silence as to real property and enchartered rights of corporations, in effect supplying what he saw as another of the Constitution's lacunae. The contracts clause aimed to secure contractual investments against the temporary passions that might sometimes sweep over state governments. In a like vein, the bill of attainder clauses (of Article I, sections 9 and 10) secure property, along with life and liberty, against impetuous hostility to particular individuals, which might sweep through either a state or national legislature.[28] Marshall's decision in these two cases saw these broader purposive principles within, or perhaps underneath, the clauses and explicated their broader reach, despite the limited wording of the clauses.[29]

The Marshall Court's other important accomplishments included establishment of the rule in *McCulloch v. Maryland* (17 U.S. 316 [1819]) that the federal government's delegated powers included those that were delegated by implication. In other words, it was of constitutional significance that the Tenth Amendment (in contrast to the Articles of Confederation formulation) removed the word "expressly" as a modifier to the phrase, "the powers not delegated to the United States by the Constitution." Also important among his accomplishments was his establishing a broad reach for the federal commerce power, such that it reached all commerce "which concerns more states than one,"[30] but a broad reach that nonetheless acknowledged a legitimate space for state legislatures to meet local needs even if such legislation might incidentally affect interstate commerce.[31]

What I am proposing is that what makes Marshall's jurisprudence the icon that it is was not his appeal to text here, to known intention of the framers there, to historical context somewhere else. It was his signal ability to find in the text, in the institutional structure, and in the principles expressed in, and/or underlying, the text, the shape of a constitution that really was "intended to endure for ages to come";[32] and that really did so endure, assisted by the enormous addition and alteration of the Civil War amendments. One might say it was in the wisdom of the principles he saw in the Constitution and articulated for the nation. His was a purposive jurisprudence, and his jurisprudence continues to endure because of the excellence of the purposes that he identified as contained in the Constitution. His wisdom in finding these principles was not the wisdom of abstract philosophy, but was a wisdom attuned to constitutional text, structure, history, and also political context, specifically the political context that gave rise to the Constitution.

The Excellence of *Brown v. Board*

Brown v. Board of Education (1954) retains a similarly iconic claim to respect. One reason for this, I believe, is that the Warren Court, too, was sensitive to the need to build respect for the rule of law as it proceeded. Because the Warren Court knew that the change it would be announcing would call for alteration of deeply entrenched customs among a large portion of the nation,[33] the justices struggled to join together into a single unanimous decision.[34] Unanimity for this case was so highly prized that Justice Jackson left his hospital bed to sit with the Court for the announcement of its decision, in order to underline physically as well as verbally that the Court was united in its view of the law.[35] If the rule of law were to prevail, the *Brown* Court recognized that it needed, at a minimum, to present a united front (as the Marshall Court generally had).

The Warren opinion for the Court in *Brown* is far from perfect, and immediately met scholarly criticism as such. The Court might have chosen to rely more closely on the higher-education precedents of 1950,[36] but instead it gave those precedents relatively little attention. In those the Court had established that de jure segregated graduate programs were unequal in such "intangible factors" as quality of education of teachers, reputation in the community, prestige of alumni, and in the opportunity to learn how to communicate with the people likely to hold influential positions in society. Surely the ability to communicate effectively with the sorts of people who run the powerful institutions of society—and in the early 1950s this meant white people—is an important skill for children to be learning. The Court might have pressed this point more forcefully. It could have done so in a way that made clear that simply spending money to upgrade the so-called "colored schools" could never overcome these intangible differences. To have done so in a way that emphasized the close ties to precedents already in place would likely have deflected some of the scholarly criticism.

Instead the Court went for the memorable rhetoric ("affects their hearts and minds in a way unlikely to be ever undone") and for reliance on social-social-science research that claimed to demonstrate that attendance at racially de jure segregated schools undermined the self-esteem of non-white children (in that they picked up loud and clear the message of de jure segregation: *viz.*, white society viewed them as inferior). This reduction of self-esteem in turn reduced the children's expectations of themselves and thus of their motivation to learn. Hence de jure segregation as to nonwhite children was producing inferior education and thereby amounted to state-imposed unequal treatment in violation of the equal protection of the laws.

Perhaps the Court emphasized the psychological damage of state-imposed segregation because relying too heavily on the Court's higher-education precedents would have made it more questionable to strike down the state-imposed Jim Crow system across the board, which the Court proceeded to do in a series of *per curiam* decisions in the immediately following years. Or perhaps the Court chose this emphasis in the misguided belief that putting an imprimatur of modern scientific research on its break with *Plessy v. Ferguson* (163 U.S. 537 [1896]) would make the break with precedent look more justified, in that it was relying on new, scientifically verified information. But the Court did not really need science to justify this new insight. It could have easily said that mid-twentieth-century Americans no longer perceive state-imposed racial separation as premised on anything other than the belief that the white race is superior, and that the use of state law to express this belief is precisely what the equal protection clause was meant to forbid and does forbid. After all, Justice Harlan the First had announced this insight with his 1896 dissent to *Plessy*,[37] and what had changed was the American public's and the Supreme Court majority's perception—or perhaps their willingness to acknowledge the perception. By 1954 the first Justice Harlan was seen as having been correct, and the rest of the *Plessy*

Court wrong, on the matter of whether state-imposed segregation expressed a message of white supremacy. Once this new understanding of the social meaning of de jure segregation prevailed, continuing to impose it had to violate equal protection.

Again, then, it was not the particular reasoning that the Court deployed in *Brown v. Board* that propelled this decision into the pantheon of nigh-universally respected judicial decisions. Rather, it was that the Court articulated the correct constitutional principle, the principle immanent in the equal protection clause, but neglected in large part for nearly a century. This was the rule that government power may not be used to subordinate one race of citizens, just because a different race controls the government and wishes to do so.[38] This was the principle finally articulated fully as of the time of *Brown* and its immediate sequelae. Since then it has evolved to cover other subordinated groups whose subordination bears certain similarities to that of African Americans. Because the clause makes no mention of race, this evolution seems appropriate. As the first Justice Harlan wrote in prophetic dissent, "There is no caste here."[39]

In addition to taking a huge step toward helping the nation fulfill the promise of the Fourteenth Amendment, the *Brown* Court furthered the rule of law not only by its studied attainment of unanimity, as already noted, but also by the gradualism of its second *Brown v. Board* ruling (1955). While the particular phrase "all deliberate speed" is a bit of an oxymoron, nevertheless practical wisdom demanded giving some sort of adjustment time to the 40 percent of the nation being asked to transform itself in the mid-1950s. Allowing fifteen years may have been overdoing it,[40] but certainly several years of adjustment time made sense in terms of giving the American public time to become accustomed to the new constitutional standards. Once Congress got on board in 1964 with real enforcement measures, it became apparent that the *Brown* ruling, for all practical purposes, would now become the law of the land.[41] And so it has. De facto segregation, to be sure, lingers and presents a myriad of social problems, but it does not carry the sting of government backing and government coercion that was present with the Jim Crow system. It does not impose a blot on the promise of the Fourteenth Amendment in the way that *Plessy* did.

Thus, the widespread admiration for the *Brown* decision as with the widespread admiration for the Marshall Court appears to result not from the precise lines of reasoning deployed by either, but from each Court's having correctly discerned and delineated the constitutional principle at stake and having deployed the judicial statesmanship required to make the principles stick as a matter of the rule of law. For courts as with individuals, discretion can be the better part of valor. Marshall may have looked more bold had he issued the mandamus to Madison that Marbury requested (the one President Jefferson had promised to ignore), and the Warren Court may have looked more bold had it announced that schools must desegregate at once, but decisions that end up so blatantly ignored that they produce an image of impotent courts, or ones that provoke legislatures to alter the law or constitution as a way of restraining courts, do not strengthen the judicial independence needed for the rule of law. Courts must sometimes walk a fine line, and both these Courts did.

What Was Wrong with the *Slaughterhouse Cases*

This brings us to our nadir example, a decision where the Supreme Court in virtually everyone's judgment crossed over the line, the *Slaughterhouse Cases* (1873). Those cases—all decided together—presented a group of challenges to a Louisiana law that restricted the slaughtering of livestock to a certain area outside the bounds of New Orleans, and set up a state-regulated monopoly, to ensure reasonable rates, for the leasing of slaughtering facilities in that place. These legal challenges claimed that the statute deprived the butchers of their right to labor in their chosen occupation and that it seriously interfered with the pursuit of the business of butchering by all who did not own the monopoly facility. Because it did these two things, went the claim, it violated the constitutional prohibitions on involuntary servitude, and on abridging the privileges or immunities of citizens, and also interfered with equal protection and due process. Before the Court majority ever got to the constitutional questions, it settled the case: It stated that the assertions that this law seriously interfered with practicing the trade of butchering or deprived people of the right to work at a trade for which they were qualified were simply unjustified assertions.[42] Thus, the Court majority had no legal reason to continue on to discuss the constitutional issues, because this case did not present these issues.

But continue on is just what the Miller majority did. And for many pages. And in these pages it presented a theory of the privileges or immunities clause that made almost no sense in terms of its congressional history or its textual context, in that the majority interpreted the clause as adding nothing to the Constitution other than to emphasize a point already covered in the supremacy clause.[43]

In Congress, leading sponsors of the Fourteenth Amendment, who had introduced it into the House and Senate, had specified on this occasion that the privileges or immunities clause would protect the fundamental civil rights of individuals against abridgment by state governments, and had said that these rights included those listed in the first eight amendments to the Constitution.[44] The speech to the Senate that made this announcement was quoted extensively or paraphrased in detail in stories on the first or second page of major newspapers all over the country.[45] Not every Congress member described the "privileges or immunities" to be protected in exactly those terms. Some spoke generally of those citizen rights that are fundamental, or that are basic in a free society. Some referred specifically to the rights listed in the Civil Rights Act of 1866. No one in Congress and no one on record in the two state legislatures that have extant ratification debates said that this clause added nothing novel and was really just underlining what the supremacy clause already did.[46]

Justice Miller's interpretation of the clause, for the *Slaughterhouse* majority of five, was brand new. It had no foundation other than his expressed view that to read the clause as saying what it said—that civil rights are to be federally protected against state abridgment now—would be too radical a change in our government system, such a radical change that for the Court to allow it would require a more explicit statement than the clause already contained. Therefore, the clause could not mean what it seemed to mean, that federal-state relations had been fundamentally restructured in the wake of the Civil War.

This majority interpretation produced unusually harsh responses among the four dissenters. Justice Field (in an opinion for all four) condemned it as a poor reading of text: it treated the privileges and immunities clause as a "vain and idle enactment, which accomplished nothing."[47] Justice Swayne in a separate dissent condemned it for its poor reading of congressional history: the Miller majority "turns what was meant for bread into stone."[48]

As a specific reading of the privileges or immunities clause, the work of the *Slaughterhouse* five endured, but as to the basic thrust of the Fourteenth Amendment it withered. By 1880, the Supreme Court (using the equal protection clause) affirmed that state legislatures may not abridge the fundamental right of (otherwise qualified) black people to sit on juries.[49] By 1897, the Court applied a piece of the Bill of Rights, the just compensation clause, to state governments by means of a substantive reading of the due process clause.[50] As is well known, in a period that ran from 1925[51] through 1968 the Supreme Court proceeded to "incorporate" most of the rest of the Bill of Rights' "privileges or immunities" against state governments via the due process clause. Thus, the reading of the privileges or immunities clause by the *Slaughterhouse* five was rendered in time a practical dead letter (although it survives as a technically valid precedent and thus continues to exercise a perverse force on the Court's compensatory readings of the equal protection and due process clauses).

Conclusions: Lessons for Judicially Guarded Constitutionalism

What can one learn from this examination of the peaks and valleys of judicially guarded constitutionalism in the United States? One lesson is the strategic one: Judges, whether protected by life tenure as in the United States or by fixed, lengthy terms as in the rest of the world, cannot simply act as philosopher kings; the correct or wisest reading of constitutional principles is not enough. Because politically dominant groups may not be ready to accept these principles, or the full-blown version of them, judicial statesmanship is needed. John Marshall's avoidance of a direct clash with the president, wherein the Court's authority would have been flouted and thereby diminished, enabled him to gradually build up judicial stature with rulings more likely to be obeyed.[52] The more often constitutional courts can arrive at unanimous decisions, the better their chances of swaying political majorities to accept the court's reading of constitutional limits on legislative power. Also, when the public is deeply divided over a constitutional interpretation, allowing societal change to proceed with a certain gradualness can be salutary for retaining judicial authority and attaining respect for the interpretation.

One should not overstate this point. In countries such as Singapore, Hong Kong, Hungary, and Russia, where governments have retaliated against ambitious constitutional courts with disempowering constitutional amendments or with transparent court-packing, it is not certain that more cautious, strategically sensitive decision making by the courts would have successfully avoided these problems.[53] Still, such judicial prudence could prove helpful, if not in every country, then at least in countries with an adequate modicum of respect for the rule of law. (What this chapter treats as a problem—resistance to constitutional courts by legislative and executive branches—is lauded in the chapter by James Stoner in this volume. But the contexts are different. For societies where the rule of law, especially in the form of the constitutional rules that aim at checking abuses of government power, is just getting off the ground and remains shaky, such opposition is far more problematic than in a country where the rule of law is firmly established.)

The second lesson to be garnered, the lesson on what makes for excellence in the decisions of a constitution-guarding court, is much more difficult to articulate. It cannot be simply the most clever reading of the constitutional text or of the lessons of constitutional history—although running roughshod over these is not going to garner admiration, as illustrated with the discussion of *Slaughterhouse*. The Marshall Court is widely admired despite its having turned somersaults with the contract clause; the *Brown v. Board* decision is similarly admired despite the opinion's reliance on psychological experiments whose conclusions underwent challenge in later experiments, and despite the historic fact that much of the U.S. public would not have accepted school desegregation in 1868.[54]

Around the world, national publics are restraining themselves by written constitutions because there are some principles, some commitments, that these publics value more highly than they value the commitment to decision-making by legislative majorities. Courts that can successfully uphold these principles will end up valued in constitutionalist systems. To be sure, differences of national culture and of political institutions and traditions will modify the particulars. Still, the shared universal trait in societies that move to constitutionalist systems would seem to be this craving for guidance by enduring principle.

Written documents can set forth these principles, but their concrete application in specific situations requires judges—as well as, obviously, for initial implementation, legislators and executive bureaucrats. Principles do not interpret themselves. As James Madison wrote in *Federalist* 37:

All new laws, though penned with the greatest technical skill, and passed on the fullest and most mature deliberation, are considered as more or less obscure and equivocal, until their meaning be liquidated and ascertained by a series of particular discussions and adjudications. Besides the obscurity arising from the complexity of objects, and the imperfection of the human faculties, the medium through which the conceptions of men are conveyed to each other adds a fresh embarrassment. The use of words is to express ideas. Perspicuity, therefore, requires not only that the ideas should be distinctly formed, but that they should be expressed by words distinctly and exclusively appropriate to them. But no language is so copious as to supply words and phrases for every complex idea, or so correct as not to include many equivocally denoting different ideas. Hence it must happen that however accurately objects may be discriminated in themselves, and however accurately the discrimination may be considered, the definition of them may be rendered inaccurate by the inaccuracy of the terms in which it is delivered. And this unavoidable inaccuracy must be greater or less, according to the complexity and novelty of the objects defined.

Multiple-member constitution-drafting and constitution-ratifying bodies (not to mention the voters listening to campaign speeches) will inevitably be laboring under a certain amount of fuzziness in their shared understanding of what they are accomplishing. Madison, the reputed "father of the Constitution," acknowledges this and states that it will be up to the makers of concrete laws and then to the judges applying these laws in concrete cases to "liquidate and ascertain" the applied meanings of this new fundamental law. Constitutional courts that exhibit the wisdom to capture the principles that their society wants from the words of its constitution will be the ones whose work is admired in the long run.

To discern the right principle, of course, the judges must study the constitutional text as a whole and also the historic circumstances that gave rise to it. Most important, this attention to constitutional origins must attain a comprehension of *the crisis that gave rise to the constitutive enterprise.* John Marshall's articulation of constitutional principle stressed the enhancement of judicial authority as against legislative or executive usurpation of rights, stressed the enhancement of national power as against states (particularly, state measures interfering with national economic development), and stressed the protection of property rights. The crisis to which the Constitutional Convention was a response was marked by abuses of state legislative power that took the form of paper-money schemes, tender laws, suspension of debt collection—these three being state legislative interferences with property rights—and also, bills of attainder, legislative interferences with trial by jury, and grants of exemption from standing laws—the latter three being legislative interferences with proper judicial process.[55] Thus, one can discern a pretty close match between the principles as Marshall developed them, and the needs that gave rise to the U.S. Constitution.

The crisis that provoked the postbellum amendments was well described, as irony would have it, by Justice Miller in the *Slaughterhouse* decision: "[T]he one pervading purpose found in them all, lying at the foundation of each, and without which none of them would have been even suggested [was] the freedom of the slave race, the security and firm establishment of that freedom, and the protection of the newly-made freeman and citizen from the oppressions of those who had formerly exercised unlimited dominion over him" (at 71).

To secure the former slaves in their new status of equal citizenship the Constitution had declared, inter alia, that no state deny to anyone the equal protection of the laws. It was precisely the perception that Southern states were using the force of their laws to keep blacks in the position of a subordinated caste that had provoked the Fourteenth Amendment. With the *Brown v. Board* decision, the Supreme Court finally redeemed the promise of this amendment, and the nation remains grateful to the Court for it. To be sure, this decision did not immediately garner universal support. Initially the country was divided over it, and admiration of it took some time to spread.[56]

A society's understanding of its own fundamental principles will naturally evolve over time, as the society encounters new challenges and witnesses new developments. A Court that correctly ascertains and articulates constitutional principle can bring public opinion to appreciate that principle in its fullness.

Moreover, publics do seem to want from their constitutional judges an ability to ascertain the societal ideals that the text aims to express, even in instances where the text may have done so imperfectly, as in the matter of Marshall's protection of vested property rights. Attention to the history of the drafting of the text can prove helpful in this endeavor, and needs to include sensitivity to the fact that some versions of text were rejected as well as to the words of the ones that were adopted. Noteworthy in this respect is Alexander Bickel's attention to the fact that the Fourteenth Amendment Congress eschewed proposed wording that would have limited the amendment's reach to racial discrimination in "civil rights," understood as embodying the specific list of rights in the Civil Rights Act of 1866, and instead Congress chose language more permissive of growth in a "latitudinarian" direction.[57]

The third lesson about judicially guarded constitutionalism that is evident from this overview must be about its risks. As societies evolve, so must the applications of their constitutional principles.[58] To insist that "equal protection of the laws" meant desegregated education in 1866 may well have doomed the Fourteenth Amendment, but both public education and African Americans as a group played a far different social role a century later—a role that made new applications of the principle in fact overdue by then.

Lodging judicial review power in a constitutional court that fails to recognize this lesson concerning societal evolution poses its own risks. The industrialized, nationally integrated U.S. economy of the twentieth century dramatically expanded the content of what amounted to "that commerce which concerns more states than one,"[59] and the Supreme Court's refusal to perceive this fact produced the confrontation with the Court-packing plan of Franklin Roosevelt in 1937.

A somewhat similar risk, one that is in a sense the other side of the same coin, is exemplified by a Court that insists on imposing its own sense of "the right thing" in lieu of the principle actually adopted into the Constitution. This is what happened in the *Slaughterhouse Cases*.

One tactic deployed by Southern state governments to maintain their slavery system had been to forbid freedom of speech and press with respect to the subject of slavery. So adamant were southerners on this point that the name of Abraham Lincoln appeared on no Southern ballot in 1860. In order to prevent such future denials of rights essential in a free society, Congress inserted the privileges or immunities clause into the Fourteenth Amendment.[60] Now the federal government would be able to protect from state governmental abridgment those citizen privileges that were fundamental. Or so the federal government and the politically attentive public believed, until the *Slaughterhouse Cases* were decided. Had the *Slaughterhouse* five succeeded, an important piece of the re-constituting of the nation attempted by the Fourteenth Amendment would have failed. This decision is emblematic of the most serious risk of judicially guarded constitutionalism. Judicial power may be used to dismantle important pieces of a constitution.[61] If it succeeds in this, it can undermine the most basic element of sovereignty—the power to make the constitution.

In sum, the appointing of judges as constitutional guardians is neither a cure-all nor free of risks. Because the public's attachment to its own enduring principles may waver, constitutional judges can prove useful. If these judges attempt to push too hard against political forces, however, or if the public at large does not retain sufficient attachment to the enduring principles, judicial review cannot save a society from itself. There is no guarantee that the Supreme Court of Pakistan, for instance, on which much media attention was focused as this book was going to press, will manage to reattain judicial independence against dictatorial forces, or that the legislatively tamed courts of Russia, Hungary, and Hong Kong will manage over time to reassert a strong commitment to constitutional checks on the political branches.

And the counterrisk of judicial guardianship lies in the fact that no judge is superhuman. Judges too may get it wrong. To be sure, they have fewer incentives to distort constitutional principle because they do not have to run for office,[62] and this freedom from immediate majoritarian pressure can strengthen a society's odds in its quest to honor enduring principles. Moreover, most, perhaps all, other countries with judicial review systems have constitutions that are easier to amend than that of the United States. This fact dramatically reduces the risk of serious harm from judicial error. On the whole, then, perhaps one should conclude that this worldwide trend is salutary. Still, like taking a vaccine, it will always carry a nonnegligible amount of risk.

Chapter Five

Who Has Authority over the Constitution of the United States?

James Stoner

"Who has authority over the Constitution of the United States?" Pose that to someone who has done no more than read the Constitution and it will seem to be a trick question, for the answer is altogether obvious: As the first words of the document make plain, the Constitution is made by the people—"ordained" and "established" are the actual terms. The ratification process specified in the final article of the original document answers the next question, "Who comprise the people?" The Constitution was to go into effect once ratified by representative conventions in nine of the existing states, among those states. "Who comprise the people now?" That's a little tougher. The Constitution provides for its own amendment, however, and that is by three-quarters of the states, through their legislatures or in convention, however Congress might direct. From the point of view of ultimate authority, then, the answer to the question, "Who has authority over the Constitution?" is *the people*, organized in and voting through their states.

But as anyone with experience in the splintering of opinion in free societies might have predicted, and as several centuries of experience under the Constitution has now made plain, constitutional amendments are difficult to pass, so the people's ultimate authority is rarely exercised; indeed, after the addition of the Bill of Rights, the Constitution has been amended only seventeen times, and most of these amendments were clustered in four decades: the 1860s, the 1910s, the 1930s, and the 1960s. So in practice, the question of who has authority over the Constitution generally means not ultimate, but *penultimate* authority over the Constitution. I want to say the answer here is the same—the people—acting now through the whole complex array of institutions established by our constitutional framework, including those established severally in the several states.

But today this answer appears to be outside the mainstream. The ordinary answer, the textbook answer, but also the usual perception of citizens, politicians, and the press, is that the Supreme Court of the United States has authority over the Constitution.[1] The Court itself, at least, seems to think so. In the 1958 case *Cooper v. Aaron*, concerning integration of the public schools in Little Rock, Arkansas, the Court wrote that its interpretation of the Constitution is "the supreme law of the land," and in a 1997 case called *City of Boerne v. Flores* the Court made clear that any attempt by Congress to substitute its interpretation of the language of the Fourteenth Amendment for the Court's would be struck down as exceeding Congress' constitutional authority, even though the amendment says, "The Congress shall have the power to enforce by appropriate legislation, the provisions of this article." Perhaps the boldest assertion by the Court came in the 1992 case of *Planned Parenthood v. Casey*, in which the Court reaffirmed its holding in *Roe v. Wade* that there is a constitutional right for a woman to abort her child. Wrote the Court:

Like the character of an individual, the legitimacy of the Court must be earned over time. So, indeed, must be the character of a Nation of people who aspire to live according to the rule of law. Their belief in themselves as such a people is not readily separable from their understanding of the Court invested with the authority to decide their constitutional cases and speak before all others for their constitutional ideals. If the Court's legitimacy should be undermined, then, so would the country be in its very ability to see itself through its constitutional ideals. The Court's concern with legitimacy is not for the sake of the Court, but for the sake of the Nation to which it is responsible.[2]

Nor is the perspective of judicial supremacy lacking academic defenders. Though not inclined to attribute to the Court the oracular responsibility the Court attributes to itself, Larry Alexander and Frederick Schauer have written a pair of prominent articles that endorse the Court's assuming exclusive or at any rate preeminent authority to define the meaning of the Constitution, on the grounds that "a central moral function of law is to settle what ought to be done."[3]

Nothing is clearer to the student of American political development, however, than that it has never been the case that the Supreme Court is the exclusive interpreter of the Constitution. Tocqueville might write that in America every political question becomes a legal question, but not every question that takes legal form becomes a case or controversy at federal law. The First Congress, meeting before the Supreme Court ever sat and indeed setting up the Court itself, had numerous debates over the meaning of the Constitution, and, however routine judicial review may have become, Congress today still holds hearings on questions of constitutionality when new forms of legislation are proposed. Since its earliest days, the Supreme Court itself has recognized what has come to be called the political question doctrine, accepting certain matters as non-justiciable. Wide range on this score has always been given to the president and Congress in relation to foreign affairs, but matters as far afield as impeachment and the ratification of constitutional amendments fall under this doctrine's purview. Indeed, many of the nation's most important constitutional crises have settled the meaning of the Constitution on matters of great importance with only limited involvement on the part of the federal courts.[4]

Precisely because the Constitution does not belong exclusively to the courts, there has been in the United States a long tradition of constitutional resistance to judicial decisions. This can range from a campaign for a constitutional amendment to reverse the rule established by an obnoxious Court decision, to efforts by other courts to restrict the reach of obnoxious precedent, to a theory of departmentalism that allows other branches of government to determine constitutional questions without regard for what the courts have said, to an insistence that the Court's ruling not be made a rule of political action, to a determination not to yield to the Court's proclamation unless forced individual by individual or town by town to pay an adverse judgment or obey a judicial decree. Of course, the doctrine of judicial supremacy casts a cloud on all this: If the Supreme Court is vicar of the Constitution, then technical doctrines that preclude Supreme Court review of any constitutional question seem to be antiquated formalities that stand in the way of constitutional justice, and resistance to judicial decisions seems an affront to the rule of law. Developments in federal law, such as section 1983 suits against recalcitrant state officials, proceed on this theory, as does the attitude frequently evident in Congress and the executive branch that would leave constitutional questions to the Court, especially when they might impede passage of popular legislation. That there has been a tradition that supported ways of challenging the Court's constitutional pronouncements does not settle the matter of whether or how it might be revived today. But it does suggest that an alternative to judicial supremacy is possible within the American regime as it still stands, at least if Americans are willing to take responsibility for the Constitution themselves, or give political authority to elected leaders willing to take responsibility in their name. In this chapter, I describe alternative assertions of constitutional authority in the early years of the republic through attention to a series of episodes that illustrate different modes of constitutional response and that develop in sequence. I begin with and later return to Abraham Lincoln, who offered the most lucid and forceful articulation of the tradition of resisting judicial supremacy, precisely in the midst of addressing a more radical claim of resistance and the constitutional crisis it provoked.

Constitutional Resistance: Lincoln and *Dred Scott*

Lincoln's argument against judicial supremacy in his First Inaugural Address in 1861 was one he had formulated in his Address on the *Dred Scott* decision in 1857 and had pressed in several interesting exchanges with Stephen Douglas during their celebrated debates; its reiteration at the moment he assumed the presidency in the crisis caused by state ordinances of secession gives it special focus and force. It is worth quoting his words at length:

I do not forget the position assumed by some, that constitutional questions are to be decided by the Supreme Court; nor do I deny that such decisions must be binding in any case upon the parties to a suit, as to the object of that suit, while they are also entitled to a very high degree of respect and consideration, in all parallel cases, by all other departments of the government. And while it is obviously possible that such decision may be erroneous in any given case, still the evil effect following it, being limited to that particular case, with the chance that it may be overruled, and never become a precedent for other cases, can better be borne than could the evils of a different practice. At the same time, the candid citizen must confess that if the policy of the government, upon vital questions affecting the whole people, is to be irrevocably fixed by decisions of the Supreme Court, the instant they are made, in ordinary litigation between parties, in personal actions, the people will have ceased to be their own rulers, having, to that extent, practically resigned their government, into the hands of that eminent tribunal. Nor is there, in this view, any assault upon the court, or the judges. It is a duty, from which they may not shrink, to decide cases properly brought before them; and it is no fault of theirs, if others seek to turn their decisions to political purposes.[5]

The gentleness of these last phrases might be accounted for by the presence of the justices of the Supreme Court on the platform with the newly inaugurated president, but the sentences that precede it are crafted with lawyerly precision. There is no claim that the rise of judicial supremacy means the end of democracy pure and simple, but "to th[e] extent" that the Court insists on having sole authority over the Constitution, self-government is diminished. There is no denying that Court decisions can assume such force as precedents that they become a settled part of our constitutional order, only that they earn that status instantly, without regard to their reception by the polity at large. There is no encouragement of a habit of angry resistance to judicial errors, but rather counsel of "respect and consideration" on the part of other "departments" of government, even as they are reminded that they are not, like the actual parties to a particular case, bound by the judicial decision of that case.

Indeed, the context of Lincoln's discussion makes clear that he thinks that this attitude of resisting an assertion of judicial supremacy is a moderate alternative to the posture of secession he was facing, the constitutional argument on behalf of which he had just discussed. Whatever position one takes on the theory of the Union he expounds to refute secession, the nerve of the argument is a sophisticated account of constitutional disagreement that acknowledges the legitimacy of differing interpretations, but insists on a peaceful settlement of disputes that turns on an appeal to the public mind. In the background, of course, is the Supreme Court's decision in *Dred Scott*, which the Republican Party could not accept without abandoning the principal plank of its platform, the call for restoring the congressional ban on slavery in the territories. Lincoln in 1860 had to make at once an argument against a constitutional claim to maximal resistance to the federal government as a whole—secession—and an argument in favor of moderate resistance to the assertion of judicial supremacy evident in the Court's *Dred Scott* decision. These two arguments are obviously related: Whatever the constitutional merits of the argument for secession, the strongest case for its political necessity in 1861 depended on showing that lawless partisans had seized control of the federal government and were preparing to do serious mischief to the constitutional order. I think that in the passage just quoted Lincoln draws his distinctions carefully and successfully, however much the Constitution would be strained in the decade that followed, especially after his assassination; and I think that the reworking of American constitutionalism implicit in the Civil War amendments does not undermine, but rather reaffirms Lincoln's case against judicial supremacy in constitutional interpretation. As much as Jefferson meant his *Declaration of Independence* to capture "the common sense of the subject . . . the harmonizing sentiments of the day"[6] regarding the first principles of political right, Lincoln meant his statement to embody the results of more than half a century of constitutional experience of the American people. For from the beginning Americans had developed a series of answers to the question, what should be done if political authorities violate constitutional principle? as well as the more specific question, what to do if the Supreme Court is wrong?

Resistance and the Founding

It is an obvious point, but it bears repeating in this context, that the United States got its start from an act of constitutional resistance, or perhaps more precisely, from a series of acts of resistance in the context of a constitutional dispute. From the Stamp Act Congress (and riots) through the Boston Tea Party to the actions of the First and Second Continental Congresses, Americans claimed their constitutional rights in spirited ways, not all of them as regular as sending a petition to Parliament or king. Among these were acts of undoubted illegality, as the riots that resulted in pulling down houses or tarring and feathering, as well as acts, such as the organization of the Congresses, that were precisely of the sort that gave rise to the constitutional dispute. With the Declaration the grounds of dispute are shifted from constitutional to revolutionary, as the Americans sever their ties with the English, or rather, declare them severed and then trust to their arms to make it stick; accordingly, the document opens with an appeal to the laws of nature and the first principles of government. But even so, much of the document refers to practices of English constitutionalism, which the Americans claim as their own, even mentioning in the middle "our Constitution," which Parliament has tried to suppress. Indeed, when James Wilson argues a few years later in his *Lectures on Law* that revolutionary principles are not, contra Blackstone, separate from the Constitution but rather part of it, he has some authority in the Declaration of Independence when it is read as an integral whole.[7]

Now one need not swear allegiance to Charles Beard in order to notice that, while the Declaration is written to defend a rebellion, the Constitution comes into being in part to oppose one. Not only did Shays's Rebellion figure in the decision of prominent figures to attend the Philadelphia Convention, but it must have been responsible in part for the clause in Article IV promising federal aid to the states "on application . . . against domestic Violence," and for the anticipation of "Rebellion" as a reason for suspending habeas corpus in Article I. Certainly the memory of Shays's is invoked by the authors of *The Federalist* as a reason for establishing a strong federal government. Still, Publius recognizes the effectiveness of the tradition of resistance in America. Without justifying resistance as a right, he often seems to suppose it as a fact. To the Anti-Federalist fear that the federal government will "accumulate a military force for the projects of ambition," he recalls that the state governments will remain independently organized and in command of their own militia: "Let us not insult the free and gallant citizens of America with the suspicion that they would be less able to defend the rights of which they would be in actual possession, than the debased subjects of arbitrary power would be to rescue theirs from the hands of their oppressors."[8] To the Anti-Federalist charge that the Constitution will occasion oppression by a small House of Representatives, he responds with reference to "the vigilant and manly spirit which actuates the people of America, a spirit which nourishes freedom, and in return is nourished by it."[9] If among the institutions of the federal government, ambition can be counted on to assert "the constitutional rights of the place," so public spiritedness in the states can be supposed to check federal excess. One way or another, there is no need for "creating a will in the community independent of the majority, that is, of the society itself" in order to prevent social injustice, writes Publius; a complex and extensive civil society, represented in "a proper federal system," will provide a less "precarious security" for free government and individual rights.[10]

Amendment and the Court: Resisting *Chisholm v. Georgia*

American constitutional law is typically traced to the Supreme Court's decision in *Marbury v. Madison*, but the truer—though less auspicious—beginning is *Chisholm v. Georgia*, the 1793 case in which the Supreme Court held that the provision of Article III of the Constitution giving the federal courts jurisdiction over "Controversies . . . between a State and Citizens of another State" authorized the executor of a citizen of South Carolina to sue the state of Georgia to force payment of a debt, a suit forbidden to a citizen of Georgia against the state of Georgia (or a citizen of South Carolina against the state of South Carolina, or a citizen of the United States against the United States) by the common law doctrine of sovereign immunity.[11] The state of Georgia took the position that, as it was immune to a suit initiated by a citizen, it was not even obliged to answer in the Supreme Court, although given a postponement, they consented to send attorneys to explain their refusal. The Supreme Court upheld its jurisdiction of the suit, over the sole dissent of Justice James Iredell, who emphasized both the lack of a jurisdictional statute and the existence of clear common law principles justifying sovereign immunity in the absence of state waiver. The *seriatim* opinions of Chief Justice John Jay and Justice James Wilson were strongly nationalistic in tone and argument, insisting that the plain words of the Constitution overrode any contrary legal principles and that the nature of the Union established by the Constitution was such as to deny sovereignty to the states in any serious sense of the term. The question of whether federal jurisdiction extended to suits for the recovery of state debts, wrote Wilson, "may, perhaps, be ultimately resolved into one no less radical than this—'Do the people of the United States form a Nation?' "[12] Jay, too, thought something fundamental was at stake: "The [sovereign immunity] exception contended for would contradict and do violence to the great and leading principles of a free and equal national government, one of the great objects of which is to insure justice to all."[13]

To this ringing invocation of nationalist first principles by the Court, the country responded unequivocally: The Federalist Congress passed, and all but three of the state legislatures ratified, the Eleventh Amendment to the Constitution of the United States: "The Judicial power of the United States shall not be construed to extend to any suit in law or equity, commenced or prosecuted against one of the United States by Citizens of another State, or by Citizens or Subjects of any Foreign State." It is hard to imagine a more decisive rebuke to the Court. The *Chisholm* case was decided in late winter 1793. With Virginia and Massachusetts in the lead, the legislatures (or single legislative houses) in almost every state had passed resolutions calling for a constitutional amendment by the time Congress again assembled at the end of the year. In early 1794, Congress sent the Eleventh Amendment to the states, where it was apparently approved within a year by a sufficient number, though formal certification of the results was delayed until 1798.[14] By then, Chief Justice Jay had resigned from the Court in discouragement. As for Chisholm and a number of similar plaintiffs, they never collected: In 1798 the Supreme Court unanimously ruled that the Eleventh Amendment had vacated the judgments they had won against the states.[15]

Nullification or Interposition: The Sedition Act

The political issue in the background of *Chisholm v. Georgia* was one that had been around since Independence: How to finance the Revolution, and then, how to repay the debts incurred. By the time the Eleventh Amendment was before Congress, however, the funding of the debt had been settled, so it was no accident that it was approved by wide majorities.[16] The next crisis over constitutional supremacy, by contrast, took place against the background of the French Revolution and its aftermath in Europe and served to lay the foundation for the establishment of permanent political parties in the United States and indeed for the politics of the new century. At issue was the constitutionality of the Alien and Sedition Acts, passed by Congress and signed by President John Adams, providing, respectively, for the deportation of aliens that the president "judged dangerous to the peace and safety of the United States," and for the punishment of "any person [who] shall write, print, utter, or publish . . . any false, scandalous, and malicious writing or writings against the government of the United States, . . . Congress . . . , or the President of the United States, with intent to defame . . . or to bring them . . . into contempt or disrepute; or to excite against them . . . the hatred of the good people of the United States."[17] Passed by the Federalists in Congress, the acts were deplored by opposition Republicans, led by Thomas Jefferson and James Madison, who found a voice in the legislatures of Kentucky and Virginia, that passed, respectively, resolutions the two leaders had drafted condemning the acts as unconstitutional. The arguments for considering the acts unconstitutional are interesting in themselves—both acts are said to exceed the enumerated powers of Congress, the "necessary and proper" clause being read strictly to permit only execution of the specific powers granted; moreover, the Alien Act is thought to violate the due process clause of the Fifth Amendment, and the Sedition Act to violate the free press clause of the First—but for our purposes here, what matters is the doctrine of what to do about unconstitutional legislative acts. Both Jefferson and Madison, and hence both Kentucky and Virginia, insist that the states, as parties to the constitutional compact, have a right to vindicate the instrument that they created, the Constitution, against the creature, the federal government, on implicit analogy to the law of nations regarding treaties thought by one of the signatories to be transgressed by another party, or an analogy to the law of principal and agent.[18] Jefferson for Kentucky writes of a right in the states to nullify such a law, though he does not ask that Kentucky now exercise the right, preferring at the moment "a committee of conference and correspondence" to communicate with other state legislatures, a process reminiscent of the actions of the colonial legislatures in response to the Intolerable Acts in 1774. Madison, ever more cautious, has Virginia assert for the states only a right "to interpose, for arresting the progress of the evil, and for maintaining, within their respective limits, the authorities, rights, and liberties appertaining to them." There, too, the call was for communication with the other states.

The response of the other states was swift but hardly satisfactory from the point of view of the Virginians. Seven northern states responded and, according to one modern historian, "all flatly condemned the protest."[19] A better document was needed, and Madison, elected in 1799 to the Virginia legislature, now produced one, in the form of a report, issued in January 1800, elaborating in detail each of the resolutions, its reasons, and its aim. His argument against the Sedition Act as a violation of what freedom of the press ought to mean in a republican government is justly famous, and the treatment of the limited applicability of common law to federal jurisprudence is also noteworthy, for it soon becomes the dominant position on the specific issue of federal common law crimes, though it is not accepted more generally until the twentieth century. Still, for our purposes, his comments on "interposition" are most significant. Madison notes that, by its terms, the resolution limits the occasions for interposition: The constitutional violation must involve a "deliberate, palpable, and dangerous exercise" of powers not granted by the Constitution. Moreover, he denies interposition will occur "either in a hasty manner or on doubtful and inferior occasions."[20] Though the argument for authoritative interpretation of the Constitution by the parties to its making depends on seeing the Constitution as a compact among the states, he distinguishes between "ordinary conventions between nations" and "an intimate and constitutional union," saying that within the latter, "interposition of the parties, in their sovereign capacity, can be called for by occasions only deeply and essentially affecting the vital principles of their political system." As for the acts of interposition themselves, Madison does not specify what form they would take. The word *interpose* means to place in between, and therefore to obstruct, delay, interfere, intervene, or interrupt.[21] He does not deny, but he also does not assert that interposition can entail nullification of an act of Congress, much less dissolution of the compact itself. Instead, he notes that the resolution in question speaks of the object of an act of interposition in a carefully restrained way: The purpose is, in Madison's near quotation, "solely that of arresting the progress of the evil of usurpation, and of maintaining the authorities, rights, and liberties, appertaining to the states as parties to the Constitution."[22] Jefferson spoke of nullification as a natural right of parties to a compact; Madison speaks more guardedly of a sort of constitutional right or duty to resist.

One of the most remarkable paragraphs of Madison's remarkable discussion is the objection he raises and answers: "that the judicial authority is to be regarded as the sole expositor of the Constitution in the last resort."[23] Here, before judicial review is even exercised to strike down a law on the federal level, is the idea of judicial supremacy that becomes familiar to Americans later on. Madison refutes it on three grounds. First, not all usurpations will be subject to judicial process; there are wrongs that will not give rise to a legal controversy or case. Second, the judiciary being only one department of the federal government, its supremacy over its cases and controversies would entail the supremacy of the federal legislative and executive powers in those matters that do not find their way to court; judicial supremacy is thus federal supremacy by another name. Finally, the doctrine of interposition is reserved for precisely those usurpations that cannot otherwise be met by ordinary constitutional means; for example, the judicial branch itself might be the usurper. In short, even if the Court might be final in relation to the other branches of the federal government, it is not final "in relation to the rights of the parties to the constitutional compact, from which the judicial, as well as the other departments, held their delegated trusts." Madison does not deny the power that comes to be called judicial review, but he does deny that it is supreme over the Constitution.

For all his protests of caution, however, Madison concludes his discussion of the interposition article with a justification of "a frequent recurrence to first principles" as "a necessary safeguard against the danger of degeneracy, to which republics are liable." Compare the present cause to the Revolution, he insists to the reader, who will be able to "determine whether the declaratory recurrence here made to those principles ought to be viewed as unseasonable and improper, or as a vigilant discharge of an important duty." The spirit of interposition, then, is the spirit of republican self-government, which is not to be reserved only for moments of extraordinary creativity, but to animate constitutional life. That the movement Madison is here defending succeeds not by means of interposition by the states, but rather by means of national electoral success in what Jefferson liked to call "the Revolution of 1800," thus seems altogether appropriate, though paradoxical. Presidential elections and politics more generally take place within the frame and according to the processes of the Constitution, but constitutional interpretation is often an issue at stake in them. "The authority of constitutions over governments," wrote Madison, "and of the sovereignty of the people over constitutions, are truths which are at all times necessary to be kept in mind."[24] That a people can be constitutional as well as sovereign, or sovereign only because also constitutional, is a truth also worth attention, and arguably the source of Jeffersonian success.[25]

Departmentalism: Jefferson, *Marbury*, and Judicial Review

The Supreme Court's decision in *Chisholm v. Georgia* and the election of 1800, which swept the authors of Republican opposition to the Alien and Sedition Acts into control of the federal government itself, are, then, the real beginnings of American constitutional law, and their lessons point more to an authoritative constitutional resistance than to judicial supremacy. In this context, *Marbury v. Madison*, the case that established federal judicial review of legislation, appears less as an assertion of judicial preeminence and more as a carefully wrought effort on John Marshall's part to preserve a place for the judiciary in constitutional interpretation.[26] As has often been explained, the case did not come to the Court as an attempt to test the constitutionality of a piece of legislation; it was not a case that pitted the judicial branch against Congress, though there was precisely such a case coming along more or less contemporaneously with it, testing the constitutionality of the repeal of the Judiciary Act of 1801.[27] *Marbury* was from the start a case of constitutional dimension, but this was because it seemed to pit the Court against the president: What Marbury sought was a court order, a mandamus, commanding President Jefferson's secretary of state, none other than James Madison, to deliver a commission sealed for him by the Adams administration. From the beginning, Jefferson made clear his intention to ignore any order that the Court might issue. He instructed Madison not to acknowledge the jurisdiction of the Court—rather like the state of Georgia in *Chisholm*, Madison only comes to Court via the attorney general, who does answer the claim but briefly testifies as a witness—and the theory of "departmentalism" was developed to explain his instructions. Each branch, according to Jefferson, is exclusively responsible for the constitutional duties placed upon its members, and each is authorized to interpret the Constitution according to its conscience in matters that concern itself.[28] We have already seen this constitutional theory in embryo in the Virginia Report of 1800, where it is used to explain the limited role of the judiciary in constitutional interpretation. Now it stands ready to defy the Supreme Court, indeed, almost to put it to a dare.

The genius of Marshall's solution in *Marbury* is that it avoids such an outcome while clearly asserting for the Court an important role in the determination of constitutional disputes. In the first place, by refusing to issue the mandamus, Marshall denies Jefferson the opportunity to defy him. Second, by speaking at length to the question of Marbury's right to the commission, Marshall seems partially to reject Jefferson's constitutional theory: There are indeed political duties of the executive that cannot be reviewed by a court of law, but the ministerial acts of an official as prescribed by statute are not among them. Third, Marshall's assertion of judicial power in *Marbury* is arguably circumscribed by a certain acknowledgment of the truth of Jefferson's departmentalism, for the *Marbury* decision can be construed in terms consistent with departmentalism: The legislative act in question was the *Judiciary* Act, of course, and the Court's constitutional ruling concerned the provision in Article III about its own jurisdiction. Whatever one thinks of Marshall's arguments construing the act and the Constitution on this matter, even Jefferson cannot reject the power of the courts to determine such things without making the case, not for departmentalism, but for legislative supremacy. From the point of view of some subsequent Democrats, Jefferson's position seems undemocratic, for it makes each branch of government—rather than, say, the people at large or through their representatives—judge of its constitutional powers and rights.[29] Without enshrining Jefferson's departmentalism as law—maybe it is a specifically executive understanding of constitutionalism, after all—Marshall prudently defines the Court's interpretive power over the Constitution in the context of the judicial function, thus invoking the departmental principle even as he reads his department's charge in a grand way.

From the Bank Veto to *Dred Scott*

The question of the constitutionality of a national bank was famously debated in the First Congress and in state papers by Secretary of the Treasury Alexander Hamilton and Secretary of State Thomas Jefferson. Only thirty years later does it make its way to the Supreme Court, where, in the case of *McCulloch v. Maryland*, Marshall writes that incorporation of a bank is within the implied powers of Congress, leaving the question of "the degree of its necessity" under the necessary and proper clause "to be discussed in another place"—that is, in Congress, not in the Court.[30] (Indeed, it was an irony of the Jeffersonian position on necessary and proper that, short of interposition, and maybe even with it—for what was Maryland's tax on the bank but an interposition?—the federal courts would be asked to invoke their power of judicial review to strike expansive federal legislation.) When thirteen years after *McCulloch* Andrew Jackson vetoes the act to recharter the Second Bank, he acknowledges Marshall's decision, but refuses to grant it the last word on the question of the bank's constitutionality. Jackson makes clear his opposition to the bank on grounds that are certainly political, charging it with favoring the wealthy and the foreign and thus denying "equal protection" to the people of the United States, but he also insists that the bank is unconstitutional, at least at the moment he acts. He invokes the principle of departmentalism, now in an official state paper, not—as Jefferson did—in "private" correspondence:

If the opinion of the Supreme Court covered the whole ground of this act, it ought not to control the coordinate authorities of this Government. The Congress, the Executive, and the Court must each for itself be guided by its own opinion of the Constitution. Each public officer who takes an oath to support the Constitution swears that he will support it as he understands it, and not as it is understood by others. It is as much the duty of the House of Representatives, of the Senate, and of the President to decide upon the constitutionality of any bill or resolution which may be presented to them for passage or approval as it is of the supreme judges when it may be brought before them for judicial decision. The opinion of the judges has no more authority over Congress than the opinion of Congress has over the judges, and on that point the President is independent of both. The authority of the Supreme Court must not, therefore, be permitted to control the Congress or the Executive when acting in their legislative capacities, but to have only such influence as the force of their reasoning may deserve.[31]

Jackson, or his reputed ghost author here, Roger Taney, is careful enough to recognize that Marshall in *McCulloch* made no contrary claim. Indeed, he says explicitly that the meaning of that opinion, and in particular of the passage from it quoted above, is that "it is the exclusive province of Congress and the President to decide whether the particular features of this act are *necessary* and *proper* in order to enable the bank to perform conveniently and efficiently the public duties assigned to it as a fiscal agent, and therefore constitutional, or *unnecessary* and *improper*, and therefore unconstitutional."[32]

In their debates in the summer of 1858, Lincoln charged his opponent, Stephen Douglas, with preparing the public mind to accept a future Supreme Court decision that would nationalize slavery by insisting on public acquiescence in the Court's decision in *Dred Scott*—despite the fact that that decision eviscerated Douglas's own principle of "popular sovereignty" by declaring unconstitutional any legislation outlawing slavery in the territories. At Galesburg, Lincoln says, "I have turned his attention to the fact that General Jackson differed with him in regard to the political obligation of a Supreme Court decision. . . . Jefferson differed with him in regard to the political obligation of a Supreme Court decision."[33] Douglas's reply seems correct on the narrow question: Jackson did indeed say, in effect, as Douglas paraphrases, "[Rechartering the bank] is unnecessary and improper, and therefore I am against it on constitutional grounds as well as those of expediency."[34] Again, Jackson had no need to resist the Court, because the Court had yielded to his and the legislature's discretion. But on the larger point of political obligation, at least if one has recourse to published statements and not only to deeds, to dicta, as it were, and not just holdings, Lincoln is surely right. Douglas seems clearly to depart from Jefferson and Jackson when he charges that Lincoln, in denouncing the decision in *Dred Scott* as mistaken and hence not binding on future legislatures and executives considering the slavery question, "is going to appeal from the Supreme Court of the United States to every town meeting," or more dramatically, that he would "raise your mobs and oppose the law of the land." Neither Jefferson nor Jackson—for that matter, neither Hamilton nor Marshall— would have said, as Douglas does, that "The Constitution has created that court to decide all constitutional questions in the last resort; and when such decisions have been made, they become the law of the land."[35]

Constitutional Resistance in Perspective

The foregoing discussion only sketches the outlines of constitutional resistance as it was understood in the early republic. Omitted are not only the other great constitutional incidents of 1832, Jackson's reputed resistance to the Court's decisions in the Cherokee cases and his facing down South Carolina's attempted nullification of the tariff, but such moments as the Hartford Convention of 1814–15 and the running dispute between the United States Supreme Court and the Virginia Court of Appeals under Spencer Roane about section 25 of the Judiciary Act and the power of the former to hear appeals from decisions of the latter. Moreover, the rich development of the law of freedom in relation to slavery is a field where resistance can be found on both sides of the question, not only among the levels of government and the branches, but even among the levels of the judiciary itself. Further, Lincoln as president put executive interpretation of the Constitution into practice, for example, in directing the State Department to issue passports to African Americans, despite the denial in *Dred Scott* that they could be citizens; and, for another example, in ignoring writs of habeas corpus even from the chief justice himself when detention of Confederate sympathizers was thought essential to the suppression of rebellion.[36] The early constitutional tradition, in short, made room for spirited defense of republican liberty by the people and their representatives. Indeed, the tradition defined constitutional liberty in precisely such terms, for resistance captures at once the two poles of constitutionalism: on the one side, the sovereignty of the people; on the other, the existence of a fundamental or higher law in whose name resistance can be justly made. The opinion that the Supreme Court has final say over the Constitution is an old one, but in the early republic, at least, its opponents carried the day.

If there is truth in the suggestion made above that our early constitutionalism was colored by the fact that the country was born of a rebellion, it should probably be expected that constitutionalism after the Civil War would be colored by the role of the federal government in the suppression of rebellion. Still, perhaps this need go no further than to require that certain constitutional determinations eventually become a settled part of the constitutional order, something Lincoln himself, in contrast to Jefferson or Jackson, seems in the passage quoted above to accept. Even the most cursory knowledge of the course of Progressive legislation indicates that unfriendly judicial decisions did not definitively thwart the Progressive cause. At the very least, Progressives succeeded in overturning the decision in *Pollock v. Farmers' Loan & Trust Co.*[37] with the Sixteenth Amendment, and they made headway against *Hammer v. Dagenhart*[38] with a proposed amendment as well. Nor did the decision in *Lochner v. New York* destroy the impetus for minimum wage or maximum hour legislation in the states, as is evident from the many subsequent occasions the Court had to revisit the issue.[39]

Though the "Constitutional Revolution" that accompanied the New Deal may have undercut the spirit of constitutional resistance by substituting a spirit of pragmatic accommodation for the more formal constitutionalism of federalism and the separation of powers, not to mention its self-conscious acknowledgment of the necessity and so propriety of judge-made law, the actual precipitant of the triumph of judicial supremacy over constitutional resistance was surely the movement of "massive resistance" that greeted the Supreme Court's decision to undo school segregation in *Brown v. Board of Education*. The assertion in *Cooper v. Aaron* that "the federal judiciary is supreme in the exposition of the law of the Constitution," that thus "the interpretation of the Fourteenth Amendment enunciated by this Court in the *Brown* case is the supreme law of the land," and furthermore that "No state legislator or executive or judicial officer can war against the Constitution [meaning the Court's interpretation?] without violating his undertaking to support it" is the defining text of modern doctrine,[40] and while it might be noted that the Court made this bold statement a full year after the original Little Rock crisis, when President Eisenhower had federalized the National Guard, it is not my purpose here to reexamine the resistance movement, much less to plead its cause. What I doubt is that the use of constitutional forms in an unattractive cause necessarily discredits those forms; on the contrary, it seems possible to me that the settled acceptance of desegregation as constitutional mandate and as public policy that is wise and just was purchased in part by resistance having had its day in the court of public opinion and having decisively lost.[41]

Today scholars speak of the Constitution as a set of legal principles rather than as a series of compromises; more precisely, they seek to expand the Constitution's principles and bury its compromises. Usually forgotten or conveniently denied is first, that what are purported to be constitutional principles are usually partisan principles, and second, that compromise is not a craven selling out of principle, but a political settlement that has its own moral structure, entailing both an acknowledgment of legitimate difference and a duty to honor one's promises and keep one's word.[42] Constitutional resistance will usually be made in the name of a principle, but the recognition of constitutional rights to resist is the precondition for genuine constitutional compromise.[43] That today it is fashionable on both sides to denigrate compromise, while our constitutionalism oscillates between assertions of judicial supremacy and threats of civil disobedience, seems to follow from the modern-day refusal to admit that there are two sides to most constitutional questions and that the genius of constitutionalism is in acknowledging this fact and providing the forms to accommodate it.

Who, then, has authority over the Constitution? The answer is still, I think, the people—at least when we have the spirit to take it back.

PART III

Comparative Perspectives

Chapter Six

The Supreme Court and Contemporary Constitutionalism:
The Implications of the Development of Alternative Forms of Judicial Review

Mark Tushnet

Discussions of the relation between judicial review and democratic self-government that take judicial review as exercised by the U.S. Supreme Court as their model quickly run up against the problem that judicial review in that form seems to place serious barriers to the ability of the people to govern themselves. It is not merely that judicial review prevents the people from implementing the policies they prefer. After all, the whole point of constitutionalism is to place some limits on the policies a nation can actually implement. The more substantial difficulty is that the U.S. Supreme Court blocks the adoption of policies in the name of the Constitution *as it interprets the Constitution* and even when there are reasonably available alternative interpretations of the Constitution under which the policy could be implemented.

One prominent resolution of this difficulty is Thayerian review, that is, a standard of review that authorizes the courts to invalidate legislation only when the legislation was manifestly inconsistent with the Constitution: "[The court] can only disregard the Act when those who have the right to make laws have not merely made a mistake, but have made a very clear one—so clear that it is not open to rational question."[1] We should distinguish between what I call pseudo-Thayerian review and true Thayerian review. Pseudo-Thayerian review occurs when the courts ask, "Did the legislature make a clear error in determining—if it did—that the legislation was consistent with the Constitution as *we* interpret it?" In this version, the courts make an independent judgment about what the Constitution means, and then ask whether a rational legislature could believe that the statute at issue was consistent with the Constitution so interpreted. In pseudo-Thayerian review, that is, the courts have the final (or only) say on what the Constitution means. True Thayerian review, in contrast, gives the (rational) legislature a role in constitutional interpretation. The truly Thayerian court asks, "Putting aside our own views about what the Constitution means, could a rational legislature believe that the statute in question is consistent with some reasonable interpretation of the Constitution—again, even if that interpretation is not one we ourselves would adopt?"

True Thayerian review involves statutes that the court believes to be unconstitutional according to the judges' independent assessment of the constitution, but which the court nonetheless refrains from striking down. It is hard to discover opinions endorsing truly Thayerian review. In recent years, the only such opinion of which I am aware is Justice Souter's opinion concurring in the judgment in *Nixon v. United States*.[2] The case involved a challenge to the constitutionality of the Senate's procedure for trying impeachments initially before a committee and then on a paper review by the Senate as a whole. Justice Souter did not find those procedures unconstitutional, but, he wrote, he could "envision different and unusual circumstances that might justify a more searching review of impeachment proceedings." These were circumstances in which "the Senate's action might be *so far beyond the scope* of its constitutional authority" that the courts should step in.[3] Justice Souter's formulation implies that the courts might refrain from intervening when the Senate acted beyond its constitutional authority, but not "so far beyond" that authority as to warrant judicial intervention.[4] This is indeed Thayerian review.[5]

The problem for which Thayerian review is offered as a solution arises because in the U.S. system of judicial review, the courts' determination of constitutional meaning is final in the medium run, at least if the hard-to-implement amendment process is not effectively deployed. Recently, constitutional designers have developed a different form of judicial review, which I have called "weak-form" review. In weak-form judicial review, the courts' constitutional interpretations are understood to be provisional and rather readily revisable by political processes that give the courts' views the deference to which they are rationally entitled, but no special authority. Courts in weak-form systems can, I suggest, exercise vigorous rather than Thayerian review without running up against the democratic-self-government objection: strong-form systems need Thayerian review because their decisions are in an important sense final, whereas weak-form systems can exercise aggressive review because their decisions are not.

In the remainder of this chapter, after showing that the United States does indeed have a strong-form system of judicial review, I describe some prominent variants of weak-form review, and then discuss some versions of constitutional interpretation in the United States that attempt to explain why strong-form review shares some characteristics with weak-form review.

Strong-Form Review in the United States

Recall that giving judges the power to enforce constitutional limitations can threaten democratic self-governance. The reason is that constitutional provisions are often written in rather general terms. The courts give those terms meaning in the course of deciding whether individual statutes are consistent or inconsistent with particular constitutional provisions. But, as a rule, particular provisions can reasonably be given alternative interpretations. And, sometimes, a statute will be inconsistent with the provision when the provision is interpreted in one way, yet would be consistent with an alternative interpretation of the same provision.

Consider here a problem that the U.S. Supreme Court addressed in the late twentieth century. Sometimes a government will adopt a rule that has particularly severe effects on a class of religious believers. The rule might require all military personnel to wear only a military uniform, in the face of religious commands to wear distinctive head-gear; it might ban the use of a psychoactive drug that plays an important role in a denomination's religious ceremonies; or it might deny unemployment benefits to those who are unable to locate jobs that would allow them to refrain from working on the day they observe as the Sabbath. Do such rules violate the Constitution's prohibition on restricting the "free exercise of religion"? In 1963 the Supreme Court held that they did, unless they were virtually the only way the government could promote important public purposes.[6] Almost thirty years later, the Court changed its mind, and held that such general rules were ordinarily perfectly constitutional, unless they were adopted with the specific aim of imposing harm on a religious denomination.[7] Now, suppose the decisions had come in the reverse order: first the Court adopts a doctrine that gives governments wide latitude, and later adopts one substantially limiting what governments can do. What if a legislature believes that the Court got it right the first time? We *know* that the constitutional interpretation favored by the legislature is not unreasonable: after all, the Supreme Court itself adopted it (for a while). No doubt, the Court's later interpretation is *also* reasonable. But, why should the Court's reasonable interpretation prevail over the legislature's (also) reasonable one?

The example I have given is not esoteric. Indeed, experience has shown that people—that is, legislatures and courts—can disagree about what a constitutional provision should be interpreted to mean quite often, and that those disagreements can, again quite often, be entirely reasonable. Strong-form review insists that the courts' reasonable constitutional interpretations prevail over the legislatures' reasonable ones. Courts exercise strong-form judicial review when their interpretive judgments are final and unrevisable. The modern articulation of strong-form judicial review is provided in *Cooper v. Aaron*, where the U.S. Supreme Court described the federal courts as "supreme in the exposition of the law of the Constitution," and inferred from that a duty on legislatures to follow the Court's interpretations.[8]

A contemporary version came in *City of Boerne v. Flores*,[9] which involved Congress' power to enact the Religious Freedom Restoration Act of 1993 (RFRA) pursuant to its power to "enforce" the prohibitions placed on state governments by Section 1 of the Fourteenth Amendment.[10] As we have seen, at the time RFRA was enacted the Court had held that states could enforce their general rules even against those whose religious views made it impossible or very difficult for them to comply with both their religious commitments and the state's law. RFRA rejected that approach, and required states to have strong justifications even for general laws that burdened religious exercise. And, again as we have seen, the rule enacted in RFRA was the one the Supreme Court itself had articulated for decades before it changed its approach.

The question for the Court was whether RFRA "enforced" Section 1. Analytically, one could take the position that the scope of Section 1 is open to reasonable alternative interpretations, the Supreme Court's prior interpretation being the first and Congress' more recent one the second. On that view, RFRA did enforce Section 1, *given* the congressional interpretation of Section 1. The Supreme Court took a different view. For the Court, the only rights that Congress could enforce were those the Court itself recognized. According to the Court, "legislation which *alters* the meaning of the Free Exercise Clause cannot be said to be enforcing the Clause." The opinion continued, "If Congress could define its own powers by *altering* the Fourteenth Amendment's meaning, no longer would the Constitution be 'superior paramount law, unchangeable by ordinary means.'"[11]

The deep assumption of strong-form review is found in the word *alter*.

A proponent of some other version of judicial review might have written, "Congress has the power to specify the meaning of the Fourteenth Amendment, at least so long as its specification is reasonable, although different from the specification we ourselves would provide." Similarly, that proponent might have written: "The Constitution defines the powers of Congress in broad terms; when Congress provides a reasonable specification of those terms' meaning in a particular context, courts should give considerable weight to that judgment. This does not allow Congress to 'alter' the Fourteenth Amendment's meaning, but rather follows from the Constitution's allocation of interpretive power to both Congress and the courts." Under a strong-form system such as that emerging from the U.S. Supreme Court's decisions, the tension between judicial enforcement of constitutional limitations and democratic self-government is obvious. The people have little recourse when the courts interpret the Constitution reasonably but, in the reasonable alternative view of a majority, mistakenly. We can amend the Constitution, or wait for judges to retire or die and replace them with judges who hold the better view of what the Constitution means.[12]

James Stoner shows that in the early years of the republic, Americans resisted courts' assertions of their exclusive (and sometimes supreme) power to interpret the Constitution.[13] Another possibility lies in designing or re-conceptualizing judicial review. Weak-form systems of judicial review hold out the promise of reducing the tension between judicial review and democratic self-governance, while acknowledging that constitutionalism requires that there be some limits on self-governance. The basic idea behind weak-form review is simple: weak-form judicial review provides mechanisms for the people to respond to decisions that they reasonably believe mistaken that can be deployed more rapidly than the constitutional amendment or judicial appointment processes.

Variants of Weak-Form Review

In weak-form systems, judicial interpretations of constitutional provisions can be revised in the relatively short term by a legislature using a decision rule not much different from the one used in the every-day legislative process.[14] I discuss here the design of weak-form review in New Zealand, the United Kingdom, and Canada.[15] I think it worth noting early on that these nations are reasonably well-functioning democracies in which civil liberties and civil rights are reasonably well protected—not perfectly, of course, according to whatever one's criteria of perfect enforcement are, but reasonably well. That observation is important for U.S. constitutionalists, who may be skeptical about claims that weak-form judicial review can even in theory be sufficient to protect fundamental rights. Perhaps one can mount theoretical objections to weak-form review, but its practice seems good enough—in the nations where it occurs. Yet, I must also acknowledge that the practice of judicial review in these nations seems to depart—sometimes only slightly, sometimes substantially—from the modesty implicit in the design of weak-form systems. As I have argued elsewhere, there is some reason to think that in operation nominally weak-form systems become strong-form ones— which in turn raises some questions about the very possibility of weak-form judicial review.[16]

The Interpretive Mandate

The New Zealand Bill of Rights Act, adopted in 1990, is in form an ordinary statute, which in theory could be repealed wholly or in part by any later legislative majority.[17] It enumerates a modern list of individual rights, such as freedom of expression and equality.[18] Those rights are not directly enforceable in the courts, though. The act specifically bars the courts from invoking its substantive provisions to hold that some statute has been repealed or is otherwise invalid, or to refuse to enforce the statute on the ground that the statute violates the act's substantive provisions.[19] Rather, the act is an *interpretive mandate*. Its key provision is this: "Wherever an enactment can be given a meaning that is consistent with the rights and freedoms contained in this Bill of Rights, that meaning shall be preferred to any other meaning."[20]

Why should a mere interpretive mandate be regarded as even a weak form of judicial review? Much turns on what we understand the mandate to require. The question of the mandate's meaning is more complex than it might seem. Initially, we can consider two scenarios in the courts. The judges begin by using the ordinary tools of statutory interpretation to determine what some provision means. They consult the statute's overall structure, its purposes, its legislative history, its relation to other statutes, various canons of statutory interpretation, and perhaps more (or less).[21] In the first scenario, the judges discover that some of the tools point in the direction of what they see as a rights-protective interpretation, others in a rights-restrictive one. The interpretive mandate urges or requires the court to adopt the rights-protective interpretation. That seems straightforward enough: the statute "can be" interpreted, without distortion, to be rights-protective,

and the act tells the courts to adopt that interpretation. The second scenario is more difficult. Here all or nearly all of the ordinary tools of statutory interpretation point in the rights-restrictive direction. Does the act give
the courts *another* interpretive tool, not simply a tie-breaker, but overriding
what "ordinary" statutory interpretation would yield?

This second scenario makes it clear that the pure interpretive requirement is a form of judicial review. The courts are saying, in essence, "The
language of this statute tells us what you wanted to do, but if we did that
you would be violating constitutional norms. You've also told us that you
don't want to do that. So, we'll interpret the statute to be consistent with
constitutional norms, even though that leads us to enforce a statute that
does something other than what the statutory language says you wanted to
do." Weak-form judicial review in the form of an interpretive mandate gives
the courts an effect on policy that is different from the effect they have using
their traditional methods of statutory interpretation.

The fundamental assumption behind weak-form review, that there can
be reasonable disagreement over the meaning of constitutional provisions,
complicates the picture even more. That assumption means that interpretations are not pre-packaged as "rights-restrictive" or "rights-protective."
Someone seeking to avoid a statute's burden will, of course, characterize the
statute as rights-restrictive. The statute's defenders might reply that it is either neutral as to rights (correctly understood) or actually rights-protective.
Libel law provides a useful example: restrictions on the dissemination of
false statements about a person restrict the right of free expression, but promote a right to human dignity.

The interpretive mandate thus directs the courts to engage in *two* acts
of interpretation: they must interpret the substantive rights protections, and
then determine whether the statutory provision at issue can be interpreted
in a manner consistent with their interpretation of the rights protections. It
would not be surprising to discover that courts cannot readily disentangle
the two interpretive steps. A judge who, going into the case, is troubled by
a challenged statute will probably be inclined to think that one of the Bill
of Rights Act's substantive provisions should be interpreted to cast some
doubt on the other statute's policy, and then will probably be inclined to
interpret *that* statute so that it does not violate the substantive provisions
as interpreted—because, for example, it does not actually apply in the circumstances. Or, perhaps more interesting, suppose the judge thinks that
all the ordinary tools of statutory interpretation point in the direction of a
rights-restrictive interpretation. The judge could throw up her hands and

say, "This statute violates substantive rights, but there's nothing I can do about it." Or, the judge could say, "If we interpret the substantive rights properly, we will see that the statute does not violate those rights."

How will *legislatures* respond to decisions invoking the interpretive mandate? Such decisions interpret statutes. Proponents of the interpretive mandate as a version of weak-form review hope that the judges' discussion of both the substantive rights and the questionable statute will induce legislatures to accept the courts' rights-protective statutory interpretation. They hope that what the judges have to say will persuade the legislature that it actually does not want to adopt a rights-restrictive policy.

Suppose, though, that the legislature disagrees. A majority might think that the courts have adopted a mistaken interpretation of the Bill of Rights Act's substantive provisions.[22] Premised on that mistaken interpretation, the courts have distorted the other statute they are purportedly interpreting, and are thereby reducing the legislature's ability to pursue policies that it prefers and that are not inconsistent with substantive rights properly understood. What can the majority do? As far as it is concerned, the statute it already enacted was perfectly fine. Should it simply reenact the same statute, running the risk that the courts will once again distort it via "interpretation"? Should it reenact the statute, adding provisions that say, in effect, "This time we really mean it"? We should note that one legislative response should *not* be available. The Bill of Rights Act is an ordinary statute, and its provisions can be amended by ordinary majorities. But, the legislature should not be expected to amend the Bill of Rights Act. As far as the legislature is concerned, the act specifies substantive rights perfectly well. From the legislature's point of view, the courts have misconstrued the Bill of Rights Act.

Normatively, making the legislature correct the judges' errors by respecifying substantive rights gives the courts a larger role than they should have in a weak-form system. And, descriptively, amending the Bill of Rights Act in the face of a judicial decision interpreting a statute to avoid a rights-restrictive interpretation seems to me a quite unlikely outcome. The reason is that proponents of judicial review, whether in its weak or strong forms, expect that a judicial statement about what substantive provisions mean will carry important weight in the political process. The language of rights matters in politics, and we can expect people to be at a political disadvantage when their opponents are able to say, "Why do you want to take away the rights the courts have told us we have?" This political dimension of even the interpretive mandate, the weakest variant of weak-form judicial review, suggests that the difference between weak-form and strong-form review may not be as dramatic as it might seem at first.

The Augmented Interpretive Mandate

The British Human Rights Act 1998 (HRA) raises similar questions.[23] The HRA is an *augmented interpretive mandate*. Briefly, like the New Zealand Bill of Rights Act, the HRA directs courts to interpret statutes to be consistent with fundamental rights. It enhances their power, though, by authorizing them to issue a statement of "incompatibility." That is, if they are unable to interpret a statute to be consistent with fundamental rights, they can declare it incompatible with those rights. That declaration has no effects on anyone's legal rights. The statute remains in effect, and can be enforced or relied on in any legal proceeding. But the HRA's proponents expected— and asserted during the debates over its adoption—that Parliament would routinely respond by amending the statute to eliminate the incompatibility. Even more, the HRA allows the minister in charge of the legislation to place it on a fast-track for amendment, bypassing some of the ordinary procedural hurdles to legislation proposed by one of the government's ministers. And, if that is not enough, under the HRA a minister who finds that amending the statute is urgently required may do so by ministerial order rather than by legislation, subject only to subsequent ratification by Parliament.

The Human Rights Act emerged out of a conjunction of interests between the Labour and Conservative parties in the United Kingdom. Historically the Labour Party and its leaders had been strongly opposed to judicial intervention in politics.[24] Early in the twentieth century the British courts had invoked common law rules to interfere rather substantially with efforts to organize workers and parallel efforts to use economic force to compel employers to engage in collective bargaining. Labour Party leaders found the contemporaneous experience in the United States, where courts were invoking constitutional principles to obstruct the adoption of redistributive legislation, to confirm their suspicion that courts—staffed by upper class professionals—would systematically disfavor Labour Party interests. In the 1970s a leading academic in Great Britain produced a skeptical study of the class backgrounds and, in his view, biases of sitting British judges that Labour Party leaders took to establish that things had not changed.[25]

What did change, though, was politics and international law. The long tenure of Margaret Thatcher and Conservative Party rule transformed the

Labour Party. Among the things the party's leaders learned was that parliamentary supremacy could devastate the policy positions they favored, and they came to believe that judicial enforcement of entrenched rights could obstruct, not the social democratic policies they favored, but the strongly conservative policies they opposed. In addition, the United Kingdom was a party to the European Convention on Human Rights, and its policies across a wide range of matters, including free press and criminal procedure, were the subject of regular, and successful, challenges before the convention's enforcement body, the European Court on Human Rights in Strasbourg, Germany. These losses embarrassed the nation's political leaders, and—they came to think—properly so: Parliament had enacted, or at least failed to eliminate, intrusions on liberties the British cherished, and the European Court actually had done a good job of identifying such intrusions. And, on the most mundane level, Cherie Booth Blair, the wife of Labour Party leader Tony Blair, was a leading human rights lawyer in Great Britain.

Tony Blair's "New Labour" platform included a pledge to adopt some sort of Bill of Rights for the United Kingdom. And, after some nervousness, Conservative Party leaders accepted the idea. Political scientist Ran Hirschl suggests an explanation: they foresaw that they were likely to lose an election in the near future, and hoped that the courts would preserve some of the policy gains the Conservatives had achieved, through enforcing entrenched rights.[26]

Exactly what would the "Bill of Rights" for the United Kingdom be? The European Convention provided a reasonably good list of the fundamental principles that constitutionalists in the late twentieth century thought important. The Human Rights Act simply made most of the convention's rights enforceable as a matter of *domestic* rather than international law. Instead of losing in the British courts and then winning in the Strasbourg Court, a litigant could now "win" in the British courts.

But what would a victory mean? The HRA adopted the "interpretive mandate" model, and then beefed it up a bit. As the HRA's supporters saw things, the pure interpretive mandate left judges with nothing to do when they confronted a statute that, in their view, *clearly* violated fundamental rights. In such cases, they simply could not interpret the statute rights protectively. That seemed inadequate. But giving the judges the power to invalidate such a statute was too strong medicine in a nation where the tradition of parliamentary supremacy had deep roots and where there remained some discomfort with giving judges too much power. The HRA's solution was the declaration of incompatibility.

The HRA raises many of the same problems of interpretation that the New Zealand Bill of Rights Act does.[27] The declaration of incompatibility poses a few modest additional problems. From a litigant's point of view, a court that issues a declaration of incompatibility has *rejected* the litigant's claim—in the sense that the litigant walks away with his or her rights still impaired. What litigants will say is something like this: "My adversary relies on a statute to justify its actions, which actions make me worse off. If you construe the statute to mean X, my adversary could not rely on it to justify its actions, and the statute would not violate my rights under the European Convention. That's what I want." Now, how does the government respond? First, of course, it will say that the statute means Y, and that Y does not violate the European Convention. But its alternative argument is this: "Hey, it's all right with us if you find that construction Y violates the European Convention, because all you can do then is issue a declaration of incompatibility, and we can still do to the plaintiff what we want to do."

Three things inhibit the government from routinely rolling over on the question of incompatibility. The first, and almost certainly the most important, is that regularly conceding that its actions violate the European Convention would eventually become a political embarrassment. A government might occasionally get away with rolling over on that question, when it could make a credible public case that the statute was really important. Try that too often, though, and the government's political standing is likely to fall.

Second, consider another aftermath of a declaration of incompatibility. The litigant walks out of the British court with nothing but the declaration in hand. Within Great Britain, that is just a piece of paper. But, it might be more important in Strasbourg. That is, the litigant can go to the European Court on Human Rights, saying that the British government has violated his or her rights, not under the HRA, but under the European Convention itself. Of course, the Strasbourg court might disagree with the British courts about what rights the convention confers. My guess, though, is that the judges on the Strasbourg court are likely to think to themselves along these lines: "If British judges think that their government has violated the Convention, who are we to disagree? We're certainly not going to get in much hot water in Great Britain if we keep saying that we're just going along with what British judges have said."[28]

Third, as noted earlier, the general expectation is that governments will regularly respond to declarations of incompatibility by amending the statute. That expectation is likely to be satisfied, at least in the HRA's early years, when the same people who supported the act's adoption are in control of the executive government. If that is so, though, a government that wants to advance a policy embodied in a challenged statute will have to defend the statute, that is, argue that it should be interpreted so as to be compatible with the European Convention. Otherwise it might win the individual case but then lose the policy by amending the statute.

Indeed, one might be more concerned about the creation of a regular practice of amending statutes in the face of declarations of incompatibility than with routine concessions of incompatibility. The degree to which that expectation is correct will provide a measure of the degree to which the HRA creates a weak or strong form of judicial review. The HRA system would be indistinguishable from strong-form review if statutes that courts declared incompatible with the European Convention were *always* amended to remove the incompatibility. Such a practice would belie the very premise of weak-form review: that there can be reasonable disagreement about what it is, exactly, that fundamental rights described in abstract terms protect and prohibit—or, equivalently, that courts will not always come up with the only reasonable interpretation of fundamental rights guarantees.

A "Dialogic" Mode of Review

The Canadian Charter of Rights, adopted in 1982, provides another version of weak-form review, notably labeled "dialogic" by the leading Canadian constitutional scholar Peter Hogg and one of his students.[29] As with the other documents I have discussed, the charter lists fundamental rights. Two provisions create weak-form review in Canada. Section 1 provides that the rights guaranteed by the charter are subject to "such limitations as are demonstrably justified in a free and democratic society."[30] Section 33 provides that Canadian legislatures can make statutes effective, for renewable five-year periods, "notwithstanding" their inconsistency with a large number of important charter provisions.[31] These provisions license two kinds of legislative response to the constitutional interpretations offered by the courts.

Consider a regulation of commercial expression—for example, a regulation of advertising for sweetened cereals, whose target audiences are children. Suppose the Supreme Court finds the regulation unconstitutional. The Court says that the goal of promoting health by diminishing children's consumption of sweetened cereals is a permissible one, but concludes that the regulation as enacted sweeps within its coverage too much expression that need not be regulated in order to accomplish a significant reduction in consumption.

How can the legislature respond? The Section 1 response is this: bolster the record supporting the legislation so that it provides a better—a more "demonstrable"—justification for the statute's scope. For example, the legislature might compile evidence, if it can, showing that narrowing the statute's scope would make it much more difficult to administer effectively, by requiring regulatory agencies to draw lines that they are not competent to draw, or that any wording that would narrow the statute's scope to accommodate the Court's concerns would actually leave advertisements on the market that contribute significantly to the demands children make on their parents. Note, though, that the Section 1 response takes the Court's *interpretation* of the charter to be correct, and disagrees only with that interpretation's application to the statute.[32] The legislature attempts to show— "demonstrate"—that the violation the Court discerned is indeed justifiable given the Court's own understandings about what is needed to justify a violation. The Section 1 response, that is, does not involve a dialogue between courts and legislatures about the *meaning* of charter provisions, but rather, and only, about how an agreed-upon meaning applies to the specific statute.

In contrast, the idealized Section 33 response does involve a dialogue about constitutional meaning. To continue the example, the parliament might enact a Section 33 override of the Court's decision because, in the legislature's view, the charter's provisions dealing with freedom of expression are simply inapplicable to commercial speech.[33] This use of a Section 33 response would be predicated on a disagreement between the court and the legislature over what the charter *means*, not merely over how it should be applied.[34]

Contrasting Strong-Form and Weak-Form Judicial Review

Strong-form review is a system in which judicial interpretations of the constitution are final and unrevisable by ordinary legislative majorities. They are not permanently embedded in the law, though. Judicial interpretations can be rejected by the special majorities required for constitutional amendment, and they can be repudiated by the courts themselves, either after new judges join the highest court or after some of the original judges rethink their position. For this reason, strong-form and weak-form review fit onto a time continuum: strong-form systems allow the political branches to revise judicial interpretations in the long-ish run, weak-form ones in the short run.

In addition, strong-form systems differ from weak-form ones in the *normative* finality they give to judicial interpretations. Here I return to some questions I raised earlier about the precise language of the Canadian "notwithstanding" clause. A legislature can make a statute effective notwithstanding the fact that, without an override, the statute would violate rights protected by the charter. In this formulation the charter has normative finality. Contrast that with the more prevalent understanding that the notwithstanding clause allows a legislature to make a statute effective notwithstanding the fact that, without an override, the statute would be held *by the courts* to violate charter rights. On *that* understanding, the courts' decisions have normative finality, which is temporarily displaced by the override.

We can combine these distinctions between strong-form and weak-form systems by reverting to the idea of dialogue. Dialogic accounts of constitutional law treat the people, legislatures, executives, and the courts in conversation. The temporal continuum identifies the time frame over which the conversation occurs. The conversation ends when the participant whose decisions have normative finality signals that the conversation is over, at least for a while.

A standard political science model of the interaction between the U.S. Supreme Court and the political branches sees a dialogue occurring over a relatively long time frame. Originating with Robert Dahl in 1957,[35] and updated by Barry Friedman and others,[36] this model has the Court being brought into line with the constitutional views held by a political coalition that sustains itself in power for a suitably long period. The mechanism for alignment is the appointment process: as older judges die or retire, they are replaced by new ones who share the constitutional views of the dominant political coalition. Notably, in this model it is irrelevant whether the dominant coalition accepts or rejects strong-form review in principle or merely disagrees with the interpretations provided by a Court that it does not (yet) control. In the end, the dominant coalition comes to live with strong-form review because it finds it pointless to argue the purely theoretical question of strong-form versus weak-form review once it has taken control of the Court.

Scholars who emphasize the role of social movements in shaping constitutional law, such as Robert Post and Reva Siegel,[37] offer a model in which the conversation can take place over a shorter term.[38] According to this view, the people influence constitutional law by organizing social movements offering distinctive constitutional visions, typically oppositional to the vision dominant in the courts when the movements begin. Social movements influence constitutional law in two ways. One returns us to the political scientists' model: the movements affect electoral politics, which in turn affects the composition of the courts. But, the social movement model offers an alternative mechanism: judges observing the social movement and its effects on society change their views about what the Constitution means. Unlike the political scientists' model, then, the social movement model does not depend on a change in the Court's composition for there to be a change in constitutional interpretation. Like that model, though, the social movement model takes the story to end when the courts come into line.

Bruce Ackerman has offered a model with an even shorter time frame. He develops a general account of constitutional transformation *within* an established constitutional system. The "switch in time" is important to that account.[39] The story, in outline, is this: a mobilized public and its political leadership enact legislation that faces constitutional challenges. The courts uphold those challenges, thereby obstructing the public's preferred policy agenda. The public and its political leaders turn their attention to getting control of the courts. Facing that opposition, the courts abandon their previous constitutional interpretations and adopt those offered by their conversational partners (here, more like adversaries). The interactions that produce the switch in time occur within a compressed time period.[40] Unlike the social movements model, here the mechanism of change is not persuasion, but submission or fear that failure to change will produce severe adverse consequences for the Court. But, as in that model, the conversation ends when the Court comes to agree with its adversaries.

Weak-form systems resemble Ackerman's model to the extent that both involve the possibility of what we might think of as "real time" conversations between courts and legislatures. They differ, though, in two ways. In Ackerman's model, switches in time are rare, and mark the transition from one relatively large-scale organization of the constitutional order to another. In contrast, weak-form systems at least allow for the possibility of routine real-time constitutional conversations. In addition, Ackerman may implicitly give judicial interpretations normative finality, at least during the extended periods of normal politics that follow the switches in time. Weak-form systems treat constitutional interpretations offered by legislatures as normatively equal in weight to those offered by courts.[41]

Conclusion

This chapter simply describes strong-form and weak-form judicial review, and to sketch their differences—and similarities. As institutions, they are different enough in terms of normative finality that we can treat them as binary alternatives. And, although they are located at points on a temporal continuum, the points are widely separated enough that it makes sense to think of them as distinct institutions. My descriptions have been rather general, and it might be that institutions that we can *describe* as quite different actually operate in practice quite similarly. Weak-form review is quite different from the form of judicial review now prevalent in the United States, and it seems unlikely that we will adopt it any time soon. Yet, Stoner's historical survey reminds us that there are alternatives to strong-form judicial review within the American tradition. Perhaps some combination of reflection on constitutional design and historical retrieval might create opportunities for the people to alter the balance between judicial supremacy and popular self-government.

Chapter Seven
The Sounds of Silence: Militant and Acquiescent Constitutionalism

Gary Jeffrey Jacobsohn

How should we understand the connection between a constitution and the social order within which it is situated? Accustomed as we are to identifying constitutionalism with written limits on power, a reasonable response would be to see a predominantly preservative role in the relationship of the first to the second. Thus the institutions that provide order to a society—for example, church, property, family—should be protected from hostile acts threatening to their essential continuity. Moreover, the framing of governing charters is not likely to culminate in a document antagonistic to the very societal structures of stability that provide ballast for the constitutional enterprise. This is not to say that constitutionally governed polities typically immunize the institutions of civil society from change, rather that the constitution itself is not the direct source of major revisions. A constitution provides protected space for institutional transformation in accordance with the actions and desires of private actors and, on occasion, of its own public standards. But the manner in which this occurs will ultimately be supportive of the existing social order, whose preservation requires an adaptive capacity to meet the needs of a changing environment.

An alternative perspective on this connection may be less familiar. In this version the constitution is a potentially subversive presence in the social order. Here the institutions of civil society are vulnerable to transformative attacks emanating from a constitution that is fundamentally antagonistic to the status quo. These institutions are not left totally unprotected, and their defenders will find ample political and legal (including constitutional) resources with which to secure them from the ravages of radical reconstruction. But to the degree that the preservative presumption is absent from constitutional design, defending the social order will be a more formidable task than in circumstances where the imprimatur of constitutional legiti-macy extends to the prevailing configurations of that order. Inherent in the constitutional condition is a gap between foundational ideals and existing realities; in this alternative understanding more is involved than just an implicit reminder of the inevitable disharmonies between law and society, namely the constitutional obligation assigned the state to resolve the sever-est of these contradictions

These approaches represent two distinctive—but not mutually exclu-sive—constitutional orientations. In this chapter I consider the Indian and American cases, both of which contain preservative and transformative ele-ments, the latter predominant in India and the former in the United States. My focus is on one bastion of civil society—the family—an institution vari-ously described in constitutional provisions around the world as "the fun-damental unit of society," "the basic nucleus of social organization," "the natural and fundamental cell of society," "the basis of society," "the founda-tion of society," "the foundation of the preservation and improvement of the nation," "the main center for the growth and edification of the human being," and "a moral institution possessing inalienable and imprescriptible rights, antecedent and superior to all positive law."[1] None of these encomia is to be found in the Indian and American constitutions, which are among the small minority of such documents without any explicit reference to the family.[2] Yet the centrality of the family to all societies—a fact recognized in political philosophy as well as practice—ensures the institution's constitu-tive prominence even where documents are silent about its societal signifi-cance. As Jean Bethke Elshtain has observed, "The question of the family and its relation to the broader social and political order has bedeviled West-ern political discourse from its inception."[3] And within this discourse one question in particular stands out: "[Are] the social relations of the family, with their competing loyalties and standards of human conduct, a threat to political order and authority or a constituent feature of that order?"[4]

The question of *a threat to political order* is critical to the contrasts drawn in this chapter. My purpose is not to present another iteration of the oft-considered distinction between constitutions of negative (or "first gen-eration") and positive (or "second generation") rights. Many modern con-stitutions include provisions for social and economic entitlements whose enforcement would require extensive state intervention within the private realm. Whether these constitutions have a transformative mission of the kind I am interested in cannot be determined solely on the basis of such inclusions. Thus even when it is difficult to dismiss their positive rights commitments as window dressing or as part of a calculated strategy of "hegemonic preservation,[5]" it does not follow that a subversive posture to the social order lies behind these commitments. As illustrated by Franklin D. Roosevelt's support for a "second Bill of Rights," these constitutional rights are just as likely to embody a preservative intent as a fundamentally transformative one.[6]

Nor does it follow that the absence of these entitlements is indicative of a comfortable fit between constitution and social order. The Indian Constitution adopted in 1949, my example of a confrontational document, does not include them.[7] By *confrontational* I refer to a particular kind of transformative constitution, one whose identity is in large measure defined by its commitment to reshape key structures of the social order. It is these structures that need to be confronted as threats to the new order envisioned in the constitutional experiment. Thus to the extent that family structure in India reflects the entrenched inequalities and arbitrariness of an ancient feudal order whose passing is constitutionally ordained, its protected status must yield to the urgency of the mission at hand. The salient features of this *militant constitutionalism* will be contrasted with a more *acquiescent constitutionalism*, the hallmark of which is a basic satisfaction with things as they are.

In the sections to follow I pursue the meanings of these contrasting approaches within a consideration of the family in constitutional jurisprudence. To avoid any initial confusion, the terminology used in this chapter is not intended to convey a judgment or a prediction about constitutional outcomes.[8] It is, for example, quite possible that as much, if not greater, change will emerge from the activity of courts in the acquiescent setting than in its militant counterpart. The very notion of a confrontational constitution hints at the magnitude and daunting nature of the challenge of reconstruction; what an eminent Indian jurist has called a "militant environment"[9] is unlikely passively to submit to the transformative designs of a hostile constitution. For that reason the success of such a constitution in delivering on its promise of radical reform is by no means assured. Moreover, as Christopher Lasch has written, "Of all institutions, the family is the most resistant to change."[10] On the other hand, the friendlier environs of acquiescent constitutionalism may ironically be conducive to significant change; with the institutions of civil society enjoying general constitutional legitimacy, innovative efforts to improve their performance—while not threatening their basic structure—may experience a similar presumption of legitimacy.

In the sections that follow I contrast these two models of constitutionalism within an analytical framework that features disharmony as endemic to the constitutional condition, if more apparent in certain places than in others. Sometimes this condition exists in the form of contradictions and imbalances internal to the constitution itself, and sometimes in the lack of agreement evident in the sharp discontinuities that frame the constitution's relationship to the surrounding society. To varying degrees these two dimensions are present in all polities; my focus in this chapter is on the second, with the greater and lesser extent of discordance corresponding with militant and acquiescent constitutions, respectively.

The next section sets the stage for the comparison by situating the family within the larger structures of inequality prevailing in society. These structures have to be studied comparatively; as Tocqueville often reminded us, inequalities that seem formidable when viewed from within may assume a very different meaning when the more entrenched and ascriptively driven hierarchical arrangements of other societies are taken into account. These meanings translate into the alternative models of constitutionalism depicted in the subsequent sections and featuring a contrast between more and less compliant constitutional orientations. Thus I explain how constitutional acquiescence in the traditional family exists as an extension of a more fundamental acquiescence in the structure of the social order. I then examine the very different circumstances of India, where the family poses a critical institutional challenge to the transformative aspirations of the nation's constitutional identity.

Born Equal . . . Or Not

Implicit in the widespread constitutional recognition extended the family is a general acknowledgment of its societal standing as a basic structure. For John Rawls too, "The family is part of the basic structure, since one of its main roles is to be the basis of the orderly production and reproduction of society and its culture from one generation to the next."[11] By some accounts this designation means that it is an institution to which principles of justice should apply. Following John Stuart Mill's argument in *The Subjection of Women* that the family—at least as constituted in his time—was a school for gendered despotism, some feminist theorists have faulted Rawls for not following through sufficiently on his appraisal of the institution's constitutive significance. "Without just families," observed Susan Moller Okin, "how can we expect to have a just society?"[12] Hard, then, was it for her to agree with Rawls's assertion that "We wouldn't want principles of justice—including principles of distributive justice—to apply directly to the internal life of the family."[13]

The debate within liberal political theory over how far the state should intrude itself into the domestic sphere is, of course, directly implicated in the constitutional question at hand. Yet important as it is to evaluate how the structure and mores of the family shape the relations among persons in the wider society, so too is it critical to consider how the family is shaped by that society and its political culture. However one finally sorts out the relative strengths of these two vectors of influence, if constitutionally encouraged and empowered actors view the latter as fundamentally unjust, the state will doubtless be less inclined to restrain itself in observing a rigid boundary protective of the family's autonomy. For surely a family structure long ensconced within a social order premised on morally compromised practices would not have escaped the taint of that order's injustice, thereby making it an obvious target for remedial politics and jurisprudence.

In the nineteenth century such a social order caught the attention of Alexis de Tocqueville, whose observations about India are less well known than his commentaries on other places. Although Tocqueville never visited India, he grasped the enormity of the challenges confronting it. "India cannot be civilized as long as she conserves her religion and her religion is so intermingled with the structure of its social state, of its customs and of its laws, that one does not know how to destroy it. Religions of this sort survive long after people stop believing in them. It is a vicious circle."[14] His account of a religiously based feudalism was tinged with a dark pessimism, the poignancy of which is underscored by his experience as an observer of a feudal order that had been destroyed. "The immense majority of Hindus belong to the lower castes. No matter what happens, their birth has placed them poor and always on the lowest rungs of the social ladder where one has little to hope from the government and little to fear from it."[15]

Tocqueville had not imagined a constitutionally based deliverance from this vicious circle. Ironically, one who many years later did was B. R. Ambedkar, the James Madison of Indian constitutional design, and a member of his society's most degraded class: the untouchables. Understanding that his country's social structure was entwined with religion in a way that rendered meaningful social reform unimaginable without the state's direct intervention into the spiritual domain, he provided the intellectual rationale for India's militant constitutionalism. Where faith and piety were widely and directly inscribed in routine social patterns, a viable constitutional approach to church-state relations would require greater attention to the substance of religious belief than in places where social conditions bore a less theological imprint.[16] Like Tocqueville, he was very clear about the connection between the religion of the majority and India's unjust caste-based social order. "The Hindus hold to the sacredness of the social order. Caste has a divine basis. You must therefore destroy the sacredness of the social order."[17] And so, consistent with this view and in anticipation of his efforts at the Constituent Assembly a decade later, Ambedkar wrote: "Unless you change your social order you can achieve little by way of progress. . . . You cannot build anything on the foundations of caste."[18]

For Ambedkar, "a caste may be defined as a collection of families or groups of families bearing a common name."[19] He argued that "the real remedy for breaking caste is inter-marriage. Nothing else will serve as the solvent of caste."[20] Families give definition to a caste, and through the custom of endogamy, the maintenance of the structure of which it is a part is dependent on particular family practices such as sati (the burning of a widow on the funeral pyre of her deceased husband), enforced widowhood, and the marriage of young girls to adult men.[21] While these notorious practices effectively dramatize the degraded condition of the family within a social structure of religiously based caste hierarchies, a multitude of lesser indignities were, as an extension of the logic of feudal arrangements, similarly sanctioned for family life. Some of them, such as the burdens and horrors of dowry demands, discriminated against women in ways largely unfamiliar to the Western experience; others involving gender inequities associated with divorce (or the lack thereof), polygamy, succession, and adoption were not tethered to the unique customs of a particular social structure. It was, however, a particular feudal structure of power that confronted India's constitution-makers and challenged their democratic aspirations. "The result," as Robert D. Baird has noted, "is that for those who want to promote the principles of traditional systems of law, their systems of religious values are in a head-on collision with the system of values promoted in the Constitution of India."[22]

The presence of a rigidly defined, hierarchically organized society may be a necessary condition for militant constitutionalism; obviously it does not make it inevitable. Indeed, the purest form of acquiescent constitutionalism should logically be found where the constitution functions as a shield against the overthrow of divinely sanctioned entrenched privilege. Nathan Brown points out that "Arab constitutions proclaim the importance of the family with a frequency and vagueness that might even make an American politician blush."[23] Where those constitutions confer authority upon the *shari'a* for the allocation of rights and privileges, the family in effect becomes a site for the enforcement of extreme inequality in the relations between men and women.[24] However vague may be the constitutional references to the family, in many of these documents the accompanying injunction to the state to protect it signals that the religiously prescribed configuration of that institution is also to be its constitutionally sanctioned form.

Viewed comparatively, both the caste system of the Indian subcontinent and the social setting of Islamic constitutionalism seem far removed from the American experience. There has, of course, been a lively debate concerning the fluidity and openness of the social structure in the United States. Tocqueville's famous insight that Americans possessed the distinct advantage of having "arrived at a state of democracy without having to endure a democratic revolution," that they were "born equal, instead of becoming so,"[25] has not gone unchallenged. Rogers Smith, for one, has countered with a powerful denial meant to correct Tocqueville as well as his latter-day disciples, most notably Louis Hartz. "America was not born equal but instead has had extensive hierarchies justified by illiberal, undemocratic traditions of ascriptive Americanism."[26] Smith points out that the law has "strengthened rather than weakened the nation's ascriptive hierarchies." This appraisal applies to the Constitution itself, explicitly with regard to racial hierarchies, but also as interpreted with respect to gender-related issues.

Yet Tocqueville's comparative perspective should not be slighted, even if one ultimately is persuaded by Smith's revisionist account. Emphasizing "the social goals [the American Revolution] did not need to achieve,"[27] Hartz and the consensus historians may very well have exaggerated the extent of the equality into which Americans had been born. Nevertheless, the ascriptive hierarchies that prevailed (slavery excepted) were of a different order of magnitude than those that characterized the *ancien regime*, to say nothing of India.[28] They were neither so severe that one should expect a constitution would be written as a charter of opposition to the manifest injustices contained within them, nor so inconsequential that one could think the beneficiaries of the existing order would be oblivious to their protection. Tocquevillian comparisons may leave some readers unconvinced by the portrayal of all aspects of American life as expressive of the equality of condition, but the comparative dimension of the undertaking may to a degree compensate for perceived descriptive inaccuracies by showing them to be revealingly significant in the context of a broader universe of possibilities.[29]

In the case of the American family, Tocqueville's depiction of relations between men and women furnishes ample material for those supportive of applying principles of justice to the domestic sphere. While he noted "a sort of equality being established around the domestic hearth,"[30] Tocqueville also was quick to observe that Americans had "carefully divided the functions of man and woman in order that the great social work be better done."[31] "Neither have Americans ever imagined that democratic principles should have the consequence of overturning marital power and introducing confusions of authority in the family. They have thought that every association, to be efficacious, must have a head, and that the natural head of the conjugal association is the man."[32] To be sure, he famously attributed American prosperity to "the superiority of women," but it was in his depiction of women's happiness in the "voluntary abandonment of their wills"[33] that he perhaps earned the enmity of many subsequent proponents of gender equality.[34]

Is this depiction, however, compatible with the enjoyment by all members of the family of their basic rights as equal citizens? Rawls insisted that as long as this condition held, the internal life of the family should be immune from state enforcement of principles of justice. He might, then, have been swayed at least partially by what Tocqueville said of men and women in the United States, but which the Frenchman would clearly not have said about India: "Americans do not believe that man and woman have the duty or the right to do the same things, but they show the same esteem for the role of each of them, and they consider them as beings whose value is equal although their destiny differs."[35] While Rawls's tolerance for the division of labor between the sexes could hardly be equated with Tocqueville's, his acquiescence in prevailing family practices (not necessarily those of nineteenth-century America) reflected a willingness to accept some departure from egalitarian norms in order to protect other freedoms. Thus he wrote: "A liberal conception of justice may have to allow for some traditional gendered division of labor within families—assume, say, that this division is based on religion—provided it is fully voluntary and does not result from or lead to injustice."[36]

What one can say, then, is that where gender distinctions result from and lead to rank injustice—for example, in India's caste system—the fact that religion may at the deepest level have caused the predicament should not obviate the need to confront and possibly dismantle the implicated institutions. When "connected with basic liberties, including the freedom of religion,"[37] the inequities of role differentiation within the family should, according to Rawls, be protected from radical legal intervention—assuming, that is, the basic justice of the system as a whole. But where these assumptions are undeserved, the argument for not acquiescing in the status quo is compelling, and thus so too is the rationale for militant constitutionalism. In this political environment maintaining the integrity of basic structures of civil society will likely be thought an indulgence too costly to embrace and too difficult to reconcile with a strong commitment to principles of a just social order.

Americans may not, as suggested by Tocqueville, have been born equal, but neither were they born so unequal as to have pursued this rationale. Unlike in India, theirs was a constitution fundamentally hospitable to the surrounding social order. In the next section I show how this nonconfrontational constitutionalism reveals itself in the constitutional jurisprudence of the family. I then turn to India for the contrasting model of militant constitutionalism.

Acquiescent Constitutionalism

A constitution's failure directly to address a subject can mean different things. One possibility is reflected in Chief Justice Marshall's famous denial that the absence of constitutional language authorizing Congress to establish a bank means that the power to do so does not exist. "[The Constitution's] nature . . . requires, that only its great outlines should be marked."[38] To comport with the kind of document "we are expounding," the Constitution should not "partake of the prolixity of a legal code."[39] Another take on constitutional silence is suggested in Justice Douglas's opinion in *Griswold v. Connecticut*. "We deal with a right of privacy older than the Bill of Rights— older than our political parties, older than our school system."[40] Here what has gone unmentioned in the Constitution—privacy in relation to marital relations—is attributable to its historic centrality; if Marshall's minimalism explains why "minor ingredients which compose . . . [important] objects" need not be "designated," Douglas's would have us accept constitutional recognition of *major* ingredients whose significance is acknowledged in their nonenumeration.

In the American constitutional tradition these are not mutually exclusive possibilities; further, the striking brevity of the document underscores their coterminous plausibility in a way that would be difficult to assert were we speaking of a book-length constitution such as exists, for example, in India. Where the governing charter is unsparing in its attention to detail, constitutional silence cannot so easily be accounted for on the basis of the above interpretive positions. Especially with regard to the family, which, in Martha Minow's apt formulation, "carries an implicit claim of universality"—"we are all members of families"[41]—the lack of attention in a constitution that is otherwise attentive to matters of much less import suggests very strongly that something else is going on. But before considering what this might be, I want to argue that the American silence with respect to the family, while consistent with the Marshall and Douglas positions, is also a mark of what I am referring to in this chapter as acquiescent constitutionalism.

To acquiesce in something is to give silent or passive assent to it. For one who is silently acquiescent, inattention should not be equated with indifference. Leaving the family constitutionally unaddressed need convey neither neglect nor agnosticism. In William Galston's account of the Constitution's inattention to the family—and, we might add, that of the *Federalist Papers*—none of the following three explanations advanced requires one to equate silence with indifference.[42]

1. The family (as well as other formative institutions) was perceived by the framers of the Constitution as having performed well, and "they assumed (or at least hoped) that [it] would remain healthy of [its] own accord."[43]
2. As a matter of constitutional design, social questions—including those involving the family—were to be addressed at the sub-national level.[44]
3. With the clearer separation of the public and private realms that accompanied the ascendance of liberal democracy over classical republicanism, "the formation of character . . . was left to institutions such as families and religious communities."[45]

While Galston's first explanation is the only one that explicitly invokes the acquiescence theme, his other two should be viewed as its corollaries. Standing alone, these latter two points are consistent with the idea that the Constitution took no position on the family, that its silence connotes a stance of neutrality; but in conjunction with the evaluative assessment in 1., they represent a tacit expression of support for and satisfaction with the status quo. Had the structure and configuration of the family been perceived as antithetical to founding societal aspirations, their constitutional choices would, in retrospect, have to be seen as misconceived. As E. E. Schattschneider famously argued nearly fifty years ago, both federalism and the public/private distinction provide important political resources to support the existing social order.[46] Limiting the Constitution's scope of conflict is in this view consistent with the idea of a document that does not include among its principal purposes the bringing about of major reform in the institutions of civil society. Such reforms as might in the course of time occur would instead be either limited in their impact (the federalism effect) or expressive of an evolving societal consensus crystallizing beyond the parameters of constitutional direction (the privacy effect).

It would of course matter a great deal if Galston's characterization of the framers' family performance assessment was wrong. But there is very little evidence to think that it is, that the family, or for that matter the larger social order (slavery again excepted), was a source of concern requiring explicit constitutional delegitimation and/or dismantling. "When the United States was founded," Gretchen Ritter has pointed out, "the law governing citizens in their daily activities drew upon English common law."[47] The common law governing family relations was most assuredly hierarchical and paternalistic, and in that way "central to the establishment and maintenance of social order."[48] However problematic this familial order may have been later perceived, Tocqueville's claim that "Americans [n]ever imagined that democratic principles should have the consequences of overturning marital power," has, at least for the formative period in American history, not been contradicted.

In time, as Ritter shows, "the centrality of marriage to civic status and [its] importance . . . as a social-ordering tool in a democracy"[49] became increasingly important to American constitutional politics, inspiring efforts to widen the circle of effective membership in the political community. Over an extended period of time these efforts were incrementally effective in altering—or at least unsettling—relations within the family and beyond.

Much of this story has unfolded in the judgments of the Supreme Court. From the late nineteenth century to the present, the Court developed a constitutional jurisprudence of the family that, as scholars of family law have noted, served multiple purposes, including, importantly, the reinforcement of various forms of traditional authority. Martha Minow has argued that "family rights have sometimes been announced to shore up patterns of authority that strengthen the forms of social stability preferred by the state or by groups in power."[50] Robert Burt has found the Court in its family jurisprudence to be "fundamentally concerned with addressing conflicting claims of individual and community, of liberty and authority."[51] Eva Rubin has discerned a common theme in the many family-related judgments of the

Court: reliance on "the traditional ideology of the family," which is present even in its more innovative rulings.[52]

Thus even when the Court has not supported the family structure "preferred by the state," as, for example, in providing constitutional protection to the extended family as against a governmental policy favoring the nuclear model, it draws upon sources "deeply rooted in the Nation's history and tradition."[53] That explains, according to the Court, why "the Constitution protects the sanctity of the family." In addition, according to Justice Lewis Powell's opinion in *Moore v. East Cleveland*, "It is through the family that we inculcate and pass down many of our most cherished values, moral and cultural."[54] Tradition both establishes the family's claim on constitutional recognition and in turn is maintained through the authority of the family. Powell was not presenting a philosophical argument, but his observation embodies an idea critical to acquiescent constitutionalism: the development of moral character, what once was referred to as the "salvation of souls," is to occur with minimum intervention by the state, or, as Harvey Mansfield has put it, the "intent [of modern constitutionalism was] . . . to restore the balance of society and enable it to function on its own with only minimum regulation and without being ruled by government."[55]

Mansfield's specific concern with this societal balance is with religion. "The religious issue *was* the social issue in its first appearance, and . . . the social issue as it appears today is the consequence of the religious issue. If politics is defined by its issues, the religious issue at the origin of modern constitutionalism is still at the heart of modern constitutionalism."[56] The "cherished values" on behalf of which the family, in the Court's depiction, is the principal conduit, are nested within historical and traditional sources heavily imbued with religious overtones. As Minow notes, "the sphere of family was . . . regulated, not by the state, but by religion,"[57] a point that underscores the integrated nature of the social order and hence the need to connect the traditions associated with discrete institutions (i.e., church and family) of civil society. The judicial invocation of "history and tradition" in conjunction with the family implicitly directs the Court to do the same with regard to the broader American religious experience of which the family is a vital part. Constitutional acquiescence in the traditional family is in this respect an extension of a more fundamental acquiescence in the structure of the social order.

This is evident in a number of the famous religion cases that implicate the family, such as *Pierce v. Society of Sisters* and *Wisconsin v. Yoder*, but most tellingly perhaps in the early and very controversial polygamy case of

Reynolds v. United States. Its standing as a respectable precedent has been compromised by the aura of intolerance that surrounds it, but as a source of insight into the relationship between Constitution and social order, and as a point of departure for comparative reflection about constitutionalism, it warrants careful attention. *Reynolds* was one of several cases in the latter half of the nineteenth century involving the efforts of the United States to curtail the activities of the Mormon Church. While the activity that was expressly targeted was plural marriages, the religiously sanctioned practice provided the Court an opportunity to affirm the supremacy of the civil law and to frustrate the determination—real or imagined—of an ecclesiastical hierarchy to wield sovereignty over territory within the United States.[58]

At first glance the polygamy cases may seem an odd fit with the argument about acquiescence. For example, in *Reynolds* the Court was considering the constitutionality of the Morrill anti-bigamy act, which was a federal statute criminalizing polygamy in the territories of the United States. Not only does this reveal national-level concern with social order questions related to the family, but it also is in tension with the commitment to having the government leave family matters to the private realm, including religious communities. As we shall see, in India the absence of constitutional language about the family is expressive of a very different sensibility and intention: to encourage the implementation of a nationally directed reform of the religiously configured family as part of a broader assault on the more flagrantly inegalitarian characteristics of the social order. What, then, is different about the American government's far-reaching intrusion into the most intimate of familial relationships among members of a particular religious community, an intervention given constitutional sanctification in the Mormon polygamy cases?

The national government's direct involvement may initially be accounted for by the urgency of the perceived threat to its authority embodied in the Mormon Church's political and territorial ambitions. The Court framed the question by deflecting attention from religion to politics. "Marriage while from its very nature a sacred obligation is nevertheless in most civilized nations a civil contract, and usually regulated by law." Emphasizing its secular motivations, the Court declared the polygamous family undemocratic. "According as monogamous or polygamous marriages are allowed, do we find the principles on which the Government of the People, to a greater or lesser extent, rests."[59] As Nancy Rosenblum has noted, "Plural marriage rested on a theory of male sexuality as the key to apotheosis, and to social order, which explains Mormon insistence on congruence among sexuality, family structure, and ecclesiastical and political community. In this sense the *Reynolds* decision can be said to be hostile to polygamy as a tenet of Mormon religion. . . . But the reasons had more to do with political ideology than heterodoxy."[60] In other words, in this particular instance—the Mormons "were not a tiny separatist community claiming toleration and free exercise exemption from laws," but a religion whose "goal was statehood"[61]—the political and social issues in play resembled more the conditions associated with militant constitutionalism than with its acquiescent counterpart. Thus the Court ruled, "Congress . . . was left free to reach actions which were in violation of social duties or subversive of good order."[62]

But this particular instance also lays the jurisprudential foundation for a constitutional model predicated on a family that serves as the cornerstone of good order. The Court's intention to protect Mormon wives from the harm that flows from patriarchal authority has been properly described by Rosenblum as "disingenuous."[63] After all, it is not as if traditional marriage was untainted by patriarchal dominance, and yet this standard familial power differential is not generally viewed as antagonistic to the democratic project. There is, however, an important difference, according to the Court. The patriarchal principle in polygamy "fetters the people in stationary despotism, while that principle cannot long exist in connection with monogamy."[64] One is reminded again of Rawls's view that the traditional gendered division of labor within families is to be acquiesced in so long as it can reasonably be described as voluntarily entered into, but where, as with polygamous relationships, the pattern of domination moves the question to a different order of magnitude, the inability to reconcile the more extreme practice with a strong commitment to principles of a just social order can culminate in a more confrontational, if exceptional, constitutional moment.[65] "An exceptional colony of polygamists under an exceptional leadership may sometimes exist for a time without appearing to disturb the social condition of the people who surround it; but there cannot be a doubt that, unless restricted by some form of constitution, it is within the legitimate scope of the power of every civil government to determine whether polygamy or monogamy shall be the law of social life under its dominion."[66]

How exceptional is the practice of polygamy? "Polygamy has always been odious among the northern and western nations of Europe, and, until the establishment of the Mormon Church, was almost exclusively a feature of the life of Asiatic and African people. At common law, the second marriage was always void, and from the earliest history of England polygamy has been treated as an offence against society."[67] This answer is what is often remembered about *Reynolds*, that its support for the government's marital policy manifested a scarcely concealed hostility toward Mormonism rooted in what today would be called Eurocentric prejudice. We should note, however, that embedded in the response is a cruder version of the substantive due process formula (as in *Moore*) for establishing the favored family order; it is the "Nation's history and tradition," here cast in terms of the cultural superiority of the West, that in effect delegitimates polygamy and leaves it bereft of constitutional protection. When seen against the appropriate historical background, the institution of plural marriage represents "an offence against society," or in the language of later cases, an attack on the nation's "cherished values, moral and cultural."

Had the practice of polygamy not been entwined in the political challenge of a geographically concentrated church with theocratic ambitions triggering national concerns, and instead been associated with a more scattered pattern of aberrant marital behavior expressive perhaps of no more than fringe beliefs, it is likely that the "offence against society" would have been addressed differently, if at all. Inasmuch as the hypothetical society offended against in this way would be the dominant Judeo-Christian social order, whose history and tradition would provide it with sufficient resources to fend for itself without the assistance of the central government, we might speculate that if there were any legislative efforts to eliminate the offense, they would occur at the local level. To speculate further, the Supreme Court's review of such legislation would rely on history and tradition to affirm the constitutionality of the ban.[68]

This hypothetical society is, of course, not difficult to imagine, since it mirrors the normal workings of the American sociopolitical order as it pertains to marriage and the family. Somewhat more difficult to imagine would be a society in which the polygamous family was at least tolerated by the country's dominant religion, and where the tolerance was consistent with other commitments of the faith that were in direct conflict with constitutional design and purpose. Family structure and functioning might in this setting be considered and evaluated within a social order heavily invested in constitutionally incorrect feudal modes of organization. "Each realm [of feudal society]," Karen Orren has argued, "exhibit[s] its own particularized morality within the larger feudal ethic of hierarchy."[69] In such a society, according to Orren, we might expect that the dismantling of the order would be marked by a major shift from a system of governance centered in the judiciary to one centered in the national legislature. "The change [is] registered as much through what [is] lost in the abandonment of government by common law—by tradition, intellect, entrenched privilege—as through the positive gains made on behalf of legislation."[70]

We will recognize change of this kind when we turn to India and reflect on the significance of the codification of Hindu law in the decade following the establishment of independence. But before leaving the United States, we should consider that, consistent with Rawls's view that radical legal intervention into the family to rectify the inequities of role differentiation should not occur unless these disparities are manifestly unjust, the family has not, for the most part, been an object of national legislative attention. It has, of course, been a frequent object of national judicial attention, and the jurisprudence that has developed, principally under the rubric of substantive due process, reflects the assumptions of acquiescent constitutionalism.[71] Thus the judicially enacted privacy right has both facilitated reform and loosened the bonds of traditional authority within the family (e.g., decisions regarding abortion and sexual activity); and concurrently, as Ritter has shown, provided a constitutional means for adapting traditional family ordering to a new legal reality in which common law status relations were no longer available to the courts.[72] "The household that had previously contained a master who governed over his wife, children, servants, and wards according to legal prescription, was now a home in which the free man apparently was left to re-create those private authority relations without government intrusion."[73]

In Orren's terms this court-centered incrementalism could mean that the feudal family structure has yet to undergo the sort of fundamental restructuring that has been the experience of American labor (her focus), or that the story of the American family is one that should not be told as a progression from dismal feudal past to happier non-feudal present. We are, then, in essence, back to the "born equal or not" question, although for our purposes a final judgment need not be rendered on that particular conundrum. One could, for example, place the family within a rigidly hierarchical ascriptive historical account and nevertheless conclude that for the framers this state of affairs did not warrant constitutional opposition. Or, with the Indian experience in mind, one could read into their acquiescence a caution that prior to labeling things "feudal," one ought to pursue the implications of a comparative consideration of familial inequality.

Militant Constitutionalism

During the discussion at the Indian Constituent Assembly of the Interim Report on Fundamental Rights, a delegate from Madras, Rev. Jerome D'Souza, made this observation: "We have nothing in these fundamental rights that safeguards or encourages or strengthens the family in an explicit way, and indeed I do not think this is necessary at this stage, because that is not a justiciable right. There are certain constitutions where the wish of the State to protect and encourage the family is explicitly declared. I hope in the second part, among these fundamental rights which are not justiciable, some such declaration or approbation of the institution and rights and privileges associated with family life will be introduced."[74] Much later, while reflecting on the draft Constitution, this same delegate returned to the earlier topic:

Now, Sir, if one thing characterizes our people more than anything else, it is the power and the sanctity of the family tie, the sacredness which we have been accustomed to attach to the sanctities that go to make up the spirit and the atmosphere of home life. Therefore, I am sure that every section of this House will feel that it is in the fitness of things that this strong and traditional spirit of our nation and race might somehow be expressed in our Constitution. Sir, I venture to say that if the virtues, the strength and manhood of our people have survived so many centuries of invasion and subjection, it is because, in spite of external and political changes, the strength of the family, its protective power, its capacity to inspire and maintain virtue and moral strength, have never been diminished, have never been completely overcome in our land. Whatever is best in the Caste system—and nobody will say that it is an unmixed evil—I venture to say is an extension of the family spirit, and the attachment to family ties that has come out of it is its best and most admirable characteristic.[75]

He went on:

Sir, in a Constitution, we undertake legislation for the organization of society. We are speaking of villages, of provinces and the Centre, of tribes and Communities, and every other forms of society. Now, the primary unit of society, one whose limits and characteristics are fixed by nature itself, is the family. The varieties and forms of external civil society may vary and change, but the limits, the characteristics, the fundamental features of the family, are fixed by natures. And it is within the bosom of the family that the social virtues, on the basis of which we are making this Constitution, and the firmness of which will be responsible for the carrying out of the Constitution, those fundamental virtues are developed and most lastingly founded in the family circle—mutual dependence, respect for authority and order, foresight and planning, and even the capacity for negotiating with other units, —qualities which would be required on a wider scale and in a wider theatre in our political and public life. Nay, Sir, patriotism itself is but the extension and the amplification of the love of the family. We call our country Fatherland or Motherland. . . . Therefore, I feel that this house will not reject this plea that in some form our respect and love for family traditions, may be reflected in this Constitution.[76]

He concluded: "I would, as a last idea which should accompany this notion of the sanctity and permanence and stability of the family, plead for respect for the rights of parents, the recognition of all reasonable authority on the part of parents in regard to their children, particularly, the right of the parent to see that his child is brought up in the traditions and in the beliefs, which are dear to him."[77]

D'Souza's speech evoked no response whatsoever. Nor did the assembly's final product reveal evidence that his remarks had had any effect on the course of the subsequent deliberations. Thus the Indian Constitution was adopted without provision for the protection of the family.

As a Jesuit, delegate D'Souza surely knew of the incorporation of Catholic doctrine on the family into the provisions of the Irish Constitution. His references to the "sanctity of the family tie" and the "sacredness" of the institution of the family in Indian history and tradition are suggestive of a desire on his part to inscribe a similar commitment into the Indian Constitution, albeit one that reflected the specific religious profile of his country. His description of the family as "the primary unit of society" closely resembles the Irish document's recognition of that institution as "the natural primary unit group of Society."[78] Unlike in Ireland, however, where protection and encouragement of the family are "explicitly declared" as rights enforceable by the courts, in India, according to D'Souza, it will suffice to provide for such commitments in aspirational terms by anchoring them in an entrenched enumeration of nonjusticiable rights. They should be placed, in other words, in a distinctively crafted corner of the document that the framers directly copied from the Irish, the Directive Principles section of the constitution.

Why was D'Souza's recommendation given such short shrift, indeed totally ignored in the assembly? Some reflection on these directive principles is instructive, as it is among them that one finds an articulation of the animating spirit of the constitution, formulated in a series of aspirational directives intended by their authors to instruct governing bodies in the achievement of a more just and egalitarian society. For example, the state is directed to pursue policies toward securing "that children are given opportunities and facilities to develop in a healthy manner and in conditions of freedom and dignity and that childhood and youth are protected against exploitation and against moral and material abandonment."[79] This pursuit, one might think, should not incur significant opposition. But what if in compliance with the directive the state should intrude upon prerogatives traditionally associated with the family and nurtured by the legal and cultural requirements of religious communities? What happens when the exploitation of which the constitution speaks turns out to be, in D'Souza's words, "an extension of the family spirit and the attachment to family ties" that embodies the caste system's "most admirable characteristic"?

Again, there is no recorded response to D'Souza's proposal, but it is easy to imagine one built around the idea that its implementation would complicate, if not render incoherent, the central thrust of Indian constitutionalism. Indeed, it could begin with a nod to Cicero: *silent enim leges inter arma*, the idea being that in the battle to be waged against the existing social order, the law of the constitution should choose its silences carefully.[80] Thus the message of the Directive Principles expresses the thematic content of the document as a whole: civil society must be dramatically transformed to accommodate the underlying mission of the constitution. As affirmed by Jawaharlal Nehru from a jail cell in 1944: "Between these two conceptions [the caste system and much that goes with it and political and economic democracy] conflict is inherent and only one of them can survive."[81]

Nehru's incarceration stemmed from activities related to his leadership role in the campaign for national independence. That movement was about many things, not the least of which was reform of the Indian family. As part of a calculated colonial governing strategy, the British had largely avoided intervening in the domestic circumstances of the many groups subject to its rule in India.[82] This policy of nonintervention was one of the major grievances animating the early participants in the nationalist movement. To be sure, over time concerns about the inequities of family life were often subordinated to other considerations, but "from [1887] the reform of the legal foundations of the traditional Indian family could not be dissociated from the struggle for national independence."[83] Indeed, the same arguments from Mill's *Subjection of Women* that were later prominently to figure in the West in feminist critiques of the family were often taken verbatim and used to good effect by nineteenth-century Indian advocates of social reform.[84]

The family, then, was not a subject notable for any lack of attention in the years preceding the drafting of the constitution; there was, in other words, no pre-constitutional silence. That may in fact help to explain why the constitution *is* silent, why it turned out not to be one of those documents "where the wish of the State to protect and encourage the family is explicitly stated." Rather, implicitly stated is constitutional encouragement for a family different from what had long existed, and attainable only if the old social order was left unprotected from state intervention. Such a commitment is prominently reflected in the documentary history of the drafting of the constitution. For example, Raj Kumari Amrit Kaur, a woman delegate and social reformer, wrote to B. N. Rau, a leading figure in the writing of India's constitution: "As we are all aware there are several customs practiced in the name of religion e.g. *pardah*, child marriage, polygamy, unequal laws of inheritance, prevention of inter-caste marriages, dedication of girls to temples. *We are naturally anxious that no clause in any fundamental right shall make impossible future legislation for the purpose of wiping out these evils.*"[85] Within the constitutional silence that flowed from such anxieties is a sociological insight of universal application, but particular relevance to the politics of national identity in India: "The family plays a crucial if not decisive role in the reproduction of the social structure, including the structure of inequality."[86] Militant constitutionalism emerges from this insight's incorporation into the argument for independence and its later absorption into the dynamic of constitutional politics.

Consider again the polygamy issue. The legal focus in India has not been on the practices of a fringe religion, even one that may have secured a local power base from which to launch a theologically inspired assault on constitutional government. Instead, the targeted group has been the Hindu majority. In the Indian analogue to *Reynolds*, a 1952 decision of the Supreme Court of Bombay that applied the provisions of the new constitution to uphold a statute forbidding bigamous marriages by Hindus, the court concluded: "If religious practices run counter to . . . a policy of social welfare upon which the State has embarked, then the religious practices must give way before the good of the people of the State as a whole."[87] There are, to be sure, similarities between the early Indian and American polygamy cases— the former, for example, explicitly rely on the latter for the importance of distinguishing religious belief and action—but there is a key difference. In *Reynolds*, Congress was left free to regulate because, as the Court put it, polygamy was "subversive of good order." In *Appa*, the state's intervention was sanctioned as part of an official program designed to create good order. The juxtaposition of the defensive rationale of the American Court and the proactive reasoning of its Indian counterpart directs our attention to the contrasting ways in which the two constitutions relate to their respective social orders.

Polygamy in India, of course, was also deemed subversive of good social order, but—and this is what lies at the heart of militant constitutionalism—for many of the framers a social order worth defending represented an aspiration, not a reality. The *constitution*, therefore, is the subversive datum to be reckoned with (and ultimately celebrated) as it confronts a social structure whose inequities are engrained in behavior that the dominant ethnoreligious group encourages, mandates, or acquiesces in.[88] The upshot is that in India, "the Nation's history and tradition" represent a dubious source from which to draw upon in protecting the sanctity of the family. To appreciate what is jurisprudentially at stake comparatively, substitute the word "Christian" for "Hindu" in the enactment under judicial review in the Indian case and then transpose the court's observation to an American setting. "The Hindu Bigamous Marriages Act is attempting to bring about social reform in a community which has looked upon polygamy as not an evil institution, but fully justified by its religion."[89]

Under the terms of this hypothetical one might wonder, for example, whether the family would find constitutional protection under the umbrella of a right to privacy. Religion's relegation to the private realm may very well lie at the core of modern constitutionalism, but to accommodate it requires, as we have seen, a comfort level sufficiently high as to justify acquiescence in what transpires within that realm. But this separation is a much costlier indulgence when, as in India, it serves to legitimate an unjust status quo. That explains why Indian justices routinely wander into the thickets of theological disputation to ascertain if morally questionable behavior is an essential part of religious identification. In polygamy cases they have determined that the sanctioning of plural marriages by "Hindu tradition" is in fact not "an integral part of Hindu religion."[90] They have, in other words, expressly renounced tradition as obstructive of the state's pursuit of a just social order. They have gone where justices in our acquiescent model have studiously avoided—to an interrogation of the essentials of religion.[91]

Such avoidance is understandable not only for the obvious benefit of minimizing awkward judicial intervention into the spiritual domain, but also for maintaining an appropriately modest profile for the court as a governing institution. There are prudential considerations that might impel Indian judges to embrace a similarly passive role in adjudicating at the borders of law and religion, but worries about being denounced for their "activism" need not weigh heavily upon them. Militant constitutionalism does not so much encourage judicial activism as it alters how we conceptualize behavior commonly associated with it. Thus the Indian Constitution, as Granville Austin has noted, makes the judiciary "an arm of the social revolution."[92] Often this requires only standing aside to allow other institutions to attempt an "extreme makeover" of the social order, but frequently the courts find themselves actively engaged in this effort. When they do, they can be seen as performing the judiciary's "mission as a radical fiduciary and redemptive institution of the people."[93] The remedial jurisprudence that flows from this role is constitutionally driven; the militancy of the document extends an aura of legitimacy to an intrusive judiciary engaged in the pursuit of its inscribed agenda.

We need, however, to look beyond the judiciary to take the full measure of militant constitutionalism. Since there is in India, in contrast with the United States, less ambiguity surrounding the use of feudalism as a descriptive term applicable to the social order, Karen Orren's argument that the dismantling of feudal institutions involves a shift from a judicial to a legislative-centered approach should, if accurate, resonate in the Indian setting. We need also to consider her (and Schattschneider's) further point that a national focus is required to eliminate the particularized moralities of the various realms that exist within the broader feudal ethic of hierarchy. This is especially pertinent to the family, which in India has been subject to a regime of personal law, laws that are the creations of the various religious communities, establishing legally enforceable obligations in accordance with the individual's communal affiliation. But unlike some other countries that have such group-differentiated rights (e.g., Israel), matters of personal law in India do not fall under the jurisdiction of religious courts.[94] One result is that these communally generated laws are in a constant state of tension with the policies of the state, which often finds its ambitions undercut or thwarted by competing communal agendas.

These state policies, particularly relating to the family, receive the constitutional imprimatur of Article 44, the Directive Principle that proclaims, "The State shall endeavor to secure for the citizens a uniform civil code throughout the territory of India." Judges who have sought to accelerate the achievement of this goal have found their efforts entangled in the combustible politics of religious nationalism.[95] On the polygamy issue, the

early judicial tolerance of Muslim exemption from the ban on plural marriage has been steadily eroded by impatience with the state's unhurried progression in realizing legal uniformity. In a 1995 case involving one of the
ingenious ways in which Hindu men have sought to circumvent the ban on
polygamous marriages—through conversion to Islam—the court affirmed
what the constitution had left unspoken: "Marriage is the very foundation
of the civilized society. . . . It is an institution in the maintenance of which
the public at large is deeply interested. It is the foundation of the family and
in turn of the society without which no civilization can exist."[96] Referring
to Article 44 as "an unequivocal mandate," the court then declared: "When
more than 80% of the citizens have already been brought under the codified
personal law there is no justification whatsoever to keep in abeyance, any
more, the introduction of [a] 'uniform civil code' for all citizens in the territory of India."[97]

The mandate may not have been as unequivocal as the court suggested,
but it did represent, in Schattschneider's scheme, a constitutional commitment to socializing conflict, to transferring a significant amount of the
decisional focus for family policy from the private to the public domain.
Moreover, a reasonable inference from the court's observation is that the
failure thus far to enact a uniform civil code has not left the social order un-
attended and untransformed. The 80 percent figure perhaps overestimates
the number of Hindus who have actually experienced a changed legal condition with respect to the personal law, yet "For the first time, the bulk of the
world's Hindus live under a single central authority that has both the desire
and the power to enforce changes in their social arrangements."[98]

The reference is to the Hindu Code laws of the 1950s. Ambedkar and
Nehru had long envisioned a radical overhaul of Hindu personal law to con-
form to the spirit of the constitution's strong emphasis on social reform. In
1951 an omnibus Hindu Code Bill was put together, essentially secularizing
various areas of the personal law—marriage, divorce, succession, inheritance, property, and women's rights.[99] The bill foundered over communal
politics and the disagreement between Prime Minister Nehru and President
Prasad on the wisdom of the proposal, the latter arguing that the legislation,
which did not include Muslims in its coverage, discriminated against Hindus. Ambedkar, then the law minister in Nehru's government, resigned from
the cabinet in protest over what he considered to be the prime minister's inadequate efforts on behalf of the bill.[100] Eventually, however, components of
the omnibus bill were separately enacted into law, first the Special Marriage
Bill of 1954 (applying to all Indians), and followed in 1955 by the Hindu Mar-

riage Act, and in 1956 the Hindu Succession Act, the Hindu Minority and Guardianship Act, and the Hindu Adoptions and Maintenance Act.

These laws were imperfect in design, and their implementation has over the years met with mixed success. The noted scholar of Hindu law J. Duncan M. Derrett long ago detailed many of their weaknesses and failures. But Derrett also suggested that his reservations should not "obscure the magnitude of the achievement effected in codifying the former system and amending it comprehensively."[101] Indeed, according to Derrett, one is obliged to recognize "India's momentous experiment, which for width of scope and boldness of innovation can be compared only with the *Code Napoleon*."[102] This evaluation has been echoed by Marc Galanter, the leading American scholar of Indian law, who wrote: "The Code marks the acceptance of Parliament as a kind of central legislative body for Hindus in matters of family and social life. The earlier notion that government had no mandate or competence to redesign Hindu society has been discarded."[103]

This is, of course, critical to the argument in this chapter. The idea of a mandate to redesign society lies at the core of the militant model of constitutionalism. When he introduced the draft constitution to the Constituent Assembly, Dr. Ambedkar responded to several questions that had arisen in regard to the document, including the worry that the Directive Principles had no legal force behind them. He readily conceded the validity of the concern, but then proceeded to argue that the constitution was, in effect, a political instrument that did in fact create obligations, though in a strictly legal sense they were not directly enforceable. "What are called Directive Principles is merely another name for Instrument of Instructions. The only difference is that they are instructions to the Legislature and the Executive." Those in power "may not have to answer for their breach in a Court of Law. But [they] will certainly have to answer for them before the electorate at election time. What great value these directive principles possess will be realized better when the forces of right contrive to capture power."[104]

Such contrivances are often unsuccessful, a fact that goes a long way to explain why in India, at least, the militant constitution has fallen short in delivering on its promise of far-reaching social reconstruction. But even when the electoral stars are in alignment, the intractability of the environment renders improbable any smooth translation of constitutional aspiration into social reality. The adoption of the Hindu Code laws—and the jurisprudence that followed in its wake—exemplifies several key elements of militant constitutionalism: the socialization of conflict, the blurring of the line separating public and private sectors, the ascendance of legislation over adjudication as the institutional focus for societal regulation. But the modest success of these laws in actually transforming the social order only underscores the inherent limits of all power—whether constitutionally sanctioned or not.

Conclusion

The contrasts drawn in this chapter between two models of constitutionalism represent a preliminary effort to highlight some of the differences in the ways constitutions imagine the relationship between the legal and social orders. The focus, however, on just two countries can only begin to establish a basis for identifying the features that distinguish acquiescent from militant constitutionalism. Constitutional provisions that are important in one setting may not perform the same role elsewhere. Indeed, they might not exist in other places. There are no directive principles, for example, in the South African Constitution, a document that must be considered an obvious candidate for inclusion in any grouping of nations where the constitution confronts a social order hostile to the document's fundamental commitments. On the other hand, the directive principles in the Irish Constitution served as a model for the framers of the Indian Constitution, but they have had practically no influence on the substance of a jurisprudence that reflects the priorities of the acquiescent constitutionalism within which it has evolved.[105]

Of equal importance are the anomalies and discontinuities that exist within specific constitutional settings. It would be surprising to find constitutional arrangements that did not include both preservative and transformational attributes. In India social reform must always be balanced against the demands of multiple cultures, whose resistance to changes threatening to their way of life finds support in constitutional provisions that explicitly endorse cultural preservation. Such provisions are as much an expression of political reality as they are a measure of constitutional acquiescence, but they do serve in arguably salutary ways to moderate and restrain the radical transformational impulse. Or stated otherwise, the presence of these preservative commitments in a predominantly confrontational document means that the enforcement of the constitution's militant agenda should occur within the parameters of feasibility. That is perhaps the best way of understanding the placement of the uniform civil code within the nonjusticiable section of Directive Principles.

In the United States, the nonacquiescent parts of the Constitution are largely embodied in the post–Civil War amendments. Acquiescence in a social order that tolerated slavery was itself an anomaly in a Constitution predicated on principles opposed to that institution.[106] It took a bloody war to destroy slavery, but to eradicate the racial hierarchies that were engrained in the social order required a new constitutional militancy. This militancy may be seen in commitments implicit (perhaps even explicit) in the three amendments—to nationalizing the issue of racial equality, to penetrating the barrier separating public and private realms, and to promoting legislative solutions to the challenge of social reconstruction.

Tellingly, however, the enforcement and interpretation of these provisions bear the imprint of a prior and more pervasive constitutional embrace of an acquiescent mindset. The words of the Fourteenth Amendment—"The Congress shall have power to enforce, by appropriate legislation, the provisions of this article"—may not be an American precursor of a directive principle, but there is in that declaration something like an "instrument of instruction" regarding national legislative engagement in dismantling the structures of racial subordination. But as early as 1883, the Supreme Court in *The Civil Rights Cases* denuded the amendment of its militancy, leading Justice John Marshall Harlan to write in his dissent:

If the recent Amendments are so construed that Congress may not, in its own discretion, and independently of the action or non-action of the States, provide, by legislation of a primary and direct character, for the security of rights created by the National Constitution; if it be adjudged that the obligation to protect the fundamental privileges and immunities granted by the Fourteenth Amendment to citizens residing in the several States, rests, primarily, not on the Nation, but on the States; if it be further adjudged that individuals and corporations exercising public functions may, without liability to direct primary legislation on the part of Congress, make the race of citizens the ground for denying them that equality of civil rights which the Constitution ordains as a principle of republican citizenship,—then, not only the foundations upon which the national supremacy has always rested will be materially disturbed, but we shall enter upon an era of constitutional law, when the rights of freedom and American citizenship cannot receive from the nation that efficient protection which heretofore was accorded to slavery and the rights of the master.[107]

That era of constitutional law has not ended, as the denial of direct and primary legislative power, with the accompanying constraints of the "state action" doctrine, has persisted well into the modern period of American jurisprudence. Thus the Court's upholding of the Civil Rights Act of 1964 was based on the indirect and circuitous methodology of commerce rather than, as Justice William Douglas argued, a "construction [that] would put an end to all obstructionist strategies and finally close one door on a bitter chapter in American history."[108] These constitutional landmarks might be construed as illustrative of the kind of friction that may result when militant constitutionalist threads are woven into a preexisting constitutional fabric whose overall design represents a wholly different conceptual structure and organization.

It is this overall design that is decisive in how we evaluate the workings of the courts in a constitutional democracy. Debates in the United States over judicial activism long ago became tedious and predictable, in part, I would argue, because they avoided genuine engagement with alternative models of constitutionalism. An American court that found unconstitutional state action when school authorities allowed their policies to reflect racial patterns in the community, that argued that purely private discrimination was no longer private when manifested in the most important policies of a public institution, would be viewed as activist by most observers. These observers might disagree about whether such activism was a good thing, but fail to appreciate how the basic constitutionalist framework establishing the relationship between the legal and social orders shaped their characterization of judicial behavior and their evaluation of it. A constitutional predisposition to acquiesce in the existing social order naturally puts judicial activism in a normatively defensive posture, but where militant assumptions dictate the constitution's relationship to the social order—where, for example, affirmative action is an explicit constitutional obligation (as in India)—neither the activist label nor its accompanying normative defensiveness need be the focus of heated debate or agonized reflection. Thoughtful and productive consideration of the judicial role begins with the recognition of constitutional democracy's contrasting conceptual possibilities and the distinctive set of institutional expectations that extend from them.

PART IV

Constitutionalism and Democracy

Chapter Eight
Constitutionalism and Democracy: Understanding the Relation

Larry Alexander

The chapters in this book address the topics of constitutionalism and the role of the United States Supreme Court from a variety of perspectives. Some look at the subjects through the prism of political philosophy, both of classical and enlightenment vintage.[1] Others take a historical approach, and more particularly, an American history one.[2] Still others look at the Constitution and Court by comparing and contrasting them to their counterparts elsewhere in the world.[3] And still others examine them using the techniques of modern political science.[4]

This chapter falls in that section of the book that takes up the relationship between constitutionalism and democracy. Are they compatible? If so, how? If not, which is prior, logically and morally?

I am not a historian, political scientist, political philosopher, or comparativist. I am not even a moral philosopher. I am an analyst, and my small toolkit consists of only modest instruments of analytical rigor and conceptual clarity. My aim is thus to clarify issues rather than to resolve them, although failure to resolve is frequently due to failure to clarify.

To begin, what is democracy? Self-rule, you will be tempted to reply, but what is *that*? When we speak of self-rule in the context of discussing democracy, we are typically referring, not to radical libertarianism or anarchy—where no one or group is recognized as sovereign over us as individuals—but to rule by contemporary majorities. More precisely, we are referring to contemporary majorities of (most) adults within a defined geographical territory. This is a purely procedural conception of democracy—democracy as majority rule.

Of course, there are more substantive versions on offer as competitors with majority rule. Ronald Dworkin's conception of democracy is one, a conception in which the master moral right to equal concern and respect and the various substantive rights derived therefrom complement and constrain majoritarian policy preferences.[5] And the purified-by-substantive-rights "procedural" conceptions of Jürgen Habermas[6] and John Ely[7] are others. And even the most ardent contemporary-majorities-rule democrat will place some limits on majority rule—limits that might be considered "constitutional." For example, no one, to my knowledge, advocates a complete lack of entrenchment of laws passed by majorities, so that a law passed one second ago can be immediately brought up for reconsideration or amendment.[8] And no one advocates the eradication of rules (such as Robert's Rules of Order) that define majority rule and impose some agenda control. Again, such rules are constitutional in a very real sense. Nor does anyone advocate completely universal suffrage, so that everyone—children, idiots, and felons included—would be entitled to vote.[9]

Moreover, not only is the majority-rule conception of democracy qualified by "constituting" rules of order and suffrage, but it is also qualified in various other ways. Foremost are the limitations of geography. Because the laws of any country affect its neighbors, can we truly have a democracy in the absence of world government?[10] Indeed, can we truly have democracy in the absence of enfranchising the future (and past) people whose interests will be affected by our decisions?[11] If the answer to these questions is "yes," does this imply that Alabama is a democracy given the restriction of its franchise to living Alabamans? Or that New York City is a democracy given the restriction of its franchise to residents of the five boroughs? Would anarchy be a democracy by the same logic?

And what about deviations from plebiscites? Is an indirect, representative democracy truly democratic? If so, is a two-house system? A two-house plus presidential approval system? And then there is Kenneth J. Arrow's problem with translating majoritarian preferences into policy, and Philip Pettit's and others' similar problem with squaring majoritarian principles with majoritarian preferences.[12] Do we truly have a democracy when no voting mechanism will align the majority's votes with its preferences or its principles?

Much of the anti-constitutional, pro-democratic critique today centers on the practice of judicial review. That is merely true of such democrats as Larry Kramer,[13] Mark Tushnet,[14] and Jeremy Waldron.[15] But one must separate judicial review from constitutionalism. Kramer, for example, objects not to the Constitution, but to judicial supremacy in its interpretation.[16] He appears to favor departmentalism, where each branch has final authority within its sphere to interpret the Constitution, or perhaps congressional supremacy.[17] But a Constitution the interpretation of which is entrusted to the legislature is still a constitution and still acts as a brake on contemporary majorities, even if *they* are its expositors. They will be tempted, of course, to try to square their current policy preferences with their constitutional interpretation, and one suspects that their self-restraint will fail. (One can surely argue that this has occurred in the case of Congress's interpretation of its commerce power.)[18] Still, when the majority succeeds in restraining itself, the Constitution will have thwarted a contemporary majority's policy preferences and arguably, therefore, thwarted democracy.

Tushnet is, in contrast to Kramer, a real anti-constitutionalist.[19] He argues for what he calls the "thin Constitution"—the platitudes of the Declaration of Independence and the Preamble—as opposed to the "thick constitution," those numerous provisions that constitute the branches of government, define their powers, and set forth the relationship between the national and state governments. Tushnet does not satisfactorily explain how the national government is supposed to function in the absence of those "thick" constitutional provisions that constitute it.

Waldron, although sometimes opposing constitutionalism in the name of democracy,[20] appears to be more exercised by constitutional bills of rights, judicially interpreted.[21] The content of our rights will always be controversial, at least beyond a settled core understanding that healthy, rights-respecting democratic majorities are unlikely to transgress. And with respect to the controversial aspects of rights, there is no reason to prefer the judicial elaborations to those of the current majority, or so Waldron argues.

There are several issues here. First, although sometimes Waldron writes as if there is but one clear right—the right of the democratic majority, after due deliberation and debate, to have its way—it is more charitable to read him as acknowledging the existence of other rights that should constrain democratic majorities.[22] Whether policies are morally right or wrong is independent of whether a democratic majority has enacted them. Or at least, per Richard Wollheim,[23] the majority in deliberating must conceive of moral correctness as a matter independent of how they vote. (This is not to take a position on how the outcome of the democratic vote might affect what one is morally obligated to do.)

If there are moral rights other than democratic self-rule, and those rights cannot be extinguished by the results of democratic decision-making, then in a very real sense they are always "constitutionally" entrenched. Indeed, they are more entrenched than any mere set of posited constitutional rights, because even supermajorities cannot amend or repeal them. Legislative majorities are always subject to constraints of moral rights whether or not there is a constitution and whether or not the constitution refers to them.

So Waldron cannot object to constitutionalizing moral rights in that sense. What he appears to be objecting to most vehemently is privileging the judicial understanding of those rights over the legislative understanding of them.

Now if the constitution implemented preexisting rights, not by direct reference to those rights as they really are, but by "rulifying" them—that is, by constructing determinate rules for their indirect implementation (much as the Supreme Court implements "freedom of speech" through a number of doctrinal rules of its own construction)[24]—then Waldron's objection to the judicial role would be misplaced. Judges are far better than legislators in interpreting determinate rules that have been posited at a specific time by specific individuals. Waldron's objection would have to be lodged against the constitutional ratifiers, the supermajority that attempted to reduce real, preexisting moral rights to determinate rules and to entrench those rules against majoritarian repeal. The objection, in other words, would be one against, not judicial review, and not against the anti-majoritarian entrenchment of real moral rights, but against the anti-majoritarian entrenchment of some supermajority's conception of how those real moral rights could be translated into determinate rules.

There are, of course, arguments for why constitutions should not incorporate real moral rights by direct reference, arguments based on the destabilizing nature of such incorporations (if those rights are not subordinated to some human institution's rendering of them). Frederick Schauer and I have recently pointed out that if real moral rights were constitutionalized rather than some institution's—the founders', the courts', or the legislature's—fallible conception of those rights, anyone could always coherently claim a *legal* (as opposed to *moral*) right to disobey the edicts of duly constituted authorities or to deny that those authorities were indeed duly constituted.[25] Morality—real morality, that is—cannot be domesticated for inclusion within a stable legal system. It can only be sufficiently domesticated by being translated into rules, rules that will be morally imperfect at best and morally wrongheaded at worst. The perennial problem of jurisprudence is that moral norms and humanly posited norms—including human interpretations of moral norms—occupy the same space in practical reasoning, namely, in determining what we are *obligated* to do.[26] Direct incorporation of moral norms by legal ones either extinguishes the latter or is incoherent.[27]

Not only are there good arguments against constitutionalizing real moral rights by direct reference, but there are also arguments for why, if moral rights are to be constitutionalized by being rulified, constitutional rulification by the founders might be preferable to constitutional rulification by courts or to nonconstitutional rulification by ordinary legislative majorities. My colleague Michael Rappaport and his coauthor John McGinnis have written on the epistemic virtues of supermajoritarianism and thus the presumptive wisdom of the supermajorities that ratified the U.S. Constitution and its amendments.[28] And, of course, there are also John Ely's arguments for a certain set of constitutional rights, judicially enforced, as preconditions for majoritarian democracy.[29]

I return now to Waldron's objection to judicial review—that is, judicial supremacy with respect to constitutional rights. Assume now that we are not talking about Ely-type constitutional rights. And assume also we are not talking about rulified constitutional rights—rights in the form of determinate rules. Finally, assume that the real moral rights are legally (if not morally) subordinated to some institution's view of them, so that whether the highest authority on their content is the legislature or the courts, the highest authority's view, right or wrong, is *legally* authoritative.[30] If we make all those assumptions, and remembering that real moral rights are entrenched and should constrain political actors whether or not those rights are constitutionalized, is Waldron correct in asserting the primacy of majoritarian institutions' view of those rights over the judicial view of them?

Now one argument that is a nonstarter here is an argument from skepticism. We are assuming that there are real moral rights to which the legislature is subject. Ontological skepticism does not produce legislative supremacy as a default. Nor does epistemological skepticism. It is odd to assume that moral rights exist but that we cannot know them. Moreover, epistemological skepticism, like ontological skepticism, is not an argument that helps the case for majoritarian supremacy. Nor does a softer epistemological skepticism, that is, humility. If judges are better epistemologically and motivationally than are legislators at discerning the content of real moral rights, then the fact that those rights are controversial and that anyone should have humility regarding her view of them does not dictate judicial deference to legislatures. If anything, it dictates the opposite.

At times, Waldron appears to rely on a moral right that majorities possess, a moral right to be morally wrong. Such a moral right would have to be superior to every other moral right. But I cannot see the argument for it. Indeed, as I have written elsewhere, I think that a belief that one is morally right when one is in fact morally wrong cannot be transformed from a false belief into a true one merely by dint of sufficient others having the same false belief. The example I use is drawn from the novella *The Ox-Bow Incident*.[31] In the story, a posse has captured two men that most believe, given the evidence before them, are guilty of cattle rustling and murder. The choice the posse faces is between taking the captives back to the nearest town with a court for the two to stand trial, with full due process, or to hold its own trial without legal due process, and if it finds the two guilty, itself administer the requisite punishment (hanging). The majority of the posse opts for the latter course of action.

There are two dissenters. In the story, they argue strenuously for taking the captives to a court for a legal trial, but in the end they lose, and the captives are adjudged guilty and lynched by the posse. And, of course, it turns out that the captives were actually innocent.

Suppose, however, that the two dissenters, employing the element of surprise, could have pulled their guns on the majority, forced it to turn over the captives to them, and then brought the captives to a court. *Would the dissenters have been wrong to do so? Did the majority have a moral right to have its morally wrong way?* Is the latter position even coherent if we assume that majorities, no matter how overwhelming, cannot alter moral rights?[32]

Remember that we are assuming that the epistemic argument has been resolved in favor of courts, not legislatures. So we are faced with this question: if it is likely that the court is morally correct and the legislature is morally wrong, is it nonetheless morally wrong to impose the likely morally correct result and thereby refuse to enforce the likely morally incorrect result? Or, to telescope, does a democratic majority have the moral right to trample others' moral rights? If we block the retreat to the epistemic question, then this is the question. And for me, "no" is the obvious answer.[33] There is no majoritarian superright to be wrong.

Even on its own terms, "the right of the majority" is misleading. Waldron is speaking of legislative majorities, not plebiscites, and surely not plebiscites involving everyone affected (children, citizens of other countries, and so on). And translating the majority of citizens into a majority of legislators, and then translating the views of moral rights of individual legislators into *the* view of those rights of "the majority," is beset by the problems identified by Arrow and Pettit.[34] Moreover, Waldron is assuming an unelected judiciary. (If the judiciary were elected, it would be another indirectly democratic body, just like the legislature.)

Some (e.g., Yuval Eylon and Alon Harel)[35] have even countered with an alleged opposing moral right, the right to a judicial tribunal. Eylon and Harel's argument rests on the insensitivity of legislative bodies to the effects of their general laws on particular individuals—that is, on the ever present possibility that legislation that is morally benign may violate moral rights in some fraction of its applications that escape the notice of the legislature. Put differently, their argument might be construed thusly: (1) Even rights-sensitive legislatures are likely to enact laws that, although not intrinsically rights-violative, will violate the rights of particular individuals in certain unforeseen circumstances. (2) Individuals have a moral right not to have their moral rights put at undue risk. (3) Even rights-sensitive legislatures will put individuals' moral rights at undue risk per (1). (4) Judicial review reduces that risk to a morally tolerable level. Therefore, (5) there is a moral right to judicial review. Eylon and Harel's argument could be viewed as a variant on the epistemic/motivational superiority of courts to legislatures, a superiority that forms the basis of a derivative moral right to judicial review.

I leave Eylon and Harel's argument for judicial review aside. What I will say is that I see no moral case for legislative supremacy regarding moral rights, unless, that is, it is based on the epistemic advantages of legislatures over the judiciary.

Waldron does make some points that go to the epistemic (and motivational) case. He describes and contrasts parliamentary debate on abortion with the Supreme Court's opinion in *Roe*.[36] He ridicules the latter's legalistic, text-and-precedent-crabbed discussion of the issue with the deeper and more relevant to the moral issue substance of the British parliamentary debate on abortion.

If Waldron's point here is that legislatures are better suited than courts to get to the truth of the matter regarding real moral rights, then he has chosen a poor example. The Supreme Court did not view itself as resolving the underlying moral issue of abortion. Instead, it was trying to determine how abortion fit into a web of precedents elaborating the phrase "due process of law" laid down in 1868. The Court performed its task very poorly in my opinion—and *Roe* is far from being the only example of the Court's poor performance in interpreting the Constitution—but its task was not, as it saw it, to answer the basic moral question about the existence and contours of a putative moral right to abort.

There are indeed good reasons to doubt that courts will be particularly good at dealing with basic moral questions. Moral philosophers cannot agree among themselves, and judges, who have many nonphilosophical tasks to undertake, are seldom trained in moral philosophy.

But neither is there reason to believe that legislatures will be better than courts at this task. They cannot escape it, of course. As I said, they are always subject to real moral rights, whether or not constitutionalized. Adding those rights to the Constitution only makes them legal as well as moral rights. It does not make the legislature more subject to them than had they not been constitutionalized.

What adding moral rights to the Constitution and hence legalizing them does do, however, is make them prima facie subject to judicial elaboration and implementation. It does not follow that the judicial view must be supreme and final. There are good reasons to have supremacy and finality located in some institution, and with respect to ordinary, legalistic parts of the Constitution, there is a strong case for having that institution be the judiciary. But that is not necessarily true of real moral rights incorporated into a Constitution. A judiciary, even if otherwise in a *Cooper v. Aaron*[37] regime of judicial supremacy, might well decide to treat the legal meaning of such rights as "political questions" on which the legislature would be final and supreme. Or, it might treat some moral rights questions as political questions and others as fitting for judicial supremacy. (It is frequently noted that courts are better at telling legislatures "You may not do *that*" than at telling legislatures or administrators, "Here are the things you must do." It is, unfortunately, quite possibly the case that the moral rights we possess do not squarely fit into "negative" and "positive" boxes; our so-called negative rights might also entail affirmative obligations of protection and not merely governmental restraint.)

The issue, then, appears to me to boil down to one of institutional competencies rather than to one of high principle. Both ordinary majoritarian legislative decision-making and judicial decision-making are to be judged by how well they perform their tasks. Institutional design, including whether legislatures should be constrained by constitutional limits, whether those limits should include individual rights, and whether courts should enforce those limits, is a matter of epistemological and motivational superiority, not a matter of moral principle.[38]

Once one pierces the high-toned rhetoric of the right of the people to rule themselves, one sees that the rhetoric belies a very complicated underlying reality. There are some matters over which we, as individuals, have a moral right to be sovereign—matters that are the legitimate concern of only us. By extension, there are some matters over which a group of likeminded individuals has a moral right to be sovereign. But when it comes to a majority having sovereignty over a minority, matters are morally complex. There may be correct answers available morally. And if there are, there will be better and worse ways of designing institutions of majority rule and placing constitutional limits thereon. Constitutional design, including both what rules and principles to entrench constitutionally and what institution will have the final say regarding those rules and principles, should be dictated only by epistemic and motivational considerations. Moral rights are at stake only in the predicted outcomes of the design. There is no moral right to constitutionally unconstrained majoritarianism, even if majoritarianism unconstrained by rules of order and franchise were conceptually possible. Nor is there a moral right that the majority be unconstrained by entrenched substantive rules designed to implement real rights or to enhance in other ways the quality of legislation and administration. And, as I have now repeated several times, the majority is always constrained by real moral rights.

Finally, if there is no moral right that majoritarianism not be constrained in these various ways, there is also no moral right that the majority be unconstrained by courts' views of these other constraints. Indeed, if what counts are epistemological and motivational advantages, then with respect to posited, determinate constitutional rules, judicial interpretations win hands down. With respect to real moral rights that a Constitution might (unwisely) incorporate by direct reference, courts are less obviously superior to legislative majorities in discerning their content. Nor is there an overweening necessity to settle and thus rulify that content—to posit and entrench that meaning—which, given *stare decisis*, courts are more likely to do. But there is no moral right against judicial review that precludes giving this job of implementing real moral rights to judges, only these concerns of lack of necessity and clear advantage.

Thus, on the question of governance by reference to moral rights, as between courts and legislative majorities, there is no knockdown winner. It all depends. A whimper of a conclusion rather than a bang, perhaps, but true nonetheless.

Chapter Nine
Active Liberty and the Problem of Judicial Oligarchy

Robert P. Young, Jr.

The topic of this volume is the Supreme Court and the idea of constitutionalism, a very broad, daunting topic considering the vast output of the United States Supreme Court since our founding, let alone considering the impact of the Court's decisions on our society. This chapter focuses more narrowly on the topic of "judicial philosophy," which I will define momentarily. The Supreme Court is the premier court in the United States because it has the final say in interpreting our Constitution and, consequently, the Supreme Court sets the tone of the American judicial culture. Therefore, I will concentrate on that Court's evolving judicial philosophy as it relates to interpreting the Constitution, and, in turn, the effect of the Court's judicial philosophy on American society.

The Constitution we have today is markedly different from the one ratified in 1789. Even considering the twenty-seven constitutional amendments that have been added to our Constitution since 1789, I submit that the more seismic "amendments" to our Constitution are largely attributable to jurists applying their improvident judicial philosophies in the course of deciding cases. What has emerged is a judicial oligarchy that rules our nation in a manner never intended by the framers and ratifiers of our Constitution. This development is not without consequences that are, in my view, largely negative. This judicial oligarchy has wrested control of major social policy decisions from the democratically accountable branches of government, the executive and the legislature, and placed itself in a policy-making role that it is not constitutionally authorized to assume, and that it is institutionally incompetent to handle. In this chapter, I attempt to trace the ascendancy of the judicial oligarchs and explore some of the repercussions of having jurists displace the people's representatives as lawmakers.

The title of my chapter, "Active Liberty and the Problem of Judicial Oligarchy," is derived in part from a book recently published by United States Supreme Court Associate Justice Stephen Breyer. Justice Breyer's book is illustrative of the judicial philosophy accompanying the rise of the judicial oligarchy. In the following passage from *Active Liberty*, Justice Breyer ruminates on his approach to interpreting our Constitution: "My thesis is that courts should take greater account of the Constitution's democratic nature when they interpret constitutional and statutory texts. . . . In a word, my theme is democracy and the Constitution. I illustrate a democratic theme—"active liberty"—which resonates throughout the Constitution. In discussing its role, I hope to illustrate how this constitutional theme can affect a judge's interpretation of a constitutional text."[1]

Certainly, as abstract propositions, "democracy" and "liberty" are laudable notions. However, beyond his invocation of these concepts, Justice Breyer's actual approach to the task of constitutional interpretation remains unclear. He obviously hears "democratic themes" in his head when he approaches the Constitution, and it is equally clear that he especially values the "active participation" of American citizens in their government. While Justice Breyer assures his readers that he is interpreting a written text, the Constitution, and disclaims the authority of a jurist to impose his personal values on the Constitution, he also freely acknowledges that he uses his "active-liberty-participatory-government" theme as an interpretive aid in making decisions about the meaning of our Constitution. This is problematic to the extent that Justice Breyer's thematic musings are essentially unrelated to any specific constitutional text. We should therefore be grateful that Justice Breyer does not hear themes of anarchy, fascism, or totalitarianism in his constitutional exegesis.

A generation ago, Justice Breyer's predecessors spoke about the "penumbras" and "emanations" of privacy in the Constitution rather than its active liberty underpinnings.[2] It surely sounds nicer that our Constitution is *thematic* rather than suffering from "emanations." But in any case, the question before us remains: Why is Justice Breyer (or any other jurist) free to select a theme of his own choosing to interpret our Constitution? My answer is that thematic interests simply should not inform an interpretation of the words of our Constitution.[3]

Lest one think that my critique of Justice Breyer's book is harsh or that my concern about judicial philosophy is overwrought, one need only look to recent political battles over judicial nominations to see evidence that judicial philosophy has become an important political question in our country. In 1987, when then–United States Court of Appeals Judge Robert Bork was nominated to the United States Supreme Court, a bitter, organized campaign of opposition to his nomination was waged by the Democratic members of the Senate and their political allies.[4] So unexpected and intense was the ultimately successful assault that the nominee and his supporters (both in and outside the Reagan Administration) provided no significant, and certainly no organized, political response. Within an hour of the nomination, Senator Edward Kennedy appeared on the floor of the United States Senate and delivered his infamous speech portraying "Robert Bork's America" as a land of back-alley abortions, segregated lunch counters, and censorship. Judge Bork, in his own word, was "incredulous." The humiliating, baseless attacks on Judge Bork were relentless. Indeed, the verb, "to be Borked," was added to the political lexicon to describe any similar public execution of a nominee for office.

Supreme Court nominations had failed and public debates about judicial philosophy had occurred before 1987. But Judge Bork's failed nomination is a useful example because the campaign against him was waged, not on his competence as a jurist (no one questioned his legal scholarship or brilliance), or on his ethical behavior, but on his *judicial philosophy.* An advocate of interpreting the Constitution according to its "original understanding," Judge Bork criticized and questioned many Supreme Court decisions from the mid-to late twentieth century as inconsistent with the Constitution's original understanding. It was this judicial philosophy, considered apostate when compared to the prevailing judicial philosophies of the time, which provoked such an impassioned opposition.

In every United States Supreme Court nomination since 1987, the specter of Judge Bork's candidacy has loomed. Each has shared an essential feature of the Bork confirmation process—the organized opposition to a nominee over his or her purported judicial philosophy usually fought on other, tenuous grounds. Most recently, we watched the Senate confirmation process concerning Justices John Roberts and Samuel Alito. Some may recall the sight of Justice Alito's wife tearfully looking on as her husband was asked at his confirmation hearing whether he was a "closet bigot" because of his association with a Princeton University alumni group. While the acrimony of these nomination proceedings never approached that of the Bork nomination, they bore an additional notable distinction. The opposition forces in these confirmation battles were now matched by equally organized and well-financed groups that supported the nominee's confirmation.

The Bork nomination probably marked one of the ugliest public manifestations of a debate about judicial philosophy that had been raging in legal academies and judicial circles for years. This is a debate about whether judges in our society play an important, but limited, role interpreting the Constitution—to act as "umpires" as Chief Justice Roberts so simply described it—or whether judges ought to function in our constitutional republic as an unelected oligarchy deciding major social policies guided by personal "themes" unexpressed in the Constitution.

Judicial Philosophy Defined

I find that most of the terms and concepts in the popular lexicon about judicial philosophy are unhelpful and tend to add confusion rather than clarity to the debate. Most popular concepts describe judges in stark *political* terms. For instance, we hear repeated the phrases "judicial conservative," "liberal activist," or "strict constructionist." I concede that jurists can be motivated by frank political goals and the results of such efforts can have partisan results. However, this is a tendency that can exist among jurists of any political stripe, whether liberal or conservative, Republican or Democrat. Thus, speaking in political terms about judicial philosophy conceals what I believe to be the underlying issue.

My view is that judicial philosophy, properly understood, is not at all a partisan belief that is necessarily aligned with one political party or another. Rather, judicial philosophy concerns a judge's beliefs about the role of the courts, particularly in constitutional matters. The debate about judicial philosophy concerns largely whether a jurist who interprets the Constitution is constrained by the Constitution's written text or whether the jurist feels free to apply nonconstitutional values that might have nothing to do with the text.

To use my own terms, this has been a debate between two main schools of judicial philosophy. *Judicial traditionalists* are jurists who believe as I do that the role of judges is guided by three fundamental principles.[5] First, judges act within a republican form of government that is assured (at least to the states) by Article IV, Section 4 of our Constitution. Second, pursuant to Article I, Section 1, it is the legislature, namely Congress, that serves the exclusive role of "law-maker" in matters of public policy. Third, beyond the enumerated rights found in the Bill of Rights, the Constitution requires public policy to be debated and resolved in the majoritarian process of the executive and legislative branches. For a judicial traditionalist, a judge's role in a constitutional republic is a circumscribed one—giving meaning to the

text of the Constitution as those words were understood by those who ratified the Constitution while refraining from deciding matters of public policy committed to the majoritarian political process. A judicial traditionalist
views the Constitution as a document with an ascertainable meaning that
is rooted in the history of its creation. He is offended by jurists who use the
power of judicial office to bend the Constitution to serve a policy agenda of
any description because the judicial traditionalist cares only about the policies *specifically expressed* in the text of the Constitution itself.

Judicial traditionalists are not monolithic. They do not always agree on
particular matters of constitutional interpretation. Most readily acknowledge that the traditionalist approach can be difficult, might not yield an obvious answer, and requires earnest effort and discipline. In short, as Justice
Antonin Scalia, who I think I can safely categorize as a judicial traditionalist, admits, this approach is "not without its warts."[6] A judicial traditionalist might make the same defense of his judicial philosophy that Winston
Churchill made of democracy: it is the worst judicial philosophy—except in
comparison to all others.

The other school of judicial philosophy consists of jurists who believe
that they have the right, or even the obligation, to look beyond the text of the
Constitution to other values in order to address the contemporary problems
of our society. I describe this latter school as the "*Rorschach school*" of interpretation, because it views the Constitution as a vague document incapable
of definite meaning and open to no certain interpretation—like a Rorschach
inkblot. Members of the Rorschach school, largely unconcerned with the
historical record of the founding, typically regard judicial traditionalists as
hidebound, quixotic troglodytes in search of the mythical intent of a long-
dead founding generation who created and ratified the Constitution more
than two centuries ago. The Rorschach school permits, even encourages,
judges to become "law-makers" rather than interpreters of the law. While
within the Rorschach school there are as many subdisciplines as there are
extra-constitutional policy values that can be projected onto our Constitution, all adherents of the Rorschach school share the view that the Constitution gives license to jurists to project onto the Constitution social, political,
and moral beliefs unexpressed in the Constitution.

Our legal academics almost universally embrace and teach the Rorschach philosophy. The United States Supreme Court, our bellwether court
in America, has, over time, also increasingly embraced the Rorschach school,
as illustrated by Justice Breyer's thematic active liberty jurisprudence. By
adopting novel methods of adjudication that are no longer tethered to our

written Constitution, the Court has equipped itself with law-making powers that extend well beyond the intended limitations of the Constitution. Consequently, the modern Court places its imprimatur on virtually any policy issue that its members desire to influence. As such, I contend the Court now functions as an unelected oligarchy.

Judicial Traditionalism in Early America

This chapter is not intended as a work of political science or history.[7] But it is imperative to frame this debate about judicial philosophy in its proper historical context. I submit that the historical record documenting the founding and the text of the Constitution suggests that few in the founding generation seriously believed, much less advocated, that judges would be empowered to behave as a quasi-legislature under the Constitution they ratified. Though members of the Rorschach school may not find the historical record relevant to the debate, the historical record undercuts their thesis that judges are authorized to remake and amend our Constitution based on extra-constitutional values.

By the time of the 1787 Constitutional Convention in Philadelphia, the leading lights of the thirteen former colonies who had prevailed against England in the Revolutionary War were largely convinced that the Articles of Confederation were inadequate to the task of ensuring survival of this newly, still independent, collection of states.[8] The unanimity requirements for action under the Articles of Confederation, and thus the reservation to each state of the power to block concerted action of the whole, had been a feature of governance carried forward in the Articles. This gridlocked, veto-laden process had been a major frustration to those who waged war against England, not the least of which was General George Washington, who lacked sufficient resources for his troops because the Continental Congress had no power to require states to contribute to the war effort.[9] Many believed that the Articles required some form of adjustment and amendment, if for no other reason than that war debts remained unpaid and the Articles seemed to provide no means to satisfy them or, importantly, advance harmonious commerce among the states.[10]

The Constitutional Convention was not, by any stretch of the imagination, "authorized" to scrap the Articles of Confederation. While the ostensible purpose of the convention was to discuss possible changes to the Articles, the delegates gathered to create a new constitution—one that was a radical departure from the ineffectual and constraining Articles.[11] They conspired under a strict ban of secrecy to create a new constitution.[12]

It is generally agreed that a few core concerns anchored and animated the Constitution that emerged from the Constitutional Convention. The colonists feared the emergence of a monarchy in the United States. They sought to avoid concentrating power in a centralized national government that might oppress the people and diminish the sovereignty of the colonies and upset the balance of power among the colonies. However, they also realized that they needed some means to avoid commercial fratricide among the thirteen colonies. The colonists also desired to preserve the rights of Englishmen under the "British constitution" they had declaimed in the Declaration of Independence with modifications forged by their experience with republican government in America while separated from the direct interference of the king of England and his government.[13] Division and diffusion of governmental power was a key concern of the founders. The sovereignty of the thirteen colonies was jealously guarded and the question of how to create a national government that would not impinge on state sovereignty was one of the great problems the Constitutional Convention had to solve.

Modern Americans who have enjoyed more than two centuries under a national government—one that has grown increasingly strong and dominant in the last century—have difficulty imagining a state of affairs that the delegates faced. There was no national government to speak of, but only thirteen independent sovereign colonies that shared a common ancestry, cultural and economic ties to England, and the shared experience of fighting the Revolutionary War. These were the common threads that provided a basis for cooperation in a new national government.

To address the concentration of governmental powers concern, two principles emerged in the proposed constitution. First, the constitution divided the national government into three branches—the executive, the legislature, and the judiciary—each with specified responsibilities committed exclusively to that branch. This separation of powers created a system of checks and balances that prevented one of the three branches from acquiring unrestrained power over the others. The Constitution also introduced the concept of *federalism*—a division of powers between the states and the national government with power of the federal government limited only to specified, enumerated powers. Federalism was conceived to allow a centralized, national government to function in specifically delegated areas without transgressing state sovereignty in the remaining areas.

Within the proposed national government, the judiciary's role was considered the weakest. It had no authority to make law. This task was committed to the legislative branch in Article I. In contrast with the extensive listing of authority given to the other two branches of government, the proposed constitution described the federal judiciary powers in fairly cursory fashion. The Supreme Court was the only federal court named in the Constitution. Its judicial authority was limited and extended only to cases and controversies listed in Article III, Section 2. The Court's jurisdiction included only cases arising under the Constitution, involving acts of Congress, foreign treaties, admiralty law and those affecting foreign officials. Its jurisdiction also extended to cases in which the United States was a party, and cases involving disputes between citizens of different states. The latter category of cases, those involving conflicts between citizens of different states, is called *diversity jurisdiction* and was especially controversial because of fear that federal courts would displace state courts and state law.

Article III, Section 2 designated that the Supreme Court had "original jurisdiction" over the small set of cases listed, but provided that any additional (appellate) jurisdiction was entirely to be determined by future congressional act.[14] There was even considerable hostility at the convention to establishing other than a federal supreme court as it was believed that lesser federal tribunals would encroach on the jurisdiction of the state courts. This point was vigorously argued by delegates to the Constitutional Convention—especially given that diversity jurisdiction arguably expanded the reach of the federal judiciary in ways that might disturb the laws of the states.[15] The challenge to whether there should be *any* lower federal courts was overcome by putting the question in the hands of Congress to decide later whether such lower courts should be established.[16]

Important to our discussion, the delegates at the Constitutional Convention also debated and forcefully rejected a broader role for the national judiciary to act as a "Council of Revision" reviewing legislative acts. The debate concerning this proposal is interesting because it reveals the contemporaneous views of the founders about how judges should function. Even those who supported a broader role for the judiciary in a "Council of Revision" did not deny that such a council would create a judicial law-making role that was a departure from the traditional role of judges as interpreters of the law.[17]

The delegates, on four occasions during their debates on the new constitution, gave consideration to adopting a Council of Revision. Edmund Randolph's Virginia Plan, drafted largely by James Madison, included a "Council of Revision" modeled loosely on the admixed judicial and legislative functions of England's House of Lords. Randolph introduced the plan in the first few days of the Constitutional Convention on May 29, 1789. Proposal 8 of the Virginia Plan read: "Resolved that the Executive and a convenient number of the National Judiciary, ought to compose a Council of revision with authority to examine every act of the National Legislature before it shall operate, & every act of a particular Legislature before a Negative thereon shall be final; and that the dissent of the said Council shall amount to a rejection, unless the Act of the National Legislature be again passed, or that of a particular Legislature be again negatived by __ of the members of each branch."[18]

Thus, the Council of Revision proposed to combine members of the executive and judicial branches, who would jointly review legislation and possess veto power over such legislation. There had been widespread belief that, during the Revolutionary War and afterward, state legislatures had acted improvidently, particularly in negating war debts. Indeed, historian Gordon Wood has observed that in these years preceding the Constitutional Convention there was a "growing mistrust of the legislative assemblies."[19] The Council of Revision proposal emerged as the delegates considered ways to check the power of reckless and profligate legislatures. The delegates to the Constitutional Convention of 1787 raised the Council of Revision proposal *four times.*[20] Each time it was rejected.

When it was first raised, the delegates voted to postpone its consideration after the idea drew criticism from Elbridge Gerry. Gerry noted, "it was quite foreign from the nature of ye. office to make [the judiciary] judges of the policy of public measures."[21] Massachusetts delegate Rufus King added that "Judges ought to be able to expound the law as it should come before them, free from the bias of having participated in its formation."[22]

Supporters of the Council of Revision tended to believe that a veto power, in the hands of a single, transitory executive, was an ineffectual check against the awesome power of the legislature.[23] Hence, the proponents believed that the veto power would be strengthened if the executive and judiciary could collectively combat the legislature. Delegate James Wilson argued for the utility of permitting the judiciary to revise laws that, although not unconstitutional, were imprudent.[24] James Madison argued that the judiciary would provide "valuable assistance . . . in preserving a consistency, conciseness, perspicuity & technical propriety in the laws, qualities peculiarly necessary and yet shamefully wanting in our republican Codes."[25] George Mason bemoaned the limited role of a federal judiciary that *could only* void a law as unconstitutional.[26]

These views drew strong opposition from delegates such as Gerry, Luther Martin, and John Rutledge.[27] After extensive debate, the Council of Revision was defeated. The idea of a council of revision was repudiated by the delegates to the Constitutional Convention in favor of the traditional judicial role that, as delegate Gerry suggested, consisted solely of serving as "expositors of the law."

Gordon Wood has argued that, in the years leading up to the Constitutional Convention, the idea of separation of powers enhanced the role of the judiciary. He argues that "at the time of Independence, with the constitution-makers absorbed in the problems of curtailing gubernatorial authority and establishing legislative supremacy the judiciary had been virtually ignored or considered to be but an adjunct of feared magisterial power."[28] However, while greater attention may have been devoted to constraining the other branches of the federal government, it appears that a confined, traditional role for the judiciary was sought within the framework of the separation of powers in a constitutional republic.

In the ratification debates that followed the Constitutional Convention, there is no indication that those who eventually ratified the Constitution contemplated or desired a judiciary with legislative or law-making powers. In fact, there was considerable hostility from the Anti-Federalists to the federal judiciary, fearing that the proposed federal judiciary was too powerful. Anti-Federalists, such as Elbridge Gerry, refused even to sign the Constitution after the convention principally because he believed that "the judicial branch will be oppressive."[29] During the ratification debates, Anti-Federalists raised alarm about the proposed federal judiciary as an unnecessary encroachment on state sovereignty and the authority of state courts. Anti-Federalists especially fought against any congressional authority to establish lower federal courts and for entirely eliminating federal diversity jurisdiction.[30]

In *Anti-Federalist Paper* 15, "Brutus," the pseudonym of the authors of the *Anti-Federalist Papers*, bluntly summarized the fears that Article III of the proposed constitution posed for the new nation. Brutus made two key points why the proposed Supreme Court was problematic. First, the proposed constitution provided no power "above" the Supreme Court to check and correct its errors. Second, under the proposed constitution, federal judges could not be removed from office or suffer a diminution of pay for merely making poor decisions; they could only be removed for conviction of treason, bribery, or other high crimes and misdemeanors. Brutus objected to a departure from the British model where, although Parliament cannot reverse the judgment in a *particular* case, it could, by legislative act, deprive the decision of binding authority in future cases. No such corrective mechanism was provided in the proposed constitution. Brutus elaborated on his concerns about the proposed Supreme Court:

This court will be authorised to decide upon the meaning of the constitution, and that, not only according to the natural and ob[vious] meaning of the words, but also according to the spirit and intention of it. In the exercise of this power they will not be subordinate to, but above the legislature. . . . The supreme court then have a right, independent of the legislature, to give a construction to the constitution and every part of it, and there is no power provided in this system to correct their construction or do away with it. . . . I have, in the course of my observations on this constitution, affirmed and attempted to shew, that it was calculated to abolish entirely state governments . . . Perhaps nothing could have been better conceived to facilitate the abolition of the state governments than the constitution of the judicial. They will be able to extend the limits of general government gradually, and by insensible degrees, and to accommodate the temper of the people.[31]

In response to these attacks on the proposed federal judiciary, the Federalists sought to allay fears that the federal judicial role was intended to be or could become a robust one. *The Federalist Papers* went out of the way to depict the envisioned national judiciary as a weak and nonthreatening branch of government. The author of *Federalist* 81 argued:

It may in the last place be observed that the supposed danger of judiciary encroachments on the legislative authority, which has been upon many occasions reiterated, is in reality a phantom. Particular misconstructions and contraventions of the will of the legislature may now and then happen; but they can never be so extensive as to amount to an inconvenience, or in any sensible degree to affect the order of the political system. This may be inferred with certainty, from the general nature of the judicial power, from the objects to which it relates, from the manner in which it is exercised, from its comparative weakness, and from its total incapacity to support its usurpations by force.[32]

Similarly, in *Federalist* 78, it was argued that

Whoever attentively considers the different departments of power must perceive, that, in a government in which they are separated from each other, the judiciary, from the nature of its functions, will always be the least dangerous to the political rights of the Constitution; because it will be least in a capacity to annoy or injure them. . . . The judiciary . . . has no influence over either the sword or the purse; no direction either of the strength or of the wealth of the society; and can take no active resolution whatever. It may truly be said to have neither FORCE nor WILL, but merely judgment; and must ultimately depend upon the aid of the executive arm even for the efficacy of its judgments.[33]

That the Federalists went to such lengths to quell the fears of the Anti-Federalists of a rampant judiciary speaks against the idea that the founders, either Federalist or Anti-Federalist, anticipated or welcomed a judiciary that would assume a law-making role.

Following ratification, the first order of business of the new Congress was the task of developing constitutional amendments to placate the Anti-Federalists' concerns that the original constitution lacked specification of certain English rights and the need to enact legislation to implement Article III. In those congressional debates, Anti-Federalists urged two limitations in the constitutional amendments under consideration to curb the power of the federal judiciary. They argued to restrict federal appellate jurisdiction to questions of law only and for eliminating diversity jurisdiction. Second, they fought to eliminate congressional authority provided in Article III to establish lower federal courts.[34]

In its first session, Congress enacted the Judiciary Act of 1789. The act created both district trial and intermediate appellate federal courts and stood as a compromise between the Federalists and the Anti-Federalists. For instance, the major Federalist victory was in preserving diversity jurisdiction, but with the concession that federal courts would be required to apply the same law the local state court would have applied. This provision was designed to reduce the possibility of federal interference with state law and sovereignty.[35]

Surely, Anti-Federalists, as illustrated by Brutus's spot-on assessment of how a national judiciary might seize power, had legitimate anxieties about what a rogue judiciary might accomplish. But the point of even Brutus's criticism is that it was a *rogue* judiciary that exceeded its proper traditional role that was to be feared. As the recounted history of the creation and ratification of the Constitution shows, there was no serious advocacy for a national judiciary to perform the role of a Council of Revision at the time of ratification or immediately thereafter. Indeed, the history of the creation and ratification of our Constitution shows that our founders intended something quite the opposite: a restrained national judiciary that interpreted the law rather than created it.

It is also worth specifically noting that on matters concerning changes to the Constitution itself, the founders emphatically made clear that amendments to the Constitution were *not* the province of jurists, but the people themselves. Article V provides that amendments to the Constitution can only be initiated by two-thirds vote of the Congress or two thirds of the state legislatures. And an amendment so initiated can be ratified only upon the vote of three quarters of state legislatures. If the founders went to the trouble of writing down how our Constitution could be amended, why do Rorschach jurists believe they have the right to do so independent of that process? The answer is, during most of our early constitutional history, it was never believed that the Constitution could be amended by judicial fiat.

Judicial Traditionalism: The Early Supreme Court

As stated, the prevailing view at the founding was that the role of judges was limited to interpreting the law, not making it. Thus, it is not surprising that the early years of the Supreme Court are marked by fidelity to the notion that a written constitution was being interpreted and that its meaning was informed by the intent of those who created and ratified it. The commitment to interpreting the Constitution in accord with its words as understood by those who ratified it was the interpretive norm. Rare was the occasion in this early era when a member of the Supreme Court, much less the Court as a whole, openly claimed the right to strike down statutes on a basis not expressly stated in the Constitution.

Notwithstanding its general fidelity to a judicial traditionalist approach, even in these early years, the judicial impulse to exceed the jurist's traditional role as expositor of the law and to become a law-maker was extant. *Calder v. Bull*[36] is illustrative of just such an impulse in the early life of the Court. The facts of *Calder* are not as important as the debate about interpretive philosophy that ensued among the Justices in their separate opinions. In short, the Connecticut legislature passed a law setting aside an earlier decree of a probate court, and the plaintiff, Calder, who benefited from the earlier court decision, argued that the law violated the ex post facto clause in Article I, Section 10. Tracing the clause's common law heritage, the Court concluded that the ex post facto clause was limited to criminal cases. As *Calder* involved a civil dispute, the clause provided no assistance to Calder.

While the Court agreed on the outcome, a split emerged among its members regarding the proper role of the judiciary when reviewing legislative acts. Justice Samuel Chase, agreeing that the Connecticut legislature's act was constitutional, still held out the possibility that a legislative act could be struck down though it violated no constitutional provision. To that end, Chase invoked extra-constitutional values of natural law to support his position : "I cannot subscribe to the omnipotence of a State Legislature, or that it is absolute and without control; although its authority should not be expressly restrained by the Constitution, or fundamental law, of the State. . . . An ACT of the Legislature (for I cannot call it a law) contrary to the great first principles of the social compact, cannot be considered a rightful exercise of legislative authority."[37]

Justice James Iredell's response to Justice Chase is one that could be made in opposition to all adherents of the Rorschach school of interpretation that rely on extra-constitutional values: "The ideas of natural justice are regulated by no fixed standard: the ablest and the purest men have differed upon the subject; and all that the Court could properly say, in such an event, would be, that the Legislature (possessed of an equal right of opinion) had passed an act which, in the opinion of the judges, was inconsistent with the abstract principles of natural justice."[38]

Marbury v. Madison,[39] written by Chief Justice John Marshall, is perhaps one of the Supreme Court's most famous cases and one of its most controversial.[40] It is a landmark case because it firmly established the right of "judicial review"—the right of the Supreme Court to assess whether laws or governmental acts violate the Constitution.

The highly politicized backdrop to the case is well known. President John Adams appointed a number of individuals to federal posts in the waning hours of his presidency, but a number of the commissions had not been delivered to those appointed. (Ironically, it was John Marshall, then secretary of state in Adams's cabinet, who failed to deliver the commissions.) When Thomas Jefferson entered office, he refused to deliver the remaining commissions authorized by his predecessor. Marbury, who had been confirmed by the Senate, sought a writ of mandamus from the Court to compel Jefferson to deliver his commission.

The question before the Court was whether it could force the president to deliver the commission by issuing a writ of mandamus. The Court noted that Marbury clearly had the right to the commission. However, the trickier legal issue was whether a provision in the Judiciary Act, which expanded the original jurisdiction of the Court to issue writs of mandamus, prevailed over the narrower original jurisdiction of Article III in the Constitution, which did not grant the Court original jurisdiction to issue writs of mandamus. Marshall, speaking for the Court, held that the provision was unconstitutional because a legislative act could not expand the original jurisdiction of the Court set forth in the Constitution. Therefore, the Court declined to order Jefferson to deliver Marbury's commission.

The legal maneuverings of Justice Marshall and the Court in *Marbury* remain controversial more than two hundred years later and are still intensely debated. What is indisputably not controversial about *Marbury* is Marshall and the Court's fidelity to interpreting the text of the Constitution, particularly Article III, according to their "plain import," giving them their "obvious meaning."[41] Marshall cannot be faulted for failing to take the words of the Constitution seriously.

Gibbons v. Ogden[42] is also illustrative. In *Gibbons*, the Court was called upon to interpret the interstate commerce clause of Article I, Section 8. The case reached the Supreme Court, and the question was whether New York or Congress had the right to issue a license to operate boats on an interstate waterway. Gibbons' license was granted by an act of Congress, while Ogden was licensed by the state of New York.

Gibbons relied on the Constitution's interstate commerce clause, which gave Congress the power "to regulate Commerce with foreign Nations, and among the several States." In Gibbons' view, his case involved interstate commerce, so New York's statutory monopoly license was void for encroaching on Congress's constitutional authority. Ogden countered that it was within New York's retained powers to create and sustain a monopoly that did not implicate interstate commerce. Moreover, Ogden argued that the Congress's commerce clause power did not extend to *navigation*, because navigation was not commerce.

The Court agreed with Gibbons and voided the New York law as an unconstitutional encroachment on federal commerce power. It is unnecessary to parse the details of Marshall's careful and nuanced analysis. Rather, it is sufficient to observe that Marshall was again guided by sound traditional principles of constitutional interpretation. That is, Marshall interpreted the words in the commerce clause as they were understood by the ratifiers, and construed those words within the context of other constitutional provisions. Marshall argued in favor of reading the words of the Constitution as those words were best understood by its ratifiers. He continued: "As men, whose intentions require no concealment, generally employ the words which most directly and aptly express the ideas they intend to convey, the enlightened patriots who framed our constitution, and the people who adopted it, must be understood to have employed words in their natural sense, and to have intended what they have said."[43] Marshall admitted that "the imperfection of human language" could create "serious doubts" as to the proper interpretation of a constitutional provision. However, even then, Marshall said he would be guided by the "objects for which it was given, especially when those objects are expressed in the instrument itself." Contrary to claims made by some members of the Rorschach school, Marshall approached the Constitution as an intelligible document whose words ought to be interpreted in their "natural sense."[44]

In *Marbury* and *Gibbons*, we see the early Supreme Court at work. Its starting point was the text of the Constitution and its emphasis was on how that text was originally understood at the time of its framing. It would be naïve to think that the Court did not behave shrewdly in those early years to assert its authority, but it cannot be said that it operated as a Council of Revision.[45]

The Rorschach School and Slavery: *Dred Scott*

In contrast to the Court's early cases, many Supreme Court commentators mark the Supreme Court's decision in *Dred Scott*[46] as the Court's most striking and blatant departure from the careful jurisprudence that marked the Court's earlier decisions. Indeed, *Dred Scott* marked the first occasion since *Marbury* that the Court held a major federal statute unconstitutional. It is a case widely reviled and believed to have been one of the precipitating causes of the Civil War.[47]

Within the first decades of the nineteenth century, the admission of states as free or slave-states repeatedly called into question the balance of political power between Northern and Southern states. Eventually, Congress settled on a compromise—known as the Missouri Compromise of 1820—to maintain the sectional balance. Without otherwise resolving the slavery question, the Missouri Compromise barred slavery in the Louisiana Purchase lands north of Missouri's southern border and paired the admission of states so that one slave state was admitted with each newly admitted free state. The compromise permitted the United States to grow without altering the North–South balance of power.

Dred Scott, a slave, was taken by his owner to Illinois, a state that forbade slavery. When returned to Missouri, a slave state, Scott sued for his freedom on the ground that having set foot in Illinois, he had thereby become a free man. He lost his case in the Missouri Supreme Court and appealed that decision to the Supreme Court.

Chief Justice Roger Taney of Maryland, joined by a Court with a majority of Southerners, not only denied Scott's claim of freedom, but went on to hold the Missouri Compromise unconstitutional (although it had been repealed two years earlier), thus declaring that the federal government was without constitutional authority to exclude slavery in United States territories—even where slavery had never existed. Taney held that slaves were property protected by the due process clause of the Fifth Amendment of the Constitution, thus creating a *substantive right* to own slaves.

The Court's decision was startling because it had no basis in the text of the Fifth Amendment's due process clause or its historical meaning. "Property," including what kind of property is lawful to own, is not defined in any way by the Fifth Amendment. The Constitution clearly protected ownership of lawful property and ensured, through the Fifth Amendment, that property could not be taken without "*due process.*" But no provision of the Constitution provided a substantive right to own slaves in a state or territory where this practice was forbidden by law.

At the time of the founding, "due process" encompassed the *processes* by which a court considered a case.[48] These include the right to a neutral fact finder, notice of the proceedings, and similar practices and procedures that assured a fair adjudication. Until *Dred Scott*, "due process" had not concerned the *substance* of the law being applied.

Thus, in *Dred Scott*, Taney—perhaps driven by a *Southern* theme of active liberty—created an unenumerated constitutional right of "*substantive* due process." In so doing, Taney impeded the democratic process by which Congress had struggled to address, albeit in compromise form, the troubling national problem of slavery. There were those, Lincoln included, who had believed that slavery, had the issue not been forced, would have eventually died in America.[49] The view is hotly contested, but the point is that such matters are placed within the purview of the *legislative* branch of government by our Constitution, not the *judicial* branch, particularly where the Constitution was largely silent on the matter of slavery.

Substantive due process, having no provenance in the common law of England from which our due process clause was derived, and unrecognized prior to 1857, has since served as the prime Rorschach inkblot onto which subsequent jurists have projected their own free-floating, nonconstitutional interpretive "themes." Modern adherents of the Rorschach school no doubt despise Justice Taney's "slavery theme," but, as will be seen, they have most assuredly appropriated his interpretive methods as well as his work product to promote their own nonconstitutional themes.

The Rorschach Influence on the Modern Supreme Court

No short essay can encyclopedically address the considerable number of modern Supreme Court cases that have employed the Rorschach school of constitutional interpretation to achieve essentially legislative policy-making goals. In matters of search and seizure, police interrogation, public obscenity, abortion, campaign finance, homosexual rights, affirmative action, free speech, religious exercise, terrorism and homeland security, to name a few, the Supreme Court has been criticized for behaving less like a court interpreting a written constitution and more like a quasi-legislature imposing its own policy judgments.

This is nowhere more evident than in recent Eighth Amendment cases grappling with capital punishment. The Eighth Amendment provides that "excessive bail shall not be required, nor excessive fines be imposed, nor cruel and unusual punishments inflicted." The last clause dealing with "cruel and unusual punishments" has been a recurrent issue in constitutional adjudication of capital punishment cases in the modern era.

It is undisputed that the founders practiced capital punishment and made specific provisions for it in our Constitution. Every state at the time of ratification in 1789 practiced capital punishment. Indeed, the number of "capital crimes"—those crimes that, at common law, warranted death upon conviction—were vastly more numerous than are recognized today in states that currently authorize capital punishment. It is not surprising then that the founders included provisions in the Constitution concerning capital punishment. For instance, the Constitution explicitly refers to the death penalty in the due process clause of the Fifth Amendment. The Fifth Amendment refers explicitly to "capital crimes" and provides that "no person shall be deprived of life . . . without due process of law." Thus, the text of the Constitution only forbids the state from taking the life of a defendant in a capital case without "due process of law."

Notwithstanding that the founders both practiced capital punishment and made explicit provision for it in the Constitution, the modern Supreme

Court has struggled with the concept whether capital punishment is itself "cruel and unusual" and thus prohibited by the very constitutional provision that recognizes it. Indeed, in an extraordinary move, in 1972, the Court actually suspended all executions by the states.[50] Although the Court four years later in *Gregg v. Georgia*,[51] confirmed the constitutionality of certain capital punishment regimes, it has since imposed a welter of conditions on its exercise, none of which can be justified on an original understanding of the Eighth Amendment's "cruel and unusual" clause.

It may be that, judged by modern sensibilities, the death penalty is no longer an acceptable practice. For instance, many states that formerly allowed the death penalty have abolished it. Other states that still allow it have drastically limited the number of crimes to which the death penalty applies.[52] However, "modern sensibilities" about capital punishment have nothing whatever to do with the *constitutional* question whether the death penalty is itself a cruel and unusual punishment prohibited by the Eighth Amendment. The two inquiries ought not be conflated.

The question of modern sensibilities about capital punishment would seem therefore to be a policy question solely for legislatures, not the Supreme Court. So why has the Court struggled with this question? The simple answer is that a number of Justices have been personally appalled by the death penalty and have been willing to exercise the power of their judicial office to restrict, if not eliminate it.[53] They have done so by a number of interpretive dodges, all of which ignore the text and history of the Constitution and require reliance on nonconstitutional values. Equally troubling is the Court's willingness to abandon precedent to accommodate its own shifting moral sentiment.

Atkins v. Virginia,[54] decided in 2002, is an illustrative case. In *Atkins*, a defendant described as "mildly mentally retarded" committed murder associated with an abduction and robbery. He was convicted of all three offenses and sentenced to death by the Commonwealth of Virginia. The question before the Court was whether it was "cruel and unusual" to put mentally retarded persons to death for the capital crimes they commit. Thirteen years previously the same question had come before the Court in *Penry v. Lynaugh*.[55] There, the Court found the practice *constitutional*. However, a majority of the Court in *Atkins* held that the practice was unconstitutional. Thus, in the span of little more than a decade, the Court found that the Eighth Amendment had *changed*.

What was the *Atkins* rationale for this flip-flop? Several decades before *Atkins*, the Court had held that what constitutes cruel and unusual punishment is not just what was considered cruel and unusual when the Bill of Rights was adopted, but cruel and unusual punishment could also be determined by "the evolving standards of decency that mark the progress of a maturing society."[56] This wonderfully high-toned phrase, the evolving standards of decency of a maturing society, cannot be found in the text of our Constitution. Nevertheless, the Court has pursued this evolving standard of decency quest by looking for "objective indicia" of such shifts. *Objective* indicia of a society's view of punishment, in the Court's opinion, could be found in state legislation or in data tracking the actions of sentencing juries.[57]

In *Atkins*, the Court took this extra-constitutional "evolving standard" fiction one step further from the original meaning of the Eighth Amendment. In its quest to discover the "evolving standards of decency" that had not existed thirteen years earlier when the Court decided *Penry*, the *Atkins* majority simply discerned new standards. Since *Penry*, it noted that several states that had allowed the execution of mentally retarded persons had banned the practice. The majority looked approvingly toward "a much broader social and professional consensus" that included professional organizations such as the American Psychological Association, world religions, the "world community" as represented by the European Union, and polling data of American citizens. *This* was the majority's "objective" justification for declaring unconstitutional a practice it had held constitutional thirteen years earlier and which was not explicitly prohibited by any constitutional text.

Even more recently, in *Roper v. Simmons*,[58] the Supreme Court repeated the "evolving standard" theme to further judicially amend the Constitution and limit capital punishment in this country. In *Roper*, the question was whether it was cruel and unusual to execute a person under the age of eighteen, where the defendant was convicted of a murder he committed at the age of seventeen. As in *Atkins*, the Court struck down the practice under the "evolving standards of decency" test. And, similar to *Atkins*, the Court reversed a case decided fifteen years earlier that upheld the constitutionality of executing criminals who were sixteen or seventeen when they committed the capital offense.[59]

The *Roper* majority justified its change not because its decision fifteen years earlier was incorrectly decided, but apparently because the meaning of the Eighth Amendment had changed in the intervening decade and a half. The *Roper* decision represents one of the most frank acknowledgments from the Supreme Court that it has the right, by judicial interpretation, to amend the Constitution. Without blushing, the majority reiterated an earlier proclamation that "the constitution contemplates that in the end *our own judgment* will be brought to bear on the question of the acceptability of the death penalty under the Eighth Amendment."[60]

There is no constitutional justification for this audacious statement. The Constitution does not "contemplate" that five Justices will assert their policy preferences and transform them into constitutional values. The *Roper* decision indicates the degree to which contemporary Justices feel free to amend the Constitution in derogation of the amendment process under the facade of interpreting it.

The *Roper* majority effectively amended the Constitution in part on the basis of a "*national consensus*" it declared was formed because fewer than 50 percent of the states permitting the death penalty prohibit the execution of minors. That is not a misprint. The *Roper* majority concluded that there was a national consensus that execution of minors was a bad policy because a *minority* of states allowing the death penalty banned the execution of minors. Apart from the odd math the *Roper* majority seized upon to forge its "national consensus," the decision seems to suggest that the meaning of our Constitution can transmogrify based upon creative polling of states' practices.[61]

More troubling was the *Roper* Court's reliance on foreign law to find "international consensus" when interpreting our own eighteenth-century Constitution. Citing, for example, the United Nations Convention on the Rights of the Child and human rights citadels such as Iran, Pakistan, and Saudi Arabia, the Court seemed embarrassed that this country stood alone in permitting the juvenile death penalty. The current Court is no longer content with ignoring the intent of those who brought our Constitution into being, but is now willing to look beyond our citizens for affirmation of its policy preferences. It is hard to suggest that the interpretive approach of the *Roper* majority deserves even to be described as a part of the Rorschach school, because it does not appear that the Court is even bothering with the pretense of looking at an inkblot. Perhaps the modern Supreme Court should be characterized as belonging to the "Gallup" school of interpretive philosophy.

If the Eighth Amendment has been judicially amended almost beyond recognition, then the same can be said of the Fourteenth Amendment's due process clause. This provision was famously cited in *Roe v. Wade* as a justification to support abortion rights. More recently, it was urged as a basis for attacking statutory restrictions on gay rights. *Lawrence v. Texas,*[62] decided in 2003, is viewed as a leading vehicle to eliminate all laws restricting homosexual activity. In *Lawrence*, the defendant was prosecuted for engaging in homosexual acts that were prohibited by the Texas sodomy statute. The defendant appealed his conviction on the ground that he had a "liberty interest" to privacy to engage in sexual acts in his own home with a consenting partner. Seventeen years earlier, in *Bowers v. Hardwick*,[63] the Supreme Court had upheld the constitutionality of sodomy laws because such laws offended no explicit constitutional provision.

The *Lawrence* majority, however, disagreed with its earlier *Bowers* decision. Without declaring homosexuality a protected characteristic such as race, or declaring that engaging in homosexual sex was a "fundamental right," the *Lawrence* majority struck down the Texas sodomy statute as violative of the due process clause. Describing due process as a "liberty interest," here is how the *Lawrence* majority presented the modern version of the *Dred Scott* substantive due process: "Liberty protects the person from unwarranted government intrusions into a dwelling or other private places. In our tradition the state is not omnipresent in the home. And there are other spheres of our lives and existence, outside the home, where the State should not be a dominant presence. Freedom extends beyond special bounds. Liberty presumes an autonomy of self that includes freedom of thought, belief, expression, and certain intimate conduct. The instant case involves liberty of the person both in its spatial and more transcendent dimensions."[64] Once again, the Court produced a contrived passage that *might* be considered lyrical were it merely a piece of literature—"*liberty of the person both in its spatial and more transcendent dimensions.*" Unfortunately, the details of that constitutional "principle" provided by the Court were as sparse as was the Court's reliance on the Constitution to justify declaring the Texas statute unconstitutional. One will search in vain for any textual reference in the Constitution protecting "intimate conduct," much less its "spatial and more transcendental dimensions."

Among the more disturbing aspects of *Lawrence* is the fact that the majority strongly hinted that normative community morality, on which every criminal law is based, might not provide a satisfactory justification to the Court: "The issue is whether the majority may use the power of the State to enforce their views on the whole society through operation of the criminal law. '[The Court's] obligation is to define the liberty of all, not to mandate our own moral code.' "[65] Ironically, the Court had difficulty giving deference to criminal laws enacted in the democratic process but had no inkling that, in striking down Texas sodomy law, the Court was, in fact, "enacting *its own* moral code" instead.

Without looking to the constitutional text for guidance on how to decide the case before it, the *Lawrence* majority was persuaded by the views of the European Court of Human Rights, which had apparently affirmed the right of homosexual adults to engage in consensual, same sex "intimate acts." As in *Atkins* and *Roper*, once again, the Supreme Court found "world opinion" in the twenty-first century more relevant than the text of our Constitution. Indeed, the majority scolded the founders for being ignorant of and failing to speak more plainly on the subject of same-sex activities: "Had those who drew and ratified the Due Process Clause of the Fifth Amendment or the Fourteenth Amendment known the components of liberty in its manifold possibilities, they might have been more specific. They did not presume to have this insight. They knew times can blind us to certain truths and later generations can see that laws once thought necessary and proper in fact serve only to oppress. As the Constitution endures, persons in every generation can invoke its principles in their own search for greater freedom."[66] This statement demonstrates a total lack of understanding of constitutional principles and the government that our Constitution created. There is simply no basis for believing that the founders sought to encapsulate in the Constitution answers to all social issues that might arise in the nation over time. The contrary is true. The founders did not need to speak more "specifically" about their views on homosexuality or any other social question of the eighteenth century or the future. That is because they created a Constitution with certain enumerated limitations—largely spelled out in the Bill of Rights—that respected and encouraged a democratic and majoritarian political process by which such social issues could be debated, decided, and redecided over time. The *Lawrence* majority misapprehended the nature of the Constitution and the Court's role as its interpreter. In assuming the Constitution purports to speak to every social issue of the day, the *Lawrence* majority (and all jurists who share its mistaken view of constitutional interpretation) created extra-constitutional doctrines that permit them to serve as a Council of Revision and pass on the wisdom, but not the true constitutionality, of democratically enacted statutes.

Consequences of the Rorschach School of Judicial Philosophy

The ascendancy of an elite, counter-majoritarian judicial oligarchy is not without its practical costs. I think the framers of our Constitution would be baffled, if not horrified, to learn that our courts, not our legislatures, were deciding such fundamental policy questions as abortion rights, gay rights, and many other controversial issues on bases that some would suggest are simply contrived constitutional grounds that have no link to the text of our Constitution. That said, some might ask: So what?

It is axiomatic that when courts signal that they are open for business to *make* social policy, political litigants—especially those who have no hope of achieving their political goals in the democratic process—pay attention. And they should. Resort to the courts is one of the cheapest political campaigns one can wage. Instead of having to convince a majority of the Congress, the president, *and* the constituencies they represent, a "political litigant" need only convince one trial judge, two judges of the Court of Appeals, or five Justices of the Supreme Court. The same is true at the state level where adherents of the Rorschach school of interpretation have also fully infiltrated the bench.

This phenomenon represents nothing short of a usurpation of political power by the judiciary and I believe that it is a dangerous threat to our constitutional framework that, with limited exceptions specifically enumerated in our Bill of Rights, respects the peoples' right of self-governance—to make their laws by the majoritarian political process, namely through the legislature.

One practical effect of judicial oligarchy is its creation of poor public policy. I contend that the judiciary is an institutionally incompetent vehicle for making sound social policy. Because the political branches of government—the executive and legislative branches—are specifically designed to create policy, it is entirely desirable that important public and social policy be made by them rather than the judiciary. These political branches are designed for robust public debate, discussion, and compromise. The judicial branch is not.

When one has a hot political issue, one can gather up like-minded citizens and storm the Congress, the state capitol, or local legislative venues such as a city council. However, by openly participating in the democratic process, one assumes the risk that equally dedicated citizens of opposing views will challenge that effort and that these opponents will prevail. Such is the nature of the majoritarian political process.

By contrast, the judicial process, though public in name, is private in its essence. The public cannot broadly petition a court to urge the court to reach a particular result, and if the public did, the court is ethically obliged to rebuff such importuning. Further, a court must consider issues largely as they are framed by the *litigants* who typically do so only in terms that serve their vested interests—to win that particular case. Moreover, members of the judiciary decide cases in the splendid isolation of our chambers, where we may be inclined to listen only to the echoes of our own voices.[67]

The legislature is free to experiment on policy questions—to try one thing and then another to reach a result satisfactory to the public at large. It is a fluid process. When the legislature makes a mistake in policy, it simply amends or repeals the law. When a court makes a mistake in social policy, and does so on constitutional grounds, its error can persist for generations.

However troubled one may be about this trend, we as a society have become enablers. Political activists on the Left *and* the Right have been guilty of resorting to the courts as a means of circumventing the majoritarian political process. If you lose in Congress or the state legislature, or if you fail to persuade fellow citizens, then "on to the court!" has been the rallying cry and strategy of far too many political activists over the years.

It is the very fact that the modern Supreme Court's judicial philosophy has encouraged the expansion of judicial policy-making into such a broad range of public issues that has, in turn, spawned a corresponding growth in interest group involvement in federal judicial confirmations and state judicial campaigns. Now, as never before, it simply matters who wears a black robe if one's goal is to ensure that one can achieve *political* results in the courts. And people are organizing politically in response to this reality. The recent confirmation battles over Justices Roberts and Alito confirm this reality.

Even at the state level where judges are frequently elected, the politicization of those elections has intensified manyfold. Professor Anthony Champagne of the University of Texas notes the following national trends in judicial races.[68] First, interest groups have had a long history of involvement in judicial selection. Second, in judicial elections, interest groups can and do play important roles in assisting candidates communicate with and mobilize voters. Third, over time, the range of interest groups involved in judicial races has broadened from a small cadre of lawyer and law enforcement groups to embrace those reflecting many different ideological interests. Fourth, more recently, interest groups involved in judicial elections have become interconnected and increasingly national in scope. Fifth, the literature on such interest groups recognizes that they have become involved in judicial campaigns in an attempt to influence courts and they do so for three primary reasons: (A) such groups believe they need to counterbalance the influence of *other* groups; (B) interest groups wish to influence judges to incorporate *their* political views into the law; and (C) they wish to hedge their bets in the event that they fail to persuade the executive and legislative branches to enact their policy preferences. Finally, and most important for my purposes here, Professor Champagne observes that interest groups today "*often draw no distinction between achieving their goals through the courts or the political process.*"

The same can be said about federal judicial confirmation battles: the interest groups formed to support and oppose judicial nominees clearly see the judicial branch as an alternative political forum for achieving their political goals. That is why the personal beliefs of Supreme Court nominees have become so critical. So widespread is the belief—based on fact—that the Courts decide social policy on extra-constitutional grounds that a partisan would be foolish to ignore a particular nominee's views on all of the important social questions of the day.

Apart from questions about the competence of courts to make social policy and their lack of constitutional authority to do so, I believe that the emergence of this broad assertion of judicial power has harmed our nation in another significant way. When a court intervenes in the democratic process and decides a social issue on questionable constitutional grounds, it destroys political accountability and frustrates the "therapeutic" benefits derived from the democratic process. The Constitution contemplates that the legislative branch makes policy. When the legislature makes a poor policy choice, it is accountable to the people for that choice. However, when the courts freely intervene to "correct" these policy choices, who should the people hold accountable—the legislature or the courts? Increasingly, the answer, I believe, is the courts.

I recently heard a radio essay on a dispute roiling in New York.[69] It appears that in the 1920s, the New York City Council banned dancing in bars. No reason was given for this ordinance and perhaps the reasons have become obscured over time. The point is that the ordinance is being enforced and bar owners are ticketed when their patrons are observed "swaying" to music. Consequently, bar owners attempt to prevent dancing and this is met with hostility from their patrons who cannot imagine why they cannot dance in a New York bar. The issue has recently prompted enough attention that a group of New Yorkers decided to challenge the law. Did they petition the City Council to amend or repeal the ordinance? No, they hired a law professor from New York University who filed a suit to overturn the ordinance on the ground that it violates the bar patrons' First Amendment rights. This is a small example, but it fully illustrates one of the distortions in our body politic when courts presume to serve as a Council of Revision and welcome all comers.

I have suggested that an expansive judicial policy-making role also harms the "therapeutic" aspects of majoritarian politics. In order to illustrate the different ways that public policy is resolved in the judiciary as opposed to the majoritarian political process, I would like to contrast the controversy over the so-called right to assisted suicide with the right to abortion. More specifically, I will consider the 1998 voter referendum in Michigan on the assisted suicide question.

By way of background, you need to understand that the liberty interest that the United States Supreme Court found to support the right to abortion is the same constitutional interest proponents asserted in support of the claimed "right" to assisted suicide. However, unlike the abortion question that the United States Supreme Court preemptively decided in *Roe v. Wade*, that Court unanimously declined to extend that same constitutional protection to the right to die.[70] That decision left the citizens of the fifty states free to decide for themselves what to do about the assisted suicide question.[71]

It is clear from the public debate on the right to die that there are compelling and passionately held beliefs on both sides of this difficult moral and social issue. Because of the odd "advocacy" of Dr. Jack Kevorkian, the debate over assisted suicide was particularly intense in Michigan. The Michigan Supreme Court had earlier declined to hold unconstitutional a statute imposing criminal penalties on one who participates in an assisted suicide.[72] The matter was eventually placed before Michigan voters in 1998 as a ballot proposal that would have legalized assisted suicide. This proposal, Proposal B, was rejected by the citizens of Michigan by a margin of 71 percent to 29 percent.

Since the failure of Proposal B almost ten years ago, Michigan has not had the kind of divisive public turmoil on the question of assisted suicide that has marked the abortion question since *Roe v. Wade* was decided in 1973. I submit that the simplest explanation for this is because, with Proposal B, all Michigan voters were able to participate in the democratic process and express their views on what was, without question, a contentious political issue. This is precisely how the political, majoritarian process works. It is responsive to the will of the people and capable of innovation. Surely, the advocates of assisted suicide were disappointed, but their frustration could lie only with their failure to persuade a majority of their fellow citizens. If, on the other hand, our courts had decided that there was a *constitutional* right to die, either in the Michigan or the federal Constitution, the public would have been excluded from participating in the decision-making process. If the issue had been elevated to constitutional status, the matter would have been forever foreclosed from further public debate and experimentation, precluding alternate ways of accommodating conflicting views on the subject.

Consider also the politically contentious issue of gay marriage. In November 2003, the Supreme Judicial Court of Massachusetts ruled that it was unconstitutional under the Massachusetts state constitution—a document drafted by John Adams in 1780—to prohibit same-sex marriages.[73] Holding that the restriction of marriage to heterosexuals violated due process and equal protection guarantees, the court *ordered* the Massachusetts legislature to respond within 180 days and remedy the problem.

The *nation's* response to that decision has been swift and decisive. The next year, 2004, voters in thirteen states—Arkansas, Georgia, Kentucky, Michigan, Mississippi, Montana, North Dakota, Ohio, Oklahoma, Oregon, Louisiana, Missouri, and Utah—amended their state constitutions to prohibit same-sex marriages, and did so by decisive, landslide margins.[74] In 2005, the people of Kansas and Texas followed suit, as did voters of Idaho, Wisconsin, South Carolina, South Dakota, Tennessee, Colorado, Virginia, and Alabama in 2006. Combine these states with three states that had already amended their constitutions prior to the Massachusetts decision, Alaska (1998), Nebraska (2000), and Nevada (2002), and a total of twenty-six states have acted in less than a decade to limit the definition of marriage in their constitutions. More significantly, twenty-three states ostensibly reacted *against* the Massachusetts decision.

When the people have plebiscite tools, such as initiatives and referenda, the majoritarian process is available to rectify a rogue judicial act.[75] At the national level, where such tools do not exist, rogue action by the Supreme Court cannot easily be therapeutically resolved in the democratic process.

As nasty and brutish as politics can be, the majoritarian political process has a potentially healing value for our society that cannot be matched by judicial edict. Those who wear black robes should be more mindful of this fact when interpreting the Constitution.

Conclusion

Having noted the flaws and dangers of the Rorschach school of interpretation, I submit that the judicial traditionalist approach is a sensible alternative, as the approach is consistent with the structure and history of our Constitution. The Constitution squarely places in the legislative branch all law-making authority. Neither the text of the Constitution nor any of the history surrounding its drafting or ratification supports the theory that anyone in 1789 advocated that judges, particularly the Supreme Court, had authority to make law, much less amend the terms of the Constitution. Judges were believed to be the "expositors" or interpreters of the laws enacted by the law-maker. Certainly, dissenting voices have surfaced in our history, for example, in *Calder v. Bull*. However, the judiciary was never intended to act as a Council of Revision as evidenced by the fact that the delegates of the Constitutional Convention raised, debated, and rejected that very proposal. Also, the basic, unremarkable fact that Article V provides an amendment process undermines the claim that judges are entitled to assume that role.

A jurist ought to be primarily constrained from imposing his views on the Constitution by the text of the Constitution itself. By interpreting the text as the text was understood by those who placed it in the Constitution, a jurist cannot easily expand or contract the policy choices expressed in the Constitution. A judicial traditionalist might at times err in his interpretation, but he is unlikely to stray as far as his Rorschach counterpart into the quicksand of faux, standardless constitutional doctrines such as the "evolving standards" fiction of *Atkins* and *Roper*.

The Supreme Court cases discussed in this chapter demonstrate how the modern Court often functions as an elite, counter-majoritarian oligarchy guided by its own extra-constitutional themes. When the Court behaves this way, it invariably undermines the democratic process and imposes these extra-constitutional themes on our American society, signifying that the Court, not the democratic process, will determine the social policy of this country. So prevalent now is the view that the Court has such powers of general "revision" that the Court's opinions now freely acknowledge that it has the authority to strike down statutes that offend no provision of the Constitution. Our Constitution, however, is no theme park.

Chapter Ten
Judicial Power and Democracy: A Machiavellian View

Rogers M. Smith

The Puzzle of Democratization and "Juristocracy"

Throughout most of globe during the past six decades, two striking and arguably contradictory trends are visible. I argue here that Machiavelli's analysis of the political dynamics of republics may help us to explain and evaluate these developments. The first trend is the spread of democracy. Depending on the definitions used, various datasets show that the percentage of the world's nations that were democratic rose from less than 40 percent at the end of World War II to between 50 percent and 70 percent by the end of the twentieth century, representing between 76 and 117 countries and much of the world's population.[1] And many countries that are not credibly democratic nonetheless claim to be so, affirming the prestige of democratic ideals, if not practices. The second trend is the rise of courts with the power to invalidate national legislation. In the midst of World War II, only the United States and Norway had judiciaries with that power. Today, courts in more than 80 nations do, even though those courts vary greatly in other ways. Scholars are increasingly calling this development "juristocracy."[2]

Although the United States was in the historical vanguard of these trends, that status does not mean that it has been unaffected by them. The 1965 Voting Rights Act and its amendments, along with the Twenty-fourth (poll tax) Amendment to the Constitution, made the franchise a reality for most nonwhite Americans for the first time since Reconstruction, and the Twenty-sixth (eighteen-year-old vote) Amendment gave the nation's younger citizen-soldiers and their peers the vote for the first time ever. These developments made the United States much more truly a democracy than it had ever been. In the same period, the Warren Court began striking down national and state laws at a rate that exceeded even that of the anti-regulatory "*Lochner*" era. The ensuing Burger and Rehnquist Courts largely sustained and sometimes exceeded those levels of judicial activism, so that post–World War II Supreme Courts have collectively produced both the highest rates and the greatest number of invalidations of national, state, and local laws in American history.[3]

How are we to understand this global, and American, pattern of expanding democracy accompanied by expanding judicial power? Many argue, as Ronald Dworkin has long done, that they are normatively linked, with constitutional courts providing the necessary protections for basic liberties that put the "liberal" in modern liberal democracies.[4] On such views, a "democracy with strong judicial power is unquestionably a stronger democracy, since it is a polity where the rights of citizens are better protected."[5] Whether or not that is so, my concern here is with how the two developments are politically linked. It is not immediately obvious why a political era that saw the adoption of democratic institutions and more expansive suffrage in many nations around the globe, old and new, should simultaneously see increased power for often unelected judges to overturn the measures adopted by the representatives of those newly broadened and empowered democratic electorates.

There are many possible explanations, including the sheer influence of the example of the United States (and perhaps Norway). Contemporary commentators are generating a range of explanatory accounts for both democratization and juristocracy, more than I can analyze here, though I draw on them. But I suggest that a highly illuminating theoretical framework for understanding these patterns derives from Machiavelli's arguments (building on analyses going back to Aristotle) concerning the inherent tensions between elites and masses in republics. Those arguments have echoed down into modern scholarship, where public opinion research, for example, regularly distinguishes between elites and masses—but with less sense of these as elements of the community that are at a deep level always in contestation with each other.[6]

Political scientists also tend to portray delegation of authority to courts as a strategy some elites may adopt in various circumstances to further their goals against rival elites.[7] Such elite contests, including efforts to win popular support against rivals, were certainly familiar to Machiavelli. As Nathan Tarcov points out in this volume, in *The Prince* Machiavelli suggests that in France, kings used a court, the parlement, to protect the people against the nobility, so that the kings did not themselves have to bear the costs of curbing the often insolent lords. In so doing, I would add, kings also used courts to make the nobility seem comparatively threatening and the monarchy comparatively benign to the people. I do not doubt that similar attempts by some elites to use courts to curry popular favor against other elites form a large part of the story of the rise of judicial power in many modern locales.

But most modern scholars, and particularly those writing in an American context, have not stressed as strongly as Machiavelli did the inescapable conflicts between elites and masses, which he saw as not only potentially threatening, but also potentially strengthening for the very survival of popular governance. Perhaps the closest approximations have come in arguments that democracies have often arisen as a means of ameliorating elite-mass clashes over economic distributions, conflicts that are certainly pertinent to the rise of judicial power as well.[8] But few of those writers have explored the linkages between elite-mass contestation and the enhancement of judicial authority. Among contemporary public law scholars, Ran Hirschl comes closest to suggesting the sort of hypothesis advanced here, and my argument can be seen as advancing a more historical and Machiavellian foundation for some of his key claims.[9]

In brief, Machiavelli suggests that elites will tolerate enhanced popular power only with institutional arrangements that make them feel that they can maintain disproportionate leverage and ensure that their interests—economic, political, cultural, and social—are effectively hegemonic, which is not to say uncontested.[10] The mass of people are content with institutional arrangements that seem likely to permit them to pursue their lives unmolested and relatively peacefully, whether or not they have any special voice in or power over those arrangements. Courts that have formal authority to invalidate legislation, but that are dependent on others to enforce their rulings, have emerged as one sustainable way to reassure both elites and masses and thereby render the tensions between them manageable, even productive—though neither these nor any other institutions can make those tensions disappear.[11] Strains between elites and masses persist in ways that, in the twenty-first century, continue to fuel the rise of greater judicial power in an era of heightened democracy in many places around the world, including the United States. Should this situation be seen as a defeat for the highest democratic aspirations, or as a viable way of perpetuating modern constitutional republics despite their inherent tensions? I suggest the answer is both.

A Machiavellian Hypothesis

Before elaborating that answer, let me acknowledge that thinkers have ana-
lyzed politics in terms of clashes between elites and masses, the few and the
many, since antiquity. There is still much to be learned from, especially,
Aristotle's arguments that the competing groups are usually best conceived
in terms of the claims of wealth versus the claims of free birth, with merit
sometimes hanging in the balance; and that in most circumstances the constitutional task is to find ways to mix these groups, their values and interests,
in stable combinations that are perceived as embodying the rule of law.[12]
But Machiavelli's reflections on the dynamics of republics have considerable
claim to be the most perceptive of those who wrote in the dawn of modern
republicanism, when foundational elements contributing to the survival or
demise of republics were, arguably, particularly visible.

In Machiavelli's political sociology, the tensions between the *grandi*
and the *popolo* were fundamental to the enterprise of republican governance, and indeed all governance. In the *Prince*, Machiavelli argued that
"in every city these two opposite parties are to be found, arising from the
desire of the populace to avoid the oppression of the great, and the desire
of the great to command and oppress the people."[13] Similarly, in the *Discourses* he maintained that in "every republic there are two parties, that of
the nobles and that of the people," and he contended again that "the first
have a great desire to dominate, whilst the latter have only the wish not to
be dominated, and consequently a greater desire to live in the enjoyment
of liberty." Yet Machiavelli also insisted that "all the laws that are favorable
to liberty result from the opposition of these parties to each other."[14] In his
view, elites seek predominance in every sphere of life, certainly in wealth,
but also in political power, social status, and all else. Those desires can stir
in the masses of people "fear to lose" and also "the wish to revenge themselves" on oppressive elites.[15] But channeled via proper institutions, the
clashing passions of elites and masses can give rise to laws that aid "public
liberty" for all.[16] Machiavelli's examples of such channeling in France and
Venice indicate that the powerful may accept being bound by laws enforced
by tribunals that provide security to the people, so long as elites are made
to feel relatively assured of their predominance and persuaded to concede
that to seek still more power is to risk popular uprisings.[17] Through these
same sorts of institutions, the populace can be made to feel relatively safe
from direct insolence and severe deprivation, and then they do not need

to be persuaded to concede anything—for such security is all that most people ask.

As that asymmetry indicates, for Machiavelli the most sustainable balance of elite and popular power is not one in which both parties are equal. Achieving even a measure of stability requires that the elites who ardently seek predominance actually have it, though not in overtly harsh forms. They will not be content otherwise—whereas most people wish only to have sufficient power to prevent abuses, and they are in any case incapable of acquiring or wielding dominant power without good leadership (which means they do not directly wield power at all).[18] Hence most "are easily satisfied by institutions and laws that confirm at the same time the general security of the people and the power of the prince" or other *grandi*. Machiavelli notes in fact that the *popolo* often choose patricians to govern them, so long as they feel confident that they will act in their interests, unlike the *grandi*, who design to control any institution to which they have access.[19] So, as John McCormick has noted, if "the *grandi* are to live and republics are to endure, the former must be granted a prominent place in the latter lest the *grandi* perpetrate oligarchic or princely coups."[20]

It follows that the more direct political power that the people gain, the more Machiavelli's elites will aim to be assured of their hegemonic status via other means; and possessing superior resources, they are likely to find ways to achieve them. This suggests a broader hypothesis than I can pursue here: that as democratization has spread in the last two centuries, we should expect elites to have repeatedly sought new ways to secure their hegemony, ways that may often include empowering courts, but that are by no means confined to them. McCormick believes these efforts are likely to have been and to remain so ubiquitous that he questions the desirability of modern democratic systems providing formally equal rights to all, instead of providing different systems of institutional representation to elites and masses. He suggests that "especially with the hindsight provided by Western history since Machiavelli's day," we might well decide that "the establishment of a single, sociologically anonymous constitutional framework" often only allows "the *grandi* to overwhelm the people in a fairly unchallenged fashion."[21] He believes that modern democracies might be well served by having some class-specific institutions, particularly some form of "Tribunate Assembly" confined to representatives of the nonwealthy.[22]

Though I have doubts about the wisdom of that recommendation, McCormick's argument should make democrats hesitant simply to celebrate the fact that most of the constitutional democracies that have proliferated since World War II have had, by and large, "sociologically anonymous" frameworks, at least from a class standpoint. Formally, political offices are equally open to all regardless of wealth. But in practice, the proliferation of courts with powers to invalidate laws may be part of the growth of nominally "anonymous," effectively elite-dominated institutions within regimes that are in other ways more genuinely democratic than ever before. If we believe that modern elites of various sorts continue to seek disproportionate power and that they experience the post–World War II spread of democracy as in some ways threatening to this goal, it is reasonable to suggest that the growth of judicial power has often been a means to safeguard their preeminence and reconcile them to further democratization in other respects. Such judicial power, unaccompanied by strong enforcement measures and promising the rule of law, also appears to have proven generally acceptable to modern democratic mass electorates. This literally "global" explanation can only be part of the story of modern judicial empowerment, since movements toward democratization and juristocracy have not occurred identically, equally, or simultaneously in every nation. But at a deep level, I suspect that is a significant part of what has been occurring for the last half century around the world.

If so, it would be no surprise to America's founders. The *Federalist Papers* famously identified the danger of "majority faction" as the greatest threat to "popular government," and they applauded an unelected federal judiciary with life tenure, armed with the power to invalidate unconstitutional laws, as a bulwark of "the Constitution and the rights of individuals" whenever "the major voice of the community" might rashly instigate "legislative invasions" of those legal guarantees.[23] There can be little doubt that Alexander Hamilton and many of the founding generation's elites, especially the more nationally minded, found it easier to embrace the cause of republican government in the United States because they believed that the increased power of the people would be joined with, and *checked* by, an enhancement of judicial power. Many were especially concerned to preserve the property rights of wealthy elites and, perhaps less transparently, the often unconventional religious views of educated elites.[24] They gained confidence from the expectation that the federal judiciary would be staffed by those "few men" with "sufficient skill in the laws" to be credible as judges, men who would almost surely be drawn from the new nation's most affluent and educated classes.[25]

Yet other leading Americans always objected to such judicial power. In practice extensive, overt judicial invalidations of state and national laws did not become common until the *Lochner* era from 1905 through 1936, and even then not as common as in our own time. Nor was the rest of the world quick to follow suit in establishing strong judiciaries. Again, most of the expansions of judicial power have come in the last half century, especially the last quarter-century. Those facts do not necessarily discredit the Machiavellian hypothesis I am advancing here, since if the United States did not display so much judicial power in the first phases of its development as it does now, neither was it so democratic then—and most of the rest of the world was even less so. But it does indicate that we need at least some evidence to judge whether there is a *prima facie* case that modern judicial empowerment has been in part an elite response to modern democratization, rather than either unrelated to or, conversely, the fulfillment of democracy, as it is widely conceived to be today.

Some Evidence

The case is perhaps easiest to make internationally. An important 1995 collection edited by Neal Tate and Torbjörn Vallinder, which included essays on the United States, the United Kingdom, Canada, Australia, France, Germany, Italy, Sweden, the Netherlands, Malta, Israel, Russia, the Philippines, and Namibia, served as the basis for Tate's essay summarizing the factors leading to the "global expansion of judicial power."[26] He contended that judicial empowerment was much more likely in systems that were democratic; had separated powers; weak parties or fragile coalitions producing policy deadlocks that judiciaries might resolve; interest groups and a political opposition that sought judicial rulings favoring their goals, and/or a majority coalition that chose to delegate difficult or unpopular decisions to the judiciary; and a rights-oriented political culture that made judicial remedies palatable. He also stressed that judges had significant agency in securing judicial power. They had to decide themselves to seize the opportunities for power that such conditions provided, by making decisions overruling the policies of other officials.[27]

In this list of facilitating conditions, all illustrated by one or more of the globe-spanning examples included in the volume, the focus is overwhelming on decisions of governing, opposition, or advocacy group *elites*—political leaders deadlocked in weak or fragile coalitions who turn to courts, or elites beset by policy issues that are politically costly to resolve who turn to courts, or political actors opportunistically seeking victories in a new venue when rival elites defeat them in legislatures or referenda. There is very little evidence from any part of the world indicating that it has sometimes been democratic movements, rather than political elites, who have taken the lead in enabling judicial elites to make important governing decisions. The views of mass electorates do play a limited role in Tate's analytical overview, when he stresses that dictators are not likely to allow powerful, independent courts, but that democratic peoples will do so when they believe in rights and respect judicial institutions.[28] Still, it is political elites of various sorts who extend chances to be major political actors to judges, and it is judges themselves who decide whether to embrace those chances.

But if judicial power appears in these studies to be primarily an elite creation, those origins do not necessarily mean that judicial empowerment is designed to achieve dominance over the populace. Again, Tate's emphasis, and that of most of his contributors, is on elites seeking to gain advantages against rival elites, not against the mass public. Still, Tate recognizes that political elites may sometimes seek to have more institutionally sheltered judges make decisions that would cost the elites popular support. That point does suggest that elites may often see judicial power as a way to protect interests and values that they see as threatened by the electorates in their democratized political systems. The same can be said of other recent comparative analyses of judicial power that are, on the whole, sympathetic to the judicializing trends they examine.[29]

Ran Hirschl has gone further. Based on extensive empirical study of four modern democracies, three long established (Canada, New Zealand, Israel) and one recent (South Africa), he explains judicial power as "a form of self-interested *hegemonic preservation*." He contends that "political, economic, and legal power-holders . . . either initiate or refrain from blocking" such empowerment because they "assume that their position (absolute or relative) would be improved under a juristocracy." How are their positions improved? Hirschl suggests that "threatened political elites . . . seek to preserve or enhance their political hegemony by insulating policy making in general, and their policy preferences in particular, from the vicissitudes of democratic politics while they profess support for democracy." He adds that "economic elites" seek judicial protection of constitutional rights that promote "a free-market, business-friendly agenda," while judicial elites seek to enhance their influence and reputation, and they often also share neo-liberal economic values. Consonant with the Machiavellian hypothesis advanced here, Hirschl maintains that even as elites prominently endorse "popular decision-making mechanisms" in "formal democratic political processes," they often shift power to "semiautonomous professional policy-making bodies" of various kinds, minimizing "the potential threat to their hegemony."[30]

In explaining why the growth of judicial power has come when it has around the globe, Hirschl stresses international economic pressures to adopt "neo-liberal," business-facilitating and property-protecting policies, reinforced by the desires of many national economic elites to have their property rights upheld. Especially since the fall of Communism, actors serving these economic interests have been major contributors to judicial empowerment in many locales.[31] Hirschl also notes that the rise in recent decades of "globalized, non-U.S. centered judicial discourse" has probably helped generate judicial elites inclined to take advantage of the opportunities to enhance their influence that their political systems may afford them.[32] The timing of increases in judicial power in particular locales is thus in part a function of the aims and activities of three sets of elites—political, economic, and judicial—in responding to international pressures, as well as problems of paralysis and popular approval that their domestic systems generate.

Yet in defining a master frame for the rise of "juristocracy," Hirschl ultimately calls attention to various forms of democratization that have occurred in recent decades, including expanded suffrages, the decline of various other forms of class, gender, race, ethnic, and religious exclusion or subordination in public institutions, and heightened movements for effective representation. He therefore sees "the current global trend toward judicial empowerment" as "part of a broader process whereby self-interested political and economic elites, while they profess support for democracy . . . attempt to insulate policy-making from the vagaries of democratic politics."[33] Powerful judiciaries are at bottom not partners of modern democracy, but efforts by elites to retain hegemony within them, as a Machiavellian analysis would lead us to expect. When we consider that Machiavelli perceived such dynamics at work at the origins of modern republicanism, and that similar dynamics were visible when some American founders first called for courts to be empowered to invalidate democratically enacted legislation, it may seem reasonable to conclude that Hirschl is broadly right in seeing the growth of judicial power chiefly as a reaction against and a check on democratization that preserves the predominance of elites, rather than as a constitutive component of such democratization.

Juristocracy as Democracy?

We cannot, however, reach that conclusion so quickly or unequivocally. For many students of modern American constitutional development in particular, this political explanation of judicial empowerment as a counter to democratization seems misguided (whatever they think of "juristocracy" normatively). Perhaps at the time of *Marbury v. Madison*, judicial review may have been in part an effort by John Marshall and other elites to check feared excesses of Jeffersonian democracy, or at least part of an effort by the unelected court to resolve conflicts among elites in accordance with property-oriented Hamiltonian principles.[34] Perhaps in the *Lochner* era, judges may have served conservative economic and political interests by striking down laws passed by legislatures dominated by different versions of "progressivism."[35] But since World War II, American judicial activism has often occurred on behalf of racial and religious minorities, urban voters, persons accused of crimes, women seeking reproductive autonomy, resident aliens, non-English speakers, the disabled, gays and lesbians, and more. Many of these groups do not look like elites engaged in "hegemonic self-preservation." In a study of Britain, Canada, and India as well as the United States, Charles R. Epp has argued instead that it has been the democratization of access to the courts—the expansion of financial and legal resources for ordinary citizens and grassroots organizations and advocacy groups, accompanied by cultural climates favorable to rights—that has made these legal victories possible. Judicial empowerment to protect rights has in his view grown "primarily out of pressure from below, not leadership from above."[36]

In a 2005 review essay evaluating five recent books, some shaped by his own arguments, Mark Graber contends that a related "new paradigm for thinking about judicial power" has now "fully formed." It holds that judicial power "is democratically as well as politically constructed."[37] But by "democratically" constructed, Graber, like Tate and his collaborators, chiefly means that "judicial activism is sponsored by elected officials," rather than by grassroots litigants. Without disputing the significance of democratized access to the courts, he does not share Epp's optimism that if rights advocates have sufficient resources, they can win effective decisions, at least in precedent-regarding judicial systems.[38] Graber notes that despite real democratization, resources to litigate remain highly unequal; and he also stresses that judges can only provide litigators with meaningful victories if other governing officials permit them to do so. Modern constitutional systems generally "contain mechanisms that enable national legislative overrides of judicial decisions." These mechanisms are "rarely invoked" only because legislators so often find judicial empowerment advantageous.

Still, to Graber these circumstances suggest that contrary to Hirschl, "juristocracy is a form of, rather than an alternative to, democracy," the result of "a democratic choice." He insists that the "crucial democratic point is judicial review rarely pits the people against the courts." Judicial power is instead involved in contests between those who want courts to decide certain issues and those who want other institutions to decide those issues, with proponents of all positions themselves possessing elite status, but with most if not all proponents also able to claim some democratic support. Graber recognizes that democratization-with-judicial-empowerment may well be a form of democracy that aids the interests of some portions of a democratic society far more than others. But for him, this is not fundamentally a choice between elite governance and democracy. It is a choice among types of elite-led democratic institutions and the particular values and interests they should advance.[39]

The Machiavellian perspective I have sketched here counsels some skepticism toward the claims of Epp, Graber, and others for the ultimately democratic character of the politics of modern judicial empowerment, though it does not require their outright rejection. There is, after all, much common ground between their arguments and Hirschl's account, as well as other more Machiavellian views. These scholars all agree that many modern polities have democratized in ways that have generated pressures for policy changes that affect all governing institutions, including courts. They all also believe that less powerful and wealthy groups are more often able to litigate than in the past, out of a combination of their increased resources and heightened judicial receptivity, and that many other government officials have come to tolerate and sometimes actively assist various forms of judicial activism, including decisions aiding long oppressed groups. The remaining debate centers on whether we should perceive this elite acquiescence and abetting as primarily representing "democratic choices" or elite "hegemonic self-preservation."

Identifying evidence that can decide this question is difficult. From a Machiavellian viewpoint, elites can be expected to make some concessions to popular wishes to still mass anxieties, but not any that threaten the elites' core interests in maintaining their predominant power, wealth, and status. Masses can be expected to accept de facto elite governance so long as they are not being materially oppressed or overtly insulted. But it is not easy to discern what constitute concrete, objective threats to these core interests in specific contexts—how extensive must inequalities in wealth, power, and social status be for elites to feel sufficiently dominant? How severe must those gaps between elites and masses be before populaces feel oppressed or simply insulted? And as those questions indicate, what counts most in Machiavelli's politics is whether elites or masses subjectively *perceive* their interests to be threatened. When that will occur is even harder to know, because both camps are capable of self-destructive errors and impulses and of being misled.[40] And elites, at least, may mislead others: if Machiavelli and Hirschl are right, elites may profess democratic goals, such as providing formally equal political rights to all citizens regardless of race, while actually being driven by hegemonic concerns, such as discrediting socialist critiques of American capitalism in order to strengthen that system of economic privilege.[41] In any case, multiple motives may be at work in the coalitions that support stronger judiciaries, and even in the psyches of individual actors. Proving what has really driven the politics of judicial empowerment in an age of democratization is thus difficult, if not impossible.

Machiavellians might try to claim an advantage in the fact that, as noted earlier, most analysts of the rise of judicial power portray it as a means by which some elites gain advantages against other elites. Writers like Tate, Guarnieri and Pederzoli, Sweet, Hirschl, Whittington, and Graber himself all note that courts benefit when dominant coalitions are so fractious or cross-pressured that leaders prefer not to resolve controversial issues through overt legislative action, or when national leaders wish to see federalism issues resolved in their favor without having to legislate on each one, or when the judiciary can provide either technical or moral legitimacy to those elites' preferred positions, among other circumstances.[42] But again, even if it is always true that judicial elites gain additional power with the aid of other elites who are serving their strategic interests, that pattern shows at best that Machiavelli's contention that masses need leaders is correct. It does not show that elites are serving their own interests at the expense of the people as a whole.

We can, however, gain somewhat more purchase on the question of how democratic the rise of judicial power has been by looking at both the processes and the results of such empowerment. In regard to process, again there is little evidence that judicial authority has increased as the result of democratic demands. Though in many locales democratic majorities have appeared content that elites have assigned great decision-making authority to judges, it is elites that have initiated and done the assigning.

And in regard to results, though the empirical evidence remains fraught with difficulties, there is considerable agreement among recent writers that activist judiciaries have increased protections for "negative liberties" such as freedom of expression and religious conscience and rights of privacy, as well as due process rights of accused persons, but modern courts have rarely done much to address severe economic inequalities.[43] In a recent survey of pertinent research, Lawrence Baum concluded that although it is difficult to assess the comparative beneficiaries of legislative, executive, and judicial policies, the Warren Court years of prominent judicial aid to the less powerful must be seen as an aberration. Over time the U.S. Supreme Court has not consistently favored "the interests of disadvantaged groups." Baum observes that in light of "the paths of recruitment to the Court and the social and political forces around it," this pattern is "not surprising."[44]

Graber himself calls attention to the fact that even the post-1937 "Roosevelt Court" that pioneered judicial support for economic regulation and minority rights "supported labor only when statutory language clearly warranted that result."[45] We might add that, as Elizabeth Bussiere has detailed, even the Warren Court did not extend its solicitude for the long oppressed to strong support for the constitutional claims of the poor.[46] And Graber, again, suggests that the activist Rehnquist Court might be understood, with Hirschl, "as behaving consistently with the global tendency of justices to engage in neoliberal" economic decisions that eschew intervention on behalf of the poor and powerless.[47] Even those conservative justices such as Antonin Scalia who contend that judicial "activism" undermines democracy (even when it aids the unemployed) often write on behalf of heightened judicial protection of property rights.[48] If McCormick is right to suggest that Machiavelli's elites may be most concerned with "the acquisition and preservation of wealth," even more than "glory and honor," judicial empowerment does not seem to have threatened the "hegemonic preservation" of modern elites' core economic interests, at least.[49] Instead, increased judicial authority may well have enhanced protection of those interests.

The lessons of the results that courts have provided are decidedly more mixed if we turn from economic rulings to cases involving the rights of racial, ethnic, and cultural minorities; women; disfranchised voters; and accused persons and general rights of privacy, where we can find in many countries rulings that appear to challenge more than to serve elite interests. Still, if we take Machiavelli at his word and assume that elites especially seek to gain and preserve political power, to "dominate" the masses, then even in these cases, proponents of Machiavellian interpretations can claim at least partial victory. Whatever their content, decisions made by courts are, after all, decisions made by tiny groups of elites, not by democratic populaces acting directly through electoral initiatives, referenda, or votes in mass assemblies. Even if they further some features of modern democratization by expanding the rights of previously oppressed or excluded groups, judicial decisions still at bottom represent elite control of how far such rights are extended to all. As Jeremy Waldron puts it, political actors resort to judicial review "when they want greater weight for their opinions than electoral politics would give them."[50] And many observers believe that even rulings that have inarguably had democratizing results have done more to entrench "progressive elite" cultural values, such as freedom for expression and personal privacy, than to threaten any core elite interests.[51]

It is nonetheless true that these decisions have resulted in part from an important democratization process, as places on judicial benches have been opened up to a wider demographic range than ever before in many countries. Yet the conditions of access remain highly constraining: around the globe, judges still tend to be disproportionately educated and affluent, people who are longtime members of the *grandi* by the time they occupy the highest judicial seats, if not by origin.[52] If we look at the results in terms of elite interests in sustaining economic privileges and elite predominance in powerful institutions, there seems to be a stronger case for viewing judicial empowerment as a check on modern democratization than as its partner.

The Perspective of the People

Even so, such a conclusion remains at best premature. Before deciding that the rise of judicial power has primarily served modern *grandi*, we should attend more closely to the fact that in Machiavelli's political sociology, the mass of people have different interests than elites. The fact that the few may have their economic and power predominance bolstered by "juristocracy" does not necessarily mean that the many have had their hopes and dreams thwarted. Most people, again, generally do not desire to hold or exercise power directly. They are not even obsessed with getting rich. They simply wish for governing arrangements that produce results that they do not find materially oppressive or stigmatizing. They can live contentedly with a considerable measure of elite hegemony so long as they feel secure that they can meet their material needs and pursue their other interests unmolested.

There is a good deal of empirical evidence to suggest that in the United

States and most other modern constitutional democracies, that is by and large what they get from courts, or at least what they perceive themselves as getting. In the United States, scholars have over time found variations in levels of attentiveness to the Supreme Court and in general approval of it as an institution.[53] Most research indicates, however, that the public supports the Court more when it is making decisions that correspond to the ideological preferences of most citizens, and less when it is not.[54] It matters little whether the Court is seen as exercising political power, so long as it is doing it in substantively popular ways. Even one of the most politically consequential decisions in history, *Bush v. Gore*, did little to diminish the Court's legitimacy in most eyes, since half the country approved the result and many of the rest were glad to get the controversy over—though when framed as an effort to end the election with Bush as the victor, the decision did, predictably, make ardent Gore supporters angry with the Court.[55]

In light of such findings in a range of public opinion research, Terri Peretti concluded in 1999 that mass "support for and obedience to the Court appears in the end to be little different from that concerning other political institutions." The Court "will receive public support or, more accurately, will not arouse or anger the public so that noncompliance or sanctions against the Court become a threat" if there is "political agreement with the policy decisions of the Court among the public"; some elite approval and limited elite condemnation; and a bit of judicial "restraint" in producing frequent, blatant political decisions.[56] Surveys in other countries similarly suggest that popular support for high courts depends over time on agreement with their decisions, and that conversely, judges in countries with comparatively little popular trust in courts are less activist than those in nations where courts are held in higher popular esteem.[57]

These accounts of the relationship of judicial activism to popular opinion are far from definitive, and they do provide some evidence that people may disapprove even of decisions whose results they favor, if they appear too blatantly partisan. But if it is true, as these analyses suggest, that courts generally do not diverge any further from dominant public opinion than most elected officials, even when judges are being "activist"; that support for courts drops when they do diverge from popular preferences; and that courts then tend to return to more popular paths, then it is likely that the masses in today's constitutional democracies do not generally perceive themselves to be oppressed by powerful courts. Some scholars add that courts can weather occasional unpopular decisions because they benefit from "highly effective legitimizing symbols," including magisterial surroundings, impressive robes, and resounding promises to provide the rule of law with equal justice for all.[58] If this is so, it suggests that judicial decisions favoring elite interests usually come with packaging that avoids the air of insult and insolence that elite domination can otherwise have. And so if Machiavelli's political sociology still holds, if modern *popolo*, like their Renaissance predecessors in the Italian republics, are content with governance that does not appear to violate their preferences greatly or frequently and that does not convey contempt toward the masses, then the level of elite predominance provided by modern democratization-with-judicial-empowerment may be fundamentally satisfactory to them. The fact that denunciations of "activist" judges have come from elites contending for power far more than any grassroots, anti-judicial movements suggests as much.

Thus on a Machiavellian analysis, even if judicial empowerment has emerged in the modern world partly as a means through which elites have preserved their dominance in the fact of many forms of democratization, that does not mean that modern populaces are being denied the political roles and the policy results that most people wish to have in their constitutional democracies. The rise of judicial power can be due to *both* elite "hegemonic preservation" and what can reasonably be called "democratic choice," for both parties are getting much of what they most want.

Living in Machiavelli's Material World

The notion that the rise of judicial power may advance the goals of both modern elites and mass publics may seem reassuring. Yet I am not entirely comfortable with it, and I suspect relatively few contemporary academics will be either. Though we are ourselves intellectual elites, most of us are neither wealthy nor powerful, and we tend to hope for more from modern constitutional democracies than relatively nonoppressive, though highly unequal, elite predominance. Many of us believe, more than Machiavelli did, that more vigorous forms of democratic self-governance are desirable and attainable. It is also possible that modern mass publics, who are in many nations more educated and affluent than in the past and more deeply socialized into democratic ideals and practices, may also not be so content with the limited forms of popular power that Machiavelli thought satisfactory to the peoples of his day—though it is not easy to find empirical evidence for that proposition. In that case modern democracies may be better positioned to achieve willing and able democratic decision-making than current arrangements as yet provide. Finally, still more hopefully but perhaps more plausibly, it may be that many of today's political and economic elites have come to embrace democratic values far more genuinely and deeply than those in Machiavelli's day. If so, his analysis of the fundamental tensions and dynamics driving republican politics may simply not be so pertinent to our own time. Elite quests for undue domination of mass populaces may today be rarer than in the past, at least in modern constitutional democracies.

Perhaps; and so perhaps modern courts should be seen as simply alternative democratic political institutions that some democratic leaders have chosen to empower at certain times for certain purposes, while other democratic leaders resist these efforts. But, leaving aside the question of whether it is psychologically realistic to adopt such a sunny view of modern elites, it is here that the patterns of history must be addressed. We still need to explain why it is only in the post–World War II period that the elites of modern democracies have decided to combat their rivals and accomplish their ends through judicial empowerment, far more than in the past, and almost everywhere that modern democratization has spread.

At a minimum, it seems likely that if elites have seen the rise of judicial power as a way to complete the construction of modern constitutional democracies, they have done so in part because they feel their core interests are likely to be better protected in democratized regimes through the strengthening of these relatively insulated political institutions. It is possible that most modern elites have become so convinced of the desirability of democratic values that democratic commitments now define their core interests, and that they are also persuaded of the propriety of strong judiciaries as institutions for realizing those values. This supposition requires us, however, to take a rather heroic view of elites throughout the world that strains credibility. Their core interests today may not be as dedicated to domination as Machiavelli suggested, but it is likely that many elites remain concerned to maintain at least some important dimensions of their elite status. And many of those elites appear to believe that they can count on courts to help them do so, a belief that the results of judicial decisions around the world largely seem to confirm.

Yet if popular desires for a sense of security and respect are also aided by increased judicial governance, is there any cause for concern? If we think the Machiavellian view I have sketched here has any force, the answer must be yes. If that analysis makes the modern joint rise of democratization and judicial power explicable as institutions that help meet the desires of both modern elites and modern masses, it also cautions against regarding these institutions as ultimate solutions to the enduring tensions between elites and masses. Machiavelli surely would have doubted that the fundamental natures of elites and masses can change dramatically, so for him, there are no ultimate solutions and the tensions never end. They can only be dealt with more or less skillfully—and skill includes modifying institutions as needed "to suit the changes of the times," something that is difficult precisely because of "the impossibility of resisting the natural bent of our characters."[59]

And though imprudent or corrupt masses certainly can present difficulties, the perennially more fundamental problem, Machiavelli stresses repeatedly, is that among elites, there will always be some at least who will not rest content for long with their current degree of domination. They will seek more and more advantages against rival elites and against the masses of people as well.[60] Machiavelli might expect many modern "democratized" elites to feel more conflicted over these desires and to engage in more elaborate discourses to justify them, but he would expect significant numbers (which need not be large) to continue to seek greater power and wealth nonetheless. To check these overweening ambitions, Machiavelli argues that masses must always remain attentive to elite abuses, actively opposing those who impose them and actively supporting those who protect popular interests. Eternal vigilance is indeed the price of liberty. But eternal vigilance is not the way most people want to spend their time; and when they are not suffering overt oppression, they are likely to relax and permit elite encroachments, sometimes even approving them. It is that complacency that Machiavelli especially terms a pernicious form of mass "corruption."[61] Again, only the engaged if constrained opposition of elites and masses provides for public liberty.[62]

These points suggest that the "new paradigm" in public law scholarship presenting judicial empowerment as a matter of democratic choice is not wrong, but it risks being unduly sanguine. Having found that modern courts are politically acceptable ways to protect and advance their interests in many modern constitutional democracies, many elites may well be tempted, consciously or not, to use judicial decision-making as an ever more aggressive vehicle to serve themselves, sometimes at the expense of popular well-being and any plausible conception of the shared public good. I do not wish to exaggerate this danger. I am enough of a believer in the Machiavellian political sociology I have deployed here to think that judicial power is actually a relatively benign way of accommodating the inescapable desires of elites for predominance, in light of the enduring inabilities and unwillingness of most of us to live up to the highest aspirations we might have for democratic civic engagement. It is also true that courts are in many ways weak institutions, and that there are many devices to curb them, which is in part why judges do not for the most depart too widely from popular preferences.[63]

Still, those devices work only so long as people are alert, or more realistically are alerted, to what courts are doing on behalf of elite interests and against their own. So though courts are not inevitably enemies of democracy and can often be its partner, partisans of democracy probably cannot afford to be complacent about global trends to judicial empowerment. As governing elites go, judges may not be so bad; but like all elites, they bear watching. Until we reach a world in which power can no longer corrupt, "a republic that desires to maintain her liberties" will still need constant "precautions" against the linked dangers that both elite restlessness and mass contentment present.[64]

PART V

Constitutionalism and Politics

Chapter Eleven
Constitutional Constraints in Politics

Keith E. Whittington

Constitutions do many things. They organize politics. They found and empower political institutions. They legitimate governments. They give voice to political aspirations. Perhaps most distinctively they bind politics.

It is this effort to bind and constrain politics that defines what we generally mean by *constitutionalism*. The rise of the modern notion of constitutionalism was intertwined with liberalism, the belief that there were limits to the legitimate power of government, and that those limitations should be made effective and real.[1] A constitutional government was a limited government, in which certain political ends and means were off limits. The adjective *constitutional* could be affixed to states that recognized and implemented this principle, regardless of the basic form of the regime. Thus, a *constitutional monarchy* was a monarchy that recognized limits to its power. A *constitutional republic* was a popular government that recognized limits to the uses to which the instruments of the state could be put. Constitutional monarchies were not oxymorons, and constitutional democracies were not tautologies, because it was possible to envision that form of political regime unbound by constitutional constraints.[2] Politics would still be structured. The organs of government would still be defined and instituted. The regime would still make claims to legitimacy. But those who wielded power would not recognize inherent limits to their power. Politically, everything could be on the table.[3]

The challenge of constitutionalism is to make those constraints effective. How can politics be bound? One tempting answer is to set constitutional mechanisms and constraints outside of politics. Politics can be bound by a neutral, external, constitutional enforcer. Though tempting, I do not believe this is an available option. It is not easy to imagine what might exist "outside of politics" in this way.[4] It is possible, though difficult, to imagine a constitutional enforcement mechanism wholly insulated from the domestic politics of the polity to be bound. For example, the enforcement mechanism might be lodged in a foreign power.[5] The English Privy Council could supervise and veto the political acts of colonial institutions.[6] A conquered nation may be subject to the will of its conqueror and find its local orders countermanded by a foreign overlord. An economically disadvantaged nation might make commitments to foreign economic actors and agree (or not) to have those commitments "enforced" by some outside arbiter.[7] A politically unstable government might treat with foreign governments to guarantee its own continuation.[8] This would seem to be a rather unattractive option for effectuating constitutional constraints. It is not only unattractive, however. It is also ineffectual, relative to the goal of creating a constitutional enforcer outside of politics.

There are two aspects of constitutional constraint that would have to be outside of politics, and both create problems for those committed to that effort. Constitutional constraints must be both interpreted and made effective. It is possible to shift the kind of politics to which these aspects of constitutionalism are subject, but it is not possible to take them entirely out of politics. We might worry that the constitutional enforcer would know the constitutional requirements, but would be infected by politics such that he would stay his hand and neglect to enforce those requirements. There is an element of this in the Hamiltonian claim that the judiciary is the "least dangerous" branch.[9] With neither force nor will, he suggested, how much trouble can the courts really cause? They can be bullied into passivity in the face of constitutional violations. A constitutional enforcer "outside of politics" would be one who was unafraid to impose constitutional constraints, political pressure to the contrary notwithstanding.

Alternatively, we might worry that the constitutional enforcer would not "know" the constitutional requirements. That is, the constitutional enforcer would not be a neutral enforcer of the constitution, but would instead be infected by politics such that politics would shape his understanding of the constitutional requirements. This is where it becomes particularly tricky to see our way to a nonpolitical constitutionalism. The military conqueror, the imperial power, or the gunboat diplomat may well be willing and able to impose his will on a polity without regard to local political pressures, but that does not mean that what is being enforced is true constitutional constraint, neutrally understood. The imperial power may be blissfully ignorant of the political forces at play within the colony, but the decisions of the imperial power will themselves be driven by considerations of imperial politics. The relevant politics has changed, but politics remains.

What does this mean for constitutionalism? Generally, it means that constitutionalism has to be understood in a political context. We cannot expect constitutionalism to operate outside of politics. It has to find a way to make itself felt within and through politics. Both the threats to the success of a constitutional project and ultimately the tools for the maintenance of a constitutional project have to be found within politics itself.

Constitutional theory has been particularly concerned with the utility of judicial review as a tool for enforcing constitutional constraints. Courts armed with the power of review hold out the promise of binding politics to constitutional requirements. At the same time, there are persistent questions associated not only with the empirical issue of how effective courts can be with making constitutional constraints effective in practice but also with the normative and conceptual issues of how much we should want to rely on courts to articulate and maintain our constitutional commitments over time. By considering such issues from a different angle—from the perspective of binding politics to constitutionalism—we might gain a different appreciation for different kinds of work that judicial review might do within the constitutional system and those different kinds of work might be evaluated normatively.

We can start by considering what the threats to this form of constitutionalism might be. Why might politics fail to be bound by the constraints of constitutionalism? We might consider four distinct threats, reasons why politics might not be informed by the notion of constitutional limitations. (1) Constitutional constraints might be resisted. (2) Constitutional constraints might be forgotten. (3) Constitutional constraints might be ignored. (4) Constitutional constraints might be contested. In each case, the solution to this problem is within politics. Constitutional constraints might fail because of politics, but they also must be maintained through politics.

Constitutional Resistance

The first threat is the most severe. Constitutional constraints may fail to bind politics simply because political actors resist constitutionalism itself.[10] They lose faith in the constitutional project and are no longer committed to the idea of constitutional constraints. I have elsewhere called this situation one of constitutional crisis.[11] The point of crisis comes when political actors no longer seek to maintain the constitutional faith. This is not the result of constitutional disagreement or interpretive error. This situation is more radical than that. In a moment of constitutional crisis, political actors *know* that they are acting against constitutional constraints and they *do not care.* They accept the existence of constitutional constraints, but they do not accept those recognized constraints as binding, not on them, not now.

The constitutional crisis may be either local or global. The crisis may be localized if political actors only refuse to accept some, but not all, constitutional constraints. They may continue to recognize the possibility of constitutional constraint and remain committed to the idea of a limited government. They may well accept other constitutional constraints that are binding in other circumstances. But at the same time they reject some constitutional constraints, regarding those as no longer binding. They effectively seek to write a set of constraints out of the constitution, but by no constitutionally recognizable manner. Many state legislatures in the early twentieth century effectively adopted this stance by refusing to comply with their constitutional requirements of periodic reapportionment. Given a choice between handing political power to the rapidly growing urban areas or ignoring constitutional rules for legislative apportionment, many state governments chose to abandon their constitutional rule. They continued to adhere to other elements of their constitutions and operate as constitutional governments, but that particular constitutional provision was, for the time being, a dead letter. The crisis may be global if political actors cease to recognize any of the existing constitutional constraints. The crisis may only be transitory. Political actors may shed the old constitution only to don a new one. The Articles of Confederation may be abandoned for the U.S. Constitution. The crisis may be permanent, a crisis of constitutionalism itself. Political actors may throw off the very idea of constitutional government and embrace some form of government unmodified by constitutionalism and its limitations.

There is no solution within constitutionalism itself to the problem of constitutional resistance. Constitutionalism only binds the willing. Constitutional safeguards can be designed so as to make such moments of constitutional crisis, of constitutional resistance, transparent. Political actors can be forced to make their choice of constitutional resistance apparent. This perhaps creates the best chance that a political opposition may mobilize in defense of the existing constitutional standards and call the constitutional resisters to account politically. The survival of constitutionalism then depends on the extent of the support for it in the broader polity, on whether a movement on behalf of constitutionalism can in fact be mobilized.[12]

What constitutional courts do best is to publicize constitutional transgressions. The efficacy of judicial review as a constitutional check depends on the political acceptance of the judiciary as an adequate arbiter of constitutional violations and on the continued political vitality of constitutional commitments.[13] Although we might well, in the abstract, embrace the active use of judicial review to sound the alarm in such cases of political resistance of constitutional constraints, the efficacy of the judicial tocsin will itself depend on the vitality of the threatened constitutional value. By intervening on an issue, however, the judiciary puts its own authority on the line and this does potentially alter the political calculus. Constitutional violations that might have been tolerated *sub rosa* might well have different implications once made visible, and particularly if the continuation of those constitutional violations becomes entangled with the judiciary's own standing and legitimacy.

More generally, many of the same considerations that are relevant to settling a constitutional rule in the first place are relevant to determining whether it will survive such a threat. Is a given constitutional principle well integrated into our general political discourse?[14] Is a particular constitutional constraint secured by pluralistic distribution of political and social power interested in its defense?[15] Does it facilitate and coordinate cooperative social and political action so as to make it valuable to others to maintain?[16] Does it have particular value to well-placed stakeholders inside or outside the political system who can be expected to muster to insist on compliance with the constitutional constraint?[17] *In extremis*, constitutionalism cannot be self-sustaining. It ultimately depends on a favorable political context. The question is how that favorable political context is constructed and maintained.

Constitutional Forgetfulness

The second threat is that constitutional constraints might be "forgotten." In such cases, constitutional constraints are disregarded, but there is no active intent to disregard them. Political actors have not chosen to reject constitutionalism. Indeed, they remain committed to the principles of constitutionalism and to the goal of adhering to constitutional constraints. Political actors have the will to be constitutionally faithful, but they lack the judgment. The difficulty is one of constitutional implementation.

This problem is not a trivial one. We often imagine the threats to constitutionalism being self-evident and high profile. Our constitutional memory is shaped by our most visible constitutional conflicts and resolutions. Constitutional teaching and discussion emphasizes something like a highlight reel of constitutional practice. The "constitutional canon" (and anti-canon) is composed of the most celebrated (or infamous) cases of constitutional interpretation and application.[18] The mundane, day-to-day work of maintaining a constitutional government is largely ignored or known only to the practitioners themselves. The constitutional implications of a law restricting access to abortions in 2006 or of a law limiting the number of hours an employee can work in 1930 are obvious. The constitutional implications of a statutory provision requiring local sheriffs to provide background checks on those seeking to purchase a firearm or imposing a federal tax on marine insurance, however, are not so obvious.[19] Preserving constitutional constraints in the latter cases is a rather different problem than preserving them in the former cases, and this difference requires some recognition.

We might imagine two sources of constitutional "forgetting." One source might be the complexity of constitutional requirements, which leads to an inadequate understanding of when constitutional constraints are implicated. Another source might be the complexity of governance, which may result in applicable constitutional constraints being overlooked in the routine press of government business. The first results from a lack of constitutional expertise. The second results from sheer oversight.

In both cases, politics slips from its constitutional binds because of particular and concrete features of the political context, and in both cases adhering to constitutional constraints requires political innovation and adjustment. There are a variety of institutional responses that can be made to minimize the problem of forgotten constitutional constraints. Each source of constitutional forgetting—lack of expertise and oversight—points toward distinct, but overlapping, responses. The complexity of constitutional requirements suggests the need to mobilize expertise to better identify applicable constitutional constraints. The complexity of governance suggests the need either to raise the salience of constitutional constraints so that they are not easily overlooked or to foster specialization in constitutional concerns so that that which is overlooked by political generalists is nonetheless noticed and addressed.

The most obvious institutional strategy for addressing these difficulties is judicial review. As Alexander Hamilton noted, it may be expected that "long and laborious study" is necessary to gain "competent knowledge" of the law, and judges may be distinguished from other government officials in their possession of the requisite skill.[20] Likewise, judges see the implementation of government policies from a different perspective, perhaps making it easier to recognize constitutional violations.[21] Whether or not they are limited to that specialized jurisdiction, courts that exercise the power of constitutional review are effectively specialists capable of focusing attention on the constitutional implications of government policy.

Two things are worth noting about this rationale for judicial review. First, it suggests only what Jeremy Waldron has called "weak judicial review."[22] Weak judicial review authorizes courts only to flag policies as being in violation of constitutional constraints, but it does not authorize them to refuse to implement those policies. Courts, operating in this mode, may scrutinize and publicize, but may not invalidate. There is no need for judges to wield a veto power in order to introduce constitutional expertise into politics or to give attention to constitutionally flawed policies that might otherwise escape notice. Second, it suggests the limitations of James Bradley Thayer's call for judicial deference. In part out of a concern that the active use of the power of judicial review would sap the legislative will to exercise constitutional responsibility, Thayer called for judges to defer to the policies adopted by legislatures with the hope that the latter could be induced to behave more responsibly.[23] Politics may still be expected to slip its constitutional bonds if legislatures lack the expertise or leisure to identify constitutional problems, even if they possess the will to behave responsibly.

There are additional strategies for attempting to realize a Thayerian politics. Judicial review relies on a "fire alarm" model, using the complaints of damaged parties to trigger scrutiny of a government policy. The ability to pull that fire alarm may not be equally distributed, however, skewing how this mechanism may be used to maintain constitutional constraints.[24] The multiplication and growth of organized groups with specialized knowledge of constitutional law can both make it more likely that such fire-alarm mechanisms will be triggered and increase the political salience of constitutional problems, reducing the likelihood that constitutional constraints will be overlooked. A political system may also set in motion "police patrols" to monitor for constitutional violations.[25] Specialized constitutional expertise and routine monitoring of proposed legislation for constitutional difficulties might be accomplished within the legislative process.[26]

Constitutional Neglect

A third threat to constitutionalism is the possibility that constitutional constraints might be ignored or neglected. I mean to distinguish the problem of constitutional neglect from both the problem of constitutional resistance and the problem of constitutional forgetfulness. Constitutional resistance involved the active and principled rejection of constitutional constraints, while constitutional forgetfulness involved the literal ignorance of relevant constitutional constraints. Constitutional neglect, by contrast, involves a failure to comply with constitutional constraints in circumstances in which political actors are both aware of the constraints and still in principle committed to them. Constitutional neglect occurs when constitutionalism is valued, but it is not regarded by political actors as the highest priority. This situation is consistent with at least one common image of normal politics, one in which politics is unprincipled and short-sighted, buffeted by "pressure groups" and governed by bargaining, compromise, and expediency.[27] Thus, some legislators, and ultimately the Clinton administration, accepted as a "kind of a game . . . as a political exercise" the Communications Decency Act regulating Internet pornography, despite recognizing its dubious constitutionality.[28] Similarly, many legislators embraced the federal Flag Protection Act as politically attractive, even as they themselves thought it was constitutionally troubling.[29] Political actors have the desire to be constitutionally faithful, but they lack the will. They are too readily seduced into straying from the straight constitutional path when it serves their immediate electoral or policy needs.

One option when confronted with this problem is to exhort political actors to behave themselves better. This is, of course, a reasonable and worthy course of action. Whether it is also efficacious is less certain. It seems unlikely. Political actors are likely to care about constitutional commitments when they have incentives to do so. When voters have an interest in a given constitutional value, for example, politicians are unlikely to trench upon it. When a given constitutional commitment promises instrumental benefits to politicians themselves, or an important subset of them, then it might well be protected against political threats. Political actors may well place an especially high value on some particular constitutional principles. That they may act on those preferences when there are few or no political costs to be paid is notable, but relatively unimportant. Senator Robert Byrd is well known for his refined sensibilities regarding the constitutional responsibilities and prerogatives of the U.S. Senate, for example, but it is not obvious that his acting on those principles carries any political costs. Of more immediate significance is how politicians behave when there are political costs to upholding constitutional principles. As the political price of constitutionalism rises, politicians will, on the margin, sacrifice constitutional principles for other political goods. When there is a choice between adhering to constitutional constraints and securing reelection, politicians will frequently choose the latter over the former. Exhortation, or more broadly constitutional education, may affect this calculus if it is aimed at either altering the utility function of the politicians themselves (raising the political price that politicians are willing to pay before sacrificing a given constitutional value) or altering the political environment within which politicians operate (by, for example, altering the utility function of voters so that they will demand more constitutional behavior and less unconstitutional behavior from politicians).[30]

Institutional design may be a more promising general strategy to curbing the threat from constitutional neglect. Thayer and, to a lesser degree, Mark Tushnet have suggested that the best approach is to heighten the political responsibility of legislators for getting the Constitution right.[31] If legislators knew that they were operating without a backstop that could catch their constitutional errors, then, the argument goes, they would have more incentive to act responsibly. By raising the cost of constitutional error, this would alter the political calculation that leads to constitutional neglect. It certainly seems likely that legislators will behave more irresponsibly and neglect constitutional values more if they know that those errors will be corrected elsewhere in the political system than if they know that their own actions will be determinative. The question is how great this effect actually is in practice and how much constitutional errors might be reduced if legislators were directly responsible for them. I am skeptical that removing the backstop would induce politicians to behave as constitutionally as we might like. It might well improve their behavior, but it is unlikely to improve their behavior enough.

Institutional designs to respond to this problem might instead be aimed at insulating pivotal political decision-makers from the political pressures that might lead them astray. There are a variety of devices that might have this effect. The Madisonian solution embedded in the U.S. Constitution, for example, sought to insulate legislators from popular pressures to transgress constitutional limits by expanding their electoral constituencies and extending their terms between elections, "republican remed[ies] for the diseases most incident to republican government."[32] More transitory and ad hoc are the strategies of political cover that legislative leaders devise for their legislative followers. Thus, constitutionally problematic proposals may also be quietly killed in committee or reconciliation conference, or they may be countermanded by other statutory provisions that are included as part of a legislative package.[33] Senior and electorally safe legislators may cast the decisive votes against popular but constitutionally dubious policies, leaving less electorally secure legislators free to vote for such measures.[34] Presidents may be expected to veto constitutionally troubled bills or gut them through administrative action and implementation, giving electorally pressured legislators a free pass to vote for them.[35]

The most obvious institutional device of this sort is the power of constitutional review exercised by politically insulated judges. Again, Hamilton recognized this possibility, observing that the "independence of judges" would be particularly beneficial in "guard[ing] the Constitution" from the "ill humors, which . . . sometimes disseminate among the people themselves" and "speedily give place to better information, and more deliberate reflection." Judicial review would be used to counter "momentary inclination[s]."[36] So long as judges are more insulated from those inclinations than are legislators, they may be less likely to succumb to temptation and help ensure that constitutional constraints remain binding.[37]

Some points are worth highlighting about judicial review in this context. First, note that the weak form of judicial review is unlikely to be adequate for addressing the problem of constitutional neglect. Simply flagging a policy as transgressing constitutional constraints is unlikely to be of much help if the political problem is one in which politicians are already aware of the constitutional difficulty, but the political price for adhering to constitutional values at the moment is seen as too high. In order to address the problem of constitutional neglect, judges will need to be armed with a veto power. Second, even though judges may be exercising a veto in such cases, they will not necessarily be acting contrary to the preferences of political majorities and political leaders. Voting against the constitutionally problematic policy may be too high of a price for the elected legislator to pay, but that does not mean that the legislator would not welcome the intervention of others to block the policy and absorb the political blame. Judicial review in this context may well be seen as "friendly," even by those who voted in favor of the policy being invalidated.[38] Third, note that this form of judicial review does not depend on a Bickelian forward-looking judiciary. In resisting the "momentary inclination" of the legislator, the judges need not attempt to guess what will "gain general assent" "in a rather immediate foreseeable future."[39] Judges seeking to overcome constitutional neglect need not attempt to lead public opinion. They need only enforce standing constitutional principles that politicians neglect to apply themselves. Fourth, constitutionalism is maintained in such cases by manipulating politics, not by standing outside of politics. The support for constitutional values in instances of constitutional neglect continues to come from within the political system. Political actors remain committed to the constitutional values that politically insulated judges are asked to apply; they simply do not wish to take the responsibility of applying those values themselves. It is the fact that those values continue to command political support that makes it possible for judges to intervene successfully. Political actors defer to the courts in such situations because the courts speak on behalf of principles that are commonly shared. These judges speak on behalf of principles that are neglected, not resisted, and thus do not invite calamitous resistance themselves.

Constitutional Contestation

A fourth threat to constitutionalism is that constitutional constraints might be contested. Constitutional constraints must not only be effectively enforced; they must be understood. The first three threats to constitutionalism considered here all bracket the question of constitutional disagreement. It could be assumed, for those purposes, that constitutional requirements are consensual, if not necessarily "clear." Constitutional meaning may be obscure, technical, or difficult to understand. It may be rejected or neglected. These difficulties primarily raise problems of enforcement and application. Accomplishing the feat of binding politics with constitutional constraints is, relative to those problems, a matter of marshaling political resources to ensure that constitutional constraints are more likely than not to be recognized and maintained.

The threat of constitutional contestation recognizes that there is not always a consensus on desired constitutional values. The possibility that the fundamental principles of the American constitutional regime may be subject to political disagreement has been recognized at various times over the course of American history, though the general tendency has been to minimize the importance of those disagreements. This is another element of Thayer's turn-of-the-century analysis of the proper scope of constitutional law, and perhaps the more enduring source of his influence within constitutional theory. The problem confronting judges by the end of the nineteenth century, amidst the rise of populist and progressive constitutional discourse, was that they were reviewing laws that did not merely reflect legislators neglecting or forgetting constitutional requirements. The problematic legislation was not the product of merely transitory "ill humors." They were the product of serious and sustained political movements, whose policy goals ran contrary to traditional constitutional understandings. At the same time, they did not (or at least, did not generally) frankly admit that some inherited constitutional commitments were to be rejected and regarded as no longer binding. Instead, they marshaled new arguments that reinterpreted inherited commitments in new ways. Judges were confronted with persistent reasonable disagreement about constitutional meaning. Thayer urged judges to defer in the face of those disagreements. Others urged judges to hold the line. What matters for the moment is that Thayer and his generation ushered in the era of legal realism, and placed the problem of interpretation, and not just the problem of enforcement, at the heart of the constitutional enterprise.

The meaning of a constitution cannot be taken for granted. It must be won, and it must be won within politics. Constitutional meaning has routinely been politically contested. Political movements have organized around divergent visions of the Constitution. Political parties have embraced controversial constitutional claims. Criticisms of judicial efforts to interpret the Constitution are regular features of American politics. Political actors do not simply leave the Constitution in the hands of the courts. They construct constitutional meaning on their own for their own purposes.[40] They sometimes respond to and displace the judicial authority to give meaning to the Constitution.[41] There are periods of relative constitutional consensus and stability, in which constitutional interpretation is characterized more by agreement on basic principles than disagreement. Likewise, the meanings of parts of the Constitution, often extensive, are uncontested and accepted as givens. Nonetheless, over time important components of the constitutional system become the subject of disagreement and political resources are marshaled on behalf of competing visions of the constitutional future. Regnant understandings of the meaning and implications of such well-established liberties as free speech and privacy, for example, were remade in the early twentieth century as reformers sought to construct a state capable of advancing their interests.[42]

Constitutional contestation ultimately leads to efforts to entrench favored constitutional understandings. The existence of disagreement puts a premium on elevating a preferred constitutional commitment above the fray. Jeremy Waldron has argued that the circumstance of disagreement suggests that politics should be open to that disagreement and that disputes should be resolved in a transparent way through majoritarian mechanisms.[43] In practice, however, political majorities seek to make the most of their victories, and the existence of mobilized opponents provides further incentive to ensure that the polity remains committed to and constrained by the constitutional values of the majority. Once constitutional politics has been reconstructed around the vision of one set of partisans, judges are unlikely to view alternatives as within the domain of "reasonable" constitutional interpretations that should receive judicial deference. Instead, judges, persuaded by and committed to the constitutional sensibilities of their political sponsors and allies, will exercise the responsibilities of their office so as to correct constitutional error and maintain constitutional fidelity as they see it. The judicial veto is one of the spoils of political war, and once captured it is likely to be actively used. In this mode, judicial invalidations are guided by a contested, but politically dominant, constitutional vision, and the value of judicial review lies in part in its utility in enforcing constitutional requirements against those who would subvert those requirements, not for the sake of expediency, but out of "misguided" principle. To be sustainable over time, however, supporters of this constitutional vision must remain politically powerful, capable of controlling the selection of judges, guiding public opinion, and protecting the independence of the judiciary. The contestation over constitutional principles creates the incentive for political majorities to entrench their own preferences and opportunities for judges to act on those sensibilities to invalidate constitutionally deviant policies, but the strength of those majorities determines how long and successfully those values will remain dominant.

Constitutionalism seeks to bind politics to a set of constraints. There is no perspective external to politics from which to define those constraints, however, and there are no mechanisms outside of politics with which to enforce them. Both the interpretation of constitutional commitments and their maintenance over time occur within politics. Attending to the threats that face constitutionalism, the various ways in which constitutionalism might fail to bind politics, gives clues to the political strategies that might be adopted in order to preserve constitutional commitments. Doing so also clarifies various rationales for turning to judicial review and the different forms of and sources of political support for judicial review. Interestingly, these rationales range from the relatively innocuous (rectifying constitutional forgetfulness) to the more hard-edged (enforcing contested constitutional understandings). They also point toward the ways in which judicial review offers a response to political dilemmas and is situated within politics, and the limitations of and alternatives to judicial review as a mechanism of constitutional maintenance.

Chapter Twelve
"The Court Will Clean It Up": Executive Power, Constitutional Contestation, and War Powers

Benjamin A. Kleinerman

In a recent editorial discussing the effects of the September 11, 2001, attacks on American constitutional law, a commentator writes: "Thus far, the Supreme Court has saved us from having, as a legacy of 9/11, a system in which the President is above the law in how he fights threats to domestic security."[1] The quotation represents a more general position: those who worry about the overextension of presidential power in the wake of 9/11 typically look to the Supreme Court to save us from its excesses. In fact, this tendency has, perhaps unsurprisingly, found its way into the very deliberations of our oft-forgotten third branch of government: Congress. For instance, in the September 2006 legislative debates concerning the bill authorizing many of the tools Bush wanted in the war on terror, Judiciary Committee Chairman Arlen Specter initially opposed the bill because it was, he claimed: "patently unconstitutional on its face." Specter's constitutional scruples caused him to seek an amendment to the legislation that would have extended the writ of habeas corpus to the detainees presently labeled by the Bush administration as "enemy combatants" and held indefinitely. After his amendment narrowly failed, Specter decided to throw aside his reservations and back the unamended bill. Why? Because, he said, the bill has several good items "and the court will clean it up" by striking the denial of habeas corpus to the detainees.[2] Even as Specter objected to what he must have continued to regard as the bill's obvious unconstitutionality, he was willing to support it because he, like so many others in the present time, thought the Supreme Court would "save us" from its excesses. He abdicates his own constitutional responsibility only because he expects the Supreme Court to exercise what he takes to be theirs. Regardless of whether the Supreme Court actually finds the legal grounds to fulfill Specter's wish, his very position illustrates an empirical reality in the present system of separated powers: members of Congress now implicitly and even, as in Specter's case, explicitly abdicate their constitutional responsibility, expecting as they do so that the Supreme Court will "clean up" their mess.[3]

In matters of war powers and other discretionary issues of presidential power of the sort contained in this bill, this development is especially problematic because our system depends on serious constitutional contestation between the executive and the legislative branches. To the extent that discretionary power truly does and should lie in the executive branch, its existence must be checked by a politically vibrant Congress that seeks both to constrain the parameters of such discretion and to contest, when necessary, its misuse. This contestation ultimately depends on the political viability of the Constitution as what might be called a potent "signaling device" by which Congress can indicate executive usurpations. Thus, the control of executive power requires a popularly treasured Constitution to which members of Congress hold the president because it is in their political interest to do so. The people's primary attachment to their Constitution rewards those members of Congress who use it over and against an executive who abuses it. The doctrine of judicial supremacy, by distancing the people from their Constitution, results in a political disincentive for Congress to prevent its abuse by the executive. So, a Supreme Court that understands itself, as I will contend John Marshall's Court did, as almost entirely an arm of legislative intent, speaking for the law by upholding it, invigorates constitutional contestation because it locates serious constitutional responsibility in Congress. This defensible form of judicial review is most closely associated with what Mark Tushnet, in his chapter, calls "true Thayerian review" insofar as it invites (demands) the legislature to have a "role in constitutional interpretation." A Supreme Court that understands itself, however, as the authoritative and final voice of the Constitution tends to eviscerate such contestation by distancing the people from their Constitution and thereby encouraging congressional lassitude and irresponsibility.

I will discuss first what I consider to be three problematic twentieth-century decisions or types of decisions in matters of war powers: the "political question" decisions, the *Curtiss-Wright* decision, and the *Hamdi* decision. Following a discussion of these three types of decisions, I will turn back to the foundations of constitutionalism itself in the thought of John Locke and James Madison, showing, through them, the problematic place of judicial power given their conception of an "Original Constitution" that the people hold as their own, and from which the people can judge the claimed authority of individuals who hold political power within it. And lastly, I will turn to what, I will argue, is a defensible form of judicial review in contradistinction to the previously discussed more problematic forms.

The "Political Question" Doctrine

The judicial branch has often in recent years invoked what it has come to call the "political question" doctrine in matters of war powers. This doctrine claims that the question before the court is incapable of being decided judicially; instead, it is a political question that must be decided by the political branches of government. This doctrine has most often been invoked in response to legal challenges to presidential wars, beginning in the Vietnam era and continuing through some of Reagan's and Clinton's wars. On the one hand, such a doctrine seems to comport with my claim that the president is best checked by Congress rather than the courts. After all, by invoking the political question doctrine, doesn't the Supreme Court invite the political struggle created, as Edward Corwin famously wrote, by the Constitution itself?

I would argue, however, that the "political question" doctrine is problematic for two essential reasons that I develop further in subsequent parts of this chapter. First, in its invocation by courts that otherwise claim final constitutional authority to say what the Constitution is, it implies that the Constitution does not apply. To be constitutionally healthy, however, the contestation between the political branches should take place with explicit and continued reference to the Constitution. If they're involved merely in "political questions," the political branches are both invited to ignore their constitutional responsibilities and, in a certain sense, precluded from citing the Constitution to show the constitutional malfeasance of the other. In other words, although the "political question" doctrine is theoretically amenable to the argument that is offered here, its invocation by courts that claim, whether implicitly or explicitly, final constitutional authority complicates and ultimately destroys its theoretical soundness. As James Stoner writes in his chapter in this volume: "If the Supreme Court is the vicar of the Constitution, then technical doctrines that preclude Supreme Court review of any constitutional question seem to be antiquated formalities that stand in the way of constitutional justice." As we will see, the Constitution expects and depends on political contestation over constitutional meaning and authority. Although the "political question" doctrine could conceivably invite such contestation, it will tend not to if it is invoked by courts that otherwise claim the final say over constitutional meaning and authority.

And second, the Marshall Court consistently held that while executives possess discretionary authority, Congress also possesses statutory authority over the execution of all branches of government. The judiciary cannot rule only if there is no controlling legislation or clear constitutional principle for it to uphold over and against executive discretion. Executive discretion only exists legally within the boundaries that Congress either establishes or fails not to preclude. The political question, beyond the Supreme Court's jurisprudence, exists in the use or abuse of that legal discretion; such political questions do not affect the Supreme Court's constitutional power to negate illegal discretion. For what it's worth, given the actual statutory content of the War Powers Act and of the Tonkin Gulf Resolution, the courts might well have come to the same conclusion about the legality of the president's actions, but done so without invoking a constitutionally questionable doctrine. By invoking a doctrine according to which all contestation between Congress and the president is a political question, not amenable to the Supreme Court's intervention, the Court invites the conclusion—a conclusion that Congress might prefer—that it is powerless in the face of discretionary executive power.

This is not to say that there is not a wide range of situations in which something that looks like the "political question" doctrine would be very useful for the courts to invoke. For instance, one might plausibly argue that the Supreme Court's prior invocation of the "political question" doctrine in matters of legislative redistricting was more constitutionally prudent than the present, post–*Baker v. Carr* world in which the courts are now regularly sought to intervene in these matters. In other words, my complaint with the political question doctrine is not with the principle underlying it: there are many conceivable situations in which the courts should refrain from intervening. In each of the problematic cases discussed, the decisive problem is not so much the decision itself, but the doctrine invoked or created by the Court to justify the doctrine.

In fact, as Stoner implies in the previous passage and as *Baker v. Carr* may reveal, a doctrine that demands constitutional abdication may be much more unsustainable than an expectation of constitutional prudence that sees the wisdom of such abdication. If constitutional matters are at stake as important as equality in voting or the deliberative decision to go to war, why shouldn't the voice of the Constitution intervene? If the Supreme Court is solely responsible for upholding such constitutional principles, why should it abide by a doctrine that leaves these important constitutional matters to branches that are not capable of this constitutional responsibility?

Curtiss-Wright

In a case in which the controlling legal question asked only whether Congress can delegate responsibility to the president in matters of foreign policy, *Curtiss-Wright* claims that the president possesses "delicate, plenary, and exclusive power" as the "sole organ of the federal government in the field of international relations."[4] Justice Sutherland derives this doctrine from a speech John Marshall made in the House of Representatives as a representative before becoming chief justice. Marshall said: "The President is the sole organ of the nation in its external relations, and its sole representative with foreign nations." The speech itself involves Marshall's attempt to delimit the power of the judiciary from interfering in the executive's extradition of a British citizen, accused of piracy and murder, to the British government. So, on the one hand, the speech does establish the executive's need for independence from the judiciary. But, on the other, in a couple of sentences after the passage cited by Sutherland, Marshall said: "Congress, unquestionably, may prescribe the mode, and Congress may devolve on others the whole execution of the contract; but, till this is done, it seems the duty of the executive department to execute the contract."[5] Although Marshall might very well agree with Justice Sutherland's claim that it is unwise of Congress "to lay down narrowly definite standards by which the President is to be governed," his argument itself does not establish this prudential consideration as a matter of principle.[6] Instead, as a constitutional principle, Marshall makes the much less problematic claim: though executive power is independent of the judiciary and discretionary in its nature, its power is neither "plenary" nor "exclusive." Where Sutherland establishes the constitutional principle that the executive has an exclusive legal power to plenary discretion—a power that, as such, cannot be infringed upon by Congress—Marshall argues only that the executive has discretionary power in his relations with other nations, the mode of which and thus the legality of which Congress can establish through legislation. From Marshall's perspective, the decisive problem with the principle in *Curtiss-Wright* would not be the claim that it is prudent to leave certain matters to presidential discretion, but that presidential discretion is always and inherently legal, and thus not susceptible to limitation by congressional legislation.

Sutherland's opinion has allowed almost every executive since to cite it as authoritative constitutional proof of his plenary and exclusive legal power in relations with other nations extending to war. As such, the case has given the president a new weapon in his arsenal in his struggle with Congress for constitutional authority.[7] And, in this particular case, the controlling question before the court did not require the broad legalization of presidential discretion for which Sutherland argues. Instead, as Justice Jackson argues in a footnote in his concurring opinion in *Youngstown*, the case did not even involve the question of the president's power to act without congressional authority, but only the question of his right to act under and in accord with an act of Congress, and so much in the opinion in the case is mere "dictum."[8] The controlling legal question in the case asked only whether Congress has the power to delegate responsibilities to the president in matters of foreign policy, and Sutherland responded by asserting that the president's power in matters of foreign policy was exclusive and plenary. One might go so far as to suggest that Sutherland's decision is not only "dictum," but also contradictory: if the president's foreign policy power is exclusive, then Congress cannot constitutionally delegate foreign policy responsibility to the president.

Hamdi

Ostensibly, the *Hamdi* plurality is one of several decisions in recent years that "save" us from the post-9/11 excesses of presidential power. In terms of the decision itself, the extent to which this is the case is a question. *Hamdi* accepts the executive branch's definition of an "enemy combatant," allowing this to include U.S. citizens, and thus also permits the executive to hold such citizens almost indefinitely without trial or release.[9] It also affirms what may be the tenuous connection the executive branch makes between Congress's passage of the AUMF and the holding of citizens, thus claiming that the executive has congressional authorization for his activities.[10] Though the decision itself worries about far-reaching executive power much more than does *Curtiss-Wright*, its similar claim, whether implicit or explicit, to speak as the voice of the Constitution has a similarly deleterious effect on Congress's willingness to exercise its own constitutional responsibility. In its role as herald of the Constitution, the Supreme Court asserts: "A state of war is not a blank check for the President when it comes to the rights of the Nation's citizens."[11] By the breadth of the decision, a question of second-order statutory legality—that is, has Congress authorized these detentions—now looks as though it has unassailable first-order support from the Constitution it-self. The decision allows the current administration and its supporters to say to their opposition in Congress: the indefinite holding of U.S. citizens as "enemy combatants" is inherently and thus unquestionably constitutional—after all, the Supreme Court has affirmed it.[12] In short, the Supreme Court's authoritative constitutional claims in the case hamper the ability of oppo-sitional legislators to use the Constitution as a "signal" with which to gain political leverage against the president's potential misuse of power.

The plurality, however, goes further. By creating a distinction between the congressionally "approved" indefinite suspension of U.S. citizens in the United States and the congressionally "unapproved" suspension of the writ of habeas corpus, the Supreme Court gives itself the room it needs "to play a necessary role in maintaining this delicate balance of governance, serving as an important judicial check on the Executive's discretion in the realm of detentions."[13] To oversee such detentions of "enemy combatants," the plurality envisions a new sort of trial in which the burden of proof has been switched from the accuser to the accused and hearsay is always accept-able. One could argue that these processes would be, at least, constitution-ally questionable if they were advanced in legislation by Congress. To be constitutionally acceptable, one has to construe the indefinite detention of citizens, without trial for treason and without the suspension of the writ, as encompassed within the "war powers" of Congress; but, such a reading of the Constitution seems at least in tension with the explicit grant of the writ of habeas corpus and the explicit statement that it can only be suspended in cases of rebellion or invasion. The court, one of whose historic roles has been to provide a constitutional check on Congress's excessive use of its war pow-ers, has, in its effort to "balance," invigorated congressional war power to a point, some would argue, beyond the bounds of the Constitution itself.[14]

Besides the questionable nature of the processes, the most troubling thing about this decision may be the extent to which it muddies the constitu-tional waters within which the debate concerning executive detentions takes place. The decision and others like it such as *Rasul* and *Hamdan* complicate and ultimately impair the constitutional dialogue in which, post-9/11, it has become absolutely necessary for the public to engage. There are essential con-stitutional questions that the American people need to answer, or at least dis-cuss, on their own apart from what Mark Tushnet calls "judicial overhang."[15] For instance, the question that Specter avoided, should the privilege of the writ of habeas corpus apply to citizens only, or to both citizens and non-citizens alike? In the aforementioned case of Senator Specter, the presence of a belief in judicial supremacy seemed to prevent members of Congress from having a meaningful debate about whether the writ should extend to noncitizens and, for that matter, citizens held in Guantanamo and elsewhere. Important senators such as Specter who "sat on the fence" on these issues could avoid them by passing off responsibility to the Supreme Court. Other important constitutional questions include: how can the government respond effectively to threats associated with terrorism while avoiding becoming so powerful and discretionary as to be dangerously arbitrary? Or, how far do we want to go in giving up our rights so as to remain secure? These are constitutional questions, admitting of no easy answer, that a constitutional government has to expect its public to be capable of at least discussing, if not answering. But, even as they are constitutional questions, they are at the same time political questions, to be debated in the political sphere—but a political sphere that's created by a constitution and infused with the spirit of constitutionalism. As it stands, however, these questions are too often simply being adjudicated by a judiciary that aims at constitutional doctrines whose authority stems in part from their claim to stand outside of politics.

Again, most deleterious is the implicit claim of courts that their constitutional rulings stand outside a political sphere that, as such, has nothing to do with the Constitution or constitutionalism; politics is thought to be independent of, though circumscribed by, the Court's own understanding of the Constitution. In other words, though Whittington simply asserts that "there is no perspective external to politics from which to define" the set of constraints imposed by constitutionalism, the Supreme Court often assumes and acts on the belief that it does, in fact, possess this external vantage point.

All of these examples suggest that the Supreme Court's effort to intervene on behalf of the Constitution has a paradoxically depressing effect on constitutionalism itself because it discourages the political use of the Constitution. In this sense, Whittington's argument itself encourages that which he seems to dismiss. That is, by viewing the Constitution merely as a set of constraints, he seems to encourage the view that these constraints can be imposed from the outside rather than created within and through the world of political contestation. So, where I would argue that the active contestation of constitutional constraints actually contributes to the healthiness of constitutionalism, Whittington classifies such contestation as a "threat to constitutionalism." Instead, one sure sign of constitutional health is when there is political contestation over constitutional meaning. To develop this argument further, I turn now to the foundations of constitutionalism where the role of an "Original Constitution" is contemplated much more extensively: the thought of John Locke and James Madison.

The Paradox of Locke's Constitutionalism: A Legal Order Without a Judiciary

I have argued in other work that Locke's *Second Treatise* wrestles with the same constitutional dilemma we are wrestling with in the present. That is, how to integrate the seeming necessity of "extra-legal" discretionary executive power with the coeval danger it poses to a constitutional order. Because of relative popular indifference to the unconstitutional exercise of discretionary executive power, Locke considers legislative elites essential to the maintenance of constitutionalism. These legislative elites can more successfully "signal" the people regarding executive usurpation and tyranny if the people hold most dear their own "original constitution." Through clear demarcations, it creates a visible means with which the people can judge the usurpation and/or abuse of power. For Locke, then, both a clearly articulated original constitution and oppositional legislators capable of using these constitutional boundaries to establish executive malfeasance are essential to the maintenance of constitutionalism.[16]

Unlike his intellectual heirs Montesquieu and Blackstone, Locke does not, however, include an independent judiciary in his liberal-constitutional order.[17] For Montesquieu and Blackstone, as Paul Carrese's recent book argues, an independent judiciary was essential to moderating and tempering politics such that individual liberty and tranquility were most secured.[18] So, if Locke is also preeminently concerned with individual liberty and tranquility, why does he fail to include a judicial power that seems most capable of securing it? After all, judges during his time had already begun to assume an independence from the crown based on their standing in the common-law tradition. By answering this question, we can begin to see, at the theoretical level, why the Supreme Court's interventions, especially when they create new constitutional principles, may complicate the relationship of constitutional contestation that limits executive power through its preservation of the Constitution itself as a meaningful signal with which oppositional legislators can reveal executive usurpations. As the Supreme Court articulates authoritative juridical claims about the Constitution's meaning in these questions of contested authority, its usefulness as a signal becomes lost upon the now-excluded public.

As a solution to this question, Paul Carrese makes the intriguing suggestion that Locke thinks judges would be as gripped by their passions as the rest and thus, like the rest, likely to misjudge and misapply the laws of nature. He writes: "Independent judges, then, would be just other predators running around, and for Locke, two are enough for keeping each other in line with the posited legal order."[19] I would amplify this argument by suggesting that it is not just that independent judges create another set of predators: the form of judicial predation is also particularly problematic. This is because, as a 2005 essay by Lee Ward argues, prior to both legislative and executive supremacy, for Locke, is constitutional supremacy.[20] And the supremacy of the constitution, which would ideally be both written and susceptible of understanding even or especially by the people, frames and delimits claims to the authority to exercise political power made by both the legislative and the executive branches.[21] Insofar as the people become attached first and foremost to *their* written constitution, they will resist any attempts at predatory usurpations and abuses of its strictures. Moreover, both branches will now have the political incentive to reveal the predations of the other. If the people are attached to it, the written constitution becomes a tool for political gain, which, at the same time, ensures its continued relevance. Because constitutional authority will be hotly contested by both sides, the constitution itself remains authoritative.

But in either their implicit or explicit claim to speak as the authoritative voice of the constitution, judges may obstruct this dynamic of constitutional contestation. On the one hand, Locke's constitutionalism forces both sides in the dispute for the exercise of political power, the legislators and the executive, to show the people the constitutional source of their power—whether that source be the standing laws made by the legislature or pressing exigencies that require the immediacy of executive power. With the entrance of independent judges claiming to speak as the authoritative voice of the constitutional order, both sides will now tend to pitch their arguments at these judges rather than at the people. So, recent presidents cite *Curtiss-Wright* as their constitutional authority for presidential war-making not so much to win the people to their sides, except insofar as it gives them an air of constitutional authority, but to win judges: this ensures that judges continue to cite the political question doctrine and refrain from becoming involved.

Moreover, the very nature of judicial power, when exercised as something more than the power to decide upon individual cases, leads it to articulate what it will tend to claim are permanent constitutional principles. When exercised, the judicial power takes a particular case and seeks to find a general constitutional rule on which to decide it. Such permanent constitutional principles all too often invite their abuse in future cases.[22] For instance, to return to the question of executive discretion, Locke claims: "The Reigns of good Princes have been always most dangerous to the Liberties of their People." They are dangerous because "their Successors, managing the Government with different Thoughts, would draw the Actions of those good rulers into Precedent, and make them the Standard of their Prerogative."[23] In managing the constitutional import of executive prerogative, an independent judge, who naturally abstracts from particulars to find general fixed rules of action, would be tempted to constitutionalize precisely those "precedents" Locke claims cannot be.[24] In short, Locke fails to include an independent judicial branch because there is no meaningful way to subordinate it to the constitutional order, given its implicit or explicit claim to final constitutional authority. Although the law must remain authoritative, the interpretation of the law must remain intrinsically contestable—it will be much less contestable if there were an institution whose very existence claims to speak for it. Perhaps this is why, with an independent judiciary in the American Constitution, the principle of coordinate review has always been suspect in the American tradition. So, even in Marshall's more restrained jurisprudence—jurisprudence that I will argue encourages constitutional contestation—there are still many scholars who claim the problem derives from Marshall himself. John Finn writes: "In Marshall's hands, judicial responsibility for the Constitution rested not on a Madisonian notion of checks and balance, but instead on the Constitution's status as law and on judicial claims of professional expertise."[25] That is, the very existence of a Supreme Court that can invalidate congressional laws based on a more fundamental Constitution seems to invite the conclusion that the Constitution is law, whose interpretation rightfully rests with legal experts.

In fact, one could go further and assert that what might be called the legal mind itself is simply incapable of accepting the contestability of discretionary action without searching for authoritative, abstract, and general legal principles that can regularize, legitimize, and, most important, legalize such action. For instance, despite his persuasive argument regarding the existence, in certain extraordinary situations, of presidential discretionary power to preserve the Constitution—an argument I think he rightly attributes to Lincoln—and his argument that the other branches "have a duty of independent constitutional review over the judgment of necessity," Michael Stokes Paulsen still implies that the power of presidential action over and against both the existing laws and the Constitution itself exists inherently.

Realizing such inherent power could be abused, he writes: "But the capacity of a constitutional power to be abused does not disprove the existence of such a power. It proves only what has just been said—that such a power is capable of misuse." In other words, despite his recognition that the power is contestable because the other branches can and should judge its use, he still tends to speak of it as inherently legal and, as such, not susceptible to judgment. The legal mind simply seems almost incapable of accepting what it truly means to say: that discretionary executive power is inherently "extralegal."[26] This is not to single out Paulsen as a law professor; I could probably level the same charge at my own attempts to articulate the constitutional principles that we can discover from Lincoln's example.[27]

Speaking generally of these extralegal models in reference to an article by Oren Gross, Louis Seidman makes an even more far-reaching claim. He writes:

Any article defending the Extra Legal Model requires some description of what it is and some norms for when it can be invoked. But as soon as the model is structured in this way, it ceases to be extra-legal. What makes conduct extra-legal is precisely its resistance to rules and norms. Without a recognition of this fact, one is led into an infinite regress. In a true emergency, one might ask, are not government officials justified in overriding the rules that Gross establishes for rule violation. But if there are rules that govern this departure, might not those rules, too, be overridden? At the bottom of the chain is the terrifying possibility of unmediated choice that cannot be contained by rules. To describe the circumstances when such choice is appropriate is to insist on the very rules that are being overridden.[28]

It is precisely the problem Seidman has identified that makes it so dangerous to view the Constitution in a purely juridical manner. As Carl Schmitt's life exemplifies, the legal mind views the alternative to law as "unmediated choice." But, when we view the Constitution as the creation of a civic culture of constitutionalism, we can see that, when exercised, extralegal discretionary power takes place in a political context that still has to justify its extralegal quality; it is not simply "unmediated choice."[29] To accomplish this constitutional civic culture in which discretionary power must justify itself, however, requires a much more engaged Congress.

Moreover, Congress, by contrast to the Supreme Court, better guards against executive abuse because it can contest the particular exercises of executive prerogative politically, refusing because of its own jealousy of power to create statutory rules or precedents by which an executive would possess the unfettered exercise of discretionary power. On the other hand, to contest executive discretion, the judiciary is almost forced to arrive either at an arbitrary and politically disastrous standard according to which discretion can never be exercised, or at a "flexible" rule by which it can be. And, given the infinite variety of the types of discretion or lack thereof necessary, such a rule would seem by its very nature either to permit abuse or to demand abrogation. In short, the judiciary simply cannot arrive at a standard which will meaningfully constrain executive power. This is not to say that such a standard is available to Congress. Instead, what is available to Congress is a far greater degree of political discretion by which it can and should judge both the intent and the necessity of questionable executive action. A political judgment must be made about the necessity of extralegal executive action; the Supreme Court is capable of determining only the legality of the action itself.[30]

Madison's Populist Constitutionalism: The Bulwark Against Executive Power

In Madison's constitutional understanding, we see the important connection between constitutional simplicity, of which the Supreme Court seems particularly incapable, and the people's understanding of and support for their constitution. For Madison, popular understanding of and support for the Constitution creates the best bulwark against the expansion of executive power. By contrast, constitutional sophistication provides the best inroads for that expansion.

Madison's series of letters under the pseudonym Helvidius, responding to Hamilton's arguments as Pacificus written in defense of Washington's issuance of a proclamation of neutrality in the war between France and Great Britain, best exemplify this strand of Madison's constitutional thinking. Hamilton asserts that executive power encompasses a degree of discretionary power that the Constitution fails to enumerate because of its intrinsic variety and unpredictability. As such, Hamilton claims the power of war is by its nature executive, but the Constitution chose to remove it from the executive because of its dangers in the hands of one person. Madison's response to Hamilton concerns not so much the proclamation itself—Madison also supported its issuance—but the doctrine by which Hamilton justifies the proclamation.[31] Madison writes: "The doctrine which has been examined is pregnant with inferences and consequences against which no ramparts in the constitution could defend the public liberty or scarcely the forms of republican government . . . no citizens could any longer guess at the character of the government under which he lives; the most penetrating jurist would be unable to scan the extent of constructive prerogative."[32] The crucial achievement of constitutional government is its ability to give citizens accountability and predictability from their government. In fact, advocates of judicial supremacy often justify it by citing precisely such accountability and predictability. But, for Madison, wanting to know what to expect from their government "admonishes the public of the necessity of a rigid adherence to the simple, the received, and the fundamental doctrine of the constitution." So, contrary to *Curtiss-Wright*, "the power to declare war, including the power of judging the causes of war" must be "fully and exclusively vested in the legislature."[33]

For Madison, to allow doctrines other than this most straightforward construction to "make their way into the creed of the government, and the acquiescence of the public" would inevitably lead to further constructions and further powers "that can be deduced from those that had already been accepted."[34] To maintain a "free and defined" Constitution, the people, Madison suggests, can neither be too vigilant "against the introduction nor too critical in tracing the consequences, of new principles and new constructions, that may remove the landmarks of power." Such landmarks of power make it easier for the public to judge when elected officials have overstepped their constitutional authority. They also force these same elected officials to use these landmarks as they justify their authority to exercise power. To maintain meaningful boundaries on the authority to exercise power, the public must be vigilantly suspicious of all creative constructions of its Constitution.

His argument leads naturally then to a complementary argument for coordinate construction. Precisely because only constitutional arguments authorize action, each branch must have at its disposal the power to interpret the Constitution in such a manner as to justify its action. Coordinate construction, then, is at the very heart of Madison's constitutionalism.[35] Political authority comes from the persuasiveness of each branch's respective constitutional arguments and not from some legalistic structure that can be maintained only by an "independent" branch's absolute authority over what the Constitution means. In this scenario, one could expect a president to advance the kind of argument one finds in *Curtis-Wright*, and one would expect the Congress to resist these kinds of arguments. Intrinsic to creating such authority is popular involvement in either accepting or rejecting constitutional arguments for political authority. How would such involvement be effectuated? Gary Jacobsohn suggests that under this model, "the jury performed a function analogous to judicial review."[36] One example is provided by Neal Devens and Louis Fisher in their book *The Democratic Constitution*. After Washington's Proclamation of Neutrality, the government tried to prosecute citizens for violating his proclamation. Jurors continuously acquitted because they refused to convict someone for a crime established only by proclamation. Washington went back to Congress to get legislation passed.[37] Although Washington claimed the power to prosecute citizens for violating the proclamation, the juries denied him this authority.

Thus, we see that Madison's constitutionalism connects political incentives to constitutional authority. The ambitious ground their exercise of power in constitutional arguments because the people hold their Constitution higher than any political actor. The control of executive power, which Madison suggests is otherwise always looking to expand, depends on popular vigilance toward the landmarks of power contained in their Constitution; such constitutional vigilance requires constitutional simplicity. A constitutionally vigilant population will refuse the executive the authority to exercise powers that are simply not his constitutionally; his legislative opposition will have tremendous political incentives to expose the executive's lack of constitutional authority. So, to the extent that the Supreme Court assumes constitutional authority and introduces "new principles and new constructions," it may, in its deleterious effect on the people's understanding of their Constitution, inadvertently destroy the very landmarks of power it seeks to create. In fact, Madison's logic goes further. By the logic of his argument, the Supreme Court constitutes the greatest danger to republican constitutionalism because, with its new interpretations and constructions, even "the most penetrating jurist" cannot "scan the extent of constructive prerogative."

By contrast to this argument, Michael Zuckert suggests that Madison originally aimed to maintain the separation of powers by proposing an elected Council of Revision in his Virginia Plan. Such a council would provide for an independent source of constitutional authority that still remained essentially political, apt to be controlled by political processes. Although the Supreme Court has evolved into something like this council, its "apolitical" character makes it ill-suited to the task. Zuckert may well be right about Madison's pre–Constitutional Convention intentions and about his relative pessimism regarding what emerged from the convention.[38] But, as Gary Rosen argues persuasively, Madison chose not to follow Hamilton's lead and surreptitiously argue into the Constitution what he had failed to achieve in the convention.[39] Instead, despite or precisely because Madison failed to get a Council of Revision, he sought to invigorate the sanctity of the Constitution as it was popularly understood at ratification. Precisely because it was not within the political spheres, Madison did not trust the Supreme Court to fulfill the role he had hoped for from his Council of Revision. Instead, he sought to give the public the role he had envisioned for his council by inviting them to participate in the politics of constitutional meaning—a politics made possible by the seriousness with which the public takes its Constitution.[40] In other words, in a certain sense, my discussion of Madison complements, rather than contradicts, Zuckert's.

In both its criticism of the corrosive constitutional effects of judicial supremacy and its lament about the loss of constitutional responsibility in the "political branches," my argument also fits within the revitalized "departmentalist" school of constitutional theory.[41] There are, however, a couple of things often, but not always, overlooked by those advocating departmentalism that, I would argue, were better understood by those who advocated the same at our founding. First, properly understood, departmentalism must include constitutional persuasion. Although Madison advocates the right and responsibility of each branch to interpret the Constitution as it understands it, he also thinks the disputes such contending interpretations create will be settled by the court of public opinion based on who they believe to have the most compelling constitutional argument.[42] In other words, constitutional powers can be claimed, but to transform into constitutional authority, these claims must be accepted. In a certain sense then, the public serves the role of ultimate constitutional authority that the Supreme Court currently claims for itself. And second, departmentalism should be practiced not just out of constitutional responsibility—his *Federalist* 51 reveals him as anything but naïve regarding the place mere responsibility possesses in human motivations—but out of political incentives. To acquire political power, one must show the constitutional basis of power; "the interest of the man must be connected with the constitutional rights of the place." Too often, the current version of departmentalism emphasizes the constitutional responsibility that should be exercised by political actors rather than the interest political actors have in exercising constitutional responsibility. That being said, incentives to behave constitutionally will not exist if the people are not themselves attentive to their constitution.

Both Locke's and Madison's concerns reveal that the problem of executive power most highlights the difficulties of a nonconstitutional people.

Where most governmental problems can still be solved legally through constitutional forms even if the people are not attached to them, the extralegal nature of executive power has never rested comfortably in a constitutional order.[43] The nature of executive power is such that it can claim most authority in those situations when the ordinary rule of law somehow does not apply. If the ordinary rule of law truly does not apply, these claims to authority are acceptable.[44] But executives will also claim an exceptional situation where none truly exists and thus attempt to assume greater power in response to the "extraordinary" situation. For instance, in the past thirty years, besides "extraordinary" regional wars that required "immediate" presidential action without congressional authorization, we have had "wars" on poverty, drugs, and now terror.[45] By claiming we are in a "war," presidents can most claim the authority to exercise the peculiar advantages of the office, that is, its secrecy, unity, and immediacy. To control such claims, we need more than a Supreme Court committed to a legalistic Constitution; we need a people committed to *their* limited Constitution. Because executive power is best controlled by the political use of the Constitution over and against executive action outside its boundaries, the court's tendency to interpret the Constitution legalistically is especially problematic insofar as its new constructions distance the people from an understanding of their Constitution—thus discouraging its political use by Congress.

Marshall's Judicial Review

Given these theoretical arguments and the deleterious effects the three types of decisions I discuss first had on constitutional contestation in their wake, one should wonder, at this point, if judicial review, of any sort, can be consonant with a constitutional order. In fact, some of those scholars advocating coordinate construction have also begun advocating the utter abandonment of judicial review itself.[46] But before taking this step, perhaps there is a form of judicial review that does less damage to the constitutional responsibilities of the other branches of government.

Recently scholars have rescued Marshall's jurisprudence of judicial review from its claimed association with the doctrine of judicial supremacy. As such, they have noted that almost uniformly, Marshall's rulings used the power of judicial review not to restrict the powers of Congress, but to enlarge them against opposition that urged the constitutional restriction of its powers. For instance, Christopher Wolfe rightly notes that Marshall's "whole discussion of adaptation appears with reference to Congress' discretion to choose appropriate means to exercise its power under the Constitution."[47]

It is this deference to the constitutional views of Congress and its resulting statutory law that has, with some exceptions, tended to characterize the majority of the Court's involvement in issues of war power. As Louis Fisher has emphasized, it is incorrect to characterize the vast majority of the Court's jurisprudence as avoiding war powers issues because such are "political questions" beyond the competency of the Court.[48] Instead, it has checked the presidency, not by acting on its own, but by upholding congressional statutes over and against contradictory executive action. Thus, for instance, in *Little v. Barreme*, Marshall's court decides against a commander of a ship of war of the United States because, though he acted according to the instructions given to him by the president, the instructions themselves were contrary to congressional legislation.[49] Outside the rest of its sweeping claims about executive power, Edward Corwin claims that this same logic—a president has acted contrary to an existing congressional statute—justifies the Court's ruling in *Youngstown*, a justification only articulated by Justice Clark's much more modest concurring opinion.[50] The doctrine of judicial review, as it has been exercised historically in this issue of crucial importance, has checked the presidency not through its own involvement, but by providing Congress with a "weapon" of sorts against the aggressive and unilateral assertion of presidential power.[51] The court has often done this, and I would submit best does this, not by articulating grand theories about the constitutional separation of powers, but merely by upholding congressional statutes over and against presidential action. In so doing, jurisprudential attention to the law (or lack thereof) invigorates the legislative authority because it locates responsibility in them, rather than the courts. As such, opposition to unwise or invasive legislation can concentrate its political attention not on the court that upheld it, but on the legislators who passed it. For instance, one might argue that had the judiciary exercised its power of judicial review and reversed the Alien and Sedition Acts, the effect would have been to concentrate attention upon those who reversed them rather than on those who passed them. In such a scenario, it is difficult to imagine the Jeffersonians becoming as ascendant as they became. By failing to exercise what would seem to have been its constitutional power to strike down unconstitutional legislation, the judiciary paradoxically benefited the opponents of the legislation more.[52]

Of course, Marshall does say in *Marbury*: "The province of the court is solely, to decide on the rights of individuals."[53] Such a statement reflects the continuing primary concern of the Court. The difference between Marshall's jurisprudence and more recent jurisprudence may lie, however, in Marshall's attentiveness to the constitutional structure and the constitutional culture in which individual rights are best secured. Leslie Goldstein claims that this attention to constitutional structure is the real accomplishment of Marshall's jurisprudence, although she might also say that I have done what she claims everyone does: ground their understanding of proper judicial review in Marshall's jurisprudence (the same might, of course, be said for her argument).[54] Marshall understood that maintaining a healthy system of separation of powers best secures individual rights over the long term and as such requires a vigorous Congress. Insofar as the contemporary principle of judicial supremacy eviscerates the constitutional power of Congress and, more generally, the Constitution's importance for the people themselves, its unintended effect is the further empowerment of the executive.[55]

Conclusion

Although my argument has concentrated on the relations between Congress, the president and the Supreme Court in matters of discretionary power, its implications are, in fact, much broader and reach to the theme of this book. Here, I attempt to show in the preeminently important case of discretionary executive power the deleterious effects of judicial supremacy and the Court's concomitant penchant for creating doctrines. Although some have argued that the authority of a Constitution can only be preserved if the courts can exercise their binding interpretations on the other branches, this chapter suggests the opposite. The absolute authority of the courts in matters of constitutional interpretation actually leads to the Constitution possessing little authority over the actions of members of the other two constitutional branches of government. In the specific, but preeminently important, question of war powers, the perception of the Supreme Court's willingness to take an absolute position of constitutional authority discourages the other branches from exercising their own constitutional responsibility. In such a scenario, as constitutional scholars dating back to James Bradley Thayer have argued, the Constitution ceases to constitute a political way of life for the American people and becomes a technical affair with little meaning to the people outside of the authoritative claims made about it by the Supreme Court justices. In other words, as the Supreme Court asserts too much constitutional sovereignty, its assertions weaken constitutionalism itself. In this volume, both Tushnet and Whittington have discussed Thayer's theory of coordinate constitutional interpretation. My argument supplements their arguments by showing in a more specific case the reasons why constitutional responsibility is essential and the dangers of judicial supremacy to that felt responsibility.

In the case of discretionary security matters, the Constitution envisions a healthy contestation between Congress and the president, whose separate functions, but overlapping powers, create a constitutional struggle for the authority to exercise power. The very ambiguity of the document promotes the vitality of the struggle and, paradoxically, the vitality of constitutionalism. Supreme Court interventions that attempt to specify the proper "balance" of constitutional powers tend to sap the vitality of Congress, whose most natural state is already relative inertia and lassitude. And to the extent that legislators' actions seem not to exhibit inertia, their assertions of "war powers" often exhibit constitutional irresponsibility, as in the Specter example, because they do not have to be responsible since they expect the Supreme Court will clean up their mess.

That the courts interpret the Constitution legalistically in a manner understood only by legal scholars and constitutional lawyers is not a new development. That such interpretations distance the people from understanding their Constitution is also not new. To some degree, I would even suggest that both developments have occurred without having the kinds of drastically deleterious effects on the polity that some critics of this mode of judicial supremacy have described. The argument here, however, suggests that this development is especially problematic in the crucial issue of controlling the growth of an overweening discretionary executive power. In this crucially important issue, control of an executive's claims to the authority to act outside of or against the Constitution depends so much on Congress's ability and willingness to use the Constitution to call into question such authority. Congress's willingness to oppose executive action depends on political incentives; such incentives only exist if the people are attached, first and foremost, to their Constitution. As the people lose their understanding of their Constitution in a haze of judicial interpretations, they lose this essential attachment.

Notes

Introduction

1. As Nathan Tarcov argues in his chapter in this volume, there were ancient constitutions and there was even an ancient "idea of constitutionalism." Tarcov's chapter situates the inquiry undertaken by the other contributors to this volume by exploring the "resemblances" between ancient and modern constitutionalism. Ancient constitutions, like modern constitutions, establish the "rule of law" and thereby seek to tame the rule of party or faction. But the differences between ancient and modern constitutions are as significant as the resemblances: the ancient constitutionalists relied on political education and on mixed regimes to achieve a politics that would "serve the common good rather than the interests of a faction"; as a result, the ancient constitutionalists were dubious about whether consent or "popular ratification alone" would be sufficient to achieve the taming of politics that is the common aim of ancient and modern constitutionalism.

2. "But every difference of opinion is not a difference of principle. We have called by different names brethren of the same principle. We are all Republicans, we are all Federalists. If there be any among us who would wish to dissolve this Union or to change its republican form, let them stand undisturbed as monuments of the safety with which error of opinion may be tolerated where reason is left free to combat it." *Thomas Jefferson: Writings* (New York: Library of America, 1984), 493.

3. We do not mean here to endorse the most pessimistic view of today's "culture wars." There are, of course, vast areas of constitutional law where most disputes are what might be called lawyers' disputes, more or less purified of politics—e.g., disputes about application of doctrine that is widely accepted or about application of competing lines of precedent, or disputes about appropriate legal or jurisprudential means to agreed ends. But there are certainly some areas of constitutional law—the constitutional law of privacy and the constitutional law of religion come to mind—where constitutional debate today approaches questions of first principle. Some years ago, Mary Ann Glendon wrote of the principal opinions in a 1986 case restricting privacy rights of homosexuals (since overruled): "it is only a slight exaggeration to say that the two main opinions in *Bowers v. Hardwick* make the case look like a battle between Yahoos and perverts" (*Rights Talk* [New York: Free Press, 1991], 154).

4. On the first issue, consider the opposing views of James Stoner and Larry Alexander in their chapters in this volume. On the second issue, consider the opposing views of Leslie Friedman Goldstein and Justice Robert Young, Jr., in their chapters in this volume. And see the chapter in this volume by Michael Zuckert for

a careful explication of Madison's understanding of the political role of the Supreme Court: "Madison's analysis helps lay bare the deeper anomaly the Supreme Court embodies: it is a legal body, with a certain legal claim . . . to the power of judicial review. But the Court's position in the system is more deeply defined by the fact that it is the body entrusted with . . . keystone political functions within the complex institutional array of the American Constitution. . . . It has the implicit duty to be more than a legal institution; it has the explicit duty to be nothing but a legal institution. . . . The Court is constantly driven beyond the bounds of strict legality in order to do its political work." (The political work of the Court is principally policing the separation of powers and federalism, including on behalf of individual rights threatened by the States.)

5. Rogers Smith, in his chapter in this volume, offers a "Machiavellian" analysis of the emergence of "juristocracy" as a favored form of modern democratic constitutional politics. The rise of judicial power in modern democracy can be understood as a partisan accommodation between elites and the people, often at the expense of democratic aspirations: "We tend to hope for more from modern constitutional democracies than relatively nonoppressive, though highly unequal, elite predominance."

6. In his chapter in this volume, Benjamin Kleinerman discusses the dangers to liberal freedoms of a failure to contest the constitution politically in the context of the president's war powers. In a different but related vein, Mark Tushnet, in his chapter in this volume, discusses various weak or "dialogic" forms of judicial review practiced in other constitutional democracies, partly with a view to the question whether these forms of judicial review might preserve liberal constitutionalism while also providing for more vigorous democratic citizenship than American-style strong judicial review.

7. Rogers Smith, in his chapter in this volume: "many elites may well be tempted, consciously or not, to use judicial decision-making as an ever more aggressive vehicle to serve themselves, sometimes at the expense of popular well-being and any plausible conception of the shared public good."

8. On the threat to democracy from judicial oligarchy or elitism, consider the very different statements of the problem in the chapters by Rogers Smith and Justice Robert Young, Jr., in this volume.

9. It is worth noting that democracy can be a threat to constitutionalism as well, and that the priority of democracy to liberal constitutionalism is itself a contested question. The chapters in this volume by Nathan Tarcov, Steven Kautz, and Larry Alexander discuss this question.

10. For treatments of the practice of constitutional politics in America in particular, see the chapters in this volume by Michael Zuckert, Leslie Friedman Goldstein, and James Stoner.

11. See the chapters by Rogers Smith, Mark Tushnet, and Leslie Friedman Goldstein in this volume.

12. Montesquieu, *The Spirit of the Laws*, book II, chapter 2.

13. See the chapters by Larry Alexander and Steven Kautz in this volume for very different justifications of constitutional limits on democratic politics. The chapter by Mark Tushnet in this volume describes a form of constitutional rea-

soning—"dialogic" judicial review—that might be said to avoid the either/or of a politics without limits and a constitutionalism without politics.

Chapter 1. Ideas of Constitutionalism Ancient and Modern

This chapter benefited from the comments of Vickie B. Sullivan and the general discussion at the conference.

1. Cf., e.g., Nathan Tarcov, "American Constitutionalism and Individual Rights," in *How Does the Constitution Secure Rights?* Robert Goldwin and William Schambra, eds. (Washington, D.C.: American Enterprise Institute, 1985), 121–22.

2. Cf. Leo Strauss, *Liberalism Ancient and Modern* (Ithaca, N.Y.: Cornell University Press, 1968, 1989), 15: "There is a direct connection between the [classic] notion of the mixed regime and modern republicanism. Lest this be misunderstood, one must immediately stress the important differences between the modern doctrine and its classic original." See also p. 24 on "the cause of constitutionalism" and *On Tyranny*, p. 194, on "liberal or constitutional democracy" as "closer to what the classics demanded than any alternative that is viable in our age" (1961; repr. Chicago: University of Chicago Press, 2000).

3. *The Laws of Plato*, Thomas L. Pangle, trans. (1980; repr. Chicago: University of Chicago Press, 1988), cited by Stephanus numbers. My quotations follow this translation except that I translate *politeia* as constitution.

4. For that universal human inclination see also Plato, *Republic* 571b, 572b.

5. See Charles Howard McIlwain, *Constitutionalism: Ancient and Modern*, rev. ed. (Ithaca, N.Y.: Cornell University Press, 1947), 29–35.

6. See Bernard Manin, *The Principles of Representative Government* (Cambridge: Cambridge University Press, 1997), 27–28, 34–41, 134–56.

7. Steven Kautz's chapter in this volume brings out more fully the ambiguities of Aristotle's case for rule of law.

8. Niccolò Machiavelli, *The Prince*, Harvey C. Mansfield, trans., 2nd ed. (1st ed. 1985; Chicago: University of Chicago Press, 1998), cited by chapter numbers.

9. For a different view of Machiavelli's understanding of the function of such courts see Rogers Smith's chapter in this volume.

10. Niccolò Machiavelli, *Discourses on Livy*, Harvey C. Mansfield and Nathan Tarcov, trans. (Chicago: University of Chicago Press, 1996), cited by book, chapter, and paragraph numbers.

11. For another analysis of the role of class conflict in Machiavelli see Rogers Smith's chapter in this volume.

12. See Nathan Tarcov, "Law and Innovation in Machiavelli's *Prince*," in *Enlightening Revolutions: Essays in Honor of Ralph Lerner*, Svetozar Minkov, ed. (Lanham, Md.: Rowman and Littlefield, 2006).

13. John Locke, *Two Treatises of Government*, Peter Laslett, ed., student ed. (Cambridge: Cambridge University Press, 1988), cited by treatise and section numbers.

14. Locke is, however, concerned in other works with education toward the

virtues required for liberty: see John Locke's *Some Thoughts Concerning Education* and *On the Conduct of the Understanding,* Ruth Grant and Nathan Tarcov, eds. (Indianapolis: Hackett Publishing, 1996) and Nathan Tarcov, *Locke's Education for Liberty* (Chicago: University of Chicago Press, 1984).

15. See Benjamin Kleinerman's chapter in this volume.

16. On this issue see Benjamin Kleinerman's chapter in this volume.

17. Nathan Tarcov, "Locke's *Second Treatise* and 'The Best Fence Against Rebellion,'" *Review of Politics* 43, no. 2 (April 1981): 198–217.

18. Alexander Hamilton, James Madison, and John Jay, *The Federalist Papers,* Clinton Rossiter, ed., with an introduction and notes by Charles R. Kesler (1961; repr. New York: New American Library, 1999).

Chapter 2. On Liberal Constitutionalism

1. See Montesquieu, *The Spirit of the Laws,* 2.1–2, 3.1–3. The liberal constitution aims to supply the defect of republican virtue. But the difference between reliance on liberal constitutionalism and reliance on republican virtue can be overstated: a sort of (liberal) virtue is, of course, required if a people is to acknowledge the necessity of supplying through a constitution the defect of more robust (republican) virtue.

2. This is the most significant difference between the ancient idea of the constitution and the modern idea. As Nathan Tarcov shows in his chapter in this volume, ancient constitutionalism relies not primarily on popular consent, but on political education and the institutions of a mixed regime, to achieve the rule of law.

3. See Locke, *Second Treatise,* §87: "Man being born, as has been proved, with a title to perfect freedom, and an uncontrouled enjoyment of all the rights and privileges of the law of nature, equally with any other man, or number of men in the world, hath by nature a power, not only to preserve his property, that is, his life, liberty and estate, against the injuries and attempts of other men; but to judge of, and punish the breaches of that law in others, as he is persuaded the offence deserves, even with death itself, in crimes where the heinousness of the fact, in his opinion, requires it. But because no political society can be, nor subsist, without having in itself the power to preserve the property, and in order thereunto, punish the offences of all those of that society; there, and there only is political society, where every one of the members hath quitted this natural power, resigned it up into the hands of the community in all cases that exclude him not from appealing for protection to the law established by it. And thus all private judgment of every particular member being excluded, the community comes to be umpire, by settled standing rules, indifferent, and the same to all parties; and by men having authority from the community, for the execution of those rules, decides all the differences that may happen between any members of that society concerning any matter of right; and punishes those offences which any member hath committed against the society, with such penalties as the law has established: whereby it is easy to discern, who are, and who are not, in political society together." See too, *Second Treatise,* §§88–89, 123–31.

4. This section of the chapter is adapted from my essay "Liberty, Justice, and the Rule of Law," *Yale Journal of Law and Humanities* 11, no. 2 (Summer 1999). I rely here on the argument in Walter Berns, "Judicial Review and the Rights and Laws of Nature," in his *In Defense of Liberal Democracy* (Chicago: Regnery Gateway, 1984), 29–62.

5. In his chapter in this volume, Nathan Tarcov concludes: "As we hold up our constitutionalism for emulation in places divided by deep ethnic and sectarian enmities, we should recall Plato and Aristotle's lesson that popular ratification alone cannot guarantee such a Constitution unless it serves the common good rather than the interests of a faction." (See, too, the harsh sequel to this remark.) Tarcov argues that today we might reasonably question whether or under what circumstances a liberal constitution can be a nonpartisan constitution, serving the common good and not the interests of a party or faction. I offer in this chapter a defense of liberal constitutionalism on this question, but I agree with Tarcov that the case for liberal constitutionalism depends on recognizing the danger that the putative nonpartisanship of "We the People" can too often prove to be a weapon of parties or sects.

6. Berns, "Judicial Review of the Rights and Laws of Nature," 40, 54. See generally, 37–54.

7. Antonin Scalia, "The Rule of Law as a Law of Rules," *University of Chicago Law Review* 56 (Fall 1989): 1175.

8. Scalia quotes Paine's *Common Sense*: "as in absolute governments the king is law, so in free countries the law ought to be king." Characteristically, he makes the argument against judicial discretion not so much on the basis of liberal fear of "private judgment," but rather from democracy: "in a democratic system, . . . the general rule of law has special claim to preference, since it is the normal product of that branch of government most responsive to the people." This democratic turn in the liberal argument seems to me misguided, for reasons that I here postpone. But for present purposes the conflation of democracy and liberalism is no trouble.

9. See Scalia's useful discussion of contributory negligence at the end of "The Rule of Law as a Law of Rules."

10. The chapters in this volume by Larry Alexander and Mark Tushnet approach the same set of questions from different directions. The case for "dialogic" forms of judicial review, presented in Tushnet's chapter, might be seen as an effort to preserve a role for judicial reason or wisdom, while offering a safety valve against the sorts of dangers discussed in the text that trouble liberal theorists. And the sorts of pragmatic judgment recommended near the end of Alexander's chapter, in thinking about the "institutional competencies" of courts and legislatures, might be seen as akin to the reasoning about judicial discretion described in the text, so long as the liberal horizon of the fear of private judgment were to frame the inquiry.

11. One might also consider the special case of bureaucratic or agency discretion, where that discretion is conferred by legislation and where the courts have embraced doctrines of deference, both of which are often justified on grounds of the superior expertise of the regulators. So far as this does not implicate controversies of a party origin, such delegation is not problematic as a matter of liberal theory, though it might be problematic as a matter of democratic theory.

12. Moreover, as Benjamin Kleinerman shows in his chapter in this volume,

there are dangers in the exercise of executive prerogative even where the case for its exercise does not depend on the superior wisdom of the ruler or executive—e.g., in cases of emergency. The question of the appropriate mix of executive discretion and popular vigilance (aided by aggressive legislative signaling and constitutional contestation across the political branches) cannot be answered by reference to the prudence or wisdom of executives, legislatives, and peoples. The contested issue is not a substantive one (who knows best), but rather a formal one (what balance of prerogative, constitutional constraint, and popular vigilance best preserves the stability of the liberal order).

13. See §111: "When ambition and luxury in future ages would retain and increase the power, without doing the business for which it was given; and aided by flattery, taught princes to have distinct and separate interests from their people, men found it necessary to examine more carefully the original and rights of government; and to find out ways to restrain the exorbitances, and prevent the abuses of that power, which they having intrusted in another's hands only for their own good, they found was made use of to hurt them." Cf. §166: "Upon this is founded that saying, That the reigns of good princes have been always most dangerous to the liberties of their people: for when their successors, managing the government with different thoughts, would draw the actions of those good rulers into precedent, and make them the standard of their prerogative, as if what had been done only for the good of the people was a right in them to do, for the harm of the people, if they so pleased." Finally, cf. §223.

14. See my "Abraham Lincoln: The Moderation of a Democratic Statesman," in *History of American Political Thought*, Bryan-Paul Frost and Jeffrey Sikkenga, eds. (Lanham, Md.: Lexington Books, 2003). But even Lincoln often speaks as a Lockean, defending prerogative not on the basis of his own superior judgment, but on the basis of some necessity (and in some cases seeking retroactive popular or legislative endorsement of his exercise of prerogative). Consider his July 4, 1861 Message to Congress, respecting the suspension of the privilege of the writ of habeas corpus: "The whole of the laws which were required to be faithfully executed were being resisted and failing of execution in nearly one-third of the States. Must they be allowed to finally fail of execution, even had it been perfectly clear that by the use of the means necessary to their execution some single law, made in such extreme tenderness of the citizen's liberty that practically it relieves more of the guilty than of the innocent, should to a very limited extent be violated? To state the question more directly, are all the laws but one to go unexecuted and the Government itself go to pieces lest that one be violated? Even in such a case would not the official oath be broken if the Government should be overthrown, when it was believed that disregarding the single law would tend to preserve it?" And his 1863 public letter to Erastus Corning: "If I be wrong on this question of constitutional power, my error lies in believing that certain proceedings are constitutional when, in cases of rebellion or invasion, the public safety requires them, which would not be constitutional when, in absence of rebellion or invasion, the public safety does not require them—in other words, that the constitution is not in its application in all respects the same, in cases of rebellion or invasion, involving the public safety, as it is in times of profound peace and public security. The constitution itself makes the distinction; and I

can no more be persuaded that the government can constitutionally take no strong measure in time of rebellion, because it can be shown that the same could not be lawfully taken in time of peace, than I can be persuaded that a particular drug is not good medicine for a sick man, because it can be shown to not be good food for a well one. Nor am I able to appreciate the danger, apprehended by the meeting, that the American people will, by means of military arrests during the rebellion, lose the right of public discussion, the liberty of speech and the press, the law of evidence, trial by jury, and Habeas corpus, throughout the indefinite peaceful future which I trust lies before them, any more than I am able to believe that a man could contract so strong an appetite for emetics during temporary illness, as to persist in feeding upon them through the remainder of his healthful life."

15. Here and elsewhere, I am indebted to Harvey C. Mansfield, "Hobbes and the Science of Indirect Government" (*American Political Science Review* 65, March 1971), and to his "Liberal Democracy as Mixed Regime," in his *The Spirit of Liberalism* (Cambridge, Mass.: Harvard University Press, 1978).

16. This picture is further complicated by Rousseau, as Allan Bloom argues in "Rousseau's Critique of Liberal Constitutionalism," in *The Legacy of Rousseau*, Clifford Orwin and Nathan Tarcov, eds. (Chicago: University of Chicago Press, 1997). "At the moment the Framers wrote 'We the people of the United States . . . ,' the word 'people' had been made problematic by Jean-Jacques Rousseau. How do you get from individuals to a people, that is, from persons who care only for their particular good to a community of citizens who subordinate their own good to the common good" (143). In the ordinary case, that transformation either will not be achieved (so that "the people" is constituted by warring interests, parties, factions) or it will be achieved perversely, by means of some ideological mystification. See especially 156–61.

17. For efforts to conceive of contemporary liberal democracy in Aristotelian terms, see Mansfield, "Liberal Democracy as Mixed Regime"; Steven Kautz, *Liberalism and Community* (Ithaca, N.Y.: Cornell University Press, 1995), especially chapters 1–3; and Martin Diamond, "Ethics and Politics: The American Way," in *The Moral Foundations of the American Republic*, Robert H. Horwitz, ed., 3rd ed. (Charlottesville: University Press of Virginia, 1986). And see too Nathan Tarcov's account of the place of the idea of a mixed regime in ancient constitutionalism in his chapter in this volume.

18. *Democracy in America*, Harvey C. Mansfield and Delba Winthrop, trans. and eds., 47. See generally 46–53.

19. *Democracy in America*, 47–51.

20. See the texts cited in note 17 above.

21. See, too, Harvey C. Mansfield, *America's Constitutional Soul* (Baltimore: Johns Hopkins University Press, 1991), especially chapter 12, "The Forms and Formalities of Liberty."

22. For a characteristic statement of the first view, from Justice Scalia's opinion in *Smith*: "Values that are protected against government interference through enshrinement in the Bill of Rights are not thereby banished from the political process. Just as a society that believes in the negative protection accorded to the press by the First Amendment is likely to enact laws that affirmatively foster the dissemina-

tion of the printed word, so also a society that believes in the negative protection accorded to religious belief can be expected to be solicitous of that value in its legislation as well. It is therefore not surprising that a number of States have made an exception to their drug laws for sacramental peyote use. . . . But to say that a nondiscriminatory religious practice exemption is permitted, or even that it is desirable, is not to say that it is constitutionally required, and that the appropriate occasions for its creation can be discerned by the courts. It may fairly be said that leaving accommodation to the political process will place at a relative disadvantage those religious practices that are not widely engaged in; but that unavoidable consequence of democratic government must be preferred to a system in which each conscience is a law unto itself or in which judges weigh the social importance of all laws against the centrality of all religious beliefs." For a characteristic statement of the second view, see Ronald Dworkin, *Taking Rights Seriously*, 149: "Constitutional law can make no genuine advance until it isolates the problem of rights against the state and makes that problem part of its own agenda. That argues for a *fusion of constitutional law and moral theory*, a connection that, incredibly, has yet to take place. It is perfectly understandable that lawyers dread contamination with moral philosophy, and particularly with those philosophers who talk about rights, because the spooky overtones of that concept threaten the graveyard of reason. But better philosophy is now available than the lawyers may remember. Professor Rawls of Harvard, for example, has published an abstract and complex book about justice which no constitutional lawyer will be able to ignore."

Chapter 3. Judicial Review and the Incomplete Constitution

1. *Federalist* 78.

2. 410 U.S. 113 (1973).

3. 505 U.S. 833 (1992).

4. Mark Tushnet, *Taking the Constitution to the Courts* (Princeton, N.J.: Princeton University Press, 2000).

5. Robert Bork, *Slouching Towards Gomorrah* (New York: Regan Books, 1997), 321; John C. Yoo and Saikrishna Prakash, "The Origins of Judicial Review," *University of Chicago Law Review* 69 (Summer 2003): 10.

6. 338 U.S. 1 (1958).

7. "James Madison to Thomas Jefferson, September 6, 1787," in *James Madison: Writings*, Jack Rakove, ed. (New York: Library of America, 1999), 136.

8. James Madison, "Preface to Debates in the Convention of 1787," in *The Records of the Federal Convention of 1787*, Max Farrand, ed. (New Haven, Conn.: Yale University Press, 1967), 3:539.

9. James Madison, Alexander Hamilton, John Jay, et al., *The Essential Federalist and Anti-Federalist Papers*, David Wooton, ed. (Indianapolis: Hackett Publishing, 2003), no. 9.

10. See esp. Madison, "Vices of the Political System of the United States, April 1787," in Rakove, ed.

11. See "The Virginia Plan," in Ferrand, ed., *Records*, vol. 1:20–23.

12. Donald Lutz, "The Relative Influence of European Writers on Late Eighteenth-Century American Political Thought," *American Political Science Review* 78 (1984): 189–97.

13. Charles de Montesquieu, *The Spirit of the Laws*, Anne Cohler, Basia Miller, and Harold Stone, eds. and trans. (Cambridge: Cambridge University Press, 1989), 11:6.

14. Ibid., 3:2, 3; 4:4–8; 5:1–7.

15. *Federalist* 39.

16. *Federalist* 47.

17. *Federalist* 39.

18. John Trenchard and Thomas Gordon, *Cato's Letters or Essays on Liberty, Civil and Religious, and Other Important Subjects*, Ronald Hamowy, ed. (Indianapolis: Liberty Fund, 1995), no. 61.

19. *Federalist* 48, 63.

20. Montesquieu, *Spirit*, XII 6.

21. *Federalist* 48.

22. *Federalist* 49.

23. Farrand, ed., *Records*, 1:21.

24. Montesquieu, *Spirit*, 9:1–3.

25. Madison, "Vices," in Rakove, ed., 69–74.

26. Farrand, ed., *Records*, 1:21.

27. "James Madison to Thomas Jefferson, October 24, 1787," in Rakove, ed., 145.

28. *Federalist* 10.

29. *Federalist* 51.

30. Martin Diamond, *As Far as Republican Principles Will Admit* (Washington, D.C.: AEI Press, 1992), 93–144.

31. Michael Zuckert, "A System Without Precedent: Federalism in the American Constitution," in *The Framing and Ratification of the Constitution*, Leonard Levy and Dennis Mahoney, eds. (New York: Macmillan, 1987), 142–45.

32. "James Madison to Thomas Jefferson, October 24, 1787," in Rakove, ed., 146.

33. Zuckert, "System," 139–42.

34. *Notes of Debates in the Federal Convention of 1787 Reported by James Madison* (New York: W. W. Norton, 1987), 66.

35. Farrand, ed., *Records*, 1:97–104.

36. *Notes of Debates*, 79–81.

37. Farrand, ed., *Records*, 1:138–40.

38. *Notes of Debates*, 336–43.

39. Ibid., 461–62.

40. Ibid., 61.

41. Robert Lawry Clinton, *Marbury v. Madison and Judicial Review* (Lawrence: University Press of Kansas, 1989), 57–60.

42. Sylvia Snowiss, *Judicial Review and the Law of the Constitution* (New Haven, Conn.: Yale University Press, 1990), 39–40.

43. Ibid.

44. *Notes of Debates*, 462.

45. Ibid., 463.

46. Ibid.

47. Farrand, ed., Records, 1:97.

48. Ibid.

49. Edward Corwin, *The Doctrine of Judicial Review* (Princeton, N.J.: Princeton University Press, 1914), 10.

50. "James Madison to Thomas Jefferson, October 24, 1787," in Rakove, ed., 148.

51. James Madison, "Observations on the 'Draught of a Constitution for Virginia,'" in Rakove, ed., 417.

52. *Marbury v. Madison*, 5 U.S. 137 (1803).

53. *Cooper v. Aaron*, 358 U.S. 1 (1958).

54. Madison, "Observations," in Rakove, ed., 417.

55. "James Madison to Thomas Jefferson, October 24, 1787," in Rakove, ed., 148.

56. Ibid., 149.

57. Ibid.

58. Ibid.

59. Ibid., 152.

60. *Notes of Debates*, 337–38.

61. Ibid.

62. Ibid.

63. Ibid.

64. Ibid.

65. Ibid.

66. *The Federalist*, no. 51.

67. James Madison, "Observations," in Rakove, ed., 417.

Chapter 4. Constitutionalism as Judicial Review

1. Neal C. Tate and Torbjorn Vallinder, eds., *The Global Expansion of Judicial Power* (New York: New York University Press, 1995). The phrase "the power of judges" itself is a title of a recent book; see note 4 below for the citation.

2. Ran Hirschl, *Towards Juristocracy: The Origins and Consequences of the New Constitutionalism* (Cambridge, Mass.: Harvard University Press, 2004).

3. Kim L. Scheppele, "Declarations of Independence: Judicial Reactions to Political Pressure," in *Judicial Independence at the Crossroads*, Stephen B. Burbank and Barry Friedman, eds. (Thousand Oaks, Calif: Sage, 2002).

4. Carlo Guarneri and Patrizia Pederzoli, *The Power of Judges: A Comparative Study of Courts and Democracy* (Oxford: Oxford University Press, 2002).

5. Hirschl, *Towards Juristocracy*.

6. Switzerland's 1848 Constitution allocated to its Tribunal Federal power to

declare unconstitutional cantonal laws, but not federal laws. The latter can, however, be voided by popular referenda. Chief Justice Carsten Smith, "Judicial Review of Parliamentary Legislation: Norway as a European Pioneer," presented at the University of London Annual Coffin Memorial, April 3, 2003; R. Ryssdal, "The Relation Between the Judiciary and the Legislative and Executive Branches of the Government in Norway," *North Dakota Law Review* 57 (1981): 527–39. The U.S. Constitution also explicitly allows judges to throw out state laws that conflict with national law, including the national constitution and national treaties (Art. VI, Para. 2). Where it was not explicit is on power to reject congressional statute or Presidential order (i.e., federal-level law).

7. Alec Stone Sweet, *Governing with Judges: Constitutional Politics in Europe* (Oxford: Oxford University Press, 2000); Guarneri and Pederzoli, *The Power of Judges*.

8. Smith, "Judicial Review of Parliamentary Legislation."

9. Guarneri and Pederzioli, *The Power of Judges*; Hirschl, *Towards Juristocracy*; Sweet, *Governing with Judges*.

10. Hirschl, *Towards Juristocracy*.

11. Hirschl, *Towards Juristocracy*, 8; Sweet, *Governing with Judges*, 31; Guarneri and Pederzoli, *The Power of Judges*, 136.

12. For an early examination of these, see Mary Volcansek, ed., *Law Above Nations: Supranational Courts and the Legalization of Politics* (Gainesville: University Press of Florida, 1997). Additional examinations of this phenomenon with particular focus on the European Court of Justice include Anne-Marie [Burley] Slaughter et al., eds., *The European Court and the National Courts—Doctrine and Jurisprudence: Legal Change in Its Social Context* (Evanston, Ill.: Northwestern University Press, 1997); Karen J. Alter, *Establishing the Supremacy of European Law: The Making of an International Rule of Law in Europe* (Oxford: Oxford University Press, 2001); Leslie F. Goldstein, *Constituting Federal Sovereignty: The European Union in Comparative Context* (Baltimore: John Hopkins University Press, 2001).

13. By "play out" I do not refer to likely policy directions. For a study that engages in such an analysis, see Hirschl, *Towards Juristocracy*, which does, in part, examine policy developments under four such recently empowered courts in order to discern likely future policy directions.

14. Suzanna Sherry, "The Founder's Unwritten Constitution," *University of Chicago Law Review* 54 (1987): 1127–77.

15. Gary J. Jacobsohn, *The Supreme Court and the Decline of Constitutional Aspiration* (Totowa, N.J.: Rowman and Littlefield, 1986), chapter 5.

16. Robert Bork, *The Tempting of America* (New York: Free Press, 1990), 21.

17. Christopher Wolfe, *The Rise of Modern Judicial Review* (Lanham, Md.: Littlefield Adams, 1994), chapter 2 and afterword.

18. Barber is in general an admirer of the jurisprudence of Ronald Dworkin (e.g., *A Matter of Principle* [Cambridge, Mass.: Harvard University Press, 1985]) but disavows Dworkin's refusal to acknowledge natural (trans-conventional) standards of right and wrong. Sotirios Barber, *The Constitution of Judicial Power* (Baltimore: Johns Hopkins University Press, 1993), especially chapter 3.

19. Sotirios Barber and James Fleming, *Constitutional Interpretation: The Basic Questions* (New York: Oxford Press, 2007), chapter 7, n. 27.

20. Raoul Berger, *Government by Judiciary* (Cambridge, Mass.: Harvard University Press, 1977), chapter 7.

21. Wolfe, *The Rise of Modern Judicial Review*, 395.

22. Wolfe specifically cites *Roe v. Wade*, 410 U.S. 173 (1973), as a long-standing precedent that nonetheless warrants being overruled. Christopher Wolfe, *How to Read the Constitution* (Lanham, Md.: Rowman and Littlefield), 188–89. Raoul Berger appears to want much of Fourteenth Amendment jurisprudence reversed, but he singles out *Brown v. Board* as particularly inappropriate for a "rollback"; see *Government by Judiciary*, 411–18.

23. For details, see Leslie F. Goldstein, "The Spectre of the Second Amendment: Re-reading *Slaughterhouse and Cruikshank*," *Studies in American Political Development* 21 (Fall 2007): 1–18 at n. 6, reviewing the history of scholarship on the Fourteenth Amendment with respect to this decision. Whatever a scholar's position on the original understanding of the Fourteenth Amendment, no one, but no one, maintains that the *Slaughterhouse Cases* correctly interpreted the privileges and immunities clause. See, e.g., David S. Bogen, "Slaughterhouse Five: Views of the Case," *Hastings Law Journal* 55 (2003): 333–98, at 384: "Although there are a number of plausible accounts of the framers' understanding of the privileges or immunities clause, Justice Miller's interpretation of the privileges or immunities clause of the Fourteenth Amendment [in *Slaughterhouse*] failed to reflect any of them." Yet the Supreme Court has never overturned the decision.

24. The law did not mention whether the Court's writ of mandamus jurisdiction would be original or appellate, saying only that the Supreme Court would have power to "issue writs of mandamus, in cases warranted by the principles and usages of law." Marshall first interpreted Article III as establishing that mandamus had to be appellate rather than original, and then read this statutory clause as *not* meaning that the Court's power to issue writs of mandamus would follow the "principle of law" conforming to this reading of Article III. This enabled him to say the statute conflicted with the Constitution and that therefore judges were obliged (and also empowered) to disallow such federal legislation, despite the constitutional silence as to a judicial power to declare void federal law (in contrast to its explicit judicial empowerment with respect to state law in the Article VI supremacy clause).

25. Article III, section 2, clause 2 states that all of the Supreme Court's jurisdiction that does not involve "ambassadors, other public ministers and consuls," or a state as party, shall be "appellate" jurisdiction, "with such exceptions . . . as the Congress shall make." Marshall then treats Section 13 of the Judiciary Act as plainly having given the Court original rather than appellate jurisdiction when its language permitted the opposite reading (see note 24) and also as not counting as one of the permitted "exceptions Congress shall make."

26. *Martin v. Hunter's Lessee*, 14 U.S. 304 (1816); Cohens v. Virginia, 19 U.S. 264 (1824).

27. As to whether Marshall justified his constitutional decisions on extra-textual law such as common law, law of nations, or natural law, see Leslie F. Goldstein, *In Defense of the Text* (Lanham, Md.: Rowman and Littlefield, 1991), arguing

in chapter 3 that judicial review *prior* to Marshall's *Marbury* decision tended to be grounded in this way, but that Marshall altered the practice to make it text-based, and that this move produced much greater political acceptance of it; also, in chapter 1 that the scholarly debate of the 1970s and 1980s over whether Marshall relied on extratextual rules of law for constitutional interpretation was clarified by G. Edward (Ted) White, who noticed that the cases up through *Dartmouth* where Justice Story or Justice Marshall relied on unwritten "general principles common to our free institutions" were all diversity of citizenship cases where the Court was free to articulate reigning common law, rather than cases where the Court was obliged to find a rule of decision in the Constitution. Edward G. White, *History of the Supreme Court of the United States: The Marshall Court and Cultural Change, 1815–1835, Volumes 3 and 4 of the Oliver Wendell Holmes Devise* (New York: Macmillan, 1988), ch. 9, 173–81, and 674–75. By the time the Court finished with *Dartmouth* it had inserted the principle of the security of individual and corporate private property into the contracts clause, and could simply refer to the written text thereafter.

28. The bill of attainder clauses protected life, liberty, and property from legislative declarations that person x is to be punished by taking away one or another of these—in other words, from the imposition of punishment by legislatures without individual trials of guilt or innocence.

29. Recent research by Mark Graber has demonstrated that the Marshall Court furthered this security of private property even against governmental transfers of ownership at the national level, for which there was no contracts clause, by means of an extratextual rule of statutory construction, rather than by flat-out declarations of unconstitutionality. His research is persuasive, but since he is uncovering a little-known aspect of Marshall's jurisprudence, it is not an aspect that can account for Marshall's iconic status, which is the concern of this chapter. Mark Graber, "Naked Land Transfers and American Constitutional Development," *Vanderbilt Law Review* 53 (2000): 73–121.

30. *Gibbons v. Ogden*, 22 U.S. 1 (1824).

31. *Willson v. Blackbird Creek Marsh Company*, 27 U.S. 245 (1829).

32. *McCulloch v. Maryland* (17 U.S. 316 [1819]), at 415.

33. In the early 1950s, the District of Columbia and 21 of the 48 states had either mandatory or local-option school segregation. Michael Klarman, *From Jim Crow to Civil Rights* (New York: Oxford University Press, 2004), 304.

34. Ibid., 299–312.

35. Ibid., 302.

36. *Sweatt v. Painter*, 339 U.S. 629 (1950); *McLaurin v. Oklahoma*, 339 U.S. 637 (1950).

37. Justice Harlan wrote in dissent (163 U.S., at 560): "What can more certainly arouse race hate, what more certainly create and perpetuate a feeling of distrust between these races, than state enactments which, in fact, proceed on the ground that colored citizens are so inferior and degraded that they cannot be allowed to sit in public coaches occupied by white citizens? That, as all will admit, is the real meaning of such legislation as was enacted in Louisiana."

38. There can be no doubt that, despite the equal protection clause, the fram-

ers and ratifiers of the Fourteenth Amendment did expect that whites in America would continue to subjugate blacks by denying them the vote. This is openly anticipated by Section 2 of the amendment. Within four years, however, the American public came to the realization that "equal protection of the laws," at least as to racial groups, could not be secured without equal access to the vote irrespective of race. It took the U.S. public fifty more years to come to this realization with respect to women.

39. *Plessy v. Ferguson,* 163 U.S. 537, at 559 (1896).

40. Not until *Alexander v. Board of Education of Holmes County,* 396 U.S. 19 (1969), did the Court officially announce that the time for "all deliberate speed" was over and schools needed to desegregate "at once."

41. In 1964 Congress both for the first time offered substantial financial assistance to American public schools with the Elementary and Secondary Schools Assistance Act, but also threatened, in the Civil Rights Act, to withdraw that money from any program that discriminated on the basis of race. Thus Congress used financial carrots and sticks to enforce *Brown v. Board* for the first time.

42. *Slaughterhouse Cases (Butchers' Benevolent Association of New Orleans v. The Crescent City Live-Stock Landing and Slaughter-House Company),* 83 U.S. 36 at 61–62 (1873).

43. The Miller majority gave a list of some examples of national-level privileges or immunities of citizens that it considered protected by this new clause, but this list came from a precedent decided before the Fourteenth Amendment was ratified— *Crandall v. Nevada,* 73 U.S. 35 (1868). This rhetorical choice by Justice Miller drove home the point that he was saying that this clause adds nothing new to the Constitution.

44. House Representative Bingham: *Congressional Globe,* 39th Cong., 1st Sess 1088–1095 (Feb. 3, 1866); 2542–43 (May 8, 1866). Senator Howard: *Congressional Globe,* 39th Cong., 1st Sess 2765–66 (May 23, 1866).

Representative Bingham makes clear his understanding that the Fourteenth Amendment would apply the privileges listed in the Bill of Rights against state governments by stating that the amendment would overturn *Barron v. Baltimore,* 32 U.S. 243 (1833), the case that had established the contrary rule. Four years later, Bingham had occasion to discuss the amendment again on the floor and at this time he said he had specifically reworded the amendment in order to make clear that it secured "the privileges and immunities of citizens of the United States, which are defined in the eight articles of amendment." *Congressional Globe,* 42d Cong., 1st Sess. 84 (1871). Senator Howard specifically referred to the first eight amendments in his 1866 speech introducing the Fourteenth Amendment.

45. Stephen Halbrook lists the following newspapers: *New York Times, New York Herald, National Intelligencer, Philadelphia Inquirer, Chicago Tribune, Baltimore Gazette, Boston Daily Journal, Boston Daily Advertiser, Springfield Daily Republican, Richmond Daily Examiner,* and *Charleston Daily Courier.* This coverage appeared less than a month before the amendment went to the states for ratification. Stephen Halbrook, *Freedmen, the Fourteenth Amendment, and the Right to Bear Arms, 1866–1876* (Westport, Conn.: Praeger, 1998), 36.

46. Bogen, "Slaughterhouse Five."

47. *Slaughterhouse*, at 96.

48. *Slaughterhouse*, at 130.

49. *Strauder v. W.Virginia*, 100 U.S. 303 (1880).

50. *Chicago B. & Q.R. v. Chicago* (1897).

51. *Gitlow v. New York*, 268 U.S. 652 (1925).

52. Not that all the rest were always obeyed. For numerous examples of state resistance to Marshall Court rulings, see Goldstein, *Constituting Federal Sovereignty*, 14–33; 161–71.

53. Gordon Silverstein, "Globalization and the Rule of Law: A Machine that Runs of Itself?" *I·CON: International Journal of Constitutional Law* 1 (2003): 427–45; Scheppele "Declarations of Independence,", 262–68 and n. 62 at 177; Kim Scheppele, "A Comparative View of the Chief Justice's Role," *University of Pennsylvania Law Review* 154 (2007): 1757–885, at 1780–86 and 1794–1840.

54. But for evidence that many sectors of the public—including substantial majorities of both houses of [the lame-duck] Congress by 1875—would have accepted it, see Michael McConnell, "Originalism and Desegregation," *Virginia Law Review* 81 (1995): 949–1140, at 1131–40.

55. Goldstein, *In Defense of the Text*, 76.

56. In 1954, U.S. public opinion was rather evenly divided on the desirability of desegregated schools, with a majority of whites opposed to it even by 1956. By the late 1960s this had changed and majorities heavily favored it.

57. Alexander Bickel, "The Original Understanding and the Desegregation Decision," *Harvard Law Review* 69 (Nov. 1955): 1–65.

58. The chapter by Justice Robert Young, Jr., in this volume would seem to take issue with this assertion, at least as it applies to the idea that there might be a constitutional principle that "evolving standards of decency" should guide the Supreme Court's decisions on what constitutes "cruel and unusual punishment." Indeed, if Justice Young does not read the word "unusual" in the Eighth Amendment as requiring justices to think about whether standards of decency have evolved such that, for example, penal sanctions such as the whipping post are no longer constitutional, then he and I do disagree.

59. *Gibbons v. Ogden*, 22 U.S. 1 (1824).

60. Bogen, "Slaughterhouse Five."

61. Of course, constitutional courts are not the only forces that can dismantle constitutional protections. Such courts are being set up around the world precisely to guard against such dismantling by forces in the legislative and executive branches. But the *Slaughterhouse* example illustrates that judges too can tear away at constitutional protections.

62. Other countries have not followed the U.S. model of lifetime appointment for judges, but appoint them either for lengthy, fixed terms or until a certain mandatory retirement age.

Chapter 5. Who Has Authority over the Constitution of the United States?

1. See Keith Whittington, *Political Foundations of Judicial Supremacy: The Presidency, the Supreme Court, and Constitutional Leadership in U.S. History* (Princeton, N.J.: Princeton University Press, 2007), chapter 1.

2. *Planned Parenthood of Southeastern Pennsylvania v. Casey*, 505 U.S. 833 (1992), at 868.

3. Larry Alexander and Frederick Schauer, "Defending Judicial Supremacy: A Reply," *Constitutional Commentary* 17 (2000): 455, at 457; Larry Alexander and Frederick Schauer, "On Extrajudicial Constitutional Interpretation," *Harvard Law Review* 110 (1997): 1359.

4. Keith E. Whittington, *Constitutional Construction: Divided Powers and Constitutional Meaning* (Cambridge, Mass.: Harvard University Press, 1999).

5. *Lincoln: Selected Speeches and Writings*, Don E. Fehrenbacher, ed. (New York: Library of America, 1992), 289–90.

6. *Thomas Jefferson: Writings*, Merrill D. Peterson, ed. (New York: Library of America, 1984), 1501.

7. *The Works of James Wilson*, Robert Green McCloskey, ed. (Cambridge, Mass.: Harvard University Press, 1967), 1:77–79.

8. Alexander Hamilton, James Madison, and John Jay, *The Federalist*, Jacob E. Cooke, ed. (Middleton, Conn.: Wesleyan University Press, 1961), 46, p. 322.

9. Ibid., 57, p. 387.

10. Ibid., 51, pp. 349, 351.

11. *Chisholm v. Georgia*, 2 Dallas (2 U.S.) 419 (1793).

12. Ibid., at 453.

13. Ibid., at 477.

14. See Clyde E. Jacobs, *The Eleventh Amendment and Sovereign Immunity* (Westport, Conn.: Greenwood Press, 1972), 65 ff.

15. *Hollingsworth v. Virginia*, 3 Dallas (3 U.S.) 378 (1798).

16. Again, see Jacobs, *The Eleventh Amendment and Sovereign Immunity*, 67 ff.

17. In James Morton Smith, *Freedom's Fetters: The Alien and Sedition Laws and American Civil Liberties* (Ithaca, N.Y.: Cornell University Press, 1956), appendix, pp. 435–42.

18. Jefferson's Draft for the Kentucky Resolutions is in *Writings*, 449–56. Madison's Virginia Resolutions are contained in his 1800 Report, reprinted in Marvin Meyers, ed., *The Mind of the Founder: Sources of the Political Thought of James Madison*, rev. ed. (Hanover, N.H.: University Press of New England, 1981), 229 ff.

19. Ibid., 230.

20. Ibid., 235.

21. These definitions are taken from *Webster's New International Dictionary of the English Language*, 2nd ed. (Springfield, Mass.: G & C Merriam, 1954), and *The Oxford English Dictionary* (Oxford: Oxford University Press, 1971). It is curious to note that in the fourth edition of *Black's Law Dictionary* (St. Paul, Minn.: West Publishing, 1968), the definition of *interposition* includes the following: "Historically, the doctrine emanated from Chisholm v. Georgia, 2 Dallas 419, wherein the state of Georgia, when sued in the Supreme Court by a private citizen of another state,

entered a remonstrance and declined to recognize the court's jurisdiction. Amendment 11 validated Georgia's position." The fifth edition (1979) replaces this last sentence as follows: "The U.S. Supreme Court rejected this doctrine of interposition in Cooper v. Aaron, 358 U.S. 1."

22. *The Mind of the Founder*, 236.

23. Ibid.

24. Ibid., 237.

25. See Harvey C. Mansfield, Jr., *America's Constitutional Soul* (Baltimore: Johns Hopkins University Press, 1994). Michael Zuckert's account in his chapter in this volume of Madison's paradoxical approach to judicial review accords, I think, with my argument; indeed, the value Madison places on interposition resolves the paradox, for it allows for a political check on legal doctrine.

26. *Marbury v. Madison*, 1 Cranch (5 U.S.) 137. See William W. Van Alstyne, "A Critical Guide to *Marbury v. Madison*," *Duke Law Journal* (1969): 1; and Robert Lowry Clinton, *Marbury v. Madison and Judicial Review* (Lawrence: University Press of Kansas, 1989).

27. *Stuart v. Laird*, 1 Cranch (5 U.S.) 299 (1803), where in a cursory opinion the repeal is upheld.

28. Jefferson to Abigail Adams, September 11, 1804, in *The Adams-Jefferson Letters*, Lester J. Cappon, ed. (Chapel Hill: University of North Carolina Press, 1988), 279; Jefferson to George Hay, June 20, 1807, and Jefferson to Spencer Roane, September 6, 1819, in *Writings*, 1179–80, 1425–28.

29. Hence Judge John Gibson's celebrated dissent in *Eakin v. Raub*, 12 Sargeant & Rawle 330 (Pa. 1825).

30. *McCulloch v. Maryland*, 4 Wheaton (17 U.S.) 316 (1819).

31. "Veto Message," July 10, 1832, in *Messages and Papers of the Presidents*, ed. James D. Richardson (Washington, D.C.: Government Printing Office, 1896) 2: 582–83.

32. Ibid., 583.

33. Robert W. Johannsen, ed., *The Lincoln-Douglas Debates of 1858* (New York: Oxford University Press, 1965), 232.

34. Ibid., 243.

35. Ibid.

36. See Whittington, *Political Foundations of Judicial Supremacy*, 34–35.

37. 158 U.S. 601 (1895).

38. 247 U.S. 251 (1918).

39. *Lochner v. New York*, 198 U.S. 45 (1905); *Morehead v. New York ex rel. Tipaldo*, 298 U.S. 587 (1936); *West Coast Hotel v. Parrish*, 300 U.S. 379 (1937).

40. *Cooper v. Aaron*, 358 U.S. 1 (1958), at 18.

41. I readily acknowledge the insight of my sometime coauthor Richard Morgan on this matter; see our "Resisting Judicial Supremacy: Prudently and 'Massively,'" paper delivered at the annual meeting of the American Political Science Association, San Francisco, California, August 31, 2001.

42. In her chapter in this volume, Leslie Goldstein accepts the modern notion that the role of the Court is to develop a jurisprudence of principle, while praising the statesmanship of judges who moderate their principles to take account of

realities of political power. But is it not a precept—I would not say a principle—of judicial statesmanship to defer to compromises struck by political branches acting within their legitimate authority? This Marshall does in several cases, for example, *Gibbons v. Ogden*, 9 Wheaton (22 U.S.) 1 (1824), where he discusses but declines to impose a principle of exclusive national authority over commerce among the states. Does he not insist upon judges' respecting compromises embodied in the Constitution itself, for example, in *Barron v. Baltimore*, 7 Peters (32 U.S.) 243 (1833), where he declines to extend constitutional protection even of property rights against the states?

43. Whittington argues in *Political Foundations of Judicial Supremacy* that departmentalism—one face of what I have called resistance—appears during "reconstructive" presidencies (that is, at moments of what political scientists used to call "critical realignment"), while support for judicial supremacy builds during normal intervals of "affiliation." Not the data, but the emphasis is different in our readings: Where I see compromise in new "constitutional regimes," he seems to see only conquest; and I think that resistance is a possibility implicit in an overarching constitutional regime that is supple enough to readjust in what he calls "political time" without being so fluid as to change its form with every new adjustment. In his chapter below, Whittington distinguishes constitutional resistance from constitutional contestation, endorsing the latter while dismissing the former, as a supporter of judicial supremacy must do. If I am right that judicial supremacy is of recent vintage, then the distinction between resistance and contestation within the constitutional tradition is recent, too. Whether we are better off without being able to constitutionally contest the justice of a doctrine announced by the Court is the question with which I conclude.

Chapter 6. The Supreme Court and Contemporary Constitutionalism

This chapter is a modified version of chapter 2 of Mark Tushnet, *Weak Courts, Strong Rights: Judicial Review and Social Welfare Rights in Comparative Constitutional Law* (Princeton, N.J.: Princeton University Press, 2007).

1. James Bradley Thayer, "The Origin and Scope of the American Doctrine of Constitutional Law," *Harvard Law Review* 7 (1893): 129–56, at 144.

2. 506 U.S. 224 (1993).

3. Ibid., at 253, 254 (emphasis added).

4. Justice Souter's formulation resonates with my own understanding of Thayerian review. An alternative understanding treats Thayerian review as imposing an epistemic requirement on a judge's determination that a statute is unconstitutional. A judge finding a statute unconstitutional must, on this understanding, conclude not simply that the statute is unconstitutional (based on a full analysis of all the relevant considerations), but that this conclusion is clear to a high degree of certainty ("beyond a reasonable doubt," for example). Applying epistemic understandings of this sort to the operation of collective institutions like courts and juries is notoriously difficult. The standard question is, How can an individual judge have the

required degree of certainty when others (dissenting judges, a minority of jurors, the majority in the legislature) not only do not have that degree of certainty, but actually draw the contrary conclusion from their evaluation of the relevant material? The Supreme Court's decisions on the permissibility of non-unanimous jury verdicts, and on the requirement that juries be unanimous in finding aggravating circumstances in death penalty cases, illustrate the difficulties. See *Schad v. Arizona* (501 U.S. 624 [1991]), upholding a capital conviction based on instructions that did not require jurors to agree unanimously on the defendant's state of mind; *Apodaca v. Oregon* (406 U.S. 404 [1972]), upholding state laws allowing non-unanimous verdicts in criminal cases.

5. True Thayerian review is rare, I believe, because it places judges in an uncomfortable psychological position. The Thayerian judge must say, "In my judgment this statute is unconstitutional, but—despite that, and despite the fact that I have the power to block the statute's enforcement—I think that this statute should go into effect because it is not too unconstitutional."

6. *Sherbert v. Verner*, 374 U.S. 398 (1963). I simplify the doctrine in this paragraph, for expository purposes.

7. *Employment Division, Department of Human Resources v. Smith*, 494 U.S. 872 (1990). For an application of the ban on targeting denominations, see *Church of the Lukumi Babalu Aye v. City of Hialeah*, 508 U.S. 520 (1993).

8. 358 U.S. 1, 18 (1958).

9. 521 U.S. 507 (1997).

10. 42 U.S.C. §§ 2000bb to 2000bb-4 (1994).

11. 521 U.S. at 519, (emphasis added), 529 (emphasis added) (quoting *Marbury v. Madison*, 5 U.S. [1 Cranch] 137, 1777 [1803]).

12. There are, of course, other mechanisms of response: The Constitution authorizes impeachment of justices, and authorizes Congress to regulate, and thereby restrict, the courts' jurisdiction. Even more than constitutional amendment, these mechanisms have not been effective as tools for ensuring that judges interpret the Constitution as the people reasonably want it interpreted. At the start of the nineteenth century, Jeffersonians attempted to impeach Justice Samuel Chase, and their failure to remove him from office has been taken to establish the proposition that a judge should not be removed simply because Congress believes that he or she has made mistaken decisions. Some minor restrictions on jurisdiction have been enacted, but none going to central disputes over the correctness of the courts' constitutional interpretations. More interesting is the enactment of a statute only marginally different from the one invalidated. Legislators might hope that the Court would change its mind, or, more likely, distinguish its prior decision and uphold the statute, perhaps in part because the reenactment was understood by the justices as a rebuke, or threat.

13. See James Stoner's chapter in this volume.

14. I insert the qualification "not much different" to emphasize that the strength or weakness of judicial review is linked inextricably to the decision rules employed in the constitutional amendment process. As the amendment process becomes easier, judicial review becomes weaker—and, conversely, as the legislative

process becomes more difficult (with respect to specific issues, perhaps), judicial review becomes stronger.

15. Stephen Gardbaum, "The New Commonwealth Model of Constitutionalism," *American Journal of Comparative Law* 49 (2001): 707–60, was perhaps the first major article to identify the emergence of an alternative to strong-form review. As the article's title indicates, Gardbaum links the alternative to the nations in which it was first implemented. I suspect that he is right in seeing a connection between the preference for weak-form review and the strength of the tradition of parliamentary supremacy in the British Commonwealth. I believe that this connection is historical rather than conceptual, and so prefer the more generic term weak-form review.

16. Tushnet, *Weak Courts, Strong Rights*, ch. 3.

17. Gardbaum, "The New Commonwealth Model," 727, describes the political background that led to the act's adoption.

18. There are some rights not commonly included in bills of rights, including a provision giving everyone a right "not to be subjected to medical or scientific experimentation without that person's consent," and a right to refuse medical treatment. New Zealand Bill of Rights Act 1990, §§ 10, 11, available at http://www.oefre. unibe.ch/law/icl/nz01000_.html (accessed January 19, 2006).

19. New Zealand Bill of Rights Act 1990, § 4.

20. Ibid., § 6.

21. There are national variations in the tools judges ordinarily use to interpret statutes, and I do not mean by the list in the text to assert that any specific court will use all of the techniques described.

22. Alternatively, the majority might agree that the statute is rights-restrictive, but want to implement a rights-restrictive policy. The questions about what sort of response such a majority might make are quite similar to those I discuss in the text.

23. Human Rights Act 1998, 1998 ch. 42, available at http://www.opsi.gov.uk/ acts/acts1998/19980042.htm (accessed January 19, 2006).

24. This summary draws heavily on the account in Michael Zander, *A Bill of Rights?* 4th ed. (London: Sweet and Maxwell, 1997).

25. John A. G. Griffith, *The Politics of the Judiciary* (London: Fontana Press, 1977). The book has gone through numerous editions, the latest to which I have access published in 1997.

26. For Hirschl's argument, see Ran Hirschl, *Towards Juristocracy: The Origins and Consequences of the New Constitutionalism* (Cambridge, Mass.: Harvard University Press, 2004). Hirschl's argument about the reasons for adopting judicial review has been confirmed for a significant number of nations, and by theoretical models. See Tom Ginsburg, *Judicial Review in New Democracies: Constitutional Courts in East Asia* (New York: Cambridge University Press, 2003); J. Mark Ramseyer, "The Puzzling (In)Dependence of Courts: A Comparative Approach," *Journal of Legal Studies* 23 (1994): 721–47; Matthew Stephenson, "'When the Devil Turns . . .': The Political Foundations of Independent Judicial Review," *Journal of Legal Studies* 32 (2003): 781–89.

27. For a discussion of interpretive questions about the HRA, see Geoffrey Marshall, "The United Kingdom Human Rights Act, 1998," in *Defining the Field of*

Comparative Constitutional Law, Vicki C. Jackson and Mark Tushnet, eds. (Westport, Conn.: Greenwood Publishing, 2002).

28. There is an additional complication. The Strasbourg court has developed what it calls the "margin of appreciation" doctrine. See *Handyside v. United Kingdom,* 1 Eur. H.R. Rep. 737 (1976). According to that doctrine, the Strasbourg court interprets convention provisions by giving member states a "margin of appreciation" to take account of distinctive local conditions and problems. See *Handyside v. United Kingdom* at 753–54 (referring to the fact that domestic authorities are in "direct and continuous contact with the vital forces of their countries"). The very fact that a domestic judge has found a violation of convention rights might count against a conclusion that the British government should be given a significant margin of appreciation with respect to the provision at issue. I discuss this and other aspects of the "margin of appreciation" doctrine in Tushnet, *Weak Courts, Strong Rights,* chs. 3 and 5.

29. Peter W. Hogg and Allison A. Bushell [now Thornton], "The Charter Dialogue Between Courts and Legislatures (Or Perhaps the Charter of Rights Isn't Such a Bad Thing After All)," *Osgoode Hall Law Journal* 35 (1997): 75–124. The Charter of Rights is the "Bill of Rights" portion of the Canadian Constitution. Formally, the charter and the Canadian Constitution as a whole are enactments by the British Parliament. Constitution Act, 1867, 30 & 31 Victoria, c. 3; Constitution Act, 1982 (U.K.), 1982 c. 11. Hogg and Bushell argue that the Canadian experience shows that dialogue actually does occur; this aspect of their argument is challenged in Christopher P. Manfredi and James B. Kelly, "Six Degrees of Dialogue: A Response to Hogg and Bushell," *Osgoode Hall Law Journal* 37 (1999): 513–28, and Christopher P. Manfredi, "The Life of a Metaphor: Dialogue in the Supreme Court, 1998–2003," *Supreme Court Law Review* (2d) 23 (2004): 104–31.

30. Charter of Rights and Freedoms, § 1, enacted as Schedule B to the Canada Act 1982 (U.K.) 1982, c. 11. The Supreme Court of Canada outlined a multistage test for determining when a rights violation is "demonstrably justified" in *R. v. Oakes,* [1986] 1 SCR 103: "First, the objective, which the measures responsible for a limit on a Charter right or freedom are designed to serve, must be 'of sufficient importance to warrant overriding a constitutionally protected right or freedom.' . . . It is necessary, at a minimum, that an objective relate to concerns which are pressing and substantial in a free and democratic society before it can be characterized as sufficiently important.

"Second, once a sufficiently significant objective is recognized, then the party invoking s. 1 must show that the means chosen are reasonable and demonstrably justified. This involves 'a form of proportionality test.' Although the nature of the proportionality test will vary depending on the circumstances, in each case courts will be required to balance the interests of society with those of individuals and groups. There are, in my view, three important components of a proportionality test. First, the measures adopted must be carefully designed to achieve the objective in question. They must not be arbitrary, unfair or based on irrational considerations. In short, they must be rationally connected to the objective. Second, the means, even if rationally connected to the objective in this first sense, should impair 'as little as possible' the right or freedom in question. Third, there must be a proportionality between the *effects* of the measures which are responsible for limiting the Charter right or freedom, and the objective which has been identified as of "sufficient importance." ¶¶ 69, 70 (citations omitted).

31. Voting, mobility, and language rights are excepted.

32. Kent Roach, *The Supreme Court on Trial: Judicial Activism or Democratic Dialogue* (Toronto: Irwin Law, 2001), 8, describes what he calls "in-your-face" Section 1 responses. These responses involve what appear to be the simple reenactment of the invalidated legislation with relatively little done to bolster it. Roach treats these responses as involving decisions by Parliament that merely purport to accept the court's interpretations, and argues that in such instances parliament should rely on the Section 33 response (see 281). For additional discussion of "in your face" responses, see Tushnet, *Weak Courts, Strong Rights*, chapter 3.

33. For an extended argument from a Canadian scholar that denying constitutional protection to commercial expression does not violate basic principles of freedom of expression, see Roger A. Shiner, *Freedom of Commercial Expression* (New York: Oxford University Press, 2003).

34. I refer to an "idealized" version of the Section 33 response because Section 33 itself does not clearly distinguish between a legislative response that concededly is inconsistent with the legislature's own understanding of the charter, and a response that is inconsistent only with the courts' understanding of the charter. The language of Section 33 might have been clearer on what was being overridden. As written, Section 33 requires the legislature to say to the public, "We are making this statute effective notwithstanding what the charter says." A better expression of weak-form review would allow the legislature to say, "We are making this statute effective notwithstanding what the Supreme Court has said the charter says (or what we expect the Court to say the charter means)." As Canadian constitutional scholars have pointed out to me, this point might be taken to demonstrate that the charter actually establishes strong-form rather than weak-form review.

35. Robert Dahl, "Decision-Making in a Democracy: The Supreme Court as a National Policy-Maker," *Journal of Public Law* 6 (1957): 279–95.

36. See, e.g., Barry Friedman, "Dialogue and Judicial Review," *Michigan Law Review* 91 (1993): 577–682; Barry Friedman, "The Importance of Being Positive: The Nature and Function of Judicial Review," *University of Cincinnati Law Review* 72 (2004): 1257–303; Robert W. Bennett, *Talking It Through: Puzzles of American Democracy* (Ithaca, N.Y.: Cornell University Press, 2003), 101–4.

37. See Robert C. Post, "The Supreme Court, 2002 Term—Foreword: Fashioning the Legal Constitution: Culture, Courts, and Law," *Harvard Law Review* 117 (2003): 4–112; Robert C. Post and Reva B. Siegel, "Legislative Constitutionalism and Section Five Power: Policentric Interpretation of the Family and Medical Leave Act," *Yale Law Journal* 112 (2003): 1943–2059; Reva B. Siegel, "Equality Talk: Antisubordination and Anticlassification Values in Constitutional Struggles over Brown," *Harvard Law Review* 117 (2004): 1470–547; Reva B. Siegel, "Text in Context: Gender and the Constitution from a Social Movement Perspective," *University of Pennsylvania Law Review* 150 (2001): 297–351.

38. Although it is not inherent in their model that it does.

39. See, e.g., Bruce Ackerman, *We the People: Foundations* (Cambridge, Mass.:

Harvard University Press, 1991), 20, providing a "five-stage process," including the switch in time; Bruce Ackerman, *The Failure of the Founding Fathers: Jefferson, Marshall, and the Rise of Presidential Democracy* (Cambridge, Mass.: Harvard University Press, 2005), 265, describing "a recurring institutional dynamic," including a switch in time.

40. This is, of course, consistent with Ackerman's metaphor of "moments," that is, short periods of time in which important political and constitutional developments take place.

Chapter 7. The Sounds of Silence

1. These characterizations are taken from the constitutions of Afghanistan and Iran and Nicaragua, Angola, Armenia, Oman, Paraguay, Turkey, Greece, Iran, and Ireland.

2. The other constitutions that do not reference the family at all are: Australia, Austria, Canada, Denmark, Finland, France, Lebanon, Nepal, Netherlands, New Zealand, Norway, Russia, Singapore, and Yemen. There is also a group of countries, for example, South Africa, Italy, and Sweden, whose constitutions make incidental references to the family without guaranteeing them any real protection.

3. Jean Bethke Elshtain, "Introduction: Toward a Theory of the Family and Politics," in *The Family in Political Thought*, Jean Bethke Elshtain, ed. (Amherst: University of Massachusetts Press, 1982), 7.

4. Ibid., 7. In either case, the constitutional order has always needed to take the measure of the family, even when, as famously regarded by Aristotle, it was a subordinate institution, albeit one essential to the existence of any polis, no matter the specifics of its constitution.

5. The reference is to the thesis in Ran Hirschl's *Towards Juristocracy: The Origins and Consequences of the New Constitutionalism* (Cambridge, Mass.: Harvard University Press, 2004).

6. See Cass R. Sunstein, *The Second Bill of Rights: FDR's Unfinished Revolution and Why We Need It More Than Ever* (New York: Basic Books, 2004).

7. A section on Directive Principles of State Policy is now being interpreted to provide it with more than hortatory significance, which is not to say that it creates judicially enforceable rights. See Mark Tushnet, "Social Welfare Rights and the Forms of Judicial Review," *Texas Law Review* 82 (2004): 1895.

8. I should perhaps say just a little more about terminology. Readers may wonder about my use of the terms "acquiescent" and "militant" to distinguish the two kinds of constitutionalism. To the best of my knowledge, neither of these words has ever been attached to constitutions, no doubt for good reason since both suggest behavior at odds with conventional ideas about the functions of a constitution. A more obvious terminological choice would be the aforementioned "preservative" and "transformative." But these words do not quite convey what it is I want to emphasize in the relationship between constitutional and social orders. Thus it is not so much the distinction between change and no change that interests me, but rather the

deeper commitments that underlie the desire to preserve or transform. For example, transformation might occur in the absence of the strongly confrontational relationship that is implied by the notion of militance. Similarly, preservation need not involve the level of satisfaction with the status quo that is involved in acquiescence.

9. V. R. Krishna Iyer, "Towards an Indian Jurisprudence of Social Action and Public Interest Litigation," in *Sociology of Law*, Indra Deva, ed. (New Delhi: Oxford University Press, 2005), 308.

10. Christopher Lasch, *Haven in a Heartless World: The Family Besieged* (New York: Basic Books, 1977), 4.

11. John Rawls, *The Law of Peoples with "The Idea of Public Reason Revisited"* (Cambridge, Mass.: Harvard University Press, 1999), 157.

12. Susan Moller Okin, *Justice, Gender, and the Family* (New York: Basic Books, 1989), 135.

13. Rawls, *The Law of Peoples*, 159. Rawls does, however, argue that these principles "do impose essential constraints on the family as an institution and so guarantee the basic rights and liberties, and the freedom and opportunities, of all its members." Ibid., 159. In this respect he held the family to the same standard as other associations, for example, the church. Not so Okin: "Rather than being one among many co-equal institutions of a just society, a just family is its essential foundation." Moller Okin, *Justice, Gender, and the Family*, 17.

14. Alexis de Tocqueville, *Oeuvres Complètes*, vol. 3, *Ecrits et Discours Politiques*, J.-P. Mayer, ed. (Paris: Gallimard, 1962), 480.

15. Ibid., 448.

16. I have discussed this in great detail in Gary Jeffrey Jacobsohn, *The Wheel of Law: Indian Secularism in Comparative Constitutional Context* (Princeton, N.J.: Princeton University Press, 2003).

17. B. R. Ambedkar, "The Annihilation of Caste," in *The Essential Writings of B. R. Ambedkar*, Valerian Rodrigues, ed. (New Delhi: Oxford University Press, 2002), 291.

18. Ibid., 287.

19. B. R. Ambedkar, "Castes in India," in *The Essential Writings of B. R. Ambedkar*, Valerian Rodrigues, ed., 243.

20. Ibid., 289.

21. These practices are "principally intended to solve the problem of the surplus man and surplus woman in a caste and to maintain its endogamy." Ibid., 252.

22. Robert D. Baird, "Gender Implications for a Uniform Civil Code," in *Religion and Personal Law in Secular India: A Call to Judgment*, Gerald James Larson, ed. (Bloomington: Indiana University Press, 2001), 146. Or stated more directly: "Instead of being seen as a vital source of India's strength, the Constitution regards [society] as an enemy who needs to be disarmed and dismantled. . . . [If] carried through to its logical conclusion, [it] would bring about the destruction of Indian society in any form." Peter G. Sack, "Constitutions and Revolutions," in *Sociology of Law*, Indra Seva, ed., 354.

23. Nathan J. Brown, *Constitutions in a Nonconstitutional World: Arab Basic Laws and the Prospects for Accountable Government* (Albany: State University of New York Press, 2002), 92.

24. For example, Chapter 3, Article 9 of Saudi Arabia's constitution: "The family is the kernel of Saudi society, and its members shall be brought up on the basis of the Islamic faith, and loyalty to and obedience to God, His Messenger, and to guardians; respect for and implementation of the law, and love of and pride in the homeland and its glorious history as the Islamic faith stipulates."

25. Alexis de Tocqueville, *Democracy in America*, vol. 2 (New York: Vintage Books, 1945), 108.

26. Rogers Smith, *Civic Ideals: Conflicting Visions of Citizenship in U.S. History* (New Haven, Conn.: Yale University Press, 1997), 36.

27. Louis Hartz, *The Liberal Tradition in America* (New York: Harcourt, Brace and World, 1955), 50.

28. With regard to the issue of race, specifically African Americans, the original Constitution tolerated their legally enforced subordinate condition. In that sense it was a form of acquiescence, although one cannot infer that all those who were a party to the compromises attendant its adoption were reconciled to the resulting inequities. I would argue that the post–Civil War amendments exemplify militant constitutionalism in the American context; in other words, they were adopted with the express purpose of directly confronting well-entrenched elements of the social order that had lost the support necessary for their preservation. Americans, according to Louis Hartz, had not had the experience common to many other places, namely "the effort to build a new society on the ruins of an old one." Ibid., 66. In many ways, however, that is exactly the effort begun in the South after the end of the war.

29. Consider France, which like the United States and India, has no protection for the family in its constitutional text. This absence is arguably traceable "[t]o the French revolutionaries, [for whom] the old feudal statuses, the Church, the guilds, and even some aspects of family organization were seen both as oppressive to individuals and as threats to the nation-state." Mary Ann Glendon, *The Transformation of Family Law* (Chicago: University of Chicago Press, 1989), 298. See also Jonah D. Levy, *Tocqueville's Revenge: State, Society and Economy in Contemporary France* (Cambridge, Mass.: Harvard University Press, 1999).

30. Alexis de Tocqueville, *Democracy in America*, Harvey C. Mansfield and Delba Winthrop, trans. and ed. (Chicago: University of Chicago Press, 2000), 561.

31. Ibid., 574.

32. Ibid., 574.

33. Ibid., 576, 575.

34. Okin, for example, cites Tocqueville as follows: He (as well as others) "bifurcated public from private life to such an extent that [he] had no trouble reconciling inegalitarian, sometimes admittedly unjust, relations founded upon sentiment within the family with a more just, even egalitarian, social structure outside the family." Moller Okin, *Justice, Gender, and the Family*, 19.

35. Tocqueville, *Democracy in America*, 576. To the extent, though, that their differing destinies did not include broader civic membership for women, Rawls could not have agreed that their value as people were equal to that of men.

36. Rawls, *The Law of Peoples*, 161.

37. Ibid., 162.

38. *McCulloch v. Maryland*, 17 U.S. 316 (1819), 407.

39. Ibid., at 407.

40. *Griswold v. Connecticut*, 381 U.S. 479 (1965), 486. The importance of marriage and the family has long been recognized by the Court. "[Marriage] is an institution, in the maintenance of which in its purity the public is deeply interested, for it is the foundation of the family and of society, without which there would be neither civilization nor progress." *Maynard v. Hill*, 125 U.S. 190 (1888), 209.

41. Minow, "We, the Family," 982.

42. William A. Galston, "Liberal Virtues and the Formation of Civic Character," in *Seedbeds of Virtue: Sources of Competence, Character, and Citizenship in American Society*, Mary Ann Glendon and David Blankenhorn. eds. (Lanham, Md.: Madison Books, 1995), 55–56.

43. Ibid., 55.

44. Federalism may suggest a third model of constitutionalism, one in which the constitutional order is neither actively hostile to the social order nor actively supportive. Accordingly, the variation—for example, with regard to the configuration of the family—that the federal solution makes possible means that the constitution in effect avoids social order questions. My view, however, is that the choice of leaving such issues for ultimate determination at the subnational level is at least indicative of an unwillingness to challenge existing social institutions. It may not indicate active support of them, but it is consistent with the idea that there is sufficient approval of the social order that some measure of variation and experimentation is tolerable at the local level. That said, I would acknowledge that there could be such deep division over a prominent social structure—slavery comes to mind—that for the sake of constitutional peace the document may be neither acquiescent nor militant with regard to it.

45. Galston, "Liberal Virtues and the Formation of Civic Character," 56.

46. E. E. Schattschneider, *The Semi-Sovereign People: A Realist's View of Democracy* (Hinsdale, Ill.: Dryden's Press, 1975).

47. Gretchen Ritter, *The Constitution As Social Design: Gender and Civic Membership in the American Constitutional Order* (Stanford, Calif.: Stanford University Press, 2006), 68.

48. Ibid., 70.

49. Ibid., 71.

50. Minow, "We, the Family," 978.

51. Robert A. Burt, "The Constitution of the Family," *Supreme Court Review* (1979), 331.

52. Eva R. Rubin, *The Supreme Court and the American Family* (New York: Greenwood Press, 1986), 192.

53. *Moore v. East Cleveland*, 431 U.S. 494 (1977), 502.

54. Ibid., at 502.

55. Harvey C. Mansfield, Jr., "The Religious Issue and the Origin of Constitutionalism," in *How Does the Constitution Protect Religious Freedom?* Robert A. Goldwin and Art Kaufman, eds. (Washington, D.C.: American Enterprise Institute for Public Policy Research, 1987), 3.

56. Ibid., 2.

57. Minow, "We, the Family," 967.

58. Marital practices were just one element—albeit the most notorious—in a regulative culture whose domain extended well into the temporal side of human experience. The Mormons made it easy for people to believe that the religion's geographic base in Utah was expected to serve as a home for illegitimate sovereign ambitions. For good discussions of this perceived threat, see Klaus J. Hansen, *Mormonism and the American Experience* (Chicago: University of Chicago Press, 1981); and Richard S. Van Wagoner, *Mormon Polygamy: A History* (Salt Lake City: Signature Books, 1989).

59. Quoted in Nancy L. Rosenblum, "Democratic Sex: *Reynolds v. U. S.*, Sexual Relations, and Community," in *Sexuality and the Law*, David Estlund and Martha Nussbaum, eds. (Oxford: Oxford University Press, 1997), 74.

60. Ibid.

61. Ibid., 75.

62. *Reynolds v. United States*, at 164.

63. Rosenblum, "Democratic Sex," 77.

64. *Reynolds v. United States*, at 166.

65. The different order of magnitude is better captured in the Court's other momentous polygamy case, *Davis v. Beason*. There the practice is described as one that tends "to destroy the purity of the marriage relation, to disturb the peace of families, to degrade woman, and to debase man. Few crimes are more pernicious to the best interests of society, and receive more general or more deserved punishment." *Davis v. Beason*, 133 U.S. 333, 341.

66. Ibid., at 166.

67. Ibid., at 164.

68. In doing so, however, it is possible to envision the Court accepting an exemption for a certain group on religious grounds. In *Wisconsin v. Yoder*, the Court upheld the claim of the Old Order Amish to be exempt from a state's compulsory school attendance law. As is now widely believed, the Amish commanded the deference of the Court precisely because they exemplified those traits that define a good American. The *Yoder* opinion, with its unabashed enthusiasm for good old-fashioned American values, is as much a vindication of authority as it is a victory for group rights. In this sense it is hard to see how it could be duplicated in a polygamy case, where the behavior in question is in blatant repudiation of those American (family) values. But the focus on an otherwise benign group's actual plural marriage experience could reveal it to be insufficiently different from the normal American family so as to justify, in the eyes of the Court, a constitutional exemption.

69. Karen Orren, *Belated Feudalism: Labor, the Law, and Liberal Development in the United States* (Cambridge: Cambridge University Press, 1991), 41.

70. Ibid., 211.

71. See especially, *Cleveland Board of Education v. LaFleur*, 414 U.S. 632 (1974); *Meyer v. Nebraska*, 262 U.S. 390 (1923); *Pierce v. Society of Sisters*, 268 U.S. 510 (1925); and *Prince v. Massachusetts*, 321 U.S. 158 (1944). To this must be added Justice Harlan's famous dissent in the 1961 case, *Poe v. Ullman*, which argued in what proved to be profoundly important ways: "The home derives its pre-eminence as the seat of family life. And the integrity of that life is something so fundamental that it

has been found to draw to its protection the principles of more than one explicitly granted Constitutional right." *Poe v. Ullman*, 367 U.S. 497 (1961), 552.

72. Ritter, *The Constitution as Social Design*, 97.

73. Ibid., 97.

74. Constituent Assembly of India, Constituent Assembly Debates: Official Report, 9.12.1946-24.1.1950 (New Delhi: Lok Sabha Secretariat, 1966–1967), vol. 3, 496.

75. Ibid., vol. 7, 513.

76. Ibid., 513.

77. Ibid., 513.

78. Article 41 of the Irish Constitution describes the family as the "necessary basis of social order . . . indispensable to the welfare of the Nation and the State." Understandably, then, the state "guarantees to protect the Family in its constitution and authority." What precedes this guarantee—a description of the family as "a moral institution possessing inalienable and imprescriptible rights, antecedent and superior to all positive law"—expresses uniquely Irish circumstances, but the legally mandated protection is an increasingly familiar feature of modern constitutional governance.

79. Article 39 (f). This language was added by the 42nd Amendment in 1976. It follows naturally from paragraph (e) in the original document, which says that children and other citizens should not be forced by "economic necessity to enter avocations unsuited to their age or strength."

80. The metaphor of war should not be considered far-fetched. Consider this comment by the English jurist Edward Jenks writing in 1898: "The two institutions, the Clan and the State, stand . . . free to face each other. Linked together against external attack, they are pledged to the deadliest internal warfare. . . . The leading characteristics of the Clan are a caste organization, a respect for the autonomy of its constituent groups, and exclusiveness. The principles of the State are precisely the opposite." Quoted in Robert Nisbet, "Foreword," in *The American Family and the State*, Joseph R. Peden and Fred R. Glahe, eds. (San Francisco: Pacific Research Institute for Public Policy, 1986), xxi.

81. Jawaharlal Nehru, *The Discovery of India* (New Delhi: Penguin Books, 2004), 277.

82. The exception to this was in regard to such practices as sati and female infanticide, abuses so horrific as to reflect badly on the British themselves. For the most part, however, as has been noted in India: "The Indians were left to live [by the British] in the cobweb of their own social superstitions, because they knew that the social emancipation of the Indians meant the end of the foreign rule in India." Haripada Chakraborti, *Hindu Intercaste Marriage in India* (Delhi: Sharada Publishing House, 1999), 134.

83. Richard Lardinois, "India: The Family, the State and Women," in *A History of the Family—Vol. Two: The Impact of Modernity*, André Burjuiere, Christiane Klapisch-Zuber, Martine Segalen, and Francoise Zonabend, eds. (Cambridge: Polity Press, 1996), 274.

84. Charles Heimsath, *Indian Nationalism and Hindu Social Reform* (Princeton, N.J.: Princeton University Press, 1964), 48.

85. Government of India Press, *The Framing of India's Constitution: Select Documents* (New Delhi: Indian Institute of Public Administration, 1967), vol. 2, 146 (emphasis added).

86. André Beteille, "The Family and the Reproduction of Inequality," in *Family, Kinship, and Marriage in India*, Patricia Uberoi, ed. (Delhi: Oxford University Press, 1993), 436.

87. *State of Bombay v. Appa*, AIR Bombay 84 (1952), 86.

88. Hinduism is a famously fragmented religion lacking an ecclesiastical hierarchy, which means that these practices have varied widely in use. The constitution, however, appears to endorse the view that intolerance for such practices as polygamy is insufficiently widespread among Hindus so as to justify sole reliance on internal reform to eradicate the associated injustices.

89. Ibid., at 88.

90. Ibid., at 86. See also *Ram Prasad v. State of U. P.*, AIR Allahabad 411 (1957) at 413 for the same assertion.

91. As Laurence Tribe has said, "[T]he most clearly forbidden church-state entanglement occurs when institutions of civil government use the legal process in order to discover religious error or to promulgate religious truth." Laurence H. Tribe, *American Constitutional Law* (Mineola, N.Y.: Foundation Press, 1988), 1232. The heterodox character of Hinduism facilitates the different orientation of Indian judges. Max Weber once commented that "the concept of 'dogma' is entirely lacking" in Hinduism. Max Weber, *The Religion of India: The Sociology of Hinduism and Buddhism* (Glencoe, Ill.: Free Press, 1958), 21. This flexibility leaves the interpretation of foundational scriptural texts arguably open to all, including judges.

92. Granville Austin, *The Indian Constitution: Cornerstone of a Nation* (Oxford: Oxford University Press, 1966), 80.

93. Krishna Iyer, "Towards an Indian Jurisprudence of Social Action and Public Interest Litigation," 297. The author was a prominent Indian Supreme Court justice, who was one of the leaders of the effort to remove legal barriers to judicial involvement in social and economic issues.

94. For a comparison see Marc Galanter and Jayanth Krishnan, "Personal Law Systems and Religious Conflict: A Comparison of India and Israel," in *Religion and Personal Law in Secular India: A Call to Judgment*, Gerald James Larson, ed. (Bloomington: Indiana University Press, 2001).

95. I have considered these efforts at length in Jacobsohn, *The Wheel of Law*, 104–19.

96. *Sarla Mudgal v. Union of India*, AIR SC 1531 (1995), 1533.

97. Ibid., at 1532.

98. Marc Galanter, *Law and Society in Modern India* (Delhi: Oxford University Press, 1989), 30.

99. In seeking passage of the legislation, Ambedkar sought to understate its reach. Thus he concluded his speech in Parliament with this appeal: "I hope that the clarification which I have given on the various points will allay the fears of members who are not well disposed towards this measure. They will realize that this is in no sense a revolutionary measure. I say that this is not even a radical measure." Rodrigues, ed., *The Essential Writings of B. R. Ambedkar*, 516.

100. Valerian Rodrigues, a prominent Indian authority on Ambedkar, says that the law inister's efforts on the Hindu Code Bill were an attempt "to effectively transform the hierarchical relations embodied in the Hindu family and the caste system and bring them in tune with the values embodied in the Constitution." Rodrigues, ed., *The Essential Writings of B. R. Ambedkar,* 15. Given the failure of the omnibus bill, Rodrigues characterizes Ambedkar's work as a "vain attempt." The subsequent piecemeal adoption of much of the original bill suggests, however, that all was not in vain.

101. J. Duncan M. Derrett, *Religion, Law and the State in India* (New York: Free Press, 1968), 326.

102. Ibid., 326.

103. Marc Galanter, *Law and Society in Modern India,* 30. Galanter, like Derrett, was keenly aware of the code's various deficiencies in addressing the needs of its purported beneficiaries. The feminist critique has been particularly severe. For example: "The codified Hindu law was hailed as providing greater legal rights to women. In reality it failed to do so." Nandini Azad, "Gender and Family: State Intervention in India," in *Family and Gender: Changing Values in Germany and India,* Margrit Pernau, Imtiaz Admad, and Helmut Reifeld, eds. (New Delhi: Sage Publications, 2003), 205. "All that can be said [of the code] in its favour is that it did to an extent help to establish the notion of women's equality as a desirable ideal to which the Indian polity became committed." Ibid., 208. In fairness, however, it accomplished much more than that, not the least of which was the abolition of the requirement that a husband and a wife come from the same caste for a Hindu marriage to be recognized as valid. Recall that for Ambedkar intermarriage among castes was the key to destroying the caste system itself.

104. Rodrigues, ed., *The Essential Writings of B. R. Ambedkar,* 490.

105. Ireland's Constitution is, in the terms of this chapter, decidedly acquiescent. Its Directive Principles reflected the incorporation of Catholic social philosophy into a document that was designed to be supportive of the existing Catholic social order.

106. For a different view see Mark Graber, *Dred Scott and the Problem of Constitutional Evil* (Cambridge: Cambridge University Press, 2006). Graber criticizes the aspirational account of the Constitution; thus, for him, the acquiescence in slavery is not an anomaly, but an essential component of the document's complicity in evil.

107. *The Civil Rights Cases,* 109 U.S. 3 (1883), 57.

108. *Heart of Atlanta Motel, Inc. v. United States,* 379 U.S. 241 (1964), 286.

Chapter 8. Constitutionalism and Democracy

I wish to thank the organizers and participants in the conference "The Supreme Court and the Idea of Constitutionalism," and especially the commentator on this chapter, Stephen Macedo, for their helpful comments and criticisms.

1. See Part One: Philosophical Perspectives in this volume.

2. See Part Two: Historical Perspectives: American Constitutional History in this volume.

3. See Part Three: Comparative Perspectives in this volume.

4. See Part Five: Constitutionalism and Politics in this volume.

5. See, e.g., Ronald Dworkin, *Sovereign Virtue: The Theory and Practice of Equality* (Cambridge, Mass.: Harvard University Press, 2000), 184–210.

6. See, e.g., Jürgen Habermas, *Communication and the Evolution of Society*, translated and with an introduction by Thomas McCarthy (Boston: Beacon Press, 1979); Jürgen Habermas, *Legitimation Crisis*, translated by Thomas McCarthy (Boston: Beacon Press, 1973). Habermas's theory purports to be purely procedural. But the procedure requires an "ideal speech situation," which in turn will require various substantive rights be guaranteed, perhaps to the extent that there will be nothing of public policy left to discuss once the ideal speech situation is achieved. See, e.g., Larry Alexander, "Liberalism, Religion, and the Unity of Epistemology," *San Diego Law Review* 30 (1993): 763, 780–84. See also David Estlund, "Democracy and the Real Speech Situation," in *Deliberative Democracy and Its Discontents*, S. Besson and J. L. Martí, eds. (Burlington, Vt.: Ashgate, 2006); Cass R. Sunstein, *Deliberating Groups Versus Prediction Markets (or Hayek's Challenge to Habermas)*, University of Chicago Law School Public Law and Legal Theory Working Paper no. 146, http://ssrn.com/abstract_id=956189.

7. See John H. Ely, *Democracy and Distrust: A Theory of Judicial Review* (Cambridge, Mass.: Harvard University Press, 1980).

8. See Larry Alexander, "What Is the Problem of Judicial Review?" *Australian Journal of Legal Philosophy* 31 (2006): 1, 3–4.

9. See ibid. at 11–12 n. 16; Thomas Christiano, "Waldron on Law and Disagreement," *Law and Philosophy* 19 (2000): 513.

10. On this point—Who comprises the demos?—see the very important article by Robert E. Goodin, "Enfranchising All Affected Interests, and Its Alternatives," *Philosophy and Public Affairs* 35 (2007): 40.

11. See ibid. at 51–55.

12. See, e.g., Kenneth J. Arrow, *Social Choice and Individual Values*, 2d ed. (New York, Wiley, 1963), 2–8; Philip Pettit, "Collective Persons and Powers," *Legal Theory* 8 (2002): 443.

13. Larry D. Kramer, *The People Themselves: Popular Constitutionalism and Judicial Review* (New York: Oxford University Press, 2004).

14. Mark Tushnet, *Taking the Constitution Away from the Courts* (Princeton, N.J.: Princeton University Press, 1999).

15. Jeremy Waldron, *Law and Disagreement* (New York: Oxford University Press, 1999).

16. Kramer, *The People Themselves*, 227–48.

17. See ibid.; Larry Alexander and Lawrence B. Solum, "Popular? Constitutionalism?" *Harvard Law Review* 118 (2005): 1594, 1609–15.

18. See, e.g., *United States v. Lopez*, 514 U.S. 549 (1995).

19. Tushnet, *Taking the Constitution Away from the Courts*.

20. See, e.g., Jeremy Waldron, "Precommitment and Disagreement," in *Constitutionalism: Philosophical Foundations*, L. Alexander, ed. (New York: Cambridge University Press,1998), 271–99, 290–92; Waldron, *Law and Disagreement*, 275–80.

21. See, e.g., Waldron, *Law and Disagreement*, 282–312; Jeremy Waldron, "The Core of the Case Against Judicial Review," *Yale Law Journal* 115 (2006): 1346; Jeremy Waldron, "A Right-Based Critique of Constitutional Rights," *Oxford Journal of Legal Studies* 13 (1993): 18.

22. Compare Waldron, "A Right-Based Critique," 49–51; Waldron, *Law and Disagreement*, 306–12, with Waldron, "The Core of the Case Against Judicial Review," 1364–66.

23. See Richard Wollheim, "A Paradox in the Theory of Democracy," in *Philosophy, Politics and Society*, P. Laslett and W. Runciman, eds. (Oxford: Blackwell, 1962), 71–87.

24. A serviceable example of "rulifying" moral principles is the translation of the general moral injunction not to create undue risks of harm to others into determinate traffic rules, such as "Stop at stop signs," "Yield the right of way to the first car in the intersection," "Do not exceed 65 MPH," etc.

25. See Larry Alexander and Frederick Schauer, "Law's Limited Domain Confronts Morality's Universal Empire," *William and Mary Law Review* 48 (2007): 1579.

26. See Larry Alexander and Emily Sherwin, *The Rule of Rules* (Durham: Duke University Press, 2001), esp. ch. 4.

27. Incorporating real moral rights into a constitution by direct reference—the target of Schauer's and my argument—not only is different from constitutionalizing rules that are meant to implement those rights, which may or may not be desirable; it is also different from constitutionalizing "standards." Standards are to be contrasted with rules. Unlike rules, standards require their interpreters to make controversial value judgments. Thus, they represent a delegation of lawmaking authority from those who promulgate the standards to those who must follow them. Standards, and the delegations they entail, may or may not be desirable. But in contrast to direct incorporation of morality, promulgation of standards, although a failure to settle what ought to be done, does not itself undermine other settlements *so long as it is clear that the evaluations standards call for take place only within the spaces between the settlements produced by determinate rules.* For more on this topic, see Alexander and Schauer, "Law's Limited Domain Confronts Morality's Universal Empire," 1589–92.

28. See John O. McGinnis and Michael B. Rappaport, "A Pragmatic Defense of Originalism," *Northwestern University Law Review* 101 (2007): 383; John O. McGinnis and Michael Rappaport, "Symmetric Entrenchment: A Constitutional and Normative Theory," *Virginia Law Review* 89 (2003): 385, 417–26; John O. McGinnis and Michael B. Rappaport, "Our Supermajoritarian Constitution," *Texas Law Review* 80 (2002): 703.

Andrei Marmor questions the legitimacy of having the constitutional founders bind future generations to the former's conception of wise and just government—though Marmor is more skeptical about tying present and future generations to the founder's conceptions of moral rights than tying them to the founder's conceptions of good governmental structures. Compare Andrei Marmor, "Are Constitutions Legitimate?" *Canadian Journal of Law and Jurisprudence* 20 (2007): 69, 76 with ibid. at 79–80. Marmor, however, does not advert to the advantages of the supermajoritarian ratification process that McGinnis and Rappaport discuss. On the other hand, Ethan Leib does dispute the claim by McGinnis and Rappaport that the supermajoritarian origin of the U.S. Constitution supports the wisdom of its original meaning. Ethan J. Leib, "Why Supermajoritarianism Does Not Illuminate the Interpretive Debate Between Originalists and Non-Originalists," *Northwestern University Law Review Colloquy* (2007): 7.

29. See Ely, *Democracy and Distrust.*

30. See Alexander and Schauer, "Law's Limited Domain Confronts Morality's Universal Empire," 1595–96.

31. Walter van Tilburg, *The Ox-Bow Incident* (New York: Random House, 1940).

32. Waldron has objected that the scenario portrayed in the story does not resemble a typical legislative procedure. The posse was adjudicating guilt (like a jury) and not legislating. There were no committees, second and third readings of bills, and so on.

These points are correct but not decisive. For suppose the posse were deciding whether to adopt the rule "lynch on the spot" or the rule "transport suspects to the legal authorities." And suppose it set up a committee, which duly reported its recommendation to the entire posse, which then debated the issue and took a succession of votes, with "lynch on the spot" prevailing overwhelmingly. The points in the text would still apply.

33. For further argument on this point, see Alexander, "What Is the Problem of Judicial Review?" 11–12 n. 16.

34. See Arrow, *Social Choice and Individual Values*, 2–8; Philip Pettit, "Collective Persons and Powers."

35. See Yuval Eylon and Alon Harel, "The Right to Judicial Review," *Virginia Law Review* 92 (2006): 991.

36. See *Roe v. Wade*, 410 U.S. 113 (1973); Waldron, *Law and Disagreement*, 289–90.

37. 358 U.S. 1 (1958).

38. David Estlund has written extensively on the epistemic qualities of democratic legislation. See, e.g., David Estlund, "Democracy and the Jury Theorem: New Skeptical Reflections" (unpublished ms., 2006); "What's So Rickety? Richardson's Non-Epistemic Democracy," *Philosophy and Phenomenological Research* 71 (2005): 30; "Book Review," *Ethics* 115 (2005): 609. See also Frederick Schauer, "Legislatures as Rule-Followers," in *The Least Examined Branch*, R. W. Bauman and T. Kahana, eds. (2006): 468–79 (discussing motivational problems that legislatures face with respect to rights that ought to constrain them).

Chapter 9. Active Liberty and the Problem of Judicial Oligarchy

This chapter is based upon remarks delivered on March 16, 2006, at the Michigan State University Symposium on Science, Reason, and Modern Democracy on the topic of "The Supreme Court in American Life." The author thanks his law clerk, Michael Bossenbroek, for assisting in the research and preparation of this chapter.

1. Stephen Breyer, *Active Liberty: Interpreting Our Democratic Constitution* (New York: Random House, 2005), 5, 6.

2. *Griswold v. Connecticut*, 381 U.S. 479 (1965).

3. Justice Breyer is not the first jurist to treat our Constitution like a "theme park." For example, Justice Thurgood Marshall advocated that our Constitution should be viewed as "evolving." He certainly saw the judiciary as the principal architects designing that evolution. Thurgood Marshall, "Reflections on the Bicentennial of the United States Constitution," delivered May 6, 1987.

4. Robert H. Bork, *The Tempting of America: The Political Seduction of the Law* (New York: The Free Press, 1990).

5. Robert P. Young, Jr., "A Judicial Traditionalist Confronts the Common Law," *Texas Review of Law and Politics* 8 (2004): 299.

6. Antonin Scalia, "Originalism: The Lesser Evil," *University of Cincinnati Law Review* 57 (1989): 849.

7. As a provincial judge from a "flyover" state, I disclaim any expertise in political science. My "career" in political science ended more than thirty years ago when a dispute with then-Dean Harvey Mansfield prompted me to attend Harvard Law School rather than the Harvard Graduate School of Government. I remain grateful to Professor Mansfield for this dispute.

8. Forrest McDonald, *E Pluribus Unum: The Formation of the American Republic 1776–1790* (Indianapolis, Ind.: Liberty Press, 1979).

9. Joseph J. Ellis, *His Excellency: George Washington* (New York: Alfred A. Knopf, 2004), 169–70.

10. Richard B. Morris, *Witnesses at the Creation: Hamilton, Madison, Jay and the Constitution* (New York: Barnes and Noble, 1996), 124–25.

11. Catherine D. Bowen, *Miracle at Philadelphia*: *The Story of the Constitutional Convention, May to September 1787* (New York: Little, Brown, 1986).

12. Michael Kammen, ed., The *Origins of the American Constitution: A Documentary History* (New York: Penguin Books, 1986), xviii.

13. Ibid.

14. U.S. Constitution, Art. III, § 2. ("In all the other cases before mentioned, the Supreme Court shall have appellate jurisdiction, both as to law and fact, with such exceptions, and under such regulations as the Congress shall make.")

15. Bowen, *Miracle at Philadelphia*, 65–66.

16. U.S. Constitution, Art. III, § 1.

17. Professor Zuckert makes the point that "judicial review may have been implicit in the logic or even the minds of constitution makers (consider the various comments in the debate over the Council of Revision) but whichever it was, judicial 'paramountcy' was not intended" (Zuckert, this volume). He also suggests that

Madison himself "never intended" judicial supremacy over the legislature (Zuckert, this volume). His points are consistent with my view that the revisionary power contemplated by Madison and rejected by the convention was a far broader power than the limited power of judicial review members of the convention apparently presumed was inherent in the judicial branch they created. The delegates' recognition and acceptance of some inherent form of judicial review coupled with their resistance to expanding traditional judicial functions *undercut* Madison's Council of Revision proposal.

18. "The Virginia Resolutions Presented to the Constitutional Convention on May 29, 1787," reprinted in *Origins of the American Constitution*, 24.

19. Gordon S. Wood, *The Creation of the American Republic 1776–1787* (New York: W. W. Norton, 1993), 456.

20. My research indicates that the delegates debated the Council of Revision proposal on June 4, June 6, July 21, and August 15, 1787.

21. James Madison, *Notes of Debates in the Federal Convention of 1787*; Monday, June 4, 1787; comments by Eldridge Gerry, http://teachingamericanhistory.org/convention/debates/ (accessed April 30, 2007).

22. *Notes of Debates*, June 4, comments by Rufus King.

23. This was, of course, the power of presidential veto that was eventually placed in Art. 1, Sec. 7.

24. Wilson suggested that "Laws may be unjust, may be unwise, may be dangerous, may be destructive; and yet may not be so unconstitutional as to justify the Judges in refusing to give them effect. Let them [the judiciary] have a share in the Revisionary power, and they will have an opportunity of taking notice of these characters of a law, and of counteracting, by the weight of their opinions the improper views of the Legislature." *Notes of Debates*, Saturday, July 21, 1787, comments by James Wilson.

25. *Notes of Debates*, July 21, comments by James Madison.

26. Mason preferred that the judiciary "giv[e] aid in preventing every improper law," which they could do because they were "in the habit and practice of considering laws in their true principles, and in all their consequences." *Notes of Debates*, July 21, comments by George Mason.

27. Elbridge Gerry countered that it "ought never to be done" to make "the Expositors of the Laws [i.e., the Judiciary] the Legislators." *Notes of Debates*, July 21, comments by Elbridge Gerry. He warned against making the judiciary the "guardians of the Rights of the people." Ibid. Another delegate argued that there was "no maxim better established" than that "the power of making [laws] ought to be kept distinct from that of expounding." *Notes of Debates*, July 21, comments by Caleb Strong. Luther Martin added that, in drafting laws, the judiciary provided no "particular advantage" nor grasped "knowledge of Mankind, and of Legislative affairs" in any "higher degree" than the legislature. Notes of Debates, July 21, comments by Luther Martin. South Carolina delegate John Rutledge urged that "Judges ought never to give their opinion on a law till it comes before them." *Notes of Debates*, July 21, comments by John Rutledge.

28. Wood, *Creation of the American Republic*, 454.

29. Russell R. Wheeler and Cynthia Harrison, *Creating the Federal Judicial System*, 2nd ed. (Federal Judicial Center, 1994), 2, http://www.fjc.gov/public/pdf.nsf/lookup/creating.pdf/$File/creating.pdf (accessed April 30, 2007).

30. Ibid.

31. Brutus, "Anti-Federalist Paper XV," March 20, 1788, reprinted in *The Origins of the American Constitution: A Documentary History*, 355–60. Brutus proved to be prophetic.

32. Alexander Hamilton, James Madison, and John Jay, "Federalist Paper 81," *The Federalist*, Benjamin Fletcher Wright, ed. (New York: Barnes and Noble Books, 1996), 508–9.

33. Hamilton, Madison, and Jay, "Federalist Paper 78," in *The Federalist*, 490.

34. Wheeler and Harrison, *Creating the Federal Judicial System*, 2.

35. Ibid., 6–7.

36. 3 U.S. 386 (1789).

37. 3 U.S. at 387–89.

38. 3 U.S. at 400.

39. 5 U.S. (1 Cranch) 137 (1803).

40. See Bork, *Tempting of America*, 20–26.

41. *Marbury*, 5 U.S. at 175.

42. 22 U.S. (9 Wheat.) 1 (1824).

43. 22 U.S. at 188.

44. This same view prevailed fifty years later in the seminal treatise on constitutional law written by one of Michigan's and the nation's preeminent jurists, Justice Thomas Cooley. Far from advocating the Rorschach approach to constitutionalism, Justice Cooley wrote that "For as the Constitution does not derive its force from the convention which framed, but from the people who ratified it, the intent to be arrived at is that of the people, and it is not to be supposed that they have looked for any dark or abstruse meaning in the words employed, but rather that they have accepted them in the sense most obvious to the common understanding, and ratified the instrument in the belief that that was the sense designed to be conveyed." Thomas M. Cooley, *A Treatise on the Constitutional Limitations Which Rest Upon the Legislative Power of the States of the American Union*, 1st ed. (Boston: Little, Brown, 1868), 66.

45. Professors Goldstein, Zuckert, and Stoner in their respective chapters in this volume all advance the notion that Marshall was particularly "astute" in his decisions to advance the place of the Court in the triumvirate of the new national government's constitutional departments. I acknowledge as much. My point is not that Marshall and his colleagues on the early Court were saints or never deviated from the "true way" of originalism. Indeed, originalism is not and can never be an exercise in applied math or the scientific method and therein lies the opportunity for principled debate as to whether a particular decision is respectful of, or even presents a persuasive case for, its purported application of the ratifiers' intent.

Rather, my point is a very modest one: that the early Court consistently acknowledged its limited role as an *expositor* of the Constitution as the expression of the ratifiers' intentions and would be shocked by the successor Court's claim of exclusive ownership of and *right* to amend the Constitution by decree according to the Court's favored policy preferences. See, e.g., our discussion of the Eighth Amendment, *infra*. If Marshall is a flawed saint, his successors on the modern Court have brazenly embraced heresy. Today, the prevailing norms of judicial philosophy admit of no limitation on a judge's power save what his gut tells him the Constitution *ought* to say based on the judge's favored personal "theme."

46. 60 U.S. (19 How) 393 (1856).

47. In drafting the Constitution, the delegates to the Constitutional Convention were unable to reach a compromise on the troubling question of slavery. Although practiced extensively throughout the South, slavery was not unknown, and was lawful, in parts of the North. Historian Joseph Ellis posits that the slavery problem was insolvable to members of eighteenth-century America because the prevailing view of the time was that, even conceding that slaves were human (not a universally recognized proposition then), they were also considered *property*. Property could not be confiscated without due process that required compensating the owner. Consequently, even if slaveholders were willing to end slaveholding, the national government would have had to purchase their slaves at market value. In 1789, the cost of such a purchase exceeded the federal budget by manyfold. Joseph J. Ellis, *Founding Brothers: The Revolutionary Generation* (New York: Alfred A. Knopf, 2000), 106. There were a few scattered references to slavery in the Constitution, for example, in Art. IV, Sec. 2, the fugitive slave clause; Art. I, Sec. 2, the apportionment clause; and Art. I, Sec. 9, the importation clause. However, the issue of slavery was deferred and the question festered as a recurring fissure in national politics from formation of the First Congress.

48. Gary Lawson, "Due Process Clause," in *The Heritage Guide to the Constitution*, Edwin Meese III, Matthew Spalding, and Davis Forte, eds. (Washington, D.C.: Regnery, 2005), 338.

49. Doris Kearns Goodwin, *Team of Rivals: The Political Genius of Abraham Lincoln* (New York: Simon and Schuster, 2005), 92.

50. *Furman v. Georgia*, 408 U.S. 238 (1972).

51. 428 U.S. 153 (1976).

52. The crimes to which the modern death penalty applies are, for the most part, limited to homicide offenses. In *Coker v. Georgia*, 433 U.S. 584 (1977), the Court held that imposing the death penalty against an escaped felon for raping an adult woman was "grossly disproportionate" and violative of the Eighth Amendment. The majority's analysis was predicated on its "abiding conviction" that the death penalty was an "excessive penalty" for the rapist who "does not take human life." The majority noted that "for the rape victim, life may not be nearly so happy as it was, but it is not over and normally is not beyond repair." Rapists everywhere were undoubtedly relieved to hear the Court's judgment on the severity of their crime. Rape victims probably had a different reaction.

More recently, five states have enacted legislation permitting the death penalty for sex crimes against children. However, in *Kennedy v. Louisiana*, 554 U.S. _; 128 S.Ct. 2641 (2008), the Supreme Court struck down as cruel and unusual punishment statutes permitting the death penalty for child rapists and held more broadly that in cases of crimes against individuals "the death penalty should not be expanded to instances where the victim's life was not taken." This is ironic because, historically, the death penalty applied to numerous crimes.

53. Justices William Brennan, Thurgood Marshall, and Harry Blackmun all famously opposed the death penalty. The latter wrote near the end of his career that he would no longer "tinker with the machinery of death." *Callins v. Collins,* 510 U.S. 1141, 1145 (1994) (Blackmun, J. dissenting). Justice John Paul Stevens apparently recently reached a similar conclusion. See *Baze v. Rees,* 553 U.S. _; 128 S.Ct. 1520, 1551 (2008) (Stevens, J. concurring)(quoting *Furman v. Georgia,* 408 U.S. 238, 312 (1972) (White, J., concurring)): "I have relied on my own experience in reaching the conclusion that the imposition of the death penalty represents 'the pointless and needless extinction of life with only marginal contributions to any discernible social or public purposes. A penalty with such negligible returns to the State [is] patently excessive and cruel and unusual punishment violative of the Eighth Amendment.'"

54. 536 U.S. 304 (2002).

55. 492 U.S. 302 (1989).

56. *Trop v. Dulles,* 356 U.S. 86, 101 (1958).

57. *Stanford v. Kentucky,* 492 U.S. 361, 370 (1989).

58. 543 U.S. 551 (2005).

59. *Stanford v. Kentucky,* 492 U.S. 361 (1989).

60. *Roper,* 549 U.S. 563, quoting *Atkins,* 536 U.S. at 312, quoting *Coker v. Georgia,* 433 U.S. 584, 597 (1977) (emphasis added).

61. As further support for its conclusion, the *Roper* majority utilized a United Nations convention that the United States *refused to ratify.* Article 37 of the United Nations Convention on the Rights of the Child prohibited capital punishment for juvenile offenders, and the *Roper* majority tartly noted "that every country in the world has ratified [it] save for the United States and Somalia." Apparently, the Supreme Court was a better judge than the president and United States Senate on which treaties our country should sign.

62. 539 U.S. 558 (2003).

63. 478 U.S. 186 (1986).

64. 539 U.S. at 562.

65. 539 U.S. at 571.

66. 539 U.S. at 578–79.

67. Because I am elected, I must at least appear periodically before the public and hear their views. A federal judge with lifetime tenure has no similar obligation.

68. "Interest Groups and Judicial Elections" (December 2000) (unpublished monograph on file with the National Center for State Courts).

69. "Profile: Lawsuit Champions Right to Dance in New York," NPR, *All Things Considered,* November 28, 2005.

70. *Washington v. Glucksberg,* 521 U.S. 702 (1997).

71. Contrary to Michigan voters, in 1994, Oregon voters passed a citizens' initiative that legalized physician-assisted suicide and rejected a measure to repeal the legislation in 1997.

72. *People v. Kevorkian,* 447 Mich. 436 (1994).

73. *Goodridge v. Department of Public Health*, 798 NE2d 941 (Mass. 2003).

74. See "Statewide Marriage Laws," (2006), Human Rights Campaign, http://www.hrc.org/marriage (accessed May 1, 2007).

75. A case in point is California. Although California recognizes civil unions between same-sex couples, in 2000, by initiative, the citizens of California enacted a statute banning same-sex *marriage*. Opponents of the statute succeeded in 2008 in having the California Supreme Court overturn the statute on state constitutional grounds. *In re Marriage Cases*, 183 P.3d 384 (Cal. 2008). In the November 2008 election, the voters repudiated the California Supreme Court decision by a new initiative (Proposition 8) that made the former statutory same-sex marriage ban a *constitutional* ban.

The policy battle over same sex marriage in California raises the very question I have posed in this chapter: who governs in our society, the people or judges? The passage of Proposition 8 after the judicially imposed death of its statutory counterpart has spawned numerous protests in California, some of which were violent and targeted at religious groups who favored the ban. The social tumult occasioned by *In re Marriage Cases* surely illustrates why our courts ought to be more reticent in removing social policy questions from the democratic arena in the guise of recognizing unenumerated constitutional rights. It remains to be seen whether the California Supreme Court's intervention in this contentious social policy arena will confound the therapeutic benefits of the democratic process.

Chapter 10. *Judicial Power and Democracy*

1. Larry Jay Diamond, "Is the Third Wave Over?" *Journal of Democracy* 7 (1996): 20–37; Tatu Vanhanen, "A New Dataset for Measuring Democracy, 1810–1998," *Journal of Peace Research* 37 (2000): 259.

2. Carlo Guarnieri and Patrizia Pederzoli, *The Power of Judges: A Comparative Study of Courts and Democracy*, C. A. Thomas, ed. (Oxford: Oxford University Press, 2002), 135; Ran Hirschl, *Towards Juristocracy: The Origins and Consequences of the New Constitutionalism* (Cambridge, Mass.: Harvard University Press, 2004), 1; Leslie Friedman Goldstein, "From Democracy to Juristocracy," *Law & Society Review* 38 (2004): 611–29.

3. Thomas M. Keck, *The Most Activist Supreme Court in History* (Chicago: University of Chicago Press, 2004), 40–41.

4. Ronald Dworkin, *Taking Rights Seriously* (Cambridge, Mass.: Harvard University Press, 1978), 277; *Freedom's Law* (Cambridge, Mass.: Harvard University Press, 1996), 34.

5. Guarnieri and Pederzoli, *Power of Judges*, 1.

6. E.g., John Zaller, *The Nature and Origins of Mass Opinion* (New York: Cambridge University Press, 1992).

7. Mark A. Graber, "The Nonmajoritarian Difficulty: Legislative Deference to the Judiciary," *Studies in American Political Development* 7 (1993): 35–73; Neal C. Tate and Torbjörn Vallinder, eds., *The Global Expansion of Judicial Power* (New

York: New York University Press, 1995); Keith E. Whittington, "'Interpose Your Friendly Hand': Political Supports for the Exercise of Judicial Review by the United States Supreme Court," *American Political Science Review* 99 (2005): 583–96.

8. Daniel Ziblatt, "Review Article: How Did Europe Democratize?" *World Politics* 58 (2006): 311–38.

9. Hirschl, *Towards Juristocracy.*

10. I use the term "hegemonic" deliberately to invoke Antonio Gramsci's later analysis of the reality "that there really do exist rulers and ruled, leaders and led" (Antonio Gramsci, *Selections from the Prison Notebooks*, Q. Hoare and G. N. Smith, eds. and trans. [New York: International Publishers, 1971], 144). But here as elsewhere, I do not identify elite status as so rooted in economics, or as quite so unconstrained, as Gramsci can be read to do; cf. Rogers M. Smith, *Stories of Peoplehood: The Politics and Morals of Political Membership* (New York: Cambridge University Press, 2003), 38–42.

11. I believe that similar arguments may help explain the rise of politically insulated central banks and other unelected "expert" institutions in modern democratizing nations, though I cannot explore these comparisons here. Amel Ahmed argues that elites in democratizing nations also have often redesigned voting systems to ensure that they retain disproportionate influence even with near-universal suffrage. See Ahmed, "Constituting the Electorate: Voting System Reform and Working Class Incorporation in France, the United Kingdom, and the United States, 1867–1913," Ph.D. dissertation, Department of Political Science, University of Pennsylvania (2006).

12. Aristotle, *The Politics*, Ernest Barker, ed. (New York: Oxford University Press, 1968), 127, 163, 180–84.

13. Niccolò Machiavelli, *The Prince and the Discourses* (New York: Modern Library, 1950), 35–36.

14. Ibid., 119, 122.

15. Ibid., 124.

16. Ibid., 120.

17. Ibid., 164, 240.

18. Ibid., 227–28, 246–50, 260–66.

19. Ibid., 164, 233–37, 240.

20. John P. McCormick, "Contain the Wealthy and Patrol the Magistrates: Restoring Elite Accountability to Popular Government," *American Political Science Review* 100 (2006): 152.

21. Ibid.

22. Ibid., 158–61.

23. James Madison, Alexander Hamilton, and John Jay, *The Federalist Papers*, Isaac Kramnick, ed. (London: Penguin Books, 1987 [orig. 1788]), 124, 438–41.

24. Ibid., 124, 128.

25. Ibid., 442.

26. C. Neal Tate, "Why the Expansion of Judicial Power?" in Tate and Vallinder, *Global Expansion*, 33.

27. Ibid.

28. Ibid., 29, 31–32.

29. E.g., Carlo Guarnieri and Patrizia Pederzoli stress more than Tate how political systems that involve proportional representation or consociational arrangements that seek to promote consensus among different groups generate conditions for judicial empowerment more often than majoritarian ones; but their explanations of why this is so track Tate's mapping of the difficulties of coalition politics. They also attend to the sorts of judicial training and selection processes that are likely to generate power-embracing judges, while agreeing that judges must choose to take power (Guarnieri and Pederzoli, *Power of Judges*, 160–67). Alec Stone Sweet suggests that explanatory lists such as Tate's fall short of coherent "theorizing" on judicial power. Building on Martin Shapiro's *Courts: A Comparative and Political Analysis* (Chicago: University of Chicago Press, 1986), he seeks to develop such a theory by stressing the need for acceptable "third party" dispute resolvers (so that judicial theorizing becomes theorizing "triadic dispute resolution" or "TDR") (Alec Stone Sweet, *Governing with Judges: Constitutional Politics in Europe* [New York: Oxford University Press, 2000], 2–3). That framework generates explanations of different levels of judicial power that focus on whether there is "an institutional environment that enables and encourages delegation to the court" and on how judges have responded to the opportunities thus provided, all in ways that are largely consonant with Tate's list (195–96).

30. Hirschl, *Towards Juristocracy*, 11–12.

31. Ibid., 46–47, 215–16.

32. Ibid., 48.

33. Ibid., 216–17.

34. Mark A. Graber, "Federalists or Friends of Adams: The Marshall Court and Party Politics," *Studies in American Political Development* 12 (1998): 231–34.

35. Howard Gillman, *The Constitution Besieged: The Rise and Demise of Lochner Era Police Jurisprudence* (Durham, N.C.: Duke University Press, 1993).

36. Charles R. Epp, *The Rights Revolution: Lawyers, Activists, and Supreme Courts in Comparative Perspective* (Chicago: University of Chicago Press, 1998), 2–3.

37. Mark A. Graber, "Constructing Judicial Review," *American Review of Political Science* 8 (2005): 446.

38. Epp, *Rights Revolution*, 8–9, 202.

39. Graber, "Constructing Judicial Review," 431–33, 447–48.

40. Machiavelli, *The Prince and the Discourses*, 233–37, 246–50, 260–66.

41. Philip A. Klinkner with Rogers M. Smith, *The Unsteady March: The Rise and Decline of Racial Equality in America* (Chicago: University of Chicago Press, 1999), 208–10, 237–41.

42. Tate, "Why the Expansion?" 28–36; Guarnieri and Pederzoli, *Power of Judges*, 167–83; Sweet, *Governing with Judges*, 194–203; Hirschl, *Towards Juristocracy*, 38–49; Whittington, " 'Interpose Your Friendly Hand,' " 583–94; Graber, "Counter-Majoritarian Difficulty," 37–45.

43. Epp, *Rights Revolution*, 202–03; Hirschl, *Towards Juristocracy*, 103–48.

44. Lawrence Baum, "The Supreme Court in American Politics," *American Review of Political Science* 6 (2003): 171.

45. Graber, "Constructing Judicial Review," 438.

46. Elizabeth Bussiere, *(Dis)Entitling the Poor: The Warren Court, Welfare Rights, and the American Political Tradition* (University Park: Pennsylvania State University Press, 1999).

47. Graber, "Constructing Judicial Review," 443.

48. Cf., e.g., Justice Antonin Scalia's opinions in *Employment Division, Department of Human Resources of Oregon v. Smith*, 484 U.S. 872 (1990) and *Lucas v. South Carolina Coastal Council*, 505 U.S. 1003 (1992).

49. McCormick, "Contain the Wealthy," 151 n. 3.

50. Jeremy Waldron, "The Core of the Case Against Judicial Review," *Yale Law Journal* 115 (2006): 1395.

51. E.g., Ken I. Kersch, *Constructing Civil Liberties: Discontinuities in the Development of American Constitutional Law* (New York: Cambridge University Press, 2004), 339.

52. Guarnieri and Pederzoli, *Power of Judges*, 18–68.

53. E.g., Gregory A. Caldeira, "Neither the Purse nor the Sword: Dynamics of Public Confidence in the Supreme Court," *American Political Science Review* 80 (1986): 1209–26; William Mishler and Reginald S. Sheehan, "The Supreme Court as Countermajoritarian Institution? The Impact of Public Opinion on Supreme Court Decisions," *American Political Science Review* 87 (1993): 87–101.

54. Robert H. Durr, Andrew D. Martin, and Christina Wolbrecht, "Ideological Divergence and Public Support for the Supreme Court," *American Journal of Political Science* 44 (2000): 768–76.

55. *Bush v. Gore*, 532 U.S. 98 (2000); James L. Gibson, Gregory A. Caldeira, and Lester Kenyatta Spencer, "The Supreme Court and the U.S. Presidential Election of 2000: Wounds, Self-Inflicted or Otherwise?" *British Journal of Political Science* 33 (2003): 555; Stephen P. Nicholson and Robert M. Howard, "Framing Support for the Supreme Court in the Aftermath of *Bush v. Gore*," *Journal of Politics* 65 (2003): 693.

56. Terri Jennings Peretti, *In Defense of a Political Court* (Princeton, N.J.: Princeton University Press, 1999), 180.

57. Lori Hausegger and Troy Riddell, "The Changing Nature of Public Support for the Supreme Court of Canada," *Canadian Journal of Political Science/Revue canadienne de science politique* 37 (2004): 23–50. Shannon Ishiyama Smithey and John Ishiyama, "Judicial Activism in Post-Communist Politics," *Law & Society Review* 36 (2002): 719–42.

58. Gibson, Caldeira, and Spencer, "The Supreme Court and the U.S. Presidential Election," 553, 555; Nicholson and Howard, "Framing Support," 692–93.

59. Machiavelli, *The Prince and the Discourses*, 443.

60. Ibid., 122, 378, 414–15.

61. Ibid., 166, 169–70.

62. Ibid., 119.

63. Peretti, *In Defense of a Political Court*, 133-60.

64. Machiavelli, *The Prince and the Discourses*, 538.

Chapter 11. Constitutional Constraints in Politics

I am grateful to the participants in the "The Supreme Court and the Idea of Constitutionalism" conference at Michigan State University and the Columbia Legal Theory Workshop at Columbia Law School for helpful discussion of earlier drafts of this chapter.

1. See Giovanni Sartori, "Constitutionalism: A Preliminary Discussion," *American Political Science Review* 56 (1962): 853.

2. Guillermo O'Donnell's "delegative democracies" are an example of nonconstitutional republics, in this sense. O'Donnell, "Delegative Democracy," *Journal of Democracy* 5 (1994): 55.

3. Of course, in practice any regime might still encounter and recognize contingent limits to its power. It may not have the capacity to achieve certain goals, and it might encounter other powerholders who could not be easily defeated or challenged. As the political realists once emphasized, the sovereign may not be "sovereign." Harold J. Laski, *The Foundations of Sovereignty* (New York: Harcourt, Brace, 1921). A nonconstitutional regime might well have to make compromises and accommodations, but those are transitory, inessential.

4. Importantly, the "what" here, a constitutional enforcer, is politically engaged. I do not mean to make claims beyond what we would normally think of as the political realm. There is certainly life "outside of politics" in the relevant senses, but constitutional enforcers are not in that domain.

5. Alternatively, constitution makers might try to create a "foreign" power within the polity. Thus, the Chilean high court established by the constitution of 1925 was functionally self-replicating, sealed off from ordinary mechanisms of influence from outside itself. Lisa Hilbink, *Judges Beyond Politics in Democracy and Dictatorship* (New York: Cambridge University Press, 2007).

6. See, e.g., Elmer Beecher Russell, *The Review of American Colonial Legislation by the King in Council* (New York: Columbia University Press, 1915); Mary Sarah Bilder, *The Transatlantic Constitution: Colonial Legal Culture and the Empire* (Cambridge, Mass.: Harvard University Press, 2004).

7. Tamir Mustafa describes a weak version of this; Moustafa, "Law Versus the State: The Judicialization of Egyptian Politics," *Law and Social Inquiry* 28 (2003): 883. North and Weingast describe a somewhat more robust version, which is relevant to a point noted below. Douglass C. North and Barry R. Weingast, "Constitutions and Commitments: The Evolution of Institutions Governing Public Choice in Seventeenth-Century England," *Journal of Economic History* 49 (1989): 803. Garth observes some recent innovations that are in this mode, but note that the power to actually enforce these rulings is limited. Bryant G. Garth, "The Globalization of the Law," in *The Oxford Handbook of Law and Politics*, Keith E. Whittington, R. Daniel Kelemen, and Gregory A. Caldeira, eds. (New York: Oxford University Press, 2008). More effective, though historically less consensual, is the reality of "gunboat diplomacy" aimed at securing Western property interests in less-developed countries. Niall Ferguson, *Empire* (New York: Basic Books, 2004).

8. See, e.g., Andrew Moravcsik, "The Origins of Human Rights Regimes:

Democratic Delegation in Postwar Europe," *International Organization* 54 (2000): 217. The republican guarantee clause in the U.S. Constitution is in this vein, though perhaps motivated as much by the desire of the other confederating partners to prevent a nonrepublican government from gaining a toehold within the boundaries of the United States as by the desire of the current state governments to prevent their own political demise.

9. Alexander Hamilton, "No. 78," in Alexander Hamilton, James Madison, and John Jay, *The Federalist Papers*, Clinton Rossiter, ed. (New York: Mentor, 1969), 465. See also Alexander M. Bickel, *The Least Dangerous Branch* (Indianapolis, Ind.: Bobbs-Merrill, 1962).

10. This is in contrast to, as Jim Stoner observes elsewhere in this volume, the "resistance" that political actors have sometimes offered to what they take to be mistaken judicial interpretations of the Constitution.

11. Keith E. Whittington, "Yet Another Constitutional Crisis?" *William and Mary Law Journal* 43 (2002): 2093.

12. Note that this does not require a "political culture" committed to "constitutionalism" in the abstract. It is sufficient if there are political interests that are capable of being mobilized and that view the current constitutional commitments as politically valuable.

13. This would be in keeping with Barry Weingast's approach to conceptualizing constitutions as coordination devices. Barry R. Weingast, "The Political Foundations of Democracy and the Rule of Law," *American Political Science Review* 91 (1997): 245.

14. See, e.g., Howard Schweber, *The Language of Liberal Constitutionalism* (New York: Cambridge University Press, 2007); Dennis Goldford, *The American Constitution and the Debate over Originalism* (New York: Cambridge University Press, 2005).

15. See, e.g., Scott Gordon, *Controlling the State* (Cambridge, Mass.: Harvard University Press, 1999); Stephen Macedo, *Liberal Virtues* (New York: Oxford University Press, 1991).

16. See, e.g., Russell Hardin, *Liberalism, Constitutionalism, and Democracy* (New York: Oxford University Press, 1999).

17. See, e.g., Moustafa, "Law Versus the State"; North and Weingast, "Constitutions and Commitments."

18. Jack M. Balkin and Sanford Levinson, "The Canons of Constitutional Law," *Harvard Law Review* 111 (1998): 963; Richard A. Primus, "Canon, Anti-Canon, and Judicial Dissent," *Duke Law Journal* 48 (1998): 243.

19. On the lack of legislative awareness of potential constitutional issues, see also J. Mitchell Pickerill, *Constitutional Deliberation in Congress* (Durham, N.C.: Duke University Press, 2004).

20. Hamilton, "No. 78."

21. James R. Rogers, "Information and Judicial Review: A Signaling Game of Legislative-Judicial Interaction," *American Journal of Political Science* 45 (2001): 84.

22. Jeremy Waldron, "The Core of the Case Against Judicial Review," *Yale Law Journal* 115 (2006): 1355–56.

23. James Bradley Thayer, "The Origin and Scope of the American Doctrine of Constitutional Law," *Yale Law Journal* 3 (1894): 108. Thayer separately argued that judges should respect legislative determinations given reasonable disagreement about the true meaning of the Constitution.

24. See, e.g., Marc Galanter, "Why the 'Haves' Come Out Ahead: Speculations on Legal Change," *Law and Society Review* 9 (1974): 95; Charles R. Epp, *The Rights Revolution* (Chicago: University of Chicago Press, 1998).

25. On these two models of oversight, see Mathew D. McCubbins and Thomas Schwartz, "Congressional Oversight Overlooked: Police Patrols versus Fire Alarms," *American Journal of Political Science* 28 (1984): 165.

26. Examples can be found in Neal Devins and Keith E. Whittington, eds., *Congress and the Constitution* (Durham, N.C.: Duke University Press, 2005).

27. See, e.g., Bickel, *The Least Dangerous Branch*, 58; Harry H. Wellington, "Common Law Rules and Constitutional Double Standards: Some Notes on Adjudication," *Yale Law Journal* 83 (1973): 246; Ronald M. Dworkin, *Freedom's Law* (Cambridge, Mass.: Harvard University Press, 1996), 344–45.

28. Keith E. Whittington, "'Interpose Your Friendly Hand': Political Supports for the Exercise of Judicial Review by the United States Supreme Court," *American Political Science Review* 99 (2005): 591.

29. Keith E. Whittington, *Political Foundations of Judicial Supremacy* (Princeton, N.J.: Princeton University Press, 2007), 139–42.

30. James Madison felt the need to take this path when he thought the Marshall Court had taken the legal restraints off Congress in *McCulloch v. Maryland*. The task for the Jeffersonians going forward was to teach legislators and voters to voluntarily "abstain from the exercise of Powers claimed for them by the Court. . . . And should Congress not be convinced, their Constituents, if so, can certainly under the forms of the Constitution effectuate a compliance with their deliberate judgment and settled determination." James Madison, "To Spencer Roane, May 6, 1821," in *The Writings of James Madison*, Gaillard Hunt, ed., vol. 9 (New York: G. P. Putnam's Sons, 1910), 59.

31. See Mark V. Tushnet, *Taking the Constitution Away from the Courts* (Princeton, N.J.: Princeton University Press, 2000).

32. Madison, "No. 10." Somewhat differently, Madison and his fellow Federalists also sought to expand the scope of conflict by nationalizing some political issues in the hope that constitutionally problematic constituency pressures would be more likely to be countered within that larger political arena.

33. Such strategies are discussed in R. Douglas Arnold, *The Logic of Congressional Action* (New Haven, Conn.: Yale University Press, 1992).

34. This was the Democratic strategy with the flag-burning constitutional amendment. See Whittington, *Political Foundations*.

35. The veto was frequently used by Jacksonian presidents. Discretion in implementing statutes has been more common among later presidents. See Whittington, *Political Foundations*.

36. Hamilton, "No. 78."

37. State judiciaries are less insulated from politics than is the federal judiciary, but even there state judges are far more insulated from electoral pressure

than are legislators. It should be noted that the focus here is on electorally driven pressures placed on constitutional constraints, but it is possible for "momentary inclination[s]" to capture the minds of government officials as well as voters. In such cases, the sociological and institutional insulation of judges (they are not the ones trying to fight the war) may be of greater relevance than their electoral insulation, but sufficient insulation may be more difficult to achieve.

38. See also Whittington, "'Interpose Your Friendly Hand.'"

39. Bickel, *The Least Dangerous Branch*, 239.

40. See Keith E. Whittington, *Constitutional Construction* (Cambridge, Mass.: Harvard University Press, 1999).

41. See Whittington, *Political Foundations*.

42. Ken I. Kersch, *Constructing Civil Liberties* (New York: Cambridge University Press, 2004).

43. Jeremy Waldron, *Law and Disagreement* (New York: Oxford University Press, 1999).

Chapter 12. *"The Court Will Clean It Up"*

I would like to thank Fred Baumann, Steven Kautz, and Dick Zinman for commenting on earlier versions of this chapter and the conference participants for their helpful suggestions and critiques. I would also like to thank the Earhart Foundation, the Bradley Foundation, and the Program on Constitutional Government at Harvard University for providing me with the resources, both financial and intellectual, to complete this project.

1. Edward Lazarus, "How Has 9/11 Affected American Constitutional Law? The Three Intersecting Cross-Currents that Have Affected Liberty, Security, and Government Accountability," September 15, 2006, http://writ.news.findlaw.com/lazarus/20060915.html (accessed September 18, 2006).

2. Charles Babington and Jonathan Weisman, "Senate Approves Detainee Bill Backed by Bush: Constitutional Challenges Predicted," *The Washington Post*, September 29, 2006, http://www.washingtonpost.com/wp-dyn/content/article/2006/09/28/AR2006092800824.html (accessed October 2, 2006). Just as this book went to press, the decision in *Boumediene v. Bush* was released and it was not possible to integrate this decision fully into this chapter. Thus, I make only a few points about it. First, the decision indicates that the judiciary can be more aggressive in striking at the decisions made under the claims of national security than my analysis of *Hamdi* in this chapter would have predicted. But second, the remaining questions left by the decision still indicate why these things are better dealt with by the political branches of government, *acting responsibly*. After all, in the wake of *Boumediene*, it is still unclear what judicial processes are envisioned for the detainees in Guantanamo. Benjamin Wittes, with amazing perspicaciousness, predicts precisely what happened and shows its problems: "The day that *Boumediene* comes down, assuming the justices rule as expected, news stories the world over will announce once again the great defeat of the administration and the rebuke to

its aggressive approach. These stories, however, will generally not discuss the mess the decision will leave—hundreds of habeas corpus suits proceeding even as direct appeals from CSRT judgments pile up in the federal courts, and all of this litigation taking place with no agreed-upon legal standards of review or substantive law guiding the key questions: Whom can the military hold? For how long? With what kind of showing? Under what evidentiary rules? America will, put bluntly, have come no closer to a coherent law of terrorism than it was the day detainees began arriving at Guantanamo. It will merely have declared—yet again—that the Supreme Court has the final word." Benjamin Wittes, *Law and the Long War: The Future of Justice in the Age of Terror* (New York: Penguin Press, 2008), 128.

3. For a very good treatment of this development and its difficulties, see Donald G. Morgan, *Congress and the Constitution: A Study of Responsibility* (Cambridge, Mass.: Belknap Press of Harvard University Press, 1966).

4. *United States v. Curtiss-Wright Export Corp.*, 299 U.S. 319–320 (1936).

5. For a lengthier discussion of both the case and a fuller version of the speech, see James Bradley Thayer, *John Marshall* (Boston: Houghton, Mifflin, 1901), 40–51.

6. *United States v. Curtiss-Wright Export Corp.*, 299 U.S. 322 (1936).

7. At a conference titled "Presidential Power in America" held at the Massachusetts School of Law in October 2006, David Adler presented both an extended critique of *Curtiss-Wright*'s legal reasoning and a discussion of its far-reaching effects on the modern presidential claim that presidents possess an inherent constitutional "war-making" power.

8. *Youngstown Sheet & Tube Co. v. Sawyer*, 343 U.S. footnote 2 (1952).

9. To see that *Hamdi* may not be the strike at presidential power that some claim it is, one might consider that John Yoo mostly supports the decision. John Yoo, "Enemy Combatants and the Problem of Judicial Competence," in *Terrorism, the Laws of War, and the Constitution*, Peter Berkowitz, ed. (Stanford, Calif.: Hoover Institution Press, 2005).

10. "The AUMF authorizes the President to use 'all necessary and appropriate force' against 'nations, organizations, or persons' associated with the September 11, 2001, terrorist attacks. 115 Stat 224. There can be no doubt that individuals who fought against the United States in Afghanistan as part of the Taliban, an organization known to have supported the al Qaeda terrorist network responsible for those attacks, are individuals Congress sought to target in passing the AUMF. We conclude that detention of individuals falling into the limited category we are considering, for the duration of the particular conflict in which they are captured, is so fundamental and accepted an incident to war as to be an exercise of the 'necessary and appropriate force' Congress has authorized the President to use." Somehow, the plurality finds, however, that their reading of congressional intent does not then constitute a suspension of the writ. *Hamdi v. Rumsfeld*, 542 U.S. 518, 536 (2004). For Scalia's argument that the AUMF could not possibly constitute either a suspension of the writ of an authorization for the indefinite detention of citizens (he thinks the distinction itself utterly meaningless), see *Hamdi v. Rumsfeld*, 542 U.S. 574 (2004; Scalia dissenting). The question that divides the plurality from Scalia revolves around whether the congressional authorization of war then implies and

thus grants to the executive a much wider range of the tools of war, including the indefinite detention of citizens suspected of fighting for the enemy.

For a fascinating historical case concerning this question about implied versus explicit congressional authorization of war powers as it relates to the condemnation of enemy property, see *Brown v. United States,* 12 U.S. 110 (1814). In the case, Chief Justice Marshall writes a majority opinion finding that British property found in the United States, at the commencement of hostilities with Great Britain, cannot be confiscated as enemy property without a specific legislative act authorizing the confiscation. Justice Story, whose understanding of the Constitution and constitutionalism more generally rivals Marshall's in its depth and acuity, writes a dissenting opinion arguing that the declaration of war implies a wide range of the tools of war, extending to the confiscation of enemy property. Whether Story would apply his reasoning to this situation, however, remains a question. He writes: "My argument proceeds upon the ground, that when the legislative authority, to whom the right to declare war is confided, has declared war in its most unlimited manner, the executive authority, to whom the execution of the war is confided, is bound to carry it into effect. He has a discretion vested in him, as to the manner and extent; but he cannot lawfully transcend the rules of warfare established among civilized nations. He cannot lawfully exercise powers or authorize proceedings which the civilized world repudiates and disclaims." Notice, however, that even as Story finds for the executive in the case, his language avoids the unilateralist assertion of constitutionally suspect principles that characterize *Curtiss-Wright* or Thomas's dissent in *Hamdi.* Story continues: "The sovereignty, as to declaring war and limiting its effects, rests with the legislature. The sovereignty, as to its execution, rests with the president. If the legislature do not limit the nature of the war, all the regulations and rights of general war attach upon it." *Brown v. United States,* 12 U.S. 153–154 (1814; Story dissenting).

11. *Hamdi v. Rumsfeld,* 542 U.S. 536 (2004).

12. To see one example of this use of Hamdi, consider Yoo, "Problem of Judicial Competence."

13. *Hamdi v. Rumsfeld,* 542 U.S. 536 (2004).

14. For a historical discussion of Congress's misuse of its "war power" and the Supreme Court's decision to intervene to prevent this misuse at the end of World War I, see Christopher N. May, *In the Name of War: Judicial Review and the War Powers Since 1918* (Cambridge, Mass.: Harvard University Press, 1989).

15. Mark Tushnet uses this word to describe the effect of Supreme Court opinions on our constitutional discussions; see *Taking the Constitution Away from the Courts* (Princeton, N.J.: Princeton University Press, 1999).

16. See Benjamin A. Kleinerman, "Can the Prince Really Be Tamed? Executive Prerogative, Popular Apathy, and the Constitutional Frame in Locke's *Second Treatise,*" *American Political Science Review* 101, no. 2 (May 2007): 209–22.

17. For a reflection on this same question, see Ross J. Corbett, "The Missing Judiciary in Locke's Separation of Powers," paper presented at the Midwest Political Science Association, April 2006.

18. See Paul O. Carrese, *The Cloaking of Power: Montesquieu, Blackstone, and the Rise of Judicial Activism* (Chicago: University of Chicago Press, 2003), 83. Car-

rese suggests that Montesquieu's cloaking of judicial power indicates that he stops far short of the modern doctrine of judicial activism; however, he also suggests that the project itself, especially when it is shorn of its prudential concern for separation of powers, plants the seeds for such activism.

19. Ibid., 24.

20. Lee Ward, "Locke on Executive Power and Liberal Constitutionalism," *Canadian Journal of Political Science* 38 (September 2005): 719–44.

21. See Kleinerman, "Can the Prince Really Be Tamed?" 218–20.

22. For a discussion of the same phenomenon, see Robert F. Nagel, *Constitutional Cultures: The Mentality and Consequences of Judicial Review* (Berkeley: University of California Press, 1989), 18–22.

23. John Locke, "The Second Treatise," in *Two Treatises of Government*, Peter Laslett, ed. (Cambridge: Cambridge University Press, 1988), XIV, 166, p. 378.

24. Cf. Nagel, *Constitutional Cultures*, 40.

25. John Finn, "The Civic Constitution," in *Constitutional Politics: Essays on Constitution Making, Maintenance, and Change*, Sotorios A. Barber and Robert P. George, eds. (Princeton, N.J.: Princeton University Press, 2001) 47.

26. See Michael Stokes Paulsen, "The Constitution of Necessity," *Notre Dame Law Review* 79 (2004): 1257–97.

27. See Benjamin A. Kleinerman, "Lincoln's Example: Executive Power and the Survival of Constitutionalism," *Perspectives on Politics* 3 (December 2005): 801–16, a charge that has been leveled at my argument already by Richard Posner. Richard Posner, *Not a Suicide Pact: The Constitution in a Time of National Emergency* (Oxford: Oxford University Press, 2006), 157–58. For my response to Posner's argument, see "9/11, the Security/Liberty Balance, and the Separation of Powers: A Review of Richard Posner's *Not A Suicide Pact: The Constitution in a Time of National Emergency*," *Criminal Justice Ethics*, Winter–Spring 2007, 62–63. Here I suggest that my initial argument regarding Lincoln is better understood as articulating constitutional standards by which to judge presidents' actions, rather than legal precedents by which to permit them.

28. Louis Michael Seidman, "The Secret Life of the Political Question Doctrine," *John Marshall Law Review* 37 (Winter 2004): 472–77; for Gross's model, see Oren Gross, "Chaos and Rules: Should Responses to Violent Crises Always Be Constitutional?" *Yale Law Journal* 112 (March 2003): 1011–134

29. I cannot take credit for this last insight. It was Nomi Lavar's formulation in her critique of those who rely too much on Carl Schmitt's terminology on a panel at the American Political Science Association, September 2006.

30. In drawing a distinction between constitutional judgments and legal judgments, my argument resembles a fascinating paper recently delivered by Jeffrey Tulis at the Miller Center of Public Affairs at the University of Virginia. Tulis suggests that the power of impeachment has been interpreted too legalistically and in an insufficiently political and constitutional manner, thus providing no effective check on the risk-seeking nature of executive power. See "Impeachment in the Constitutional Order," http://webstorage1.mcpa.virginia.edu/library/mc/apd/colloquia/pdf/col_2006_1027_tulis.pdf (accessed April 18, 2007).

31. In his Helvidius letters, Madison writes: "The existence of war among sev-

eral nations with which the United States have an extensive intercourse; the duty of the executive to preserve peace by enforcing its laws, whilst those laws continued in force; the danger that indiscreet citizens might be tempted or surprised by the crisis, into unlawful proceedings, tending to involve the United States in a war, which the competent authority might decide them to be at liberty to avoid, and which, if they should be judged not at liberty to avoid, the other party to the eventual contract, might be willing not to impose on them; these surely might have been sufficient grounds for the measure pursued by the executive: and being legal and rational grounds, it would be wrong, if there be no necessity, to look beyond them." James Madison, *The Writings of James Madison*, Gaillard Hunt, ed., VI, 181–82. For a fuller discussion of Madison's agreement on the policy, but disagreement on the principle by which the policy was justified, see Gary J. Schmitt, "Washington's Proclamation of Neutrality: Executive Energy and the Paradox of Executive Power," *Political Science Reviewer* 39 (2000): 121–59.

32. Ibid., 152.

33. Ibid.,, 174

34. Ibid.,, 171.

35. For instance, in 1789 in a debate in the House of Representatives concerning who possesses the constitutional power to remove executive officers (a debate in which Madison was on the side of the executive), Madison says: "But the great objection drawn from the source to which the last argument would lead us is, that the Legislature itself has no right to expound the Constitution; that wherever its meaning is doubtful, you must leave it to take its course, until the Judiciary is called upon to declare its meaning. I acknowledge, in the ordinary course of government, that the exposition of the laws and Constitution devolves upon the Judiciary. But I beg to know, upon what principle it can be contended, that any one department draws from the Constitution greater powers than another, in marking out the limits of the powers of the several departments? The Constitution is the charter of the people to the Government; it specifies certain great powers as absolutely granted, and marks out the departments to exercise them. If the Constitutional boundary of either be brought into question, I do not see that any one of these independent departments has more right than another to declare their sentiments on that point. . . . There is not one Government on the face of the earth, so far as I recollect, there is not one in the United States, in which provision is made for a particular authority to determine the limits of the Constitutional division of power between the branches of government." Joseph Gales, Sr., comp., *The Debates and Proceedings in the Congress of the United States* (Washington, D.C.: Gales and Seaton, 1849), I, 500–501. For a very good treatment of the consistent principle that unites Madison's *Helvidius* essays with his support for something like the presidential power of removal, see Ruth Weissbound Grant and Stephen Grant, "The Madisonian Presidency," in *The Presidency in the Constitutional Order*, Joseph M. Bessette and Jeffrey Tulis, eds. (Baton Rouge: Louisiana State University Press, 1981).

36. See Gary J. Jacobsohn, *The Supreme Court and the Decline of Constitutional Aspiration* (Totowa, N.J.: Rowman and Littlefield, 1986).

37. Neal Devins and Louis Fisher, *The Democratic Constitution* (Oxford: Oxford University Press, 2004), 38.

38. See Michael Zuckert's chapter in this volume.

39. Gary Rosen, *American Compact: James Madison and the Problem of Founding* (Lawrence: University Press of Kansas, 1999).

40. For an argument similar to my own, see George Thomas, "Recovering the Political Constitution: The Madisonian Vision," *Review of Politics* 66 (2004): 233–56.

41. For a very nice summary and discussion of the arguments of those scholars advocating constitutional departmentalism, see Susan R. Burgess, *Contest for Constitutional Authority: The Abortion and War Powers Debates* (Lawrence: University Press of Kansas, 1992), 12–27.

42. In a 1796 speech in the House of Representatives, discussing a situation where "two of the constituted authorities interpreted differently the extent of their respective powers," Madison says, "if the difference cannot be adjusted by friendly conference and mutual concession, the sense of the constituent body, brought into the Government through the ordinary elective channels, may supply a remedy." *Debates and Proceedings*, V, 772.

43. For the best and most penetrating discussion of this problem, see Harvey C. Mansfield, Jr., *Taming the Prince: The Ambivalence of Modern Executive Power* (New York: Free Press, 1989). For instance, Mansfield writes: "Locke's political science shows that the modern constitution and the modern executive are mutually dependent and yet antithetical" (81).

44. See Kleinerman, "Lincoln's Example."

45. For a persuasive argument regarding the corrosive effects of such rhetorical "wars" on policy itself, see Jeffrey Tulis, *The Rhetorical Presidency* (Princeton, N.J.: Princeton University Press, 1987).

46. Mark Tushnet's important book *Taking the Constitution Away from the Courts* also suggests that the principle of judicial review should simply be abandoned because its political costs outweigh its benefits. See the chapter "Against Judicial Review," 154–76. This dissatisfaction with judicial review, however, is challenged by Jeffrey Rosen's recent book, *The Most Democratic Branch: How the Courts Save America* (New York: Oxford University Press, 2006), which suggests that the problem is not judicial review, as such, but the aggressive and unilateral exercise of judicial review in the midst of a constitutionally contested issue. Thus, Rosen suggests that the difference between, for instance, Marshall's exercise of judicial review, and the way in which it is often exercised currently, is that Marshall tended to defer to the constitutional opinions of Congress, "closely scrutinizing only laws that threatened federal power or judicial prerogative." See *The Most Democratic Branch*, 16.

47. See Christopher Wolfe, "John Marshall and Constitutional Law," *Polity* 15 (Autumn 1982): 7.

48. See, e.g., Louis Fisher and Nada Moutada-Sabbah, *Is War a Political Question?* (Huntington, N.Y.: Novinka Books, 2001). For a discussion of Fisher's concomitant and problematic belief in both coordinate construction and the constitutional support for congressional superiority in war powers, see David Gray Adler, "Judicial Power, Coordinate Construction," in *Political and Constitutionalism: The Louis Fisher Connection*, Robert J. Spitzer, ed. (Albany: State University of New York Press, 2000), 91.

49. *Little v. Barreme*, 6 U.S. 177, 178 (1804).

50. See Edward S. Corwin, "The Steel Seizure Case: A Judicial Brick Without Straw," *Columbia Law Review* 53 (January 1953): 65–66.

51. Other cases which come to similar decisions about Congress's ability to provide guidelines for the exercise of war powers include *United States v. Smith*, 27 F. Cas. 1192 (C.C.N.Y. 1806); *Brown v. United States*, 12 U.S. 110 (1814); *Jecker et al. v. Jecker et al.*, 54 U.S. 498 (1851). As mentioned above, the majority opinion in *Milligan* could also be included in this category. See note 12 above.

52. Cf. "To Thomas Jefferson," May 20, 1798: "It may however all be for the best. These addresses to the feelings of the people from their enemies, may have more effect in opening their eyes, than all the arguments addressed to their understanding by their friends." James Madison, *Papers of James Madison, Volume 17*, David B. Mattern, J. C. A. Stagg, Jeanne K. Cross, and Susan Holbrook Perdue, eds. (Charlottesville: University Press of Virginia, 1991), 134.

53. *Marbury v. Madison*, 5 U.S. 164, 170 (1803).

54. See Leslie Goldstein's chapter in this volume.

55. Robert Scigliano claims the opposite, namely, that only the doctrine of judicial supremacy can control the growth of executive supremacy. Robert Scigliano, *The Supreme Court and the Presidency* (New York: Free Press, 1971).

Contributors

Larry Alexander is Warren Distinguished Professor of Law, University of San Diego School of Law. He teaches and writes in the areas of constitutional law, criminal law, and jurisprudence. He is the author of many scholarly articles and several books, including *Is There a Right of Freedom of Expression?*; *Demystifying Legal Reasoning* (with Emily Sherwin); and *Whom Does the Constitution Command?* (with Paul Horton). He is also editor of *Constitutionalism: Philosophical Foundations.*

Leslie Friedman Goldstein is Judge Hugh M. Morris Professor, Department of Political Science, University of Delaware. She specializes in American constitutional law, comparative law and courts, gender and law, and American political thought and political philosophy. She is the author of *Constitutional and Legal Rights of Women* (with Judith Baer); *Constituting Federal Sovereignty: The European Union in Comparative Context*; and *In Defense of the Text: Democracy and Constitutional Theory.* She has been Visiting Professor at the University of California at Berkeley, at Fordham University, and at Bryn Mawr College.

Gary Jeffrey Jacobsohn is Patterson-Banister Professor and H. Malcolm Macdonald Professor in Constitutional and Comparative Law, Department of Government, University of Texas. He specializes in comparative constitutionalism and constitutional theory. He is the author of several books, including *The Wheel of Law: India's Secularism in Comparative Constitutional Context*; *Apple of Gold: Constitutionalism in Israel and the United States*; and *Pragmatism, Statesmanship, and the Supreme Court.* He has been a Fulbright Research Scholar (India) and he received a Woodrow Wilson International Scholars Fellowship in the Humanities and Social Sciences.

Steven Kautz is Associate Professor, Department of Political Science, Michigan State University. He is the author of *Liberalism and Community* and of articles on the political philosophy of liberalism and American political thought. He is currently working on projects on the political thought of Abraham Lincoln and on democratic citizenship and the culture wars.

Benjamin A. Kleinerman is Assistant Professor, James Madison College, Michigan State University. He is the author of two recent articles on executive power, "Lincoln's Example and the Survival of Constitutionalism" (*Perspectives on Politics*) and "Can the Prince Really be Tamed? Executive Prerogative, Popular Apathy, and the Constitutional Frame in Locke's *Second Treatise*" (*American Political Science Review*), and of a forthcoming book, *The Discretionary President: The Promise and Peril of Executive Power*. He was a Visiting Scholar in Harvard's Program on Constitutional Government (2006–2007).

Rogers M. Smith is Christopher H. Browne Distinguished Professor of Political Science, Department of Political Science, University of Pennsylvania. He teaches American constitutional law and American political thought, with special interests in issues of citizenship and racial, gender, and class inequities. He is the author of several books, including *Stories of Peoplehood: The Politics and Morals of Political Memberships* and *Liberalism and American Constitutional Law*. His book *Civic Ideals: Conflicting Visions of Citizenship in U.S. History* won the Ralph J. Bunche Award of the American Political Science Association and the Merle Curti Intellectual History Prize of the Organization of American Historians, and was a finalist for the 1998 Pulitzer Prize in History.

James Stoner is Professor, Department of Political Science, Louisiana State University. He is the author of *Common-Law Liberty: Rethinking American Constitutionalism* and *Common Law and Liberal Theory: Coke, Hobbes, and the Origins of American Constitutionalism*. From 2002 to 2006, he served on the National Council on the Humanities, to which he was appointed by President George W. Bush. He is currently at work on a book titled "Resisting Judicial Supremacy," with Richard Morgan of Bowdoin College, and on a study of St. Thomas More.

Nathan Tarcov is Professor, Social Thought, Political Science, and the College, University of Chicago. He is the author of *Locke's Education for Liberty* and of many articles on Machiavelli, Locke, Leo Strauss, and American political thought and foreign policy. He edited and translated, with Harvey C. Mansfield, Machiavelli's *Discourses on Livy*. He has been a Carl Friedrich von Siemens Fellow at the Siemens Stiftung and a Research Fellow at the Naval War College. He served on the policy planning staff of the Department of State.

Mark Tushnet is William Nelson Cromwell Professor of Law, Harvard Law School. He is the author of many books, including a two-volume work on the life of Justice Thurgood Marshall; *A Court Divided: The Rehnquist Court and the Future of Constitutional Law*; and *The American Law of Slavery, 1810–1860: Considerations of Humanity and Interest*. He is also co-author of several casebooks, including *Constitutional Law* (with Stone, Seidman, and Sunstein) and *Comparative Constitutional Law* (with Vicki Jackson). He was elected a fellow of the American Academy of Arts and Sciences in 2002 and he was President of the Association of American Law Schools in 2003.

Keith E. Whittington is William Nelson Cromwell Professor of Politics, Department of Politics, Princeton University. Professor Whittington has published widely on American constitutional theory and development, including *Constitutional Interpretation: Textual Meaning, Original Intent, and Judicial Review*; *Constitutional Construction: Divided Powers and Constitutional Meaning*; and *Political Foundations of Judicial Supremacy: The Presidency, the Supreme Court, and Constitutional Leadership in U.S. History*. He has been a Visiting Professor at the University of Texas School of Law.

Justice **Robert P. Young, Jr.**, has been a member of the Michigan Supreme Court since 1999; he was elected in 2002 to a term that will expire January 1, 2011. Before joining the Supreme Court, Justice Young served as a judge of the Michigan Court of Appeals. Justice Young has been an adjunct professor at Wayne State University Law School for a number of years and is a co-editor of *Michigan Civil Procedure During Trial*, second edition, and *Michigan Civil Procedure*.

Michael P. Zuckert is Nancy Reeves Dreux Professor, Department of Political Science, University of Notre Dame. Professor Zuckert is the author of many books and articles on liberal political philosophy, American political thought, and constitutionalism, including *The Natural Rights Republic*; *Launching Liberalism: John Locke and the Liberal Tradition*; and the forthcoming *Completing the Constitution: The Civil War Amendments*. He is co-author, with Catherine Zuckert, of *The Truth About Leo Strauss: Political Philosophy and American Democracy*. He has been a Visiting Scholar at Liberty Fund and a Woodrow Wilson Center Fellow in American Studies.

Index

Acknowledgments

This is the seventh volume of essays published by the LeFrak Forum and the Symposium on Science, Reason, and Modern Democracy. Established in 1989 in the Department of Political Science at Michigan State University, the symposium is a center for research and debate on the theory and practice of modern democracy. It sponsors lectures, conferences, publications, and teaching, as well as graduate and postdoctoral fellowships. Its specific mission is to explore the intersection of philosophy and public policy: to place theoretical issues in practical context and policy issues in philosophical perspective.

This volume grew from a lecture series, "The Supreme Court in American Life," held during the 2006 spring semester, and a conference, "The Supreme Court and the Idea of Constitutionalism," held in January 2007.

Ten of the chapters in this volume appear here for the first time. An earlier version of James Stoner's chapter appeared in *Claremont Review of Books*, 6, no. 3 (Summer 2006). A somewhat different version of Mark Tushnet's chapter was published in his book *Weak Courts, Strong Rights: Judicial Review and Social Welfare Rights in Comparative Constitutional Law* (Princeton, N.J.: Princeton University Press, 2007). And a section of Steven Kautz's chapter is adapted from an essay that appeared in the *Yale Journal of Law and the Humanities* 11 (1999): 435–68. We thank these contributors and their publishers for permission to reprint.

The symposium's programs in 2005–2006 and 2006–2007 and, indeed, all its activities, were made possible by a "We the People" challenge grant from the National Endowment for the Humanities; and by grants from the Bradley Foundation of Milwaukee, Wisconsin; the Carthage Foundation of Pittsburgh, Pennsylvania; the Earhart Foundation of Ann Arbor, Michigan; and the Scaife Foundation of Pittsburgh, Pennsylvania. We are grateful for their generous support.

Michigan State's Department of Political Science and College of Social Science have been home to the symposium since its founding. We thank our colleagues in these institutions. In particular, we thank Marietta Baba, dean of the college, and Richard Hula, chair of the department. As always, we are especially grateful to Karen Battin, the symposium's administrative assistant, for her fine work.

In addition to the authors whose essays are included in this volume, the following individuals took part in the 2006 lecture series and 2007 conference: Walter Berns, Montgomery Brown, John F. Burleigh, James W. Ceaser, Bruce Cole, Shikha Dalmia, Werner J. Dannhauser, Ingrid A. Gregg, Brian C. Kalt, Alex Kozinski, Thomas Lindsay, Harry Litman, Stephen Macedo, Richard Primus, Lou Anna K. Simon, Kathleen M. Sullivan, and Vickie B. Sullivan. We thank them for their valuable contributions.

We also thank Peter Agree, editor of the University of Pennsylvania Press, and Rogers M. Smith, editor of Penn Press's series on Democracy, Citizenship, and Constitutionalism, for their support of this project.